SIXTEENTH-CENTURY EUROPE

This study of sixteenth-century Europe is designed for sixth-form pupils in schools, and other mature readers who have only limited experience of this topic. The author gives a clear and comprehensive survey without cluttering up the text with excessive footnotes or other scholarly impedimenta. His concise system of cross-referencing offers the reader a choice of entry points to the account, links the chapters neatly and avoids undue repetition. For those who require fuller detail on important aspects of the period, the bibliography gives suggestions for further reading.

SIXTEENTH-CENTURY EUROPE

Leonard W. Cowie

OLIVER & BOYD

Oliver & Boyd
Robert Stevenson House
1–3 Baxter's Place
Leith Walk
Edinburgh EH1 3BB

A Division of Longman Group Ltd.

First published 1977
Third impression 1981

ISBN 0 05 002828 6 paperback
ISBN 0 05 002829 4 cased

Library of Congress Cataloging in Publication Data

Cowie, Leonard W
    Sixteenth-century Europe.

    Bibliography: p.
    Includes index.
    1. Europe—History—1492-1648. I. Title.
D228.C68   940.2'3   76-23419
ISBN 0-05-002829-4
ISBN 0-05-002828-6 pbk.

Printed in Hong Kong by
Wah Cheong Printing Press Ltd.

CONTENTS

ACKNOWLEDGMENTS

The Valencia Mariner's Astrolabe and the detail from the 'Drake Map' by Hondius are incorporated in the cover design of this book by permission of the National Maritime Museum, London and the British Library Board respectively.
Maps and genealogical trees were drawn by Tim Smith.

MAPS

PREFACE

The main purpose of this book is to offer a clear and simple survey and discussion of the history of Europe in the period between 1494 and 1598 for students in sixth forms, particularly those who are studying history at the Advanced level of the General Certificate of Education, though it is hoped that it will interest other readers as well.

The same plan has been followed as in the author's *Seventeenth-Century Europe*, *Eighteenth-Century Europe* and *Hanoverian England*. The first eight chapters are devoted to such introductory subjects as population, science, social and economic development, war and diplomacy, and these include chapters on the medieval Church, the Renaissance and overseas discovery and exploration to provide the background for the great themes of the century. Readers who prefer to begin the book by reading the narrative of the sixteenth century in Europe, however, may start with Chapter 9 and consult any necessary explanations by referring to the footnotes, which throughout the book have been confined to indicating complementary passages in the book so that repetition is avoided and the chapters are linked together. The aim has been to confine the narrative to the essential events and characters of a period and subject rather than to tell a detailed story, so that as much space as possible may be given to the discussion of the issues involved in a consideration of the important topics of the period.

An indication of the many writers on this period to whom the author is indebted would be too lengthy to include. The bibliography is, therefore, short and selective and consists largely of the leading authorities in English which may be used for further information on the most important aspects of the period, and at the same time is confined to those books which may be found in most libraries.

	FRANCE	GERMANY	ITALY
1500	1494 Start of Franco-Spanish Wars	1493-1519 Maximilian I, Holy Roman Emperor	1494 Start of Franco-Spanish Wars
	1498-1515 Louis XII	1508 Luther goes to Wittenberg	1508 League of Cambrai
			1511 Holy League
	1515-47 Francis I 1516 Concordat of Bologna	1517 Luther's 95 Theses published 1519-56 Charles V, Holy Roman Emperor	
		1524-5 Peasants' Revolt	
1525	1525 Battle of Pavia	1526 Diet of Speyer	1525 Battle of Pavia
			1527 Sack of Rome
		1530 League of Schmalkalden	1529 Treaty of Cambrai
		1532 Peace of Nuremberg	
	1534 'Day of the Placards'		
			1540 Society of Jesus founded
		1546 Death of Luther	1544 Treaty of Crespy 1545-63 Council of Trent
	1547-59 Henry II	1547 Battle of Mühlberg	
1550		1552 Convention of Passau	
	1559 Treaty of Cateau-Cambrésis 1559-60 Francis II 1560 Conspiracy of Amboise 1560-74 Charles IX	1555 Peace of Augsburg 1556-74 Ferdinand I, Holy Roman Emperor	1559 Treaty of Cateau-Cambrésis 1559 Papal Index instituted
	1563 Pacification of Amboise	1563 Jesuits at University of Ingoldstadt 1564-76 Maximilian II, Holy Roman Emperor	1566 Roman Catechism published
	1572 St Bartholomew's Massacre		
	1574-89 Henry III		
1575	1576 Peace of Monsieur	1576-1612 Rudolf II, Holy Roman Emperor	
	1585-9 War of the Three Henries 1588 Henry of Guise murdered 1589 Henry III murdered 1589-1610 Henry IV	1579-97 William V, Duke of Bavaria	
1600	1598 Edict of Nantes and Treaty of Vervins		

NETHERLANDS	SPAIN	SWITZERLAND	
			1500
	1494 Start of the Franco-Spanish Wars	1499 Swiss independence gained	
	1516-56 Charles V	1518-31 Zwingli in Zurich	
	1520-1 Revolt of the Comuneros		
3 First heretics burnt at Brussels 4 Introduction of the Inquisition			
			1525
	1526 Peace of Madrid 1527 Sack of Rome		
9 First Placards against heresy	1529 Treaty of Barcelona	1529 Colloquy of Marburg	
		1531 Death of Zwingli	
7 Revolt of city of Ghent		1536 Calvin's *Institutes* published 1536-7 and 1541-64 Calvin in Geneva	
			1550
		1553 Execution of Servetus	
59-67 Regency of Margaret of Parma	1556-98 Philip II 1559 Treaty of Cateau-Cambrésis	1559 University of Geneva founded	
66 The Compromise 67-73 Governorship of Alva 68 Egmont and Hoorne executed			
72 Revolt of Holland and Zeeland; William of Orange elected Stadtholder 73-6 Governorship of Requescens	1568-70 Revolt of the Moriscos 1571 Battle of Lepanto		
			1575
76 Sack of Antwerp; Pacification of Ghent 76-8 Governorship of Don John of Austria	1580 Conquest of Portugal		
78-92 Governorship of Parma 79 Unions of Arras and Utrecht			
	1588 Defeat of the Armada		
84 William of Orange murdered			
	1598 Treaty of Vervins		
			1600

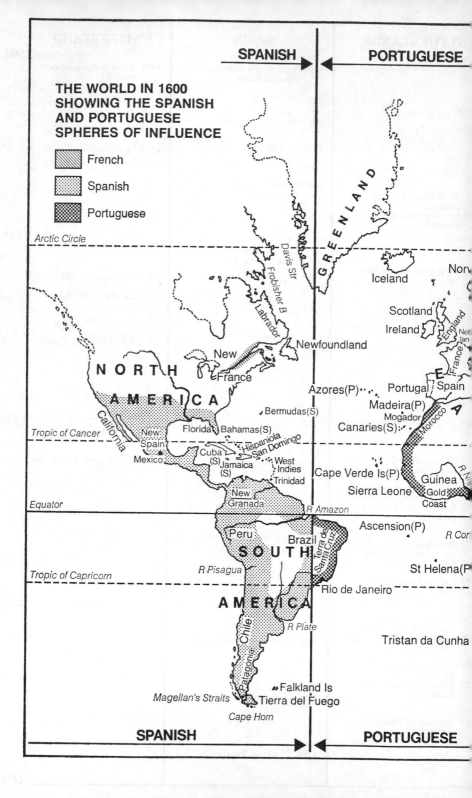

THE WORLD IN 1600
SHOWING THE SPANISH
AND PORTUGUESE
SPHERES OF INFLUENCE

French

Spanish

Portuguese

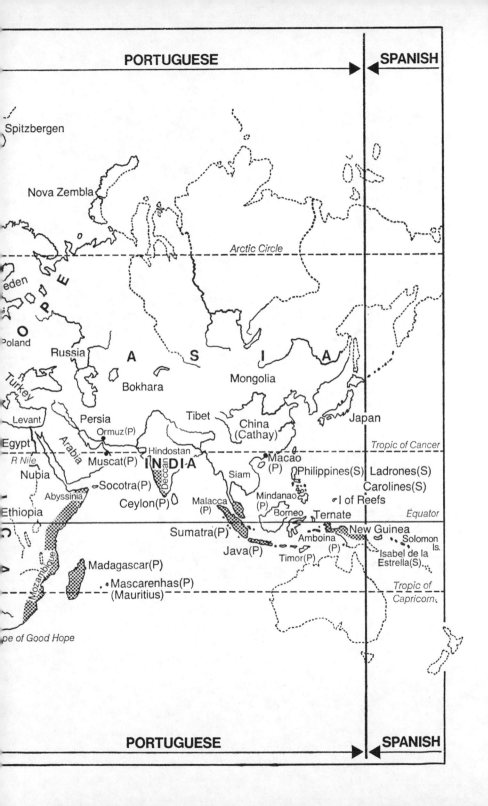

PORTUGUESE

SPANISH

Spitzbergen

Nova Zembla

Arctic Circle

eden

E

O

Poland

Russia

Turkey

A   S   I   A

Bokhara

Mongolia

Levant

Persia

Tibet

China
(Cathay)

Japan

Tropic of Cancer

Egypt

Arabia

Ormuz(P)

Hindostan

R Nile

Muscat(P)

I N D I A

Macao
(P)

Philippines(S)   Ladrones(S)

Nubia

Deccan

Siam

Carolines(S)

Abyssinia

Socotra(P)

Mindanao
(P)

I of Reefs

Ceylon(P)

Malacca
(P)

Ethiopia

Borneo

Ternate

Equator

Sumatra(P)

New Guinea

Mozambique

Amboina
(P)

Solomon
Is.

Madagascar(P)

Java(P)

Timor(P)

Isabel de la
Estrella(S)

Mascarenhas(P)
(Mauritius)

*Tropic of
Capricorn*

pe of Good Hope

PORTUGUESE

SPANISH

I
SIXTEENTH-CENTURY EUROPE

The century in history

The sixteenth century in European history is commonly regarded as marking the end of the Middle Ages and the beginning of modern times and is represented as one of unprecedented change. It saw the two great intellectual and religious movements of the Renaissance and the Reformation, the establishment of new trade routes and the discovery of another continent in the world and the rise of nationalism and the development of the sovereign nation-state. It was an age which gave western Europe an ascendancy in the world that was to last for over three hundred years.

For historians, what are the approximate limits of the sixteenth century? A commonly-accepted year for its beginning is 1494, when Charles VIII of France entered Italy and conquered Naples. Though he lost it within the year, this first French invasion of Italy was to initiate the struggle for domination of the peninsula between France and Spain, which lasted throughout the first half of the sixteenth century. In Italy, too, it was the year when Savonarola set up his theocratic republic in Florence, which foreshadowed some aspects of the coming Reformation. It was also the year of the Treaty of Tordesillas, in which Spain and Portugal divided the New World between them, and in which the Venetian press of Aldus Manutius issued its first book. In European politics, in religious revolt, in overseas exploration and in the spread of ideas, these events are signposts to developments which were to do much to determine the character of this century.

At the other end, the century is commonly regarded as terminating in 1598 with the Treaty of Vervins, which brought peace between France and Spain and recognized Spanish domination of Italy. In that year also, the death of Philip II of Spain brought to an end a reign which had made his kingdom supreme among the nations of the world, and the issuing by Henry IV of France of the Edict of Nantes,

which granted toleration to his Huguenot subjects, indicated a determination to permit religious diversity in order to restore national
unity and strength after internal strife. The fourth navigation of the
world by the Dutch sailor, John van Noort, and the closure of the
Hanseatic Steelyard in London, further events in this year, indicated
the changes in national fortunes in colonization and commerce that
were coming about as the result of the development of new trade
routes during the sixteenth century. The understanding of these
events lies in the sixteenth century, though their consequences were
to be seen in the next period of European history.

The states of Europe

The sixteenth century has been called the 'Spanish century', it was the
period when Spain's power came to be extended over the whole of the
south-western peninsula of Europe, the Netherlands and the greater
part of Italy, the whole of South and Central America, a large part of
North America and her possessions in the East Indies and in Africa;
when she had the most formidable military and naval forces in Europe;
when she checked the advance of Turkish power at the Battle of
Lepanto; and when she enjoyed great artistic, literary and religious
achievements. In the first half of the century, Charles V united in his
person the positions of King of Spain and Holy Roman Emperor,
and thereafter the Spanish royal family was linked through marriage
with the important house of Habsburg, the holder of territories in
Central Europe and the Imperial position. Moreover, the Counter-
Reformation made Spain the leading Roman Catholic power, sending
missionaries overseas, dominating the Council of Trent and seeking
to destroy Calvinists in the Netherlands and Huguenots in France.

Yet Spain's greatness was only a little more recent than her existence
as a state. Between the years 714 and 732 the Moors had crossed from
North Africa and conquered almost all the peninsula. Gradually they
had been subdued, and Christian kingdoms had come into being which
had been absorbed by the kingdoms of Castile, dominant in the heart
of Spain, and Aragon with its Mediterranean empire. These were
united with the accession of Ferdinand of Aragon in 1479 who had
married Isabella of Castile ten years earlier. Only in the reign of these
two 'Catholic Kings', when a single Spanish kingdom was at last
achieved, did Spain's greatness begin. The unification of the peninsula
was completed with the conquest of Moorish Granada in 1492 and of
Portugal in 1580. Thus, the state which became the greatest in Europe
was also the newest, and this rapid rise to power was an important
cause of her equally rapid decline, signs of which were apparent even
before the end of the sixteenth century.

Spain's rival was France, whose territory was almost the same as it is now, except that her eastern boundary ran somewhat farther west, being west of the three bishoprics of Metz, Toul and Verdun, west of Franche Comté, just east of Lyons and again west of Savoy and Nice. France might have been the one kingdom strong enough to challenge Spain, but the Treaty of Cateau-Cambrésis in 1559 forced her to yield to Spain her ambitions in Italy, and the death of Henry II in the same year was followed by political disorder and religious strife which crippled her for almost the rest of the century. Only when Henry IV came to the French throne was internal peace secured and the way prepared for a successful challenge to Spanish supremacy in Europe.

While Spain and France were national states seeking future aggrandizement, the Holy Roman Empire was rendered confined and impotent by its medieval beginnings and misfortunes. It originated through the persistent dream of medieval thinkers that all Christendom might be brought together under a single ruler, who would restore to Europe the unity it had enjoyed in the time of the ancient Roman Empire. In 800 Charlemagne, the ruler of the Carolingian Empire of the Franks, which stretched from northern Germany to southern Italy and from the Atlantic to western Hungary, was crowned in St Peter's, Rome, as 'Carolus Augustus, Emperor of the Romans' by Pope Leo III as a reward for supporting him against his rebellious Italian subjects. This was regarded as a revival of the Roman Empire in the west, but Charlemagne's empire and the Carolingian monarchs both vanished. The idea was revived when Otto the Great, king of the recently-united German tribes, was crowned Emperor in Rome by Pope John XII in 962, and henceforward the Holy Roman Empire, as it was later called, was combined with the German monarchy.

Though both popes and Emperors agreed in supporting the idea of a single Christian empire in Europe, they disagreed about its nature. The Emperors considered themselves the successors of the old Roman rulers who had possessed complete secular and religious power, while the popes thought of the new Empire as a theocracy in which the Emperor (and all other princes) received their authority from the Papacy, which derived its position from God Himself. This disagreement frustrated the realization of the Empire's claim to renew the imperial authority of Rome all over Europe. In the eleventh century, the conflicting claims between the two authorities resulted in a long and violent quarrel which prevented successive Emperors being strong enough to gain either control of Italy for a short period or effective authority over all Germany.

Moreover, constant fighting and absence from the country weakened the position of the Emperors as German monarchs. They had to make concessions to the German princes, which increasingly enabled them to become virtually independent of Imperial rule. When, therefore, the Emperors at last abandoned the aim of universal dominion, Germany had become no more than a loose confederation of principalities, ecclesiastical domains and free cities, which defied all attempts to unite them into a single national state.

In addition, the German kingship remained elective according to the old Germanic tradition. Originally all the German princes could participate in the election, but this right became limited to a group of seven princes who were known as Electors and claimed to be the successors of the Roman Senate; the voting procedure was finally fixed by the Golden Bull issued by the Emperor Charles IV in 1356. There was a Diet, an assembly composed of three colleges—of Electors, of ecclesiastical and lay princes and of representatives of the free cities. It deliberated on Imperial questions, passed laws with the Emperor's assent and issued the ban or outlawry of the Empire against recalcitrants; but rivalries between the three colleges and between the Diet and the Emperor prevented effective legislation, while the independence of the princes made it even more difficult to secure the enforcement of laws or the imposition of bans. Some reforms were made. The Empire was divided into Circles (*Kreise*) in 1500, each with its local diet to deal with military and fiscal matters. The Emperor Maximilian I (1493-1519) was compelled to set up a Supreme Court of Justice (*Reichskammergericht*) and an Imperial Council (*Reichsregiment*)—a standing body of princes to control the central administration—but they met with little success owing to the dislike felt for them by successive Emperors and the rivalries of the princes.[1]

On election, the German king assumed the title of the 'King of the Romans'. He did not receive the title of 'Holy Roman Emperor' until his coronation by the pope in Rome. Frederick III, however, was the last to be crowned in Rome (in 1452), and with papal approval Maximilian I assumed the title of 'Holy Roman Emperor elect' in 1508. After Charles V, who was crowned at Bologna in 1529, no Emperor sought papal coronation, and from 1562 they were crowned Emperor at Frankfurt.

From 1440 the Electors chose an almost unbroken succession of Emperors from the Habsburg family;[2] and it became customary for an Emperor to maintain this quasi-hereditary possession of the Imperial throne by having his son elected King of the Romans during his own lifetime. Because the Imperial power had become so weak, Emperors often paid more attention to their hereditary family domains than to their Imperial claims. During the sixteenth century, Maximilian added Burgundy to the Habsburg possessions. His grandson, Charles V, ruled Spain and tried to restore the Empire to its former medieval

[1] P. 283.   [2] P. 279.

glory; but the Empire remained basically a collection of disunited German states, incapable of acting as a great European power.

At the beginning of the sixteenth century, the boundaries of the Empire nominally enclosed much territory in central Europe. It consisted largely of German-speaking states, though Prussia in the east was not in it. The Habsburgs' own hereditary domains—Austria, Tyrol, Styria, Carinthia and Carniola—were included in it, but not Hungary, an elective monarchy which became subject to them in 1526. It included the Netherlands and Switzerland and also Lombardy in northern Italy.

Within Germany itself, there were some 360 separate political entities, all supposed to hold their territory from the Emperor. Among the princes the most important were the seven Electors—the three Archbishops of Mainz, Cologne and Treves, the Archduke of Saxony, the Margrave of Brandenburg, the Count Palatine of the Rhine and the King of Bohemia. The Reformation and Counter-Reformation were to divide the German princes in their religious persuasion and sharpen their antagonisms, among which contention over the secularization of the prince-bishoprics presented an acute problem.

Below the princes were the Imperial Knights, who were entirely excluded from the Diet. Each owned a castle and some acres of land and dominated the nearby villages. They claimed to hold their estates immediately from the Emperor and refused to pay taxes imposed by the Diet. Perhaps two hundred had enough lands and wealth to be financially secure, but at least two thousand of them were in some sort of difficulty. The decay of feudalism, the aggrandizement of the princes and the growth of commerce were disadvantageous to them, and rising prices proved a final blow to many. They sought to support themselves by levying tolls and exactions in the countryside, taking service with the princes or raiding each other's strongholds. In the parts of Germany where they were most numerous, they formed confederations among themselves and vainly tried to take advantage of the Lutheran movement by organizing a revolt in 1522 which was suppressed by the princes.[3]

Finally, there were the Imperial free cities, some eighty-five in number, which also recognized no authority except that of the Emperor. Some, such as Nuremburg and Ulm, had considerable landed possessions, but others, such as Nordhausen and Wetzlar, owned only small orchards and gardens round their walls. In the early sixteenth century a number of these cities were important trading centres since Germany had become the centre of the European economic system with the decline of France in the wars of the previous two centuries and of Italy in the Franco-Spanish wars of the previous thirty years.

[3] P. 160.

These were Hamburg, Lübeck, Bremen and others in the north, where the Hanse, the association of trading towns, dominated the Baltic and the North Sea; and Augsburg, Nuremburg, Ratisbon and others in the south, where they controlled the great commercial routes over the Alps into Italy and from France and Burgundy in the west to different parts of Europe. During the century, however, these cities were adversely affected by changing economic conditions. In particular, the Hanse lost its supremacy to the Dutch.[4]

As well as Germany, the Italian peninsula was another part of Europe without national cohesion and for a similar original cause. While the development of a single German state had been frustrated by the determination of the Emperors to gain universal authority, similar consequences had attended a like policy adopted by the popes in Italy. On the eve of Charles VIII's expedition in 1494, there were five Italian states, amid the numerous smaller ones, which had assumed special prominence. These were Milan and Venice in the north, Florence to the south of them, the Papal States in the centre and the Kingdom of Naples forming the southern part of the peninsula.

The Duchy of Milan, in the centre of the plain of Lombardy, had, under the rule of the Visconti family during the fourteenth century, greatly increased its territory and taken over most of the smaller states of the plain which had not come under the rule of Venice. Following the death of the last Visconti duke in 1447, the Sforza family seized power, and during the last part of the fifteenth century the court of Francesco Sforza, the patron of Leonardo da Vinci, became the most brilliant in Europe. The sixteenth century, however, saw the end of Milan's independence. On the death of the last Sforza duke in 1535, it reverted to Charles V as an Imperial fief; he conferred it on his son, Prince Philip, in 1540, and thereafter it remained attached to the Spanish crown.[5]

Eastwards of Milan was the Republic of Venice, which was governed by an oligarchy of merchants through a system of elected councils. During the Middle Ages it had become the leading trading city of the Mediterranean and possessed Crete, Corfu, many Aegean islands and much of the Dalmatian coast. In the fifteenth century it extended its territory in north-eastern Italy almost as far as Milan and became involved in the wars of the mainland, losing much of its Aegean territory in 1479. The sixteenth century saw it faced with the competition of the new oceanic routes to India discovered by the Portuguese, but its decline was not as rapid during this period as has often been supposed.[6]

The chief city of Tuscany, Florence, was a republic which also had become a great commercial city, enjoying a prosperity from textiles, leatherwork and banking; it had entered into trade by obtaining the

[4] P. 311.   [5] P. 150.   [6] P. 269.

port of Pisa. From the fifteenth century, the Medici, a rich banking family, gained increasing control over the affairs of the city, though the outward symbols of the republic were maintained. The family were prominent patrons of art, and during the supremacy of Lorenzo the Magnificent from 1469 to 1492 the city became a brilliant centre of artistic achievement and classical learning. From 1494 to 1498 the reforming friar, Savonarola, dominated the republic. Later the Medici were restored, and by the Treaty of Cateau-Cambrésis in 1559 Florence became the capital of the Grand Duchy of Tuscany to which was added the territory of the free city of Siena.[7]

Encircling the territories of Siena and Florence on the east and stretching across the centre of the peninsula from coast to coast were the Papal States consisting of the Patrimony of St Peter, the Campagna, the Duchy of Spoleto, the March of Ancora and the Romagna. Their beginnings dated from the edict of the Emperor Constantine in 321, which allowed the Church to own property. In succeeding centuries large estates, including much Imperial property, were given to the Papacy, which later strengthened its title to them by reliance upon the forged Donation of Constantine.[8] When Pepin, King of the Franks, defeated the Lombards in 754, he gave the Papacy additional lands and recognized the supreme political authority of the pope over his territory. This marked the real foundation of the Papal States. By the fifteenth century, the effective rule of the pope, apart from Rome itself, was confined to the Patrimony and the Campagna, and even there his authority was continually being defied by powerful noble families. In Rome the popes had become much like other Italian princes since they were elected by the cardinals, who formed a small oligarchy similar to that of Venice and came from the Medici and other leading Italian families. The popes of the Renaissance, like other Italian princes, became artistic and literary patrons and, following the example set by Sixtus IV (1471-84), made it their policy to strengthen their position by aggrandizing their family and consolidating their rule over their territory.

South of the Papal States and occupying the extremity of the peninsula and the island of Sicily was the Kingdom of Naples, the largest of the Italian states. It was also the most disturbed and during the Middle Ages was contested by rulers from the French house of Anjou and the Spanish house of Aragon, who had at times divided the mainland territory and Sicily between them. The kingdom was reunited in 1443 by Alphonso V of Aragon, but was divided again on his death in 1458 between his legitimate and illegitimate sons, a situation which gave Charles VIII of France an opportunity to assert the Angevin claims in 1495. His brief occupation of the kingdom was followed by a joint occupation by his successor, Louis XII, and by Ferdinand of

[7] P. 272.   [8] P. 31.

Aragon, but differences between the two soon led to the expulsion of the French and the establishment of lasting Spanish rule in 1503.

In north-western Europe, the Netherlands formed a state united only in the person of the ruler. Its inhabitants were peoples of differing race and language—Dutch in the north-east, Flemish in Brabant, Walloon and German in the west and south. In the Middle Ages it had been divided into numerous counties, dukedoms and bishoprics. During the fifteenth century the Dukes of Burgundy acquired these by marriage, cession and conquest and sought to coalesce them into seventeen provinces which were represented in a central States-General. When the Emperor Maximilian I married Mary, the Burgundian heiress, the Netherlands had passed to the house of Habsburg. The son of this marriage, Philip, married Joanna, the daughter of Ferdinand of Aragon and Isabella of Castile, and their son, Charles V, united the Netherlands with Spain. On his abdication in 1555, however, he resigned them with Spain and her empire to his son, Philip II, at the time when the revolt, which was to split the Netherlands by the end of the century, was coming to a head.

The largest state in eastern and northern Europe at this time was the Kingdom of Poland which, in common with the Netherlands, possessed a lack of natural frontiers and a diversity of races among her inhabitants. Her territory occupied the vast plain extending from the Western Dvina, a river flowing into the Gulf of Riga, to the great Austro-Hungarian mountain range, the Carpathians, and from the Baltic almost to the Black Sea and the Sea of Azov. She lacked defensible boundaries on several sides, and her frontiers were artificial. Her inhabitants included Poles in the west, Lithuanians in the east, Ruthenians in the south and numerous Germans and Jews in the cities. During the greater part of the sixteenth century, Poland was stable and prosperous and suffered less severely than other countries from the impact of the Reformation, but her inability to develop a strong national government continued, and signs of the decay of her power were apparent in her later years.

Across the Baltic, Scandinavia was a single state at the beginning of the sixteenth century. The three kingdoms of Norway, Denmark and Sweden were united under the Danish monarchy in 1397, but this union became increasingly unpopular with the Swedes. They achieved independence in 1523 as the result of a rebellion led by a Swedish nobleman, Gustavus Vasa, who was elected King of the newly-separated state. Denmark not only still ruled over Norway and Iceland, but her territory also included Jutland and the maritime provinces of Halland, Scania and Bleking round the southern extremity of the Scandinavian peninsula, which gave her control over both sides of the entrance to the Baltic and enabled her to impose tolls on shipping.

Sweden possessed Finland and acquired Estonia in 1561, and grew in internal strength throughout the sixteenth century. Scandinavia was the only important area in Europe outside of Germany which became Lutheran during the Reformation.

Russia in the sixteenth century was only just beginning to make contacts with western Europe. The territories of Sweden, Poland and Turkey, stretching across Europe from north to west, still blocked her access to the sea and the rest of the continent. The Princes of Moscow in the fourteenth century had gradually achieved supremacy over the neighbouring principalities, but until 1480 they had continually to pay tribute to the Tatar tribes, who had become overlords of the whole region. The sixteenth century was to see the continued expansion of the Muscovite state; Ivan the Terrible in 1547 assumed the title of Tsar of All Russia.

While during the sixteenth century the impact of Russia upon Europe still lay in the future, that of the Ottoman Turks, nomads from Asia who had become Moslems, was urgently menacing and dangerous. Their capture of Constantinople in 1453, which brought the Byzantine Empire to an end, was followed by the conquest of Bosnia, Herzegovina and Albania, the seizure of many of the dependencies of Venice in the Aegean and the subjection of the Tatars of the Crimea. The phase of conquest in Europe continued with the capture of Belgrade in 1521, Rhodes in 1522, Buda in 1527 and Cyprus in 1571. By then the Ottoman Empire was at its height. From the last quarter of the sixteenth century, however, its gradual but steady decline began, distinguished notably by the Battle of Lepanto in 1571 which checked further encroachments by the Turks in the Mediterranean.

The population of Europe

Knowledge of the total number of Europe's inhabitants rests on very uncertain foundations. Reliable figures only became available during the nineteenth century, and estimates for the population of sixteenth-century Europe must allow for a considerable margin of error because of the scarcity of trustworthy data upon which they can be based. Only a few wealthy Italian cities undertook censuses of their citizens, but in other parts of Europe taxation returns, parish registers and militia lists are among contemporary enumerations which make some calculations possible. The views about population totals or trends expressed by people at the time are generally not of much value.

It does seem certain, however, that there was a general rise in population of most parts of Europe during the sixteenth century. The total population of Europe increased perhaps from about 60 000 000 in 1500 to 85 000 000 in 1600, and this was accompanied by a marked growth in the size of towns. Some towns even doubled in size. In 1500 there were probably only five European cities with 100 000 inhabitants or more, but by 1600 the number of such cities may have increased to twelve or thirteen. Contemporary writers, while hopelessly uncertain about figures and often wishing to support some political or social cause in what they said, do agree in recognizing a rising rather than a falling population, although the reasons for this increase, apart from the absence of serious outbreaks of plague and famine during the century, are not easily ascertainable.

The most populous country in Europe during the sixteenth century (and for long afterwards) was France. Recovery from effects of the double disasters of the Black Death (1347-50) and the Hundred Years War (1337-1453) brought her an increase in population during the period, though at what rate is uncertain. It has been estimated that she grew from about 10 000 000 to 15 000 000 or 16 000 000, but it has been suggested that this increase would have been larger had it not been for the sixteenth-century Wars of Religion. Some calculations place the loss due to this cause as high as 2 000 000 between the middle and end of the century. Similarly, Paris, the largest city in Europe, may have increased its numbers from 120 000 to almost 300 000 by the middle of the century, but war probably reduced this to about 220 000 by the time Henry IV besieged it in 1590. It is difficult to assess the truth. The losses of the Wars of Religion were heavy, but contemporaries and historians after them have often tended to over-estimate the numbers lost by a country in war in past times.

A similar problem arises over the population of Spain. Contemporaries seem to agree that it increased during the first half of the century, especially in Castile, but declined during the second half, particularly because of emigration to America. Yet estimates based upon such figures as can be obtained do suggest that the population of the Iberian peninsula had increased by the end of the century. In 1492, after the conquest of Granada, the population of Castile perhaps approached 6 000 000, while that of Aragon was 1 000 000 and of Portugal possibly about the same; about a hundred years later, Castile's population had risen to about 8 300 000, Aragon's to just over 1 300 000 and Portugal's to 1 500 000.

What is the explanation of this discrepancy? Several factors must be noticed. Castile comprised two-thirds of the area of the peninsula and was three times the area of Aragon. Nowadays its countryside is empty and deserted; then it was the most thickly settled part of Spain. Nowadays most of the Spanish people live in the coastal areas; but then they were concentrated in the centre, and it was here that contemporaries observed a process of depopulation. Was this caused by emigration to America? Figures for the New World are particularly a matter of guesswork, but there may have been about some 50 000 settlers in Spanish America in the middle of the century and as many as 118 000 by the end. Even if this implied an emigration of twice that number to account for deaths at sea and in the colonies, this would not have involved a proportionately large loss of population at home.

It may well be that what contemporary observers regarded as depopulation was rather a redistribution of population brought about by internal movements. Indeed, the population of twenty of the thirty-one towns of Castile increased between 1530 and 1594, while that of only eleven decreased (nine of which were in the northern part of Spain where the war in the Netherlands and increasing piracy in the Bay of Biscay were likely to have affected them adversely). It seems likely, therefore, that there was a decline in the population of northern Castile, which had been the most prosperous area in the earlier part of the century, when the Spanish population as a whole was still increasing. But the population did, indeed, decline at the end of the century. The great plague, which first appeared in northern Spain in 1596 and coincided with a series of bad harvests in the last years of the century, moved steadily southwards, devastating the crowded Castilian cities, wiping out much of the population increase and initiating a period of stagnation and perhaps of declining population in Castile.

Notable among the Spanish cities to increase in size was Seville. Situated on a navigable river fifty miles from the Atlantic, it had the monopoly of trade with the Indies in the sixteenth century.[9] In 1500 it had about 65 000 inhabitants, but by 1588 this had risen, despite epidemics and emigration to the New World, to 150 000, making it the largest Spanish city, surpassed in Europe only by Paris and Naples. Its new greatness was exemplified by its magnificent archiepiscopal cathedral, the largest Gothic church in the world; built on the site of a mosque, it was finished in 1519, and contained the tomb of Columbus. To Seville came many foreign sailors and merchants as well as people from northern and central Spain, who were attracted by its wealth and overseas connections.

Madrid, which had about 4 000 inhabitants in 1500, grew rapidly after 1561 when Philip II made it his capital because of its position in the centre of the peninsula; by 1594 it had 37 000 inhabitants. The establishment of the court there stimulated the building of palaces by the nobility and monasteries by the religious orders; before the end of the century it was criticized as an extravagant drain on the Spanish economy.

The population of England perhaps increased from about 3 500 000 in 1500 to 4 500 000 in 1600. London steadily felt the effect of increasing trade during the century. Its population may have gone up from 60 000 to 200 000. This was much larger than any other English town,

[9] P. 73.

though they too were growing. Estimates for other English towns during Henry VIII's reign (1509-47) include 12 000 for Norwich, 10 000 for Bristol, 7 000-8 000 each for perhaps a dozen others, including York, Coventry, Exeter and Salisbury, 3 000 for a few like Northampton and Leicester, and 2 000 or less for most of the rest. It has been suggested that the population of Wales numbered rather less than 252 000 in the mid-sixteenth century and 275 000 by the end. The population of Scotland may have been about 500 000 in 1500 and about 700 000 in 1600. Of Ireland, it can only safely be said that its population was probably not much more than 500 000 at the end of the century.

The population of the Netherlands was about 3 000 000 in 1560. Holland, the largest of the northern provinces, had about 200 000 inhabitants in 1514; Brabant, the largest of the southern provinces, had 500 000 in 1526. Early in the sixteenth century, Antwerp had overtaken Bruges as an industrial and commercial centre and become the largest city in the Netherlands. Its population rose from 88 000 in 1526 to about 110 000 in 1550, but its prosperity was ruined by the iconoclastic riots of 1566, the 'Spanish Fury' of 1576, the blockade of the River Scheldt and other incidents of the revolt of the Netherlands. At the end of the century, its population had perhaps fallen by a half, and it had been overtaken in the north by Amsterdam, which by then may have had a population of nearly 100 000 and was sometimes called the 'new Antwerp'.

The Italian cities and states were the first to take censuses, some as early as the middle of the fifteenth century, but most not until a century later. This makes it possible to give more accurate figures for some of them during the period, and they show an increasing population in this peninsula also. The city of Verona had 27 000 inhabitants in 1473 and 52 000 in 1548. The Kingdom of Naples, without the capital city itself, grew from 1 870 000 in 1501 to 2 910 000 in 1548. The city of Naples doubled its numbers from 100 000 to 200 000 during the sixteenth century. Milan rose from about 100 000 to 180 000 in the same period. The Republic of Venice increased from 1 650 000 in 1550 to 1 850 000 in 1620 and the Duchy of Florence from 586 000 in 1551 to 649 000 in 1622. During the century the city of Venice rose from nearly 100 000 to 168 000 and the city of Florence from 45 000 to over 60 000. The population of Rome fluctuated considerably. It was said to have been about 55 000 in 1521, was reduced by the sack of 1527 to 32 000, but thereafter rose rapidly to 45 000 in 1558 and to 100 000 in 1590. The total population of Italy is estimated to have risen from about 10 000 000 in 1500 to 13 000 000 in 1600.

The population of Germany, on the other hand, is difficult to estimate, but that of the territories of the Holy Roman Empire as a whole may have grown from about 12 000 000 to 20 000 000 during the century. Though none of the German cities were among those in Europe which had more than 100 000 inhabitants by the end of the century, some had increased rapidly in size during the period. These included Erfurt, Cologne, Nuremburg, Augsburg, Strasburg and Vienna, all of which had about doubled in size to 40 000-50 000 by 1600. Danzig had about 21 000 in 1550, and Hamburg rose from 12 000 in 1521 to 19 000 in 1594. The declining importance of Lübeck was shown by its rise during the century of only about 10 000 to 40 000. In Switzerland, only Geneva had more than 10 000. When Calvin went there in 1535 it had no more than 13 000 inhabitants, but between 1549 and 1559, no fewer than 5 000 foreigners settled in the city.

For the Baltic countries it is not easy to make any estimates of population. It has been suggested, however, that in 1600 Poland with East and West Prussia had about 3 000 000 inhabitants, Denmark 600 000 and Sweden, Norway and Finland 1 400 000. The population of Russia at this time must remain virtually unascertainable. It was probably not more than 7 000 000 at the end of the century. Moscow, before the Tatars burned the city in 1571, was reputed to have 40 000 houses, which may have meant as many as 200 000 inhabitants.

It would seem, therefore, that the increase in the population during the sixteenth century was fairly general among the countries of Europe though the growth of the size of towns was most marked in prosperous, fertile regions like Italy or France or in maritime, commercial areas like the Netherlands and England, and was less marked in remote, northern countries like Norway, Sweden and Denmark. This difference is shown by the various densities of population among the European states at the end of this period. It has been estimated that the average number of persons to the square kilometre at about that time over the whole of Europe was under 20 and for Italy 44, the Netherlands 40, France 34, England and Wales 30, Germany 28, Spain and Portugal 17, Denmark 15, Poland with Prussia 14, Scotland and Ireland 12.5, Sweden, Norway and Finland 1.3. Considerable though these differences are, the fact remains that every European country at this time was thinly-populated in comparison with modern conditions. The population density of Elizabethan England, for instance, approximated to that of European Russia in the nineteenth century. Yet the increase of population in the sixteenth century, combined with inadequate methods of food production, was the most important factor behind the inflation of the time.[10]

[10] P. 82.

2

THE
MEDIEVAL
CHURCH

The Roman inheritance

The Reformation of the sixteenth century was not a sudden and wholly unexpected event. It came about as the result of long-standing forces and developments—some going back in origin to the early days of Christianity—in the history of the Church and the Papacy. 'The Papacy is not other than the Ghost of the deceased Roman Empire, sitting crowned upon the grave thereof,' wrote Thomas Hobbes (1588-1679) in a well-known phrase in his *Leviathan*. To a considerable extent, indeed, this description applied, not merely to the Papacy, but to the Catholic Church as a whole in western Europe at the beginning of the sixteenth century. Since the fifth century, the attempt to revive the ideal of unity, destroyed by the barbarian tribes, had found expression in the Holy Roman Empire and the Church, but the Empire was largely a phantom creation rather than a political reality. Its territory was confined to central Europe, and even here the Emperor possessed but scant authority. The Church, on the other hand, exercised very real power and did most to maintain that European unity which had existed under the old Roman Empire. At its head was the Roman Papacy, which through its bishops and law-courts exercised an authority in the various kingdoms upon clergy and laity alike which temporal rulers could do little to dispute.

This came about not so much by the carrying out of any prearranged policy in the Church as through the circumstances surrounding its origins and early development. Jesus Christ even at birth was enrolled as a Roman subject, though not a Roman citizen. His mission was confined to Palestine, which was a small province of the Roman Empire. After his death, his task was continued by Jews who were Roman subjects, some of whom, notably St Paul, were Roman citizens, and they worked within the Roman Empire. The Church, therefore, came into being as a Roman institution, and was so regarded by the imperial authorities, who recognized the danger of the rival authority it exerted over its members who were also Roman subjects. It was almost inevitable that Christians should soon find themselves exposed to persecution by the imperial authorities.

During the first centuries of its existence, the Church had to struggle not only against persecution from without, but also, in an age of religious uncertainty and speculation, against diversity of belief within. The result was a strengthening of its organization to stiffen resistance against repression and a tightening of its system of doctrine to establish orthodoxy against heresy. One feature of this development was the ever-increasing power of the clergy and a growing distinction between them and the laity. The bishop, as the centre of unity and the protector of the apostolic faith, became continually more important; and bishops of leading cities soon began to gain a superiority over the rest. In particular, the bishops or popes of Rome, the imperial capital, began to claim some sort of primacy.

The granting of toleration to Christianity by the Emperor Constantine in AD 312 hastened these developments. Since his policy was to unite the Church with the state,[1] Constantine insisted that it must possess unity of doctrine so that it could exercise a unifying influence within his dominions. Though unbaptized, he himself presided over the Council of Nicea in AD 325, and the great age of creed-making began. Moreover, the removal by Constantine of his capital to the new city of Constantinople, on the shores of the Bosphorus, in AD 330 further increased the power of the pope. Later, Constantine's action came to be regarded as deliberately favouring the Papacy, a belief expressed in the forged Donation of Constantine in which the Emperor purported to confer on the pope primacy over other Churches and supremacy in Rome and Italy;[2] but the legend was based upon the situation which had developed. The departure of Constantine from Rome did not destroy the age-long universal regard for the city as the centre of civilization, and the bishop came to take the place of the Emperor there. The continuing doctrinal controversies also exalted the Papacy. Most of them occurred in the east, and the disputants, anxious to gain support from neutral Latins, appealed to the Bishop of Rome, who thus became an arbiter in disputes affecting the whole Church and a source of pronouncements upon doctrinal questions.

The final collapse of the Roman Empire in the west in 476 further strengthened the Church, which was the one stable institution to survive from the former age. When the authority of the Roman officials vanished with the barbarian invasions, there remained that of the clergy who were superior in culture and education to the new invaders. Gradually not only education, but administration and statecraft as well, passed into ecclesiastical hands. The power of the clergy was thus further increased, and the distinction between them and the

[1] P. 33.   [2] P. 23.

laity became yet more pronounced. They inherited the traditions of the class of officials who had given the Roman Empire its reputation for efficient government. And when the Church began to take the Gospel to the barbarian peoples, its expansion was practically contained within the frontiers of the old Roman Empire or at least of the Roman imperial influence; and so it was to remain for some fifteen hundred years. During this time also the Church was substantially an institution which organized its officials, method, spirit and aims on the imperial modes of ancient Rome. Its dioceses corresponded to the empire's territorial divisions; its canon law was strongly influenced by Roman legal ideas; and Latin remained the language of its worship, administration and scholarship.

The exaltation of the spiritual power

The period in the history of western Europe extending from the decay of classical culture during the fifth century to the beginning of medieval culture during the eleventh century is commonly known as the Dark Ages. During this time it was intellectually inferior to the civilization of both Byzantium and Islam and was beset by Moslem invaders and Slav, Hungarian and Viking raiders. Plague, famine, destruction and decline of trade reduced the life of its people to poverty and insecurity.

The Church, which had become bound so closely to the Roman Empire, suffered severely materially and in morale; its great days of power and expansion seemed to be over. The troubled times contributed to the rise of monasticism, which owed its origin to the wish to lead a life of perfection in greater security than was possible in the constricted circumstances of ordinary existence in the west. John Henry Newman described this period, from the point of view of ecclesiastical history, as the Benedictine age, and this well recalls the predominant religious ideal of the time. By the middle of the eleventh century the hold of the rule of St Benedict upon the popular mind was complete; the greatest figures of the previous three centuries had been connected with the order.[3]

In this age of uncertainty, people sought security through the physical association with eternity that the veneration of the relics of saints brought them. By the eighth century, such was the demand for these relics, the alleged bodies of early saints and martyrs were broken up and the fragments bought and sold; the cult increased during the Crusades (1095-1204) when numerous relics of all sorts were brought back from the Holy Land. They were encased in shrines, kept in reliquaries, carried in processions and visited by pilgrims in search of acts of healing and answers to their prayers. Every church collected them, sometimes in great quantities. In the mid-thirteenth century

[3] P. 34.

York Minister had nearly two hundred which included bones and pieces of clothing of apostles, martyrs, popes and bishops, stones from the Holy Sepulchre, pieces of the Cross, some of the manna which fed the Israelites and a fragment of the staff of Moses. Many relics also were in the possession of monarchs, who sought to support their authority with the power of the saints. Charlemagne's throne in Aachen, constructed to the dimensions of Solomon's throne, was made with cavities to contain relics; and the Holy Lance, which had pierced the side of the Saviour and was said to have belonged to Constantine, was the most important political possession of the tenth-century Emperors. In the sixteenth century, King Henry VII of England treasured a leg of St George, his kingdom's patron; and the Elector Frederick, Archduke of Saxony and Luther's patron, had made a collection of relics in the Church at Wittenberg, which in 1509 was listed as containing 5 005 items, including 204 corpses of the innocent children slain by Herod, a piece of the burning bush of Moses, a part of the cradle of Jesus and thirty-three fragments of the Cross. Even the pope, though his claims were based upon Scripture, came in practice to owe most of his authority to the fact that he was the guardian of the body of St Peter so that from Rome the Apostle spoke through his representative on earth.

Yet the possession of relics was not enough to uphold the exercise of authority by rulers. They needed some form of direct sanctification of their office, and this they obtained through their coronation at which the reception of the crown, the anointing with holy oil and the putting on of official vestments gave them a sacred character and put them as much above bishops and priests as the pope himself. The nature of the coronation service is a reminder that at this time the idea of Church and State as two separate, competing societies did not exist.

As well as its organization and outlook, the Church inherited from the Roman Empire its position in the community. The Roman Empire had been a single, all-absorbing, omnicompetent power which recognized no rival authority. At first the Church had claimed freedom and so endured persecution, but when it triumphed, it virtually abandoned this claim. Under Constantine, the only change made was that the state became Christian instead of pagan, and when Theodosius the Great in AD 380 proscribed paganism, the unity of the imperial authority was in fact restored. This Church-state conception was inherited by the kingdoms that succeeded the fall of Roman power. In all of them, every member of the state was a member also of the Church and was ruled by two official hierarchies, the king's officials and the pope's, clerical and lay. These two sets of officials normally worked closely together. Royal officials enforced ecclesiastical discipline, and the clergy acted as royal clerks and ministers; kings exercised

B

authority within the Church, and popes had rights in every kingdom. In these circumstances, when Church and state came into conflict, it meant a clash between the ecclesiastical and civil hierarchy of officials, a dispute over their respective spheres of authority.

Such a situation arose during the tenth and eleventh centuries when Europe gradually regained its political and military, economic and cultural power, culminating in the medieval Renaissance of the twelfth century.[4] The Church shared in this renewal of strength, in which monasticism took an important part. The Benedictine movement continued to flourish and reached its height in the Abbey of Cluny in Burgundy, which was founded in 910. Among the ideals held by the Cluniacs was the freeing of the clergy from dependence upon lay rulers and the exalting of the spiritual power above the temporal. One of their number, Hildebrand, became Pope Gregory VII in 1073 and two years later forbade the practice of investiture by which the Emperor and other lay princes claimed to invest a bishop-elect with the ring and staff of his office and to receive homage from him before his consecration, a practice which had led to the bestowal of ecclesiastical office upon unqualified persons. He was defied by the Emperor Henry IV, but by excommunicating him and releasing his subjects from their allegiance to him, the pope compelled the Emperor to submit to him at Canossa. By the end of the twelfth century, as the result of the policy of Gregory and his successors, the Papacy had power and influence which rivalled that of any lay ruler and was wider in its international scope.

At the same time, the authority and prestige of the clergy, which distinguished them from the laity, increased. Clerical celibacy, which had long been required of all the higher clergy, was from the beginning of the twelfth century gradually extended to all in holy orders, depriving them of the ties of citizenship and family and uniting them by common participation in another way of life. Again, canon law (the collection of ecclesiastical rules imposed by the Church in matters of faith, morals and discipline) had developed by 1300 into a complete system which was enforced by bishops' courts upon both clergy and laity. Of great importance also was the definition at the Lateran Council of 1215 of the doctrine of trans-substantiation (the conversion in the Mass of the whole substance of the bread and wine into the Body and Blood of Christ so that only the 'accidents' or appearances of the bread and wine remained) and the requirement that all adult Christians were to confess to their parish priest at least once a year. Every priest, even if illiterate or immoral, was now invested with the immense spiritual prerogative of calling down Christ from Heaven and making Him to be present among the people, together with the power to determine their eternal future by absolving them from their sins. A further distinction, which

[4] P. 32.

had been gained by the clergy by the thirteenth century, was that they alone communicated in both kinds—they received both the bread and the wine at the Mass and the laity only the bread.

The monopoly of education enjoyed by the medieval clergy further increased their power, and the period of two centuries, which ended with the death of St Thomas Aquinas in 1274, saw the establishment of Scholasticism, the system of philosophy that buttressed the control of the Church in the realm of scholarship and thought. It assumed that all the conceptions of the divine mind could be arranged in a human system which should include all knowledge; and by the application of the logic of Aristotle to Christianity, it offered a coherent account of all phenomena and returned a theoretically consistent answer to every enquiry.[5] In the sixteenth century Erasmus and Luther were not alone in finding Scholasticism a lifeless system, irrelevant to the knowledge of God,[6] but in the twelfth and thirteenth centuries it flourished and became closely identified with Christianity itself, one of its postulates being the supremacy of papal power. In this way, this aspect of the medieval Renaissance contributed towards the growth of ecclesiastical influence and authority.

The decay of medievalism

This period was not only a time of European intellectual revival, but also one of increasing population, wealth and general vitality. The new spirit found expression in the military drive to the east in the form of the Crusades undertaken to recover the Holy Land from Islam. The natural leader of the Crusading armies should have been the Emperor, but he was excluded because of the quarrel with the Papacy, and so the popes took control of the movement into their own hands and gained further prestige. The Crusades were a military and religious failure; they neither saved the Sepulchre of Christ nor gained the commerce of the east.

In fact, the resurgence of Europe was short-lived. The thirteenth century began another period of semi-decline; similarly, the Papacy, despite its increasing pretensions, could not retain the actual authority it had acquired in previous generations. The signs of the change were not, however, immediately apparent. Pope Boniface VIII proclaimed the year 1300 a Holy Year. Thousands of pilgrims came to Rome to claim the indulgence granted to them,[7] and the power of the Papacy seemed as strong and assured as ever. During the great pontificate of Innocent III (1198-1216), the reduction of King John of England to the position of a vassal of the Papacy was but one instance of the many uses made of papal authority in nearly every kingdom of Europe; and in 1266 the Papacy, by bringing the French into Italy, won its

[5] P. 96.   [6] Pp. 61, 155.   [7] P. 39.

final triumph over the Empire.[8] Yet events, which would have been hardly imaginable during the previous two centuries, were at hand and foreshadowed changing circumstances that were not favourable to ecclesiastical authority. The violent attack on Boniface VIII in 1303 by French troops, who defied the threat of excommunication and stormed his palace at Anagni, was a sign of the growth of national feeling which had occurred during the later part of the thirteenth century and was increasingly to reduce the political influence of the popes.

It now seems that Innocent III's pontificate marked the climax of the medieval Papacy and, indeed, of the whole medieval ecclesiastical system. The summer of the Middle Ages was passing into its autumn. Even at the great Lateran Council of 1215, which was the culmination of papal success, there were those who urged that the high claims made for the clergy were not matched by their fitness for office or devotion to duty, and the Council sought to encourage the establishment of schools, preaching in cathedrals and higher standards of clerical conduct.

Censures of the corruptions of the clergy and calls for a return to apostolic purity were by no means infrequent in the Middle Ages. At this time the most vehement were made by the Albigenses, a sect in the south of France who rejected the sacramental system of the Church and revived the ancient Manichaean heresy, which believed in two divinities, one good, the other evil, struggling for mastery of the world. Since the body was the work of the spirit of evil, the Albigenses held that true Christians must renounce all the pleasures of the flesh, and the asceticism and self-denial displayed by many of them, when compared with the self-indulgence and privileges of the clergy, gained them widespread influence. As they were a threat to both the Church and the social order, the condemnation of the Albigenses was inevitable. It was a sign that the twelfth-century cultural resurgence was now turning inwards, instead of expanding further, that the Papacy was able to divert the crusading zeal, previously directed against the infidels in the east, to suppressing such efforts to purify the Church. In 1208 a crusade, often conducted with great brutality and cruelty, was launched against the Albigenses and resulted in their final extirpation by the end of the fourteenth century.

The Albigensian crusade inaugurated a new era in the history of the Church. Pious, devout-minded lay people were in conflict with the clergy, a development which was to continue for the rest of the Middle Ages, and the use of military force to combat heresy was accompanied by the establishment of the Inquisition, an organization to prevent its reappearance. Up to this time bishops had been responsible for the suppression of heresy in their dioceses, but many of them had neither the time nor the inclination to do this thoroughly, and in 1233 Pope

[8] P. 19.

Gregory IX appointed papal inquisitors to go round the parishes, seeking out heretics, admonishing them to repent, and trying and punishing the contumacious. The medieval Inquisition was essentially an institution devised and controlled by the Papacy, but its efficacy depended upon the attitude of rulers of states towards its activities. It was most energetic and powerful in France, Germany and Italy, but even there it had by the sixteenth century become virtually extinct or moribund after its first century of success.

Another development, which also changed the medieval Church, followed upon the collapse of the Benedictine monopoly in monasticism during the late eleventh century, a collapse which coincided with the beginning of the period of rapid commercial and cultural expansion in western society. This expansion made possible a new diversity of life and opportunity in many enterprises, including monasticism, and the twelfth century saw the successful growth of the Carthusians, Cistercians and other new monastic orders. Numerous monasteries were established, especially in England and France, but within a century a decline had set in. No longer were new orders founded to amend the defects of the older ones. The abbots and monks of all orders beautified their churches, but none went forth in search of a stricter life than was possible in the old monasteries. Every generation saw fewer new monasteries established and a steady decline in the number of monks in the existing ones.

Indeed, the monastic ideal was losing its attraction. For centuries monasteries had provided a refuge in which individuals could pursue the quest for the purification and salvation of their souls by privation and self-denial—to medieval Christianity this was the highest form of religious life. Now, however, the desire to seek communion with God in mysticism and seclusion was declining. This changed outlook was seen in the early years of the thirteenth century with the appearance of the friars, who were something completely new in the religious life of Europe. They took the same vows of poverty, chastity and obedience as monks, but did not live enclosed in a monastery; they offered devout men the opportunity to exercise their piety by being useful and active in the world. Of the two greatest orders, the Dominicans were founded to combat heresy by study and preaching and the Franciscans to share the poverty of the urban slums and evangelize their inhabitants. They were thus brought into being by the revival of learning and trade in the twelfth century which produced two features hitherto unknown in medieval Europe—universities and great towns. And with the decline of the monastic ideal, the spirit of true medievalism disappeared, never to reappear. The new orders of the Counter-Reformation were to model their aims upon those of the friars rather than the monks.[9] The friars did not produce saints of the monastic type, but from their

[9] P. 203.

members later came religious rebels and visionaries, some of them forerunners of Luther, who himself belonged to an order of friars.[10]

The triumph of papal government

Such movements of protest were fostered among the friars by the bitter sense of disillusionment felt by many at the failure of their high hopes during the thirteenth century. But the original call for reform of the religious life and return to evangelical poverty was quenched. The Franciscan ideal of poverty was seen by the Papacy to be as dangerous a threat as that of heretics to the foundations of society and the Church as a great property-owner. The Spiritual Franciscans, who wished to follow a literal interpretation of the ideal, were condemned in favour of those who upheld the corporate ownership of property by the order. Moreover, the Papacy succeeded in converting the friars into a kind of irregular papal army, exempt from all control except that of the pope himself. Inquisitors were appointed from among their numbers, especially from the Dominicans, whose scholarship was devoted to strengthening the intellectual influence of the Church.

At the same time as the Papacy was seeking to strengthen its monarchic rule in the Church, it continued to lose its political influence. Indeed, the two developments were closely connected. The Papacy was convinced that its power over the Church could only be assured if Rome itself were under its strict control and removed from any threat by the Emperors. Thirteenth-century popes, therefore, devoted their efforts to the work of keeping a client king in southern Italy—the Kingdom of Naples—and ruling central Italy with the assistance of their own relatives. So, instead of dreaming of dominion over all the rulers of Christendom, they were driven by necessity to intrigue in the restricted area of Italian politics.

Even after the defeat of the Empire, however, Rome remained anything but a safe papal residence, and in 1309 Pope Clement V moved for safety to Avignon in southern France, which belonged to the Kingdom of Naples and became papal property in 1348. Thus began the period in the history of the Papacy commonly known as the 'Babylonian Captivity'. It is true that in a sense the Avignon popes were captive to the French monarchy, which had previously brought the Papacy both victory and humiliation in Italy. Being close to the French kingdom, they needed French protection, and every one of them during these years was French by birth and culture; but the extent to which the Papacy suffered through this move must not be exaggerated.

During the two centuries before the move, the reverses it had suffered

[10] P. 153.

during the bitter struggle in Italy had been such that the papal court had not, in fact, been in Rome for half that time. The removal to Avignon was not, therefore, a great change for the Papacy, which could function there with less interruption than amid the distractions of the Italian scene. Moreover, the new seat of papal government was in a better geographical position, being on the strategic southernmost route across the Rhône and easier of access for the great majority of the people of western Christendom. Previously it would have been impossible to have thought of dissociating the Papacy from its mystical association with Rome, but now such a tie was no longer strong enough to prevent it moving to a place which possessed important political and other advantages.

The reason for this changed attitude was that the papal court had now become mainly a body which transacted administrative business. Innocent III had reorganized its machinery of government and began a new era in its history. His reforms included the establishment of specialized departments, the appointment of clerics trained in law and office routine and the initiation of the great series of papal registers. Among his extensions of its activities were the encouragement of appeals from lower ecclesiastical courts to Rome, the frequent employ- ment of papal legates who had supreme ecclesiastical authority in the countries to which they were sent, and papal intervention in the appoint- ment and translation of bishops. Subsequent popes had continued this work of centralizing the administrative framework of the Church, and the quieter atmosphere and more convenient position of Avignon assisted its further development.

The increasing bureaucracy this entailed and the enlargement of the papal palace at Avignon to contain it, together with continued political campaigning in Italy, involved growing expenditure, and the Papacy had, therefore, to seek means of obtaining greater revenue. The two most important ways adopted to achieve this were the issue of indul- gences and the increase of direct papal nominations to ecclesiastical posts with an accompanying system of clerical taxation.

The development of indulgences was connected with the change in the Church's penitential system by which confession by sinners before the whole congregation gave way to regular private confession to a priest, a process formalised at the Lateran Council of 1215.[11] This involved also the change from public to private penance (or punish- ment) for sins committed and an inevitable relaxation in the severity of the penalties imposed, since lengthy fasting, severe flogging or distant pilgrimages proved insupportable in ordinary life. A penance could be commuted by the payment of money, and from this practice probably came the idea of indulgences, which remitted the punishment imposed on the sinner. Later medieval belief held that in purgatory,

[11] P. 34.

the state of suffering after death for souls capable of salvation but
insufficiently purified at death, the time spent in the final expiation of
sin could be shortened by the prayers and good works of the living
performed on behalf of the dead. This led naturally to the idea that the
saints, by performing works of piety and virtue in excess of what was
required for their own salvation, had bequeathed to the Church an
inexhaustible 'treasury of merit' which could be transferred to sinners
by indulgences remitting not only penances in this life but also the
pains of purgatory in the next.

The dangers involved in using such a power led popes to reserve it
to themselves, but this resulted in the granting of papal indulgences
on a large scale. The first such general indulgence was proclaimed by
Urban II in 1095 to all who participated in the First Crusade and later
indulgences were granted to those who performed a particular action,
particularly a pilgrimage, or contributed a sum of money to a pious
purpose, a development which did much to turn the practice into an
abuse. Though official teaching always insisted that repentance and the
acceptance of absolution on the part of the sinner were essential before
an indulgence could be granted, in practice this was little observed.
By the fifteenth century most people regarded papal indulgences as a
way of hastening the ascent out of purgatory into heaven of themselves
and their dead relatives by means of a simple money payment. They had,
in fact, become an important source of papal revenue and were sold
without restriction by professional salesmen, such as John Tetzel
whose activities in 1517 infuriated Luther.[12]

The seventy years during which the popes were at Avignon saw
also the culmination of the long struggle to secure papal control of
ecclesiastical appointments. From the middle of the twelfth century
the determination to influence the appointment of bishops, which had
been displayed by Gregory VII, was continued by successive popes
until Gregory XI (1370-78) reserved all bishoprics for his own
nomination, although actually in most countries an arrangement had
to be made between popes and kings which allowed royal wishes often
to prevail. The right of the canons of a cathedral to elect their bishop
was ignored by both. Similarly, a claim to make lesser appointments
was also asserted by the Papacy. Clerics were intruded into cathedrals
and parish churches contrary to the rights of bishops and other patrons.
Often such papal nominees were foreigners and absentees who performed administrative functions at Rome or Avignon. This arrangement not only provided the Papacy with bureaucrats, but also gave it a
substantial income in the form of fees, dues and taxes imposed upon
the clergy to whom it gave appointments.

The popes were not able, however, to pursue these policies without
opposition. The fourteenth and fifteenth centuries were beset by

[12] P. 156.

cultural decline and spiritual malaise, plague and war, loss of population and economic recession; people looked for support during these years to their monarchs. A new national consciousness began to appear, particularly in northern Europe, and the rulers of some states were able to pass laws against papal aims. Both England and France sought to check papal appointments and taxation, although Imperial ineffectiveness and princely disunity prevented such measures in Germany. Indeed, Germany suffered increasingly from papal interference and exactions because of the very success achieved in limiting them elsewhere.

The growing nationalism of the times affected the Papacy disastrously. During its long residence in Avignon, all the cardinals, the ecclesiastics who formed the Pope's council and elected a new Pope, had come to be French. They were suspected in England and Germany and resented by the local Roman noble families, who had formerly dominated papal elections. In 1378 the cardinals unwillingly elected an Italian pope, who resided in Rome, but a few months later proceeded to elect another pope. For thirty years there was a pope at Avignon and another at Rome, each with his own cardinals. The resulting Great Schism not only raised deep questions of conscience and ecclesiastical authority for Christians but, since the Avignon pope was recognized by France and her allies and the Roman pope by her enemies, indicated the passing of the medieval belief in a universal order resting upon the Papacy and foreshadowed the national divisions of the Reformation.

When the cardinals of both sides at last met at Pisa in 1409 to end the Great Schism, the efforts failed so completely that for the next five years there were three popes with three papal bureaucracies. Then national rulers and their bishops took the initiative by compelling the pope with the greatest support to summon the Council of Constance (1414-18), which was attended by delegations of national representatives. The Council began by asserting that it had supreme authority in the Church, which it derived directly from Christ and so was superior to the pope. The three rival popes were replaced by a new one residing at Rome and proceedings taken against the contemporary Wycliffite and Hussite heresies.[13] Some attempt was made to remove ecclesiastical abuses and establish a conciliar system of government over the Church in the future. A number of decrees were passed condemning such abuses as clerical neglect of duty and delinquency, and restricting papal exactions, but the Council failed, through national differences and insufficient desire for general reform, to initiate administrative machinery and continuity of policy needed to perpetuate such a change. The Council of Basle (1431-49), which met to continue its work, had to submit to the Papacy, which was able to use its reunited resources and bureaucracy to regain its administrative power and

[13] P. 44.

supremacy. The medieval Church had failed to reform itself by agreement and in unity. The Reformation, when it came less than a century
later, was in part a movement of the clergy against this growth of
centralization in the Church.

The eve of the Reformation

During the later part of the fifteenth century far-reaching economic,
political and cultural changes began to take place in Europe which
inevitably affected the Church and increased its problems. Economic
depression had not halted the development of trade and the growth
of towns, and now economic conditions were improving.[14] Schools
were established everywhere, and universities grew in size. The
increasingly important bankers, merchants and manufacturers, rich
and educated, were jealous of the wealth and power of the Church
and disliked the monopoly by the clergy of positions in the state which
they wished to fill. Again, commercial undertakings needed capital in
the form of investment and loans.[15] In an agrarian society, money is
largely borrowed for consumption and need, to enable the farmer to
survive a drought or to buy seedcorn to sow, but in a trading and
manufacturing society, it is for production and profit, to finance
enterprises that can be expected to make a high return on their outlay.
For the greater part of the Middle Ages, therefore, the money-lender
was suspected as one who took advantage of his neighbours' necessities,
and the Church accepted this popular sentiment by condemning the
exaction of interest on loans.[16] By the end of the fifteenth century,
however, both an Italian archbishop, Antonio of Florence, and a
German theologian, Gabriel Biel, taught that, since loans were essential
for the productivity of an undertaking, money-lenders were entitled
to a share in its profits. This was, in fact, a recognition of the situation
in economic life where the teaching of the Church was receiving less
and less regard.

The weakening of religious sanctions appeared also in politics where
the rise of the national state was challenging the medieval conception
of the relationship between ecclesiastical and civil authority.[17] The
decline in papal and Imperial prestige gave determined monarchs an
opportunity from about 1480 to extend their power within their
kingdoms. They were able not only to check papal intervention in
ecclesiastical matters, but even achieve it themselves. By the Pragmatic
Sanction of Bourges in 1438 and the Concordat of Bologna in 1516,
the French kings secured the right of appointment to all the higher
posts in the Church of France.[18] Other monarchs were more or less
successful in gaining control of ecclesiastical offices to reward their
ministers and administrators, while in 1478 the pope granted to the

[14] P. 88.   [15] P. 89.   [16] P. 86.   [17] P. 109.   [18] Pp. 111, 221.

Spanish sovereigns the right to set up their own Inquisition.[19] The result of this development was twofold. On the one hand, there came into being bishops, abbots and other ecclesiastics who were royal officials rather than clerics, absentees from their dioceses and monasteries and dependent upon their king rather than upon the pope. On the other hand, as the Papacy became weaker and governments became stronger, reformers looked to their rulers to reform the Church, and the Church's hold over its vast wealth and possessions became more insecure, particularly as growing populations everywhere demanded its lands.

European rulers sought also to increase their power externally by aggressive wars. When Charles VIII led the French armies into Italy in 1494, he inaugurated a lengthy contest that destroyed the political isolation of the peninsula in which the Papacy had been able to play a part and exposed the unreality of its claims to domination over the rulers of Christendom. The need to establish efficient control over their own territories meant that the popes were now Italian, and so were most of the cardinals. Despised everywhere, particularly in northern Europe, they made the international role of the Papacy seem even less convincing. The Sack of Rome in 1527 showed up its diplomatic weakness. It could sometimes still secure what it wanted, but only by negotiation and not by decree. To achieve anything important in most European states, it had to gain the support or approval of their rulers whose subjects were increasingly looking to them for leadership and security.

By the beginning of the sixteenth century, the moral prestige of the Papacy had also seriously declined. It had become an institution committed to maintaining a large bureaucracy and engaging in diplomatic alliances and military adventures. This had inevitably led to a considerable degree of secularization in its character. The popes had come to occupy the position of princes of one of the Italian states, and they were elected from a small oligarchy of leading families, notably the Borgias and the Medicis. Indeed, in their personalities, ambitions and ways of life, the Renaissance popes were not inappropriate to the papal court as it actually existed as an institution, but visitors to Rome, including Erasmus in 1509 and Luther in 1511, found the atmosphere shockingly irreligious and worldly.

The Renaissance and Humanism were not in themselves anti-Christian, and by the early sixteenth century artists and scholars were increasingly influenced by the religious revival of the times.[20] Nevertheless, the improved education of the intelligent minds of the western world, which accompanied it, made thinkers and writers more critical of the Church's failings and, through the invention of printing, able to express their views more widely. The corruption and abuses of the

[19] P. 211.   [20] P. 55.

Church were not new. Immorality and neglect of duty by the clergy, superstition and ignorance in the religion of the common people, had existed for centuries, but what was changing was the attitude of educated people and leaders of opinion towards them. The indignation of Erasmus, when he visited Canterbury Cathedral in 1513 with Thomas More, at the variety of skulls, jawbones, teeth and other relics, which were engaging the attention of crowds ignorant of the teaching of the Gospel, typified the growing impatience of such men with the religious situation. Both Erasmus and More sought to persuade the Church to simplicity of life and efficiency of organization and a greater awareness of Christ's message through a renewed study of the Bible.

Nevertheless, the real signs of religious revival tended to be divorced from the system of the Church. The Great Schism had encouraged the heresies of John Wycliffe (c 1325-84) in England and John Huss (c 1369-1415) in Bohemia, who combined criticism of the wealth and worldliness of the Church with a desire to submit its teaching to the authority of Scripture. Their followers had apparently been suppressed, but still existed in both countries. In Germany and the Netherlands groups of mystics sought union with God through prayer and meditation rather than through the sacraments and penitential system of the Church. Among them was the German friar, Master Eckhart (c 1260-1327), who asserted that God was not to be found 'in thoughts, prayers, pious offices,' but rather 'by keeping silence and letting God work and speak.' Very different was the passionate protest of the Italian friar, Girolamo Savonarola (1452-98) at Florence;[21] but it, also, was an expression of the desire, among the zealously pious, for a purer, more vital form of religion than the Church seemed able to offer.

Yet there were signs of successful reform within the Church. The Brethren of the Common Life, an order of laymen founded in the Netherlands under the influence of the mystical movement, encouraged a personal piety which was inspired by *The Imitation of Christ* of Thomas á Kempis (c 1380-1471), and established schools at which both Erasmus and Luther were educated.[22] There was a growing movement towards self-reform within the religious orders, and by the beginning of the sixteenth century many of them were internally divided between those who obeyed their rules strictly or laxly. The new and reformed orders of the Counter-Reformation began to appear during the years Luther was making his first protests.[23] Cardinal Ximenes, Archbishop of Toledo from 1495 to 1517, had already carried out important reforms in the Spanish Church.[24]

These, however, were efforts so isolated and limited in their results as to increase rather than satisfy the needs of the devout and the aspirations of reformers. The superstitions of popular piety flourished

[21] P. 271.   [22] Pp. 59, 153.   [23] P. 203.   [24] P. 202.

as never before. There was a marked growth during these years of the veneration of relics, the making of pilgrimages and the elaboration of the cult of the Virgin Mary and the saints. Bishops continued to act as administrators rather than spiritual counsellors and leaders. Monasteries enjoyed their rich endowments from the past though the life of the cloister was attracting fewer and fewer entrants. Above all, the popes, owing to their very characters and current absorptions, were incapable of being able to provide the religious reform and renewal so widely demanded.

Indeed, the very absolutism within the Church, which the popes had secured for themselves, meant that every denunciation of abuses or attempt at reform was likely to be pronounced heretical or irreligious. Ecclesiastical authority adopted the same methods it had used before. The Wycliffites were persecuted like the Albigensians; Savonarola was executed as Huss had been. The Papacy expected this policy to discourage heretics and reformers as it had done in the past. Discontent had existed for a long time in the Church, but it had been subdued and could still be rendered harmless, therefore, in the future. By the sixteenth century, however, a new situation and fresh forces had produced a movement which successfully challenged beliefs and practices that had grown up during the centuries of Christian history, and this movement destroyed the unity of the medieval Church.

3
THE
RENAISSANCE

The nature of the Renaissance

While the term 'Reformation' was used contemporaneously with the movement in the sixteenth century, the term 'Renaissance' does not seem to have been adopted until about 1840. Europeans, who lived in the years of the Reformation, were aware that important religious changes were taking place around them, but they do not seem during the period of the Renaissance to have appreciated its significance to the same extent. The term was coined by nineteenth-century historians to express their conception of it as the great revival of arts and letters in the fifteenth and sixteenth centuries which brought the Middle Ages to an end and ushered in a new era.

The view commonly held about the nature of the Renaissance was that it was the recovery of Europe from the consequences of the fall of the Roman Empire. Since the barbarian invasions of the fourth century not only destroyed the power of Rome, but also swept away practically all the accumulated knowledge and culture of ancient Greece and Rome, the progress of European civilization was seen to have been checked for a thousand years and most of the achievements of the past to have been forgotten. Men's minds were dominated by the doctrines of the Church, which regarded the old pagan ideas as sinful and subjected art and learning to its control. An event sometimes held to have begun the Renaissance, the rebirth of culture in Europe, was the capture of Constantinople by the Turks in 1453, which compelled Greek scholars to flee for refuge to Italy and even farther west, taking with them their precious manuscripts of the Greek classics so long lost to western Europe. From them, first the Italians and then others rediscovered the literature and learning of the ancient world and so inaugurated the modern age, which was believed to be a time of almost continuous European progress.

In recent times, however, the unique simplicity of this view has been criticized in a number of ways. Modern historians insist that the revival of ancient learning was neither sudden nor concentrated in this period. There were several Renaissances, not just this one. There was the Carolingian Renaissance of the ninth century, which brought about a revival of the study and correct writing of Latin and even of prose and verse composition. More important was the medieval Renaissance of the twelfth century, which saw the establishment of Scholasticism.[1] This Renaissance was also marked by the revival of the study of Roman law in Italy, which had long been part of the Byzantine Empire where this law had been preserved in the great code of the sixth-century Emperor Justinian, and by contact with the learning of ancient Greece mainly through the Arabs in Moslem Spain.[2] The one led to the incorporation of elements of Roman law into the laws of continental countries, the other to the production of Latin translations from Arabic versions of Greek works. It would appear, therefore, that the recovery of antiquity in Europe was accomplished through a number of periods of revival rather than in a single one.

Consequently, the Renaissance of the fifteenth and sixteenth centuries must, contrary to common supposition, be seen as not unique. It was the culmination rather than the initiation of the movement towards cultural revival in Europe. It is equally clear that it did not start in 1453. The most that can be said about the effect of the fall of Constantinople is that it accelerated a process which had already begun. Long before this event occurred, teachers of Greek had found their way to Italy, notably Manuel Chrysoloras, the Byzantine diplomat and scholar, who taught Greek at Florence between about 1395 and 1398 and produced the first Greek grammar used in western Europe. During the time of Francesco Petrarch (1304-74), educated Italians became interested in searching for the lost works of Greek and Roman writers, in imitating the style of the Romans and in learning Greek. Petrarch himself not only discovered ancient manuscripts, but also sought to restore a taste for writing in classical Latin and to encourage through his historical work in prose, *De Viris Illustribus*, an admiration of the qualities of the famous men of antiquity. He also inspired others to share his interests, among whom were Giovanni Boccaccio (1313-75), whose *De Genealogia Deorum* became the principal source-book on classical mythology for Renaissance writers and painters. The roots of the Renaissance can be seen, therefore, to go back into the Middle Ages and, indeed, Hugh Trevor-Roper has described it as 'that last brilliant efflorescence of medieval Italy'* rather than a movement which ushered in the present age.

A further argument in support of this idea is that, if the Renaissance did mark the beginning of modern times, then it should have been largely concerned with natural science, since it is this that has changed

P. 35.   [2] P. 18.   * *The Rise of Christian Europe* (1965).

men's lives out of recognition and become by far the most important
influence at work in the world today. But it is difficult to see the
Renaissance as the transition to the age of science. Renaissance thinkers
paid no attention to science; none of them produced any important
mechanical inventions in this period, and even the greatest of the
architects made no advances in engineering over the Middle Ages.
The first scientific societies were not founded in Italy until the later
part of the sixteenth century, more than a century after the establishment of the literary societies.[3] The first epoch-making event in the
development of scientific knowledge did not take place until 1543
when Copernicus published on his death-bed his De Revolutionibus
Orbium Coelestium.[4] Neither the scientific discoveries nor the revolution
in thought in western Europe were a feature of the Renaissance.

Similarly, the geographical explorations accomplished by European
seamen have little connection with the Renaissance. European expansion by sea, which began in the fifteenth century, was not a departure
from the past, but rather a natural continuation of the Crusades of
the medieval centuries which were motivated by religious zeal mingled
with the desire for political power and commercial advantage. Throughout the Middle Ages the religious and military contest between
Christendom and Islam had been a constant aspect of European politics.
The struggle took place in the Mediterranean area, where the European
armies were unable to prevent the advance of the Ottoman Turks.
Indeed, it was they and not the European peoples who were most
obviously engaged in successful expansion during the fifteenth century.
Portugal's African maritime and commercial activities, from the early
years of this century, were an effort to attack Moslem power and
divert Moslem trade by initiating operations elsewhere. Their undertakings were a product of the hopes and frustrations of the past and
not derived from any new contemporary outlook.

The geographical discoveries should not be regarded as contributing
towards the outlook of the Renaissance. The voyages of Columbus
and Vasco da Gama, which were to have the most far-reaching and
fundamental consequences, did not take place until the last decade of
the fifteenth century, and the impact of the New World and the oceanic
trade routes upon Europe as a whole did not occur until a century
later. Not until then did the decline of the Mediterranean, as the great
artery of European commerce, become apparent. Nor did such
discoveries widen European thought any earlier and, in particular,
cast doubt upon the universality of Christian doctrine. It was not until
the seventeenth century that writers such as John Locke appealed to
the differing customs and religions in various parts of the world as
evidence to support his arguments against the idea that certain beliefs,
such as a belief in God, are innate.

[3] Pp. 101, 105.   [4] P. 103.

The invention of printing was similarly more gradual in its effect than is often stated. There is no evidence that the earliest printers brought about rapid multiplication or wide circulation of either the ancient classics or the new humanist writers. The books produced, for instance, by William Caxton, the first English printer, between 1474 and 1491 were mostly English versions of works of devotion and romances of chivalry, which had been the general reading in the courts of the Middle Ages. The edition of *Aristotle*, published in 1495-9 by Aldus Manutius (who also was the first to print Greek accurately), was a sign of the future contribution of printing to the cause of the new learning, but throughout Europe the output of the presses was predominantly of popular medieval books until the second half of the sixteenth century. Nor did printing play an immediate part in the spread of education; rather, printed books could be produced because of the demand resulting from the growth of education which had already begun in the fifteenth century. Later the increasing number of books further stimulated the development of schools and universities, but this also was not until well into the sixteenth century. It is easy to exaggerate the immediate connection between the invention of printing and the Renaissance, which was not a revolutionary movement in the realms of popular reading and general education.

Even as late as the opening years of the sixteenth century, the well-established medieval Latin grammars and textbooks were still in use in schools and colleges. In itself, Latin grammar was not a new contribution to education as a result of the Renaissance. It was the only sort of grammar that had been studied in western Europe for over a thousand years, and the methods of instruction remained fundamentally the same. The main contribution of Renaissance scholarship to the study of Latin itself was the preparation of better texts of the Roman writers and making available a greater number of authors to be studied. It also continued the spread of the study of Greek, which was becoming recognized as a university subject by the beginning of the sixteenth century, and gave some attention to Hebrew.

In many respects, therefore, the Renaissance of the fifteenth and sixteenth centuries appears as a continuation of the revival of the knowledge and culture of ancient Greece and Rome which had been already taking place over a number of past centuries. Yet it would not be correct to consider that there was not more than that to this Renaissance. Despite its strong links with the revivals of the Middle Ages, it was also different in character to an important extent. This is to be seen in comparing the medieval scholars with the humanist scholars of the Renaissance. Medieval scholars had been mindful of the question asked by St Augustine of Hippo in the fourth century,

'What is there in common between Athens and Jerusalem?'; and, like him, their aim had been to 'spoil the Egyptians', that is, to take from pagan learning what could be suitable for a framework of thought based upon Christian doctrine. This was done most notably by St Thomas Aquinas (c 1225-74), who tried to combine the philosophical system of Aristotle and Christian theology into a harmonious whole. He accepted, for instance, Aristotle's distinction between substance and accident which was used to explain the doctrine of trans-substantiation.[5]

What distinguished the scholars of the fifteenth and sixteenth centuries from their predecessors was not their continued study of the ancient languages and literature, but rather their attitude towards them, which became known, again in the nineteenth century, as Humanism. The humanists studied the literature and philosophy, art and antiquities of the Greeks and Romans and also admired the human culture these embodied. They accepted with enthusiasm the moral, social and aesthetic standards these proclaimed. They no longer thought, as medieval writers had done, of man as destined to do God's will on earth and live to His glory, but to seek to develop his own accomplishments and enjoy all that the world could offer him—an idea set out by Count Castiglione in *The Courtier* (1528).[6] And Humanism had a similar influence upon Renaissance art.[7] Though this attitude was inspired by a love of antiquity, it was no mere imitation. The achievements of Humanism in art, literature and thought were original and distinctive. The extent to which the outlook, standards and accomplishments of this age ushered in the modern world have been exaggerated, but its uniqueness is without doubt. As Jacob Burckhardt, the historian of the civilization of the Italian Renaissance, has said, it was 'not the revival of antiquity alone'. It was a new birth as much as a rebirth.

The Italian Renaissance

Italy occupied a central position in the Renaissance. It started there, and Italian leadership of the movement persisted in European philosophy, literature and art throughout the sixteenth century. Among the reasons for the Italian origins of the Renaissance, was the continuing reminder of her great past provided by the ruins of temples and villas, particularly in the city of Rome. For centuries these had been destroyed to provide lime and building materials for contemporary houses, but in the fifteenth century a new appreciation of these classical remains appeared. A Roman declared in 1443, 'The beauty of Rome is in its ruins', and the Renaissance popes ordered their preservation and encouraged their excavation. Pius II (1458-64)

[5] P. 34.   [6] P. 51.   [7] P. 53.

himself conducted antiquarian surveys, and Julius II (1503-13) appointed Raphael to be Conservator of Roman Antiquities. Popes and princes vied with each other in making collections of ancient objects. Even more important, the interest in Greek thought and literature of those who discovered and collected ancient manuscripts was also stimulated by contacts with the Byzantine Empire through Venetian and Genoese traders and Chrysolora and other diplomats.[8]

Such an interest in scholarship and art, however, required material resources to sustain it, and this was made possible by the expansion of Italian trade and industry during the fifteenth century,[9] which produced a greater degree of wealth and urban life than in the rest of Europe. This economic development was accompanied by political and social circumstances of equal importance in the origins of the Italian Renaissance. The lack of a strong central power in the peninsula meant that, particularly in northern and central Italy, where neither pope nor Emperor could assert their authority, most cities became virtually independent city-states, able to manage their own affairs. Moreover, their prosperity had attracted many of the Italian nobility to move into neighbouring cities and form with the leading manufacturers and merchants a common ruling class divorced from feudal and ecclesiastical influences. This combination of urban material wealth, political independence and social unity fostered a civic pride and rivalry which took the form of a desire on the part of each city-state to become as far as possible a centre of the art and learning of the Renaissance. Their rulers were ready to spend their wealth on supporting scholars and artists, collecting pictures and books and erecting and embellishing buildings. It was a situation congenial to the development and expression of new ideas in culture and learning.

The ideal behind this development was expressed most effectively by Baldassare Castiglione (1478-1529), a Mantuan nobleman, in his book, *The Courtier*, which he based upon his experiences at the small court of Urbino, where the Duke in the late fifteenth century had collected a fine library and established a cultured court. Castiglione set out the ideal of the Renaissance courtier, trained in both court and camp, who was to be learned and cultured, civilized and urbane, excelling in music and dancing, in scholarship and sports and, not least, in warfare.[10] It was a book which had an immense influence in the courts and among the nobility of the sixteenth century.

In the early fifteenth century the most important centre of the Italian Renaissance was the city of Florence, which had been a republic since the thirteenth century and was now one of the great commercial cities of Europe, its wealth being founded on the wool trade and banking. During this century the princely merchant family, the Medici, held power and brought the city to the height of its magnificence.

[8] P. 47. [9] P. 269. [10] P. 125.

Most of the members of the family were great art patrons, but outstanding were Cosimo de Medici and Lorenzo the Magnificent, whose power and influence extended over the greater part of the century.

Florence nurtured three leading protagonists of the Early Renaissance—in architecture, in sculpture and in painting. Filippo Brunelleschi (1377-1446) was the initiator of the new style of architecture. He went to Rome with Donatello to study classical architecture and on his return to Florence began its transformation into a Renaissance city. He had, however, to adapt Roman architecture to churches and other buildings for which there was no classical precedent. Arches over columns, which he introduced in the Church of San Lorenzo, came from early Christian basilicas which themselves were derived from later classical buildings. Similarly, the dome which he added to complete the Cathedral of Florence, was Byzantine in inspiration. The same is true of his facade of the Foundling Hospital, which has been described as 'the very first building in Renaissance forms': the pediments over the windows and the delicate Corinthian columns are Roman features, but the arches on these columns come from the native Romanesque style of eleventh-century Florence. The most important way in which he pioneered the Renaissance revival of the ancient manner of building was in basing his buildings on a coherent scheme in which the proportions and relationships of each part were carefully considered. Thus, the basic measurement of the whole of his Church of San Lorenzo is the square of the crossing: the nave measures four times this square and the side aisles a quarter, the complete effect being one of serene order and harmony.

The greatest Florentine sculptor of this time was Donatello (c 1386-1466), who was a pioneer among artists in rediscovering the antique. On his visit to Rome with Brunelleschi, he explored the Forum and broke into the chambers of the Great Baths to study the paintings and marble statues buried in the rubbish. He may be regarded as the founder of modern sculpture because he was the first since classical times to produce statues which were complete and independent in themselves and not simply adjuncts of their architectural surroundings. He developed three-dimensionally conceived sculpture, and his monument to the Gattemalata in Padua was the first bronze equestrian statue since classical times. With its realism and vitality it strongly influenced Italian art.

The most important painter was Masaccio (1401-28) who, despite the shortness of his life, influenced all artists who followed. Of his few surviving works, the most influential were his frescoes in Santa Maria Novella and in the Brancacci Chapel in Santa Maria del Carmine. They were among the first paintings to employ the new discovery of perspective, which Brunelleschi had used in designing his buildings.

His figures are no longer flat, but round and appear to stand out from the wall. Moreover, his paintings express the spiritual significance of Humanism. His subjects are religious, but the symbolic image has been replaced by a new realism: the qualities of his figures are expressed in purely human terms of everyday experience. After him, a succession of Florentines developed the art of the Early Renaissance. Fra Angelico (1387-1455), the 'heavenly painter', executed frescoes in the Convent of San Marco which expressed a feeling of spiritual serenity. Fra Lippo Lippi (1406-69) and Domenico Ghirlandaio (1449-94) in the Church of Santa Maria Novella both painted Biblical subjects modelled upon scenes from contemporary Florentine life. Andrea del Sarto (1486-1530), the 'faultless painter', was an accurate draughtsman and had a refined feeling for harmonies of colour. And Paolo Uccello (1397-1475) developed still further the use of perspective.

By far the greatest of the Florentines was Leonardo da Vinci (1452-1519), who has been called 'perhaps the most gifted man in history'. In his art, he was hardly at all influenced by the antique. His practice was rather based upon a patient and thorough study of nature, including anatomical studies and dissections. The details of the hair and hands of his *Mona Lisa* are most beautifully observed. His paintings are remarkable also for their careful composition, and a characteristic feature of his composition, to be seen, for instance, in the *Virgin of the Rocks*, is the arrangement of the figures in pyramid form to point the eye to the most important part of the picture. Similarly, in the *Last Supper* the disciples, as they lean across each other, show in a few telling gestures their distress at the betrayal of Jesus. Though its light and atmospheric colour resemble an antique fresco, these tensions within its grouping are modern, and it is truly the first picture of the High Renaissance, the culmination of the Italian Renaissance in the opening years of the sixteenth century.

His delight in investigation, restless imagination and wide interests led him to fill his notebooks with detailed observations on nearly all natural, scientific and mathematical subjects, and also to undertake ambitious engineering feats and attempt inventions which were not developed until centuries later. He investigated the circulation of the blood, the laws governing the transmission of light and the theory of aeronautics. He invented a number of improvements in water-works and mills, canals and locks, and he designed a giant ballista, a steam-gun, bombs, armoured chariots, multi-barrelled guns, an underwater-craft and a flying-machine. His delight in nature and its mysteries led him to consider its conquest by man, but his ideas remained theories because the scientific and technical discoveries that would make them possible still lay in the future.

Before the death of Leonardo da Vinci, Florence was ceasing to be the leader of the Italian Renaissance. This was partly due to the disorder to which the city-state had been reduced by the French invasions, the fall of the house of Medici and the dictatorship of Savonarola, but it was due also to the interest and support accorded to art and literature by the Renaissance popes.[11] By the time of the High Renaissance the cultural supremacy of Florence had passed to Rome. The Papacy had become Italianized and secularized in the fifteenth century;[12] and the popes, who belonged to the leading families of the peninsula, became like other Italian princes generous patrons of scholars and artists, even though these might be men who damaged the reputation of the Church and the Papacy. For instance, a papal librarianship was conferred upon the Italian humanist, Lorenzo Valla (*c* 1406-57), who was suspected of heresy, upheld the Epicurean view of life and proved the spuriousness of the Donation of Constantine.[13] Martin Luther was not alone among visitors to Rome at being shocked by scandalous tales about the popes, by the concern of cardinals for scholarship and good living rather than for morality and religion and by the immorality, laziness and irreverence of the priests.[14] This was the effect of the Renaissance upon the city and court of Rome, which had not yet experienced the religious revival that was making itself apparent elsewhere in Europe.

With the exception of Pius II (1458-64), who was one of the most eminent humanist scholars of his age, the Renaissance popes were not men of particular learning or intellectual ability, but they were determined to make Rome culturally worthy of her importance and history. Notable in doing so was Nicholas V (1447-55), who used papal funds to despatch agents east and west to copy or purchase important Greek and Latin manuscripts and founded the Vatican Library of almost five thousand manuscripts, so making Rome the leading centre of the new learning in all Italy and, therefore, in all the western world. The Library was enriched by Sixtus IV (1471-84), who also founded the Sistine Choir, built the Sistine Chapel and was a munificent patron of painters and scholars. Rome finally displaced Florence as the centre of the Renaissance under the two Medici Popes, Leo X (1513-21) and Clement VII (1523-34), both of whom supported outstanding artists and undertook magnificent building projects. But the way had been prepared for them by the warrior pope, Julius II (1503-13), probably the most imaginative patron of all, who within the short period of four years commissioned the three leading accomplishments of the High Renaissance—Bramante's rebuilding of St Peter's, Raphael's decoration of the Vatican apartments and Michelangelo's frescoes on the Sistine Chapel ceiling. And the men who undertook these projects were the predominant figures of this stage of the Italian Renaissance— their achievements illuminate its nature and development.

[11] P. 277.   [12] P. 43.   [13] P. 31.   [14] P. 154.

The first known accomplishment in Rome of Donato Bramante (1444-1514) is the small Tempietto of San Pietro, which is the first building of the High Renaissance and as important in architecture as Leonardo's *Last Supper* was in painting. Compared with the churches and palaces of the fifteenth century, it is remarkably severe. Its sole decoration consists of a frieze of crossed keys, the symbol of St Peter, who was supposed to have been crucified on the spot where the building was erected. Bramante largely discarded antique decorative devices and relied here for effect upon a simple compactness based on circular shapes and the noble relationship between the outer ring of severe Roman Doric columns and the inner core which it partly masks.

In 1506, only four years after he had completed the Tempietto, he was appointed by Julius II to replace the old basilica of St Peter with a new building. He rejected the usual longitudinal plan in which the building culminates in the high altar, and designed the church in the shape of a Greek cross with four apses and a large dome at the crossing. His conception symbolized both the decay of medievalism and the culmination of the Renaissance. It abandoned the conception of the medieval churches with their atmosphere of worship and prayer in favour of a splendid design which upheld the power and grandeur of the Catholic Church ruled by the pope as the successor of St Peter and Vicar of Christ on earth. The focal point of the building was to be the central cross from which all the points would radiate and it would be crowned by a vast dome. The massive piers supporting the central dome, which were the only parts of Bramante's plan that were executed, still stand and give an idea of the grandeur of his conception. It represents the combination of the spirit of Humanism with the weakened spirituality and unconcealed secularization of the Roman Curia and society.

Yet this mood was beginning to change as a result of the teaching of Savonarola and the growing religious revival which was to produce the Reformation and Counter-Reformation. The effect of this is to be seen in the work of Raphael Santi (1483-1520), the most famous of the Renaissance painters. When in Florence, before he was summoned to Rome in 1508 by Julius II, he painted in the common classical style, but his well-known *Sistine Madonna*, painted about seven years later, depicts the Virgin, not on a throne amid calm philosophical saints as had been usual since the fifteenth century, but floating on clouds like a heavenly apparition between Pope Sixtus II and St Barbara, while from below two angels gaze upwards in fervent adoration; it has been called by J. A. Symonds 'the sublimest lyric of the art of Catholicity'.* Raphael's series of paintings for the walls of the Vatican apartments are not only so harmonious, serene and balanced as to make them the

The Renaissance in Italy (1886).

finest expression of Renaissance art, but also significant in that their subjects are themes upholding those doctrines which were to be denied in the Reformation. His last important work, the *Transfiguration*, conveys this sense of changing, troubled times. The actual transfiguration, a symmetrical group illuminated in celestial radiance, is typical of the High Renaissance, but below it confused figures gesticulate in murky gloom. Renaissance clarity and harmony are replaced by confusion and uncertainty.

This change is apparent also in the frescoes in the Sistine Chapel painted by Michelangelo Buonarroti (1475-1564). He, too, was originally a Florentine, and his appreciation of the classical ideal of sensuous beauty had long to contend with the principle of religious asceticism taught by his older contemporary, Savonarola. His years of experiment in the 1490s finally produced the *Pieta* (now in St Peter's) which perfectly combined classical beauty with Christian harmony. By then he was inspired by a profound mysticism and concentrated his whole attention on the great theme of man and his relationship to God, which he expressed in his Sistine frescoes. Their subject is the preparation for Christ, leading from the Creation of the world through temptation and sin to the prophets of the Old Testament and the sybils of the Gentiles. The two frescoes representing the *Creation of Adam* and the *Separation of Light from Darkness* are grandiose paintings full of power, hope and light. These compare strikingly with the fresco on *The Last Judgment*, which he added between 1534 and 1541. The light, clear hues of his earlier paintings had given way to darker, obscurer tones and calm confidence to fearful confusion in a picture dominated by Christ the Judge amid the swirling bodies of the doomed and the saved. It reflects the changed mood of Rome after the Reformation and the Sack of Rome in 1527 had destroyed the optimism and self-confidence of Humanism.

Michelangelo's concern with the question of man's ultimate destiny was expressed in the sonnets he wrote at this time, which are full of devotion and religious feeling. For the last eighteen years of his life, he was engaged in completing St Peter's, but he did not share the spirit of Bramante's work, and, as Nikolaus Pevsner has said of his dome, 'the eternal city is crowned, not by a symbol of Renaissance worldliness, but by the overwhelming synthesis of Antiquity and Christianity'. As he regarded his work at St Peter's as an offering to God, he would not take any salary and offered to give his services without payment to the newly-founded Society of Jesus. He also joined a group of zealous reformers within the Church (which included Cardinal Pole, Archbishop of Canterbury during Queen Mary's reign), who had contacts with contemporary humanists; but the piety of the Roman Catholic Church of the Counter-Reformation was hostile to the Italian Renaissance, and the austere Pope Paul IV (1555-9) had the nude figures of Michelangelo's *Last Judgment* draped.

The successor of Rome to High Renaissance art was Venice, which remained politically independent and commercially active, escaped the consequences of the struggle between Francis I and Charles V and was sufficiently distant from Rome to be less immediately affected by the Reformation and Counter-Reformation. During his long life, Titian (1490-1576) led Venice to the forefront of the Renaissance and attracted many artists to the city from north-eastern Italy. His first paintings were full of vivid blues and reds; some of the finest were poetical or allegorical, and he was much in demand as a portrait-painter. Later, he painted in more sombre colours and produced numerous and magnificent religious pictures, including *Christ and the Tribute Money*, which an Italian contemporary called 'something stupendous and miraculous'. The Counter-Reformation was steadily exerting its influence on Italian art. Tintoretto (1518-94), the last great artist of the Venetian Renaissance, devoted himself increasingly to religious subjects; his most important work was the *Narration of the Life of Christ* for the rooms of the Scuola di San Rocca, which includes the vast *Christ before Pilate* and *Last Supper*, and all his works reveal his genuine faith in what he painted. On the other hand, another Venetian artist, Paolo Veronese (1528-88), whose gigantic pictures including his religious works exhibit a love of pomp and worldly splendour, came into conflict with the contemporary religious atmosphere. He was commissioned by the Dominican friars of the Church of San Zanipolo to paint a *Last Supper*, but it was so opulent and Venetian in its character that he only escaped condemnation by the Inquisition for sacrilege by renaming it *The Feast in the House of Levi*.

The classical style of the Renaissance did not, indeed, suit the revived Roman Catholic Church. During the next century it was to be succeeded, at first in architecture and then in painting, by the massive, ornate, splendid Baroque style, which asserted the claims of the Counter-Reformation in a Christendom that had partly denied them. The earliest clearly Baroque building is usually held to be the Church of the Gesù, built for the Jesuits in Rome between 1568 and 1584, and there is a certain appropriateness that it should be connected with the Society which did so much to sustain the new movement.

The Northern Renaissance

Renaissance Italy was well placed to spread the movement to the rest of Europe. Rome was the centre of the Catholic Church; Padua, Bologna, Pavia, Salerno and other universities attracted foreign students, particularly in law and medicine; foreign merchants came to

Florence, Milan and Venice; and artists crossed the Alps to learn from
the great Italian painters and sculptors. The leading kingdoms of
France and Spain both experienced its cultural and artistic influence;[15]
but the most important and distinctive development occurred in
northern Europe which, under German leadership, was by the early
sixteenth century the centre of European trade.[16] The courts of German
princes and the families of Dutch merchants patronized artists and
scholars and made possible the Northern Renaissance which, while
inspired by Italian influence, was essentially a native growth.

The intermingling of German and Italian artistic elements are to
be seen in the work of Hans Holbein (1497-1543), the German painter,
who produced at Basle his great altarpiece, *The Virgin with the family
of Burgomaster Meyer* in which, it has been said, 'German realism and
Italian dignity are blended'. Albrecht Dürer (1471-1528) similarly has
been described as achieving 'a genuine fusion of German strength and
character with Mediterranean breadth and nobility.' This is perhaps
best seen in the fusion of the noble and the macabre in his famous
engraving, *Knight and Death*, in which the knight on his charger has
at his side a skeleton holding an hour-glass and mounted on a broken-
down horse. Nevertheless, Lutheranism and Calvinism were hostile to
the continuance of religious art which had everywhere predominated.
With introductions from Erasmus, his friend, Holbein went to the
court of Henry VIII in England which he found more congenial than
the Protestant Swiss cities or German states; and Dürer was unable
in his last important work, the two panels representing *The Four
Apostles*, to found a tradition of Protestant art.

The Northern Renaissance was not, therefore, marked by flourishing
artistic developments like those of the High Renaissance in Italy. Its
emphasis was rather upon a scholarly and literary Humanism, which
owed much to the humanists of the south, to the diffusion of whose
works the Germans contributed the use of movable type in printing.[17]
Nevertheless, northern Humanism did not take the same direction as
that of the south. It was not inspired by the same delight in the rediscovery of the Greek and Roman classics and the desire to adopt from
them a morality which emphasized the uniqueness of man; rather, it
was guided by a Christian inspiration of its own. Northern scholars,
too, considered that they were emerging from the ignorance and mistakes of the Middle Ages and found the ideas of the ancient world a
welcome guide for the future, but at the same time they sought to
apply these ideas to the teaching of Christianity. The Northern
Renaissance, it has been said, was 'an intellectual revolution with
religious overtones.'

An important reason for the direction taken by northern Humanism
was supplied by the influence in this part of Europe of the Brethren

[15] Pp. 90, 202.   [16] P. 88.   [17] P. 17.

of the Common Life.[18] They represented what was called the *Devotio Moderna*; this insisted that the essence of Christianity was spiritual communion with God through Christ, which would transform the characters of men and enable them to lead a more moral life inspired by the message of the Gospel. For them Christianity was to be apprehended, not by scholastic arguments, but through the reading of Scripture. It was important, therefore, that Christianity should endeavour to discover, as accurately as possible, the truth about the Bible—its text, its meaning and its interpretation—and the methods of the Italian scholars of the Renaissance provided the means of doing this.

For the Old Testament, the pioneer work was undertaken by John Reuchlin (1455-1522), who travelled in Italy and learnt Hebrew from a Jewish court-physician so that he might study the Old Testament in its original language. He published a Hebrew grammar, the first to be compiled by a Christian and showed that there were a number of inaccuracies in the text of the Vulgate, the official Latin version of the Bible of the Medieval Church. Because he believed that study of the Hebrew language and literature was necessary to understand the sources of Christianity, the Dominicans accused him of heresy in 1511. His books were condemned by the Inquisitors at Mainz and solemnly burnt at Cologne. Pope Leo X finally upheld this condemnation of his books in 1520. This treatment of him seemed to be a glaring example of the bigotry and ignorance of the supporters of the old learning which was to be one of the causes that led many German humanists to support the Reformation.

The other and greater northern humanist, Desiderius Erasmus (1466-1536), was more closely influenced by the *Devotio Moderna*. Born in Rotterdam or Gouda, the illegitimate son of a priest, he was educated at a school of the Brethren of the Common Life and was influenced by both their personal piety and their respect for classical scholarship. After leaving school, alone and unsupported, he joined the community of the Augustinian Canons of Sion near Delft, but monastic life did not suit him, and he seized the first opportunity to obtain his release and pursue his own studies. Between 1498 and 1514 he lived in Paris, Oxford and Italy, taught for two years at Cambridge and then spent most of the rest of his life at Basle. He had an acute intellect and a strong moral sense. The freshness and interest of the new classical learning attracted him, and he wanted to promote it among the northern universities which he considered to be in a condition of 'barbarism'. At the same time, he was deeply concerned with the reality of religion and wished to free it from all that concealed its truth and degraded its moral tone. To him the promotion of scholarship was primarily designed to achieve this end. He wished to establish a more

[18] P. 44.

rational Christian doctrine and to emancipate believers from the ignorance and superstition of the past.

Probably the most important scholarly work of Erasmus was his edition of the New Testament published in 1516, which included not only a revised Greek text, but also a new Latin version and notes and comments on the matter. Like Reuchlin, whose Hebrew grammar had been published shortly before, Erasmus was among the first to apply the new critical methods to the study of the Bible. In undertaking this task, Erasmus was inspired by the hope that as many Christians as possible should become acquainted with the New Testament for themselves. In an often-quoted sentence in the introduction to his New Testament itself he wrote, 'I long for the husbandman to sing parts of them to himself as he follows his plough, for the weaver to hum them to the accompaniment of his shuttle, for the traveller to beguile the tedium of journeying with them.'

Next to the Scriptures in authority and value, Erasmus placed the ancient Fathers of the Church, and he sought to recover also the authentic texts of their writings. He published editions of the complete works of Jerome, Cyprian, Augustine, Hilary, Irenaeus and Ambrose, besides editing parts of Chrysostem, Athanasius, Basil, Origen and other patristic writers. This work was devoted to the same wish that knowledge of the real nature of Christianity would lead men to the true practice of it. To study their writings was, he declared in his preface to Jerome, a better way of worshipping the saints than 'kissing their old shoes and dirty handkerchiefs'.

Such words indicate that Erasmus was not merely a scholar, writing for a limited, learned readership. More than any other humanist, he was a popular writer who produced polemical, satirical books vigorously exposing with irony and ridicule the religious evils of his time, and these reached many northern homes and parsonages. A bookseller in Paris, who had heard that his *Familiar Colloquies* might be condemned by the university as heretical, immediately had a single edition of 24 000 copies printed and soon sold them all.

Among the objects of his attacks were the abuses of the Church's administration and especially those of the Papacy. In 1506, when he made his long-desired visit to Italy, he was present when Pope Julius II subdued Bologna and he saw him, clothed as a warrior, make his triumphal entry at the head of his army, a spectacle which he viewed 'with a mighty groan'. And in *The Praise of Folly* he spoke of the great benefits that would be gained by the Church 'if the Popes of Rome, who pretend themselves Christ's Vicars, would but imitate his exemplary life.' He went still further and criticized the whole system of the Medieval Church—'Truly the yoke of Christ would be sweet and his burdens light, if petty human institutions added nothing to what He

Himself imposed. He commanded us nothing save love for one another.'
He attacked also the monastic life as useless and wasteful, though his
own youthful and hated experience of the cloister led him to an
exaggerated condemnation of all who entered the religious life. He
said, for instance, that 'most of them have had no other call than
stupidity, ignorance, despair, laziness and the hope of being fed.'
Again, he ridiculed popular superstitions. In the vows and offerings
made by pilgrims and worshippers to popular saints, he saw merely a
pagan survival of the practice of sacrificing a cock to Aesculapius or a
bull to Neptune—'the names are changed, the intention is the same.'
And, finally, he joined in the contemporary criticism of Scholasticism,
believing that its attempt to comprehend all knowledge and truth
within the limits of a single system of thought had obscured the
simplicity of the Gospels and the Early Church 'with a kind of crude
and barren subtlety.' He accused Schoolmen of discussing such
questions as 'whether God could have taken upon Him the form . . .
of a cucumber . . . and supposing He had taken the form of a cucumber,
how He could have preached, performed miracles or been crucified.'
In answer to his critics, he declared, 'By identifying the new learning
with heresy, you make orthodoxy synonymous with ignorance.'

As a popular writer, Erasmus exerted a considerable influence.
The constant attacks he made with every weapon of invective and
ridicule upon the abuses and shortcomings of the Church and its
officials did much to undermine the self-confidence and prestige of
the older order. His influence as a scholar added authority to his
criticisms and accusations and gained the Protestant reformers a
more ready hearing when they repeated many of his denunciations.
In learned circles, his Christian Humanism was not without effect.
There were many Erasmians in the University of Alcalá which was
founded by Cardinal Ximines to restore learning to the Spanish
Church;[19] and there were several of them at the court of Charles V,
many of whose own ideas for ecclesiastical reform were in agreement
with those of Erasmus.[20] Many of the reforms later carried out by
the Council of Trent (1545-63) had been suggested by Erasmus or
were designed to remove abuses he had condemned. Yet his influence
upon the universities was limited, and his attacks upon the obscurantism
of Scholasticism were generally ignored. Similarly, the clergy were not
to be ridiculed by him into piety and conscientiousness or mocked
out of lucrative abuses.

When the Reformation came, it embittered the last years of his life.
He wanted the Church reformed, its abuses abolished and the primitive
faith of the Early Christians revived; but he never criticized the current
orthodoxy, sacraments or form of government of the Church. He
disliked controversy and argument and believed that Christian unity

[19] P. 202.   [20] P. 189.

must be maintained—'I cannot help hating dissension and loving peace and harmony. I see how obscure all human affairs are. I see how much easier it is to stir up confusion than allay it.' His detachment and tranquillity meant that he was tolerated and sometimes even patronized by the authorities, but it brought him sharp condemnation from Luther, who accused him of 'making fun of the faults and miseries of the Church of Christ instead of bewailing them before God with deep sighs.' The bitter quarrel between the two men was probably inevitable. At first Erasmus praised Luther because he 'had attacked the crown of the pope and the bellies of the monks', but later he said truly, 'I laid a hen's egg; Luther hatched a bird of quite a different breed.'

4

OVERSEAS
EXPLORATION
AND
COLONIZATION

Navigation, ship-building and gunnery

The oceanic discoveries and expansion of sixteenth-century Europe were a continuation of those of the previous century. These had been made possible by an earlier period of technical developments, the most important of which were three new branches of knowledge. One was the study of geography and astronomy, particularly as applied to problems of navigation, as well as the improvement of the means of navigation. Another was an advance in ship-building and the management of ships, and the third was the development of ship-borne artillery and new naval tactics.

The Renaissance revival of classical learning assisted a great deal in the development of scientific geography during the fifteenth century. In 1410, the *Geography* of the Hellenized Egyptian, Ptolemy (*c* AD 150), which summarized the knowledge of the world in his time, was recovered and published in a Latin translation. Educated men now believed that the earth was a sphere and had a fair knowledge of the region of the old Roman Empire and its neighbouring countries, but beyond this their knowledge was so limited and uncertain that it discouraged maritime exploration. By then, too, charts for the known areas of sea were reasonably practical, but the long ocean voyages of the sixteenth century meant that a way had to be found of representing the spherical surface of the earth on to a flat map—a problem solved by Mercator's projection which appeared in 1569.

Owing to the interest in astronomy the Arabs had preserved another work by Ptolemy, commonly known by its Arabic title, the *Almagest*, which catalogued the bright stars. The Arabs were more concerned with the use of astronomy in cosmography and astronomy than in navigation, but they were able to sail a roughly accurate course in their ships by following the bearings upon which prominent stars were known to rise and set. When Portuguese navigators began to make longer voyages, they needed more exact observations. In 1462 the altitude of the Pole Star was used to determine a ship's latitude, but as explorers approached the equator the star disappeared on the horizon, and observation of the height of the sun at midday was used instead. For this calculation, the distance of the sun's zenith north or south of the equator at noon on any day had to be known. Jewish contacts with the Arabs made this possible. The first practical almanac, containing such tables, was compiled in 1478 by a Portuguese Jew, Abraham Zacuto, and was a great advance in navigation, although the determination of longitude was not satisfactorily achieved until the eighteenth century.

For measuring the height of heavenly bodies, Arabs and Europeans had used the astrolabe in the Middle Ages, but this was difficult to manipulate on the deck of a rolling ship, and when the Portuguese sailed down the African coast they made their observations on land whenever possible. The fifteenth century devised the quadrant, which was slightly easier to use and was taken by Columbus on his voyages. For determining a ship's direction, the mariner's compass, a graduated circular card attached to a magnetized needle balanced on a pivot in a glazed box, had been used since about 1250. To gauge a ship's speed mariners used the log, a slab of wood towed behind the ship on the end of a regularly knotted line which was paid out, and the speed at which the knots ran out over the stern was timed with a sand-glass. These instruments enabled navigators to sail quite an exact course by combining observed latitude with dead-reckoning, the estimation of a ship's position from the distance run by the log and the course steered by the compass, marked out on a chart.

During the first part of the fifteenth century, a revolutionary change took place in the design of European ships. These years, indeed, have been described as 'the time when the development of the sailing-ship went on at a faster pace than at any other period in history.' In the Middle Ages the most common type of ship was the cog, which was short, broadly built with a roundish prow and stern and a single mast carrying a square sail. Such a square-rigged ship was difficult to navigate and could not sail with an oblique wind. The Arabs devised the lateen, a triangular sail set fore and aft inside the rigging, which made it possible to bear into the wind, and this was rapidly adopted throughout the Mediterranean world. Lateen-rig, however, had two serious disadvantages: it was difficult to go about, and the area of sail that could be carried was limited. Portuguese and Spanish ship-designers, therefore, set about combining the advantages of square-rig with the lateen in one ship, and by the middle of the fifteenth century they had produced the carrack, the first full-rigged ship. It usually had three masts and carried square sails on the fore and main masts, a lateen rig on the mizzen mast and a sprit-sail on the bow-sprit. Such ships were built longer, to carry the additional masts, and so were more seaworthy, but a fifteenth-century carrack was not normally longer than three times its width. The *Santa Maria*, the largest of Columbus's ships, was only 29 metres long by seven and a half metres wide, which was not much larger than most modern trawlers.

Medieval warships carried soldiers, and a naval battle consisted largely of bringing ships alongside enemy vessels to enable the soldiers to board them and fight hand-to-hand on deck in conditions approximating to fighting on land. The ships were built with a battlemented fore-castle hanging over the bow and an after-castle rising up from the stern, which provided both high parapets from which to fight and accommodation for the soldiers. The Venetians in the fourteenth century were probably the first to mount small guns on these castle superstructures to rake the enemy's deck, and other European countries followed their example. In the later part of the fifteenth century, embrasures were cut in the gunwales through which guns ranged along the deck could fire, and early in the next century guns were mounted between decks, and the ship's side was pierced with ports. The Portuguese pioneered the substitution of big guns and the broadside for foot-soldiers and deck-fighting in naval warfare. They appreciated that guns should be used against the enemy's ships rather than against his men. Such weapons and tactics were very important factors in their overseas triumphs—their naval victories in the Indian Ocean were the first won by sinking ships by gunfire.[1]

The Portuguese Empire

In the middle of the twelfth century, a group of English and Flemish military adventurers, who were sailing towards the Mediterranean to participate in the Second Crusade, reached the mouth of the River Douro on the Atlantic coast of the Iberian peninsula. They were persuaded to assist in the local campaign against the Moors, and captured Lisbon in 1147. Many remained as settlers, together with Spanish migrants, in the thinly-peopled reconquered lands, and so the Kingdom of Portugal came into being. The new state, comprising a narrow strip of territory along the Atlantic coast, in area a little larger than Ireland, escaped from the economic control of Castile later imposed upon the rest of the peninsula and was compelled to support itself by turning to the sea. It engaged in trade with northern Europe and fishing and whaling in the Atlantic. In the middle of the fourteenth century, Italian merchants, driven from the mercantile cities of the Mediterranean by the economic depression of the time, came to Lisbon and, after the massacre of Jews in Spain in 1391, were joined by the Jewish cartographers of Majorca, who were the best in Europe.[2]

[1] P. 67.   [2] P. 64.   c

They united with the native shipbuilding industry to make Portugal an important maritime and commercial state. This, together with successful Portuguese participation in the Hundred Years War (1338-1453) as the naval ally of England, made possible a unique political and economic revolution in the country. While in the rest of Europe, feudal princes asserted their power and extinguished civic liberties, the Portuguese mercantile and maritime classes, led by the city of Lisbon, were able to gain power in the state.

These were the factors which, together with the contemporary growth of population, brought about the great movement of overseas expansion and colonization by Portugal, which set a new example soon followed by the other maritime powers of Europe. The leader of this enterprise was Prince Henry 'the Navigator' (1394-1460) who has achieved an almost legendary importance. What inspired him is not known. It may have been a crusading fervour to destroy the power of Islam in Africa, or a consuming interest in the possibilities of maritime exploration or the dream of discovering an oceanic route to the spice markets of India. Perhaps his thoughts were first turned in such directions by the Portuguese capture of Ceuta in Morocco in 1415, which brought them information about Africa not then known to other Europeans. At any rate, from about 1420 until his death he sent out fleet after fleet into the Atlantic and down the west coast of Africa although he never went to sea himself.

His contribution to the Portuguese urge to explore this region was to set up a sort of seafaring academy on the rocky shores of Sagres Bay on the southern tip of Portugal. To this academy he attracted navigators and mariners, scientists and cartographers, Portuguese and Italians, Jews and Moslems, who provided sailors with all possible information and techniques. During his lifetime, the Portuguese settled Madeira in 1419 and the Azores in 1431, doubled Cape Bojador on the west coast of Africa in 1434, and occupied the Cape Verde Islands in 1441 and Senegal in 1445. The first consignment of slaves was brought to Lisbon in 1434, and Pope Nicholas V in 1454 authorized the Portuguese 'to attack, subject and reduce to perpetual slavery the Saracens, pagans and other enemies of Christ southward from Cape Bojador . . ., including all the coast of Guinea.'

After Prince Henry's death, there was a reaction in Portugal against the national concentration on these unprofitable oceanic expeditions. The ruling nobility preferred to revert to fighting the Moors on land, and it was not until the reign of John II (1481-95) that vigorous direction was given to the promotion of further exploration. By then the hazardous voyages had begun to produce regular gains; the Portuguese had a flourishing trade with West Africa, sending out some forty carracks a year, and to press on and share in the trade with Asia would be still more profitable. A new generation of noblemen were prepared to support John II's commercial policy which led other jealous European monarchs to nickname him 'the Grocer'. The climax of his reign came in 1488 when Bartholomew Diaz doubled the Cape of Good Hope, and the sea route to the east was at last discovered. In the same year, a·Portuguese expedition followed the course of the Nile through Egypt and reached Abyssinia, where they heard of Arab ships trading along the East African coast. To sail in these waters and go beyond to India now became the prime Portuguese aim.

In 1492, however, Christopher Columbus made his first voyage across the Atlantic and was thought to have forestalled the Portuguese in discovering a sea route to India. Their disappointment was naturally great. John II made hurried preparations for a fleet to sail across the Atlantic to challenge the Spanish claim, but war was averted by negotiations resulting in the Treaty of Tordesillas in 1494 by which the Papacy established a line of demarcation running north and south 370 leagues west of the Cape Verde Islands. This deprived the Portuguese of access to the West Indies, but reserved for them the discovery of Brazil, the existence of which they had come to suspect since their ships had penetrated into the South Atlantic.

By the time of the accession of Manuel I (1495-1521), the belief that the Spaniards possessed the western route to India was fast fading. The Portuguese decided, therefore, to renew the search for an eastern route, and in 1498 Vasco da Gama reached the western coast of India. A sea route to India had been found. Manuel exultantly assumed in 1500 the title of 'Lord of the Conquest, navigation and commerce of India, Ethiopia, Arabia and Persia'. In that year a fleet of thirteen ships under Pedro Cabral sailed to Brazil, which he claimed for Portugal, and then back across the south Atlantic and round the Cape of Good Hope to open up trade with India, returning with the first cargoes of pepper and other spices. Regular trading fleets were now despatched, and within three years the price of pepper at Lisbon was only a fifth of that charged at Venice by merchants who had bought it at inflated prices from the Arabs at Alexandria. Portuguese trading activities inevitably meant that they had to establish themselves in India and intervene in Indian affairs. Commercial transactions had to be combined with the building of trading posts and forts along the western coast and the waging of campaigns on behalf of their native allies. The Portuguese also established a fleet in eastern waters and, in destroying the opposition of the Arabs in sea battles, demonstrated the superiority of their ships and guns.[3] Portuguese power in this region was firmly established by Alfonso d'Albuquerque, who was Viceroy of the new possessions from 1509 to 1515. He conquered Goa, which he made the seat of the Portuguese government, gained

[3] P. 65.

control of the Straits of Malacca, which connected the Indian Ocean with the Chinese Sea, and captured Ormuz, the key-port to the Persian Gulf. His successors established commercial relations with Japan in 1542 and with China in 1557.

The scattered Portuguese empire in Asia, like the settlements they had by now founded also on the western and eastern African coasts, consisted of small, dispersed units. Portugal was too small a country to attempt territorial dominion and large-scale settlement; Brazil, her largest colony, was not developed beyond its coastline during the sixteenth century. Hers was a maritime empire, founded and maintained by the sea on which her fleets established their supremacy. It was also a trading empire. It came to monopolize the maritime trade between Europe and the east for a time and also to organize trade within the east itself. And since the original impulse to expand overseas had come from the monarchy, the empire remained under royal control during this period.

New institutions were organized in Lisbon to supervise overseas trade and administration—the India House for shipping, outward cargoes and the sale of imported spices; the Arsenal for the supply of crews and pilots, equipment and arms for the ships; the High Court of Appeal for judicial appointments and overseas cases; the Board of Conscience and Military Orders for religious matters. Imperial political and economic policy and development were controlled by the Council of Ceuta, the Council of Guinea, the Council of the Indies and other specialized royal councils. The Crown claimed a monopoly in the trade in pepper, ginger, silk and other valuable commodities, while most royal officials were forbidden to engage in private trade. Few Portuguese went overseas on their own account. Most were administrators, soldiers, mariners or priests, who were all to some extent directed by official agencies.

Commerce was organized upon a regular, annual routine. Each March a royal fleet left Lisbon carrying bullion, copper and silverware to pay for the oriental wares, as well as arms and supplies for the trading-posts. It arrived at Goa in September and left in December if it were to sail back along the east African coast or in January if it sailed directly to the Cape. On its arrival at Lisbon in the autumn, the cargoes were either sold by the Crown to merchants or shipped to the royal factory at Antwerp to be bought, mainly by German traders, for distribution in Europe. Portuguese expansion farther eastwards made possible additional trade—the 'country trade'—by which the products of the Spice Islands of Indonesia were obtained in return for exported Indian cottons.

The spiritual revival aroused by the Counter-Reformation and the work of the Society of Jesus brought a new religious aspect to the

Portuguese Empire. From the first, there were priests in the overseas settlements, but they ministered to the Portuguese officials and their families and were not missionary-minded. This situation was transformed, however, by Francis Xavier (1506-52), one of the first of the Jesuits, who arrived at Goa in 1542 and for ten years laboured among the native populations of the East Indies and also founded a mission in Japan.[4] From him and his successors the Portuguese gained an ideal of Christian evangelization for their empire to replace the fading ideas of religious crusading which had previously animated them in their wars against the Moors. Converts were made, missions established and churches built wherever Portuguese traders and administrators went. It was said that by 1583 there were some 600 000 Christians in the Asian area.

This religious development took place, however, at a time when Portuguese enterprise in the east was declining through the difficulties it encountered. The Counter-Reformation itself contributed towards them through the introduction of the Inquisition in Portugal in 1536 and the persecution and later expulsion of the Jews. By then the Portuguese Empire was already past its prime. The system of royal trade was failing. The Portuguese ships making for Antwerp increasingly attracted French attacks, and German merchants suffered from Dutch competition. In 1548 the Portuguese factory at Antwerp had to be closed and the trade carried on less profitably from Lisbon. Even more serious was the revival of trade with the Arabs by the Venetians, who enjoyed several economic and geographical advantages.[5] The Portuguese government was unable to meet these threats because it had insufficient resources to develop properly the commerce between Lisbon and Goa. In the 1530s it had to spend heavily on ships and armies, which brought it no direct profit, and it had to borrow large sums which got it deeply into debt. The Portuguese administration in Asia became steadily weaker and could not even employ the number of men it needed. Its financial difficulties were made worse by corruption among colonial officials, who deprived it of its rightful Asian revenue and overcharged it for goods and services, and were also determined to engage in private trade and even smuggling with the Arabs who supplied Venice with its spices.

The eleven years of regency which followed the reign of John III (1521-57) further undermined the power of the Crown, and in 1578 King Sebastian had to relinquish the royal monopoly of trade; but Portuguese merchants, weakened by the expulsion of the Jews, could not develop a flourishing trade, much of which fell into the hands of Arabs and Asians. At the same time, the basis of power upon which Portuguese participation in the seaborne trade of Asia had been established—the fortresses and ships—began to fail. Increasingly

[4] P. 206. [5] P. 269.

manned by unskilled Indian and half-caste seamen, the Portuguese
fleet lost its efficiency and pre-eminence. From 1500 to 1580 ninety-
three per cent of the ships sailing from Portugal reached the east
safely, but from then to 1610 only sixty-nine per cent. Meanwhile,
the whole course of Portuguese history had been changed by a royal
reversion of policy. The romantic young King Sebastian was determined on a crusade in Morocco, but royal finances could only provide
him with an inadequate army, which was overwhelmed by the Moors
at the Battle of Alcazar-el-Kebri in 1578; he himself was killed and
succeeded by his great uncle, the senile Cardinal Henry. The union of
Portugal with Spain[6] followed in 1580, and she thus became involved in
Spain's wars and economic troubles, including those connected with the
inexorable stalemate in the Netherlands. In 1595 the arrival of the Dutch
in the east heralded the destruction which overtook her empire in the
next century.

The Spanish Empire

Unlike the Portuguese Empire, the establishment of the Spanish one
was not the result of a century of national effort and persistent voyages
of exploration. It began with the first crossing of the Atlantic by the
Genoese navigator, Christopher Columbus (1451-1506), who was a
secretive man and did not expound his aims at all fully. In his agreement with the Crown of Castile in 1492, he undertook 'to discover and
acquire islands and mainland in the Ocean Sea.' As far back as 1484
he had unsuccessfully sought financial support for a similar proposal
from the Portuguese government, but in 1492 the Castilian army
captured the city of Granada thus completing the centuries-old reconquest of Spain from the Moors, and a mood of patriotic and
religious exuberance prevailed. Portugal's monopoly of the profitable
West African trade was resented. A successful expedition by Columbus
would bring Spain the possibility of commercial gain and of relieving
the poverty of the royal treasury. It might also open up a new way of
waging the crusade against Islam with fresh allies and the prospect of
establishing a great Christian mission in the east. Queen Isabella
overcame her hesitation and agreed to finance his voyage, grant him
the hereditary title of Grand Admiral and the right to a tenth of the
merchandise and produce of the new lands.

On his first voyage, Columbus discovered the two largest islands of
the Antilles, Cuba and Hispaniola (Haiti), which he claimed lay off the
coast of eastern Asia. Ferdinand and Isabella sufficiently believed him
to despatch him in 1493, even before the demarcation negotiations
with Portugal were completed, with a fleet of seventeen ships carrying
neither guns nor trade goods but twelve hundred people with tools,

[6] P. 248.

seeds and animals to be settled in Hispaniola. While Columbus accepted Portuguese and Italian notions and imagined that his discoveries would be followed by the establishment of a commercial undertaking, the Spaniards, imbued with their soldiering, crusading tradition, thought of military conquest, division of lands and conversion of infidels. This conflict of intentions, together with his own failure as an administrator and colonizer in Hispaniola, broke Columbus. He was allowed to make a third and a fourth voyage during which he added the discovery of the coast of South and Central America to his original discovery of the West Indies, but the Spanish government sent out its own governors and would not permit him to exercise the office of viceroy and admiral to which he thought himself entitled.

By the time of the death of Isabella in 1505 and of Columbus one year later, it was clear that the New World, as it was coming to be called, was not part of Asia. The hope of immediately challenging the prosperous Portuguese connection with the Indies was fast fading; and in 1513 Vasco Nunez de Balboa (c 1475-1517) crossed the Isthmus of Panama and saw the Pacific for the first time. It was clear now that Asia lay beyond yet another ocean, but the hope of reaching it by sailing westwards still remained, and in 1519 Charles V accepted the offer of the Portuguese explorer, Ferdinand Magellan (c 1470-1521), to find for Spain a way round the southern part of the American continent to the East Indies. Magellan's voyage, however, which cost him his life, did not bring Spain the desired prize. The Strait of Magellan, separating South America from the islands of Tierra del Fuego, proved impossible as a regular channel for trading ships, and Spanish imperial activity was henceforward confined, except for the Philippines annexed in 1569, to the Americas.

Spanish control over Hispaniola was asserted by 1508 and over Cuba by 1511, while Panama was settled soon after Balboa's expedition. A twenty-year period of conquest followed which established the Spanish Empire in America. It was achieved by the conquest of the two native empires of the Aztecs and the Incas. The Aztecs, the ruling people of Mexico, were defeated between 1519 and 1521 by Hernan Cortes (1485-1547), who set out from Cuba with six hundred soldiers and sixteen horses; and the Incas, the possessors of a great empire covering Peru, much of Ecuador, Chile, Bolivia and north-western Argentina, were overthrown between 1531 and 1533 by Francisco Pizarro (c 1478-1541), who set out from Panama with one hundred and eighty men and thirty-seven horses. By 1540 all South America, except Brazil, was Spanish.

Not a great deal is known about the Spanish *conquistadores*, who were so few in number and subjugated these vast American territories so rapidly. They came mostly from Castile and belonged to the lesser nobility rather than the important noble families, who took no interest in the conquest. They were men seeking their fortunes in the New World whose sole skill was in fighting. They came with the way of life and the outlook their class had acquired in the *Reconquista*, the war to free Spain completely from its Moorish rulers, which had only recently ended. They were tough, professional soldiers, ruthless and brutal. At the same time, they were still animated by the crusading zeal of the *Reconquista*, now strengthened by the spiritual revival destined to bring about the Counter-Reformation in which Spain took such a prominent part. To them their campaign was also a 'spiritual conquest'. Native idols were thrown down and temples destroyed to be replaced by cathedrals and monasteries. And, as in earlier crusades, they displayed a mixture of religious and material motives. 'We came to America,' wrote one of them frankly, 'to serve God and the king and also to become rich.' Lands and wealth, titles and social distinction were the object of their personal ambitions. It was these qualities, and not military superiority, which gave them victory: Cortes invaded Mexico with a few small cannon and thirteen muskets. Both the Aztecs and Incas went down before their powerful combination of discipline, bravery, religious zeal and desire for riches and distinction.

Spain's conquest of South America was followed by its settlement. Colonization rather than trade remained the motive of her domination. Throughout the sixteenth century an average of about 1 500 Spaniards emigrated to the New World each year, and by 1600 these people were ruling a subject Indian population estimated at over seven millions.[7] There were also about 40 000 negro slaves and many *mestizos* (of mixed Spanish and Indian parentage) and *mulattoes* (of mixed Spanish and negro parentage).

All were regarded as subjects of the Spanish Crown, which had been determined from the start of the overseas enterprise to assert its control over the new dominions. The Castilianizing policy of the Crown was firmly extended across the Atlantic. The conquered territories did not become colonies of Spain, but possessions of the monarchy, which granted authority first to individual commanders and then to the viceroys who represented it and exercised its authority. Representative institutions, local autonomy or federal government were never considered. The territories were controlled from Castile by a separate royal council, the *Consejo des Indias*, organized by Charles V, which appointed and supervised colonial officials, made laws for the new territories and heard appeals. There were two viceroys—the Viceroy of New Spain ruling from Mexico City and the Viceroy of New Castile from Lima. Each of these two vice-royalties was divided into districts, presided over by a governor, who was aided by an administrative and judicial tribunal called the *audencia*.

[7] P. 27.

Isabella had asserted in her will that since the overseas countries had been discovered and conquered 'at the expense of my kingdoms and settled with nationals of these kingdoms, it is right that all their trade and traffic should belong to my kingdoms of Castile and Leon and be conducted from them; and that everything brought from the Indies should go to them and be for them.' As with Portugal, all imperial trade was controlled by the Crown. This was done through the *Casa de Contratacion* or Board of Trade, set up by Ferdinand at Seville to direct colonial trade, shipping and travel. Only Castilians could settle in or trade with America, and commerce was organized on a system of two fleets each year and went through a single Castilian port, at first Cadiz, but from 1503 Seville.[8] The monopoly was retained throughout the century, and a petition by the city of Barcelona in 1522 for permission to trade with America was rejected.

Royal control over the trade of the Spanish colonies was exercised in the interests of the home country. The *Consejo des Indias* encouraged the growth of sugar and other tropical products in the West Indies and Philippines, which used native labour and supplemented it by importing negroes from Africa. On the other hand, the cheap wines of Chile and Peru and the olive industry of Peru were checked to prevent competition with the raw material exported by Spain to pay for her colonial imports. At first the colonists had to import food from Spain, but by the middle of the century they were able to feed themselves and increasingly required silks, textiles, gloves, leather, arms, cutlery and other manufactures which she produced. But Spain's industry could not expand rapidly enough to meet her own needs because of the rigidity of the country's economic structure; and Spanish shippers could not supply the colonists with sufficient negro slaves.[9] The result was that English, Dutch and other foreign merchants and slavers began to trade illegally with the colonies. In addition, the annexation of the Philippines in 1569 began an equally illegal trade across the Pacific in which the colonists exchanged American silver for silks and spices brought by merchants from Macao, and this diversion of bullion from Spain caused growing official anxiety.[10]

The export of gold and silver from America to foreign countries was absolutely forbidden. The abundance of precious metals discovered in the colonies became particularly important in Spain's economy from the 1520s onwards. They, above all else, provided her with wealth and became essential to her dominance in Europe. Without them neither Charles V nor Philip II could have maintained her important role in the history of the time. Yet, as her dependence upon them increased, these imports of bullion were ultimately harmful to Spain's economy, political constitution and international position.

During the opening years of the sixteenth century, however, such

[8] P. 27.   [9] P. 76.   [10] P. 252.

harmful effects were not yet apparent and Spain was triumphantly rebuilding the New World in her own political and social image. In no way was this more clearly seen than in the towns she established in the parts of the continent settled by her people. Society in Spain was urban. Noblemen drew their income from the land and the possession of flocks and herds, but they had their town houses, and the peasants, many of whom were Moriscos, were the only true rural dwellers.[11] The garrisoning of fortified towns had been important in accomplishing the *Reconquista*, and the Castilian *conquistadores* inevitably established themselves in America in this way. By the end of the sixteenth century, there were some two thousand towns in the Spanish overseas territories. Many of them were still little more than collections of thatched huts, but they were not regarded primarily as military forts or trading posts. From the start they obtained legal incorporation and the establishment of the usual municipal offices and organization of contemporary Spanish towns. Their essential purpose was social and administrative. They were the strongholds of the Spanish ruling class, controlling and supported by the surrounding districts.

These towns were not only organized and administered as those of medieval Castile, but the largest also possessed the same principal buildings—the church or cathedral, the town hall, the law courts, the prison, the university and the palace of the Inquisition, all fronting on to the *plaza mayor*, the large square in the middle. At the same time, they did not come into being through the needs of commerce or travel as in the past. They were founded in accordance with regulations laid down by the *Consejo des Indias* and built upon a regular, spacious plan. Careful consideration was always given to the choice of a site for a new town, and often it was surrounded by a shallow depression to allow water from tropical rainstorms to drain away rapidly without damage from flooding. Whenever possible, the layout followed the rectangular, gridiron pattern of an ancient town, an idea probably derived from the Renaissance interest in classical town-planning. Radiating from the *plaza mayor*, the straight streets were laid out at right angles, the land divided in lots among the settlers and places found for churches, monasteries and schools. The soldiers of the conquering armies became the first *vecinos* or legally enrolled householders and elected from among themselves the municipal councillors and magistrates.

The *vecinos* were not prepared to support themselves by urban crafts or trade. They were mostly soldiers, who had gone to America and endured the hardships of conquest at their own expense, and now they expected to live by the labour of the native population. Here again they sought to achieve this by adopting a practice used in the *Reconquista*. This was the *encomienda*, by which, after land had been recovered

[11] P. 244.

from the Moors, the Morisco inhabitants were 'commended' to Castilian settlers, who protected them in return for receiving labour services from them. The system was introduced to America by Columbus in Hispaniola and thereafter organized throughout the rest of the Spanish territories. But the Crown did not want the development of a feudal autocracy overseas to challenge its power. The American *encomienda*, therefore, was not a landed estate, but a lordship granted on a temporary, non-hereditary basis (theoretically at any rate) over a village or group of villages, the native inhabitants of which formally retained the ownership of their land. The Spanish settlers protected them and instructed them in Christianity and in return received from them tributes of their produce and labour services.

As the Spanish population grew, there was an increasing demand for native labour for both farming and building work, and the *encomienda* inevitably came to approximate slavery in many areas. This aroused the opposition of the friars, whose missionary fervour brought them in large numbers to the New World. Here they were the strongest religious influence for forty years after the conquest until the secular clergy, who were more amenable to control by the Crown, became more numerous. The friars were deeply influenced by humanist ideas and hoped to lead the American Indians into that simple Christian way of life to which they believed the contemporary Church had failed to dedicate itself. Outstanding among the friars was Bartolomé de las Casas (1474-1566), 'the Protector of the Indians', who became the first Bishop of Mexico and repeatedly travelled to Spain to denounce at the court the iniquities of the *encomienda* system. Since the Crown itself continued to fear that the system would develop feudal tendencies, it listened to the pleas of the friars and passed laws which led to the virtual emancipation of the Indians before the death of Las Casas.

Meanwhile, Spanish settlers had already sought an alternative supply of labour by importing negro slaves from Africa. The first shipload of slaves was landed in Hispaniola in 1510 and in Cuba in 1521. Though he bitterly regretted it later, Las Casas at first supported their introduction to the American mainland so as to rescue the Indians from the abuses of the *encomienda*. Accordingly Africans were brought across the Atlantic in growing numbers to work on the plantations and in the silver mines. By then the Portuguese had done the same in Brazil, obtaining the slaves from their colony of Angola. Moreover, since Portugal controlled the places on the West African coast from which slaves were exported, the supply of negroes to the Spanish colonies was largely in her hands. In 1580 she obtained from the Spanish government the *Assiento* or contract for a monopoly in the trade, but this very lucrative concession did not go unchallenged by the other sea-going nations of Europe.

English, French and Dutch ventures

The Portuguese and Spaniards were the only European peoples to establish overseas empires during the sixteenth century, and the Spanish Empire was by the end of the century, through its absorption of the Portuguese one, the only existing colonial empire. By then, however, Spanish exploration and expansion in the New World had diminished. This was mainly due to the deliberately restrictive and cautious policy adopted by Philip II, whose huge debts and extensive commitments in Europe made him ever more dependent upon the revenue obtained from the royal silver tax and other impositions levied on the colonies. He was anxious, therefore, that existing profitable American mines and other activities should be developed rather than that the frontiers of existing colonies should be extended.

Though no other nation succeeded in founding overseas colonies during this century, determined attempts were made by several to obtain a share in the profitable proceeds of the Spanish Empire. The colonists needed slaves and manufactured goods, which Spain could not herself supply, and they had plenty of bullion with which they were prepared to defy the royal monopoly by trading with foreigners to get what they wanted. The New World presented, therefore, an alluring opportunity to illegal traders who judged the risks worth the possible profits. In the first years of Elizabeth I's reign, when relations with Spain were relatively friendly, English seamen were well placed to seek participation in the American trade. The English produced cloth themselves and could purchase slaves in West Africa, and these were the two most urgent requirements of the Spanish settlers. The lead was taken by John Hawkins (1532-95), who organized four trading voyages to the Caribbean between 1562 and 1568 to exchange slaves and textiles for sugar, hides and silver which, in their turn, were in high demand in Europe. Hawkins believed that he could engage as a lawful trader in the Spanish Empire, and he found that the planters and local officials were prepared to do business with him, but during his last voyage he was attacked by a Spanish fleet in the Gulf of Mexico and lost three of his five ships.

The experience of Hawkins made it clear that the Spanish government would not allow interlopers in American waters. English seamen's attempts to trade gave way, therefore, to privateering expeditions, even though England and Spain were not openly at war until the sailing of the Armada in 1588. Best known and most active among these privateers was Francis Drake (1541-96), whose most famous voyage, which took him round the world between 1577 and 1580, brought back Spanish treasure and East Indian spices worth nearly five thousand times as much as he had spent on preparing for the expedition. Both Hawkins and Drake had their English imitators, notably John Oxenham (d 1575), who raided Central America, but was captured and hanged by order of the Inquisition, and Thomas Cavendish (1560-92) who also sailed round the world and took much treasure in the Pacific. In addition, French privateers had already operated in American waters, especially during the long period of almost continuous war between France and Spain from the election of Charles V as Holy Roman Emperor in 1519 to the signing of the Treaty of Cateau-Cambrésis in 1559. They, too, took considerable prizes from the Spaniards, their most successful season being in 1537 when they captured nine of the twenty-two Spanish ships that sailed from the New World that year. In the later years of the century, the English and French were joined by the Dutch, who both made profits and suffered from Spanish retaliation.

Indeed, the loss of treasure and still more of prestige inflicted upon the Spaniards by the foreign privateers led them in the second part of the century to take counter-measures. A convoy system was organized for their ships, and fleets of frigates were stationed on the main sea lanes. These steps met with considerable success and were responsible for the failure of the last Indies voyage of Drake and Hawkins in 1595. By the Treaty of the Hague in 1596 England, France and the Netherlands formed an alliance which might have been strong enough to assert their will over the Spanish Empire (a combined Anglo-Dutch fleet destroyed a complete American convoy in Cadiz harbour, so interrupting communications between Spain and the Indies for almost two years), but the alliance came to an end when Henry IV of France made peace separately with Spain through the Treaty of Vervins in 1598.[12] By the end of the sixteenth century the commercial monopoly and territorial possessions of the Spanish Empire remained largely unharmed. The successes of the foreign privateers have tended to be exaggerated, but the prizes that seemed to await them were so attractive that raiding and smuggling continued despite all the dangers.

It was their preoccupation with the West Indies trade that largely accounted for the failure of England and France to establish colonies of their own in parts of the New World unoccupied by Spanish settlers. Monarchs and ministers, merchants and patrons, believed that better profits were to be made from privateering voyages than from colonial ventures, particularly as many believed that the Spaniards had established themselves firmly in all the best lands of the new continent. John Cabot (d 1499) discovered Newfoundland and Nova Scotia and claimed them for Henry VII of England in 1497, but these northern regions seemed ill suited for profitable schemes of settlement. By the middle of the sixteenth century, England appeared to have a surplus population which needed more land, but settlement in Ireland was

[12] P. 235.

accepted as the best solution for this problem. The two Englishmen who were interested in American colonization during the 1580s— Humphrey Gilbert (1539-83) and his half-brother, Walter Raleigh (1552-1618)—both had experience of Ireland, but Gilbert's colony in Newfoundland and Raleigh's in Virginia alike lacked official support and failed. Meanwhile, in 1534 the French explorer, Jacques Cartier (1494-1557), had sailed up the St Lawrence River and penetrated to the interior of Canada. After the Treaty of Cateau-Cambrésis, however, there was little French interest in the idea of colonization except among the Huguenots in the Atlantic ports, who, in the prevailing religious situation, could expect no official support.

The attraction of a share in the trade of the Spanish Empire did not prevent English merchants from wishing also to intrude upon the Portuguese in the commerce of the East Indies. In 1581 a group of London merchants founded the Levant Company, an early example of the joint-stock company which was to be so important in commerce and colonization during the next century.[13] Largely as the result of reports supplied by Drake and Cavendish, the first English expedition to the East Indies was despatched in 1591 under the command of James Lancaster (d 1618). This was followed by the establishment of the larger East India Company in 1600 and the appointment of Lancaster to command its fleet. Meanwhile, though the Dutch were not to found their East India Company until two years later, they had already begun operations in eastern waters on a larger scale. Between 1595 and 1601 fifteen Dutch expeditions sailed for the East Indies; they were to be the first to challenge successfully the overseas territorial and commercial advantages gained by the Iberian nations. Before that, however, the establishment of the Muscovy Company in 1555 had initiated English trade into another profitable direction.[14]

[13] P. 89.   [14] P. 309.

5
SOCIAL
AND
ECONOMIC
CHANGE

Rural society

Despite the growth of towns in some regions, European society remained, as it had been for centuries, predominantly rural. Most people lived in small villages and were engaged in agriculture or occupations connected with it. The majority of countrymen were peasants, dwelling in cottages or hovels and each having a small holding of land, which might, in a normal year, suffice to support a family. Originally they had been serfs, bound to their feudal lord by service which was attached to the soil and transferred with it. By the beginning of the sixteenth century, serfdom had come to an end in England, but the situation on the Continent varied from country to country.

The French countryside in the early sixteenth century was recovering from the effects of the Hundred Years War.[1] Rural depopulation and ravaging had weakened the feudal system in many parts of the kingdom, and peasants escaped from their servile obligations. Recovery had a similar effect because the lords, hampered in restoring the cultivation of their lands by the shortage of labour, made concessions to their serfs, emancipating them and leasing estates to them. Other lords were forced by debts to sell their lands, often to peasants who sometimes achieved considerable wealth. As a result of these developments, those who owned their land formed about a twentieth of the peasantry by the end of the century and those bound to the land in full serfdom about another twentieth. Most of the rest paid their lord, either in kind or money, part of the yield of their holding, which was becoming increasingly recognized as their own freely disposable property.

In Spain, a royal decree of 1480 had released Castilian peasants from all surviving servile bondage and allowed them to sell their land, but they continued to be subjected to feudal dues and jurisdiction. Most of them only had small holdings and lacked the resources to undertake irrigation and other measures necessary for corn-growing.

[1] P. 26.

Increasing population, especially in the towns, made corn more
expensive during the sixteenth century, but the government responded
by price-fixing and importing foreign grain, a policy which assisted
the consumers but not the food-producers, who suffered also through
official support for the *Mesta*, the large Castilian corporation dominated
by the nobility, which monopolized sheep-farming. The Aragonese
peasantry suffered additionally from unrelieved feudal rights and
exactions. Their lords could treat them as they liked without fear of
royal interference, and in 1585 the Cortes (Parliament) imposed an
automatic death-penalty upon any peasant who took up arms against
his lord. Consequently, the peasantry welcomed the royal army which
Philip II sent into Aragon in 1592 to put down the revolt.[2]

In western Germany the position of the peasantry was much the
same as in most of France. The Black Death in the fourteenth century
had caused a considerable decline in population and farming, and
many peasants had ceased to perform their servile obligations. When
the countryside began to recover in the middle of the fifteenth century,
the peasants had been able to exploit the shortage of labour by obtaining
from the lords reductions in their dues and rents. Rising prices,
increasing population and economic difficulties in the sixteenth century
led the lords to attempt to reimpose their feudal rights. This brought
about a number of rural risings, culminating in the great Peasants'
Revolt of 1524-5 and, though it was crushed by the princes, the lords
found that they could not increase their rents and other rights. Most
peasants now held their land on a hereditary basis, and the lords had
to employ direct labour more and more to farm their own estates.

North and east of the River Elbe, however, (and, indeed, also in
Poland, Bohemia and Hungary) the situation was different. The lords
here, especially those whose lands had been obtained by knights of
the military orders conquering the Slavs, were in a stronger position
than elsewhere. Many had large estates which they farmed with both
household servants and forced peasant labour. Since the lake and
river systems connecting eastern Germany with the Baltic and the
North Sea made it possible for corn to be transported cheaply to meet
the growing demands of western Europe, they were presented with a
profitable market and were able to supply it by increasing the labour
services exacted from their tenants. So a 'new serfdom' gradually
came into being from the later sixteenth century, and the lords were
supported by the princes, who depended upon them for grants of
money and the performance of military service.

In Russia also, serfdom increased in both extent and exactions during
the sixteenth century, partly as a result of the policy of Ivan the
Terrible (1530-84) in establishing the *Oprichnina*.[3] In return for service
to the Crown, the members of this new ruling class were given lands

[2] P. 243.   [3] P. 306.

and were enabled to exact labour services from the peasants in order to cultivate them. Serfdom was further spread by the conquest of Kazan on the Volga and the enforced removal of princely landowners from the central regions of Muscovy to the new border areas. Here they were established on estates with the right to exact labour from the peasants, both as workers on the land and as domestic serfs in their households. Another feature of Russian serfdom was the power of discipline legally possessed by the lords, including the frequently-used right to inflict whipping as a punishment on both male and female serfs.

The price rise

Since the social basis of much of the European population remained a predominantly rural one in which goods were often obtained by barter or for services, the inflation of the sixteenth century was only gradually noticed by contemporaries. Moreover, prices, and particularly food prices, had always varied in agricultural communities with the seasons and the yield of harvests, and the annual rate of increase in prices during the century as a whole averaged between two and three per cent, though it was not the same in all countries. The later Middle Ages, however, had been a time of stable or falling prices, so from the middle of the sixteenth century, when the cumulative effect of rising prices was being felt, concern and resentment were evident.

In seeking to discover the cause of the situation, popular resentment turned upon the individuals engaged in food-production, finance or trade, such as landlords and grain merchants, monopolists and trading companies, usurers and bankers. Preachers thundered against their greed, and governments, anxious to preserve social stability, sought to legislate against price-rises and monopolies, but neither succeeded in checking the general inflation. A more reasoned explanation of the continuous rise in prices came independently in the middle years of the century from the Spanish theologians of the University of Salamanca and the French political writer, Jean Bodin (c 1530-96), both of whom concluded that it was due to the falling value of coinage, because more was being minted and put into circulation as a result of the import of American gold and silver into Europe.

This view has been supported by many modern economic historians, particularly Professor Earl J. Hamilton who, as a result of collecting and studying the figures for American silver imports and Spanish prices, concluded that 'the extremely close connection between the increase in the volume of treasure and the advance of commodity prices throughout the sixteenth century, particularly from 1535 on, demonstrates beyond question that the "abundant mines of Spain" were the principal cause of the Price Revolution in Spain,'* and that this had an inevitable effect on the rise in prices in western Europe as a whole. Recently, however, his explanation has been queried. It has been shown that he ignored the fact that much of the silver that entered Spain was rapidly transferred abroad again to pay for Spanish imports, the maintenance of Spanish troops in other countries and the interest due on loans to the Spanish government from German and Genoese bankers. Moreover, Spanish prices rose most rapidly in the first half of the sixteenth century, when bullion imports were only just beginning, and more slowly in the second half, when imports took place on a larger scale. Possibly, therefore, the considerable re-export of bullion reduced the rate of inflation during that period.

It would seem likely that Spanish treasure had some effect on the increase in prices in Spain and western Europe, but there were probably local causes as well. In Spain, for instance, Imperial loans and increasing demands for goods, both at home and in the New World, may well have had an inflationary effect upon the undeveloped Spanish economy and sent up prices of both food and manufactures. Again, debasement of the coinage, which took place in England under Henry VIII (1509-47) and in France under Francis I (1515-47), inevitably caused inflation in those countries. Moreover, if the general price-rise in Europe had been mainly brought about by an increase in the circulation of coinage, then the price of all commodities should have risen more or less evenly, but this was not so. In fact, agricultural products, particularly grain and wool, rose most steeply in price, while manufactured goods increased by only about half as much.

From this it would seem likely, therefore, that the most important cause of the European price-rise was the increase in population which occurred during the century.[4] Existing methods of farming were inadequate to meet the demands of the greater numbers of people and the increased proportion of food-consumers to food-producers resulting from the growth in size of the towns. While increasing demand for food put its price up, so also did the rise in the value of land and labour, which brought higher rents and wages, and the cost of extending farming to less easily farmed land. The only two countries which exported wool at this time were England and Spain, and in both these kingdoms wool prices in the first half of the century rose even more rapidly than food prices, and consequently arable land was given over to sheep-farming. Later in the century, however, the demands of the continually rising population sent food prices up higher. Arable farming became more profitable again, and the Spanish government gradually withdrew its support of the *Mesta*.[5] Throughout the sixteenth century, the growth of Europe's population seems to have outpaced food supplies and it did not slow down until the next century.

* *American Treasure and the Price Revolution in Spain* (1934).
[4] P. 29.   [5] P. 25.

Social results of the price rise

The effects of rising prices upon the rural society of western Europe are not easy to determine because of the lack of reliable statistical evidence. Since rents fixed by custom tended, however, to fall behind rising prices, the landowning classes, particularly those with smaller estates, found themselves faced with financial problems and had to find new sources of income. Usually the higher nobility were most successful, since they were able to rely upon patronage from rulers who required their military and administrative services; they also possessed considerable feudal privileges inherited from the past and benefited from the increased demand for agricultural production.

Thus in Spain, Charles V succeeded in establishing his power over his kingdoms largely by making, in effect, an alliance with the greater nobility, the grandees, who in Castile were exempt from most taxation. For a time they were able to benefit considerably from the profitable sheep-farming activities of the *Mesta*; but by the end of the century they were in serious difficulties.[6] In France, the feudal privileges of the nobility were very great: they were exempt from all national direct taxation, from the *taille* (the main property tax) and from the *gabelle* (the salt-tax). As inflation made these privileges more valuable, they were determined to retain them solely for their caste, and in 1560 they induced the Crown to legalize the principle of *dérogeance*, which deprived noblemen of them if they engaged in any form of trade or handicraft. Many, however, still found it difficult to escape impoverishment, particularly at a time when inflation was combined with their extravagant spending inspired by the Italian Renaissance.[7]

In western Germany, the price-rise imposed considerable difficulties upon landowners, particularly because of the security enjoyed by the peasants. Several princes protected them in the interests of social stability through laws forbidding the raising of rents and the conversion of long leases into short ones. Most seriously affected were the lesser nobility, the Imperial Knights, many of whose small domains had never been economically viable. Rising prices, added to the difficulties they were already experiencing, provided the final cause of the Knights' War of 1523.[8]

Those who suffered most seriously from inflation, however, were the wage-earners, both rural labourers and urban artisans. As with rents, custom tended to keep wages below increasing prices, and in some places unemployment had the same effect. By the 1530s the plight of the lowest paid workers in the towns, who might face starvation through unemployment or a bad harvest, had become desperate, and they began to manifest signs of violent discontent. Upper class town councils in Germany were compelled by popular pressure unwillingly

[6] P. 90.   [7] P. 90.   [8] Pp. 21, 160.

to accept Lutheranism with its accompanying spoliation of the Church, and in 1534 the Anabaptists established their communistic and polygamous Kingdom of the Elect at Münster in Westphalia with the help of unemployed artisans from the nearby Netherlands.[9] The shock of this event led town councils throughout Europe to lay up stores of grain in municipal granaries to be issued to the hungry in times of scarcity. Other outbreaks followed, in which social discontent was united with religious fervour, such as the image-breaking riots in the Netherlands, which followed the 'hunger-winter' of 1565-6, and the popular domination of the Holy League in Paris in 1589-90.[10]

The middle classes

Charles Smyth said (in a pamphlet long out of print), 'All history scholarship candidates appear to know two things: that the peculiar and distinctive character of any century of European history is "the rise of the middle classes"; and second, that the Reformation was an important factor in the political, social and economic history of the sixteenth century, intimately connected, of course, with the rise of the middle classes, but what it had to do with the Christian religion is neither here nor there.' Many historians have, indeed, held that the period of the Reformation was one of important social transformation, that it brought about the rise in numbers and importance of this new class which gained its wealth from trade instead of land and came to replace the old feudal nobility in social and political preeminence within the state. The Reformation itself is regarded as an accompaniment of this development, the determination of the middle classes to secure the endowment of the Church and to assert their will over the clergy in worship and ecclesiastical government.

If, however, there had been such a rise to power by the middle classes, it would have produced egalitarian social developments. But European society remained hierarchic in character with no fundamental change in its conception of ordered ranks. Kings retained their authority and continued to rely upon the landed noblemen to act as their courtiers and diplomats, ministers and soldiers. That this class sustained its importance was shown by one of the most influential books of the Renaissance, *The Courtier*, published by Count Castiglione in Italian in 1528 and within the next forty years translated into Spanish, French, English, Latin and German. In it, the count set out his picture of the ideal gentleman of the Renaissance, who developed his accomplishments and used his gifts to the best of his ability. Such a man, trained at both court and camp, was soldier, sportsman, athlete, scholar, artist and musician, and Castiglione not only thought of him as a courtier, but also insisted that the first pre-requisite of the

[9] P. 233.   [10] Pp. 256, 234.

perfect courtier was that he should be of high birth and noble blood. The humanistic notion of the cultivation of a rounded personality, built on the training of the body and the mind, was not applied to any new class, but rather to the old noble class which had previously claimed to be inspired by ideals of chivalry and service and whose members had been accepted as the natural recipients of social honours and political authority.

Far from displacing the nobility, those who made money in trade or the professions sought to enter its ranks by ennoblement and marriage and purchase of estates. In this they were assisted by the need of monarchs for both more administrators and more money, which led to the sale of royal patents of nobility and public offices. The Spanish monarchy increased the number of grandees during the sixteenth century from 77 to 119, though this was modest compared with the numbers that were to be created in the next century. Henry III of France sold four seats in the *Conseil du Roi* for 15 000 francs each, and in this kingdom the feudal *noblesse d'epée* were joined by a growing number of *noblesse de robe*. This new nobility of the gown not only enjoyed the same tax exemptions as the old nobility of the sword, but also secured estates and exacted their feudal dues so vigorously as to produce the later *réaction seigneuriale*, which was to play an important part in the development of the French Revolution. In these countries, successful middle-class men did not try to increase the power and prestige of their own class, but rather to rise above it and become prominent members of the superior, hereditary governing class.

If the middle classes had become more important in the sixteenth century, the towns would have been expected to have increased in power and influence, but the reverse, in fact, took place. Though many towns grew in size and wealth, this was a period in which their political independence declined. In Spain, the towns of Valencia formed a *Germania* or armed alliance in defence of their rights in 1519, which lasted precariously until 1523 when the grandees finally suppressed it. The more serious revolt of the league of the *Comuneros*, formed in 1520 by the towns of northern Castile, which expelled royal officials and refused to pay taxes, was similarly defeated in 1521.[11] In Germany, the Swabian League, founded in 1488 by the cities of the south-west, after enjoying considerable armed power, passed into dissolution soon after 1530. Other European towns, notably Ghent and Antwerp, Augsburg and Strasburg, which had once enjoyed much freedom and influence, lost their importance during the century. Everywhere during the age of the Reformation the urban middle-classes showed hardly any sign of asserting themselves against the growing power of the state exercised by the nobility under their king.

In fact, the Reformation was essentially a religious revival, not a

[11] P. 195.

political or social movement. Inevitably it became associated at times with other aspirations and grievances, but the few religious groups, notably the Anabaptists, that definitely sought to overthrow the existing political and social order were expressions of the discontent of the lower rather than the middle classes. As a religious movement, the Reformation gained the support of people of various classes in different countries—German princes, Genevan merchants, Scottish noblemen, Flemish craftsmen, French peasants and Italian artisans. It assumed different forms and experienced varying fortunes in Europe, but its background must be seen against the religious situation of the time and not against a supposed middle-class social revolution.

Capitalism

The Reformation has often also been associated with another social and economic question—the rise of capitalism or the capitalist spirit. Since capitalism is commonly regarded as both an economic and a social phenomenon, its nature is not easy to define. It may be said, however, that a capitalist is one who supports trade or the production of goods by means of capital, often obtained as credit based upon existing financial wealth, the motive behind his enterprise being to make a profit. A capitalist society, therefore, is a market society in which those who wish to buy certain commodities do business with those who wish to sell them either as producers or merchants.

It would be wrong to suggest that capitalism did not exist during the Middle Ages. Nevertheless, medieval social and economic life was largely dominated by small-scale and limited manufactures for local use and by agricultural activity that often hardly went beyond subsistence farming; and neither required great amounts of money to be put into operation. During the sixteenth century most of the population continued to live in these circumstances. They dwelt in isolated, mainly self-supporting, rural communities, governed by the manorial system; trade affected only a very small proportion of them. They continued to accept the medieval notion of the principles governing trade, profit and credit.

Influenced partly by Greek ideas of harmony, the Medieval Church thought of society as an organism whose members had the duty of serving one another. In commerce this principle was expressed in the notion of the just price. It was considered that every article had, in any particular circumstances, a proper value, and to seek more than this was condemned as sinful. A man who made or grew anything must not sell it for more than its just price, which should cover his expenses and give him a fair compensation for his own labour. Money itself, however, was not regarded as something that could earn such a measure of compensation. Money was held to be solely a medium of exchange for articles of consumption, the use of which in credit was adequately repaid by the return of a sum equal to that which had been lent.[12] This doctrine was based upon Aristotle's theory of the 'barren' nature of money and was elaborated by the Schoolmen, especially St Thomas Aquinas. It did not recognize the nature of interest as payment for capital needed to produce wealth and compensation for the risk facing the lender. Consequently, the practice of usury, the exacting of interest on money lent out, was formally condemned at the Third Lateran Council in 1179 and the Second Council of Lyons in 1274, though it was allowed to Jews by the Fourth Lateran Council of 1215.

Since official ecclesiastical strictures would seem to be a hindrance to trade and industry, it has been suggested that the Reformation had a strong influence upon the development of capitalism in the sixteenth century. This idea has been most fully expressed by two writers, though they did not share the same attitude towards the question. The first was the German sociologist, Max Weber, who wrote *The Protestant Ethic and the Spirit of Capitalism* in 1904. In this he asserted that while the Medieval Church condemned the world and profit-making and usury in particular, the Protestants, especially the Calvinists, saw worldly activities as acceptable to God and, therefore, to be undertaken as energetically and profitably as possible. He saw this as producing a new outlook of mind, the 'capitalist spirit', which distinguished post-Reformation Europe and was most marked in Protestant countries. The second writer was the Christian Socialist, R. H. Tawney, whose *Religion and the Rise of Capitalism* was published in 1926. He argued rather differently that Protestantism did not *produce* the capitalist spirit, which existed in human nature already, but rather that it stopped attempting to restrain and control it. Protestantism even encouraged it by representing industry, thrift and enterprise as cardinal virtues and the success and prosperity gained through their application to business as a sign of godliness and divine favour.

Despite their differences, both writers agreed in linking the growth of Protestantism and the development of capitalism. It is difficult, however, to find geographical justification for this idea in the sixteenth century. There is no sign of capitalism establishing itself first or more strongly in countries where Protestantism was gaining adherents. The origins of modern capitalism date back to the growth of banking in the city-states of northern Italy and to the rise of industries, such as the wool-weaving of Florence, in the later Middle Ages. During that time the Papacy itself became the centre of a complex financial system; and the kings of France and municipal authorities in other countries officially regulated the legal amount of interest which could

[12] P. 42.

be charged in their areas without any reference to ecclesiastical rulings. By the beginning of the sixteenth century, the greatest single capitalists in Europe were in southern Germany and the Tyrol. The Fuggers were the wealthiest family. Their head, Jacob Fugger, boasted to a Spanish cardinal that he had lent money to every see in Germany to pay the first-fruits required by the Papacy on the appointment of each new bishop—and to some sees twice or thrice. This, he said, was even more profitable than his silver mines and other sources of income. When he died in 1525, a respected Catholic and a Count of the Empire, his firm had been paying a dividend of fifty-four per cent for the previous sixteen years.

Moreover, the Protestant reformers were less ready to tolerate the practices of capitalism than the orthodox theologians who, in the words of G. G. Coulton, 'were accustomed to regard the law as a pious aspiration rather than a solid fact',* and by the end of the fifteenth century some theologians were openly speaking in favour of interest on loans.[13] Protestantism wished to purge Christianity of its corruptions, and it regarded the easy tolerance of cupidity and usury as being among them. The reformers had no sympathy with the monastic ideal, that men could best serve God by withdrawing from the world, but they taught that their efforts in the world should be to the glory of God and not to their mutual advancement. Luther, Zwingli and Calvin all condemned usury as thoroughly as any medieval canonist, though Calvin in 1545 did come to agree that interest at five per cent might be taken in certain circumstances. He argued that, since a complete prohibition of usury was impossible, financial transactions must be regulated by the law of charity, which would condemn excessive rates of interest as contrary to Christian love for one's neighbour, and his arguments were gradually accepted among European divines.

The only sense in which there was a connection between Protestantism and capitalism is probably that Protestants, being less bound by precedent, were eventually more ready to accept officially the ways of the new economic system. Those who practised the Protestant insistence upon applying Christian principles in the world, and who gained experience in practical affairs through participating in the organization of their religious body, were likely to be more successful in business than those without this background. The fact remains, however, that capitalism developed in Europe during the sixteenth century, not because of the effect of any religious teaching and practice, but through the increase of trade and the greater availability of capital, and that this was a development which had already begun before this period.

For the greater part of the sixteenth century, European capitalism

* *Medieval Panorama* (1938)   [13] P. 42.

was practised by the great merchant dynasties, especially those of
Italy and Germany, very much in the traditional way of the later
Middle Ages. Towards the end of the period, however, efforts were
made to develop institutions which broke away from this pattern and
were to become closely involved in the workings of capitalism. One
such institution was the public bank, a means of facilitating the making
of payments and the raising of capital. Venice provided herself with
the Banco della Piazza di Rialto in 1587, but France failed in her
attempt to found a bank in 1604 and so did Spain in 1607. The most
famous and successful of them all, the Wisselbank of Amsterdam, was
founded in 1609. The other new capitalist institution, the chartered or
joint-stock company, began in England with the granting of a charter
to the Levant Company in 1581.[14] This was an organization to which
the members contributed a common, permanent capital, in return for a
share in the profits of its collective activities, unlike earlier regulating
companies in which each member traded in his own goods, used his
own methods and made his own gains or losses. The success of the
Levant Company encouraged the formation of the East India Company
in 1600, the challenge of which was met two years later by rival Dutch
merchants who formed their own more immediately successful East
India Company. The establishment in these countries of these new
organizations, so different from the older family undertakings, was a
sign that the most powerful growth of capitalism was moving away
to those parts of northern Europe best situated to make use of the
oceanic routes which led to the exploitation of trade with the east,
the West Indies and, eventually, the North American mainland.

The nobility

The European nobility, despite their importance in politics, their
continued social pre-eminence and their comparative success in consolidating their position and privileges, nevertheless encountered
serious financial and economic difficulties, particularly in the later part
of the century. The benefits they obtained from royal patronage and
better returns from their lands were often nullified by the continual
rise in prices throughout the period. To this was added the effect of
the Renaissance extravagance in which they indulged themselves often
beyond their means. Again, since the growing complexity and
specialization of government made legal or university training
increasingly necessary for service under the Crown, nobles now had
to face considerable costs in educating their sons. For some noblemen
the oldest aristocratic occupation of all, serving in a royal army,
provided a measure of financial relief from their problems, but such
military service and its rewards were intermittent—a cessation of

[14] P. 78.

hostilities might at any time deprive them of most of their income.

This was particularly true of the French nobility. Although the Italian wars ended unsuccessfully for the French, who were unable to maintain themselves in the peninsula, the nobility returned with an unbounded admiration for the works of art of the Italian Renaissance and determined to imitate its costly way of life. They spent large sums on food, clothes, furniture and, above all, buildings. A Huguenot leader observed in 1587, 'it is only in the last sixty years that architecture has been re-established in France.' (The magnificent Renaissance *châteaux*, such as Chambord, Blois, Amboise and Chenonceaux, were erected at this time in the valley of the Loire between Orleans and Angers.) This same Huguenot considered that the financial difficulties of the French nobility were due mainly to 'the mistakes it has committed in the spending of its wealth.' For a time fighting in the French army had lessened their problems, but the signing of the Treaty of Cateau-Cambrésis in 1559 brought many of them near to poverty at a period when prices were still rising, and yet the urge to spend was as great as ever. Their reaction to this situation was one of the reasons which led them to support the royal and religious factions that plunged the country into civil war.[15]

In Spain a comparison of the annual incomes of thirteen ducal families between the early sixteenth century and 1600 shows that their incomes had hardly doubled over the years while costs had quadrupled. By the end of the century many noble families were deeply in debt; a Venetian ambassador at the Spanish court asserted that the grandees probably received no more than a fifth of their revenues because the rest went to pay the interest on their mortgages and loans. The fifth Duke of Infantado, who died in 1598, left large debts, one of the biggest items being caused by expenditure on repairs and improvements to the ducal palace at Guadalajara.

In both countries, the impoverishment of the nobility led them to seek much the same source of alternative income in royal patronage. It was traditional for the French nobility, in times of monarchical weakness, to take advantage of the situation by revolting, not so much to gain political power as to secure gifts and pensions, offices and benefices, from the Crown; and during the civil wars they were able to obtain them as the price of their support for one side or the other. When the succession of Henry IV became certain in 1593, those who had received appointments under the Catholic League began to desert to him, because they were anxious about the legality of their position, and so they assured his successful establishment upon the throne. Moreover, the Concordat of Bologna of 1516 made the French Church part of the patronage system of the Crown with the result

[15] P. 222.

that it was said that 'bishoprics were like cinnamon and pepper to the nobility.' In Spain, when the parsimonious Philip II was succeeded by his extravagant son, Philip III, in 1598, the nobility were quick to benefit from his enormously increased royal household and splendid court. The royal treasury was plundered, corruption became common and redundant office-holders multiplied. Throughout the century, the Spanish nobility made determined efforts to stop the Crown appointing men of humble origin to high office in the Spanish Church.

The clergy

Nevertheless, the general effect of the Reformation and the Counter-Reformation was to diversify the social status of the clergy. This may be observed in the occupants of the Papacy during the period. Of six popes elected between 1503 and 1550 all except one (Adrian VI) belonged to distinguished Italian families, and of these, two were Medicis (Leo X and Clement VII); but of five popes elected between 1559 and 1591 two were of humble origin, one the son of a middle-class bankrupt, one of a minor nobleman and one of a good family from Bologna. Tenaciously though the nobility sought to maintain their hold upon the high offices of the Church, the widening basis of society as a whole and the greater spread of education presented them with serious competition.

In Roman Catholic countries, where the Church retained its endowments, the clergy remained more numerous than in Protestant ones. At the end of the sixteenth century, there were in France 136 archbishops or bishops, 40 000 parish priests with as many secular clergy in subordinate positions, 24 000 canons, 34 000 friars, 2 500 Jesuits, 12 000 monks and 80 000 nuns. The spiritual leadership of the French Church, however, was greatly weakened by the control exercised over it by the Crown, which possessed the patronage of some 600 bishoprics and abbeys. It enabled the monarchs to reward favourites and provide for their diplomatic service, but it meant that the country's ecclesiastical leaders had secular interests, were swayed by court factions and cared little for their dioceses or religious houses. Attempts at reform were paralysed, and there was widespread pluralism and non-residence. One of the most notorious pluralists was Charles de Guise, Cardinal of Lorraine (1524-74), who became all-powerful during the reign of Francis II (1559-60). He was Archbishop of Rheims, Bishop of Metz and Verdun and the Abbot of eleven abbeys; offices which gave him an income of 300 000 livres a year. He had inherited most of his appointments from his uncle, becoming Archbishop at the age of fourteen and Cardinal at twenty-three. Most of the lower clergy inherited their benefices in the same way for they were part of the patrimony of local families. Many of them were non-resident also, and their parishes at the best were in the charge of poorly-paid curates.

In Spain there were seven archbishops and forty bishops and by the end of the century some 200 000 regular and secular clergy. The growth in the number of new religious orders, brought about by the Counter-Reformation, had increased the number of men and women under vows. The older orders enlarged their membership as well; there were said to be 32 000 Dominicans and Franciscans. During these years of religious revival in Spain, the Church received large gifts of money, jewels and real estate, which increased the incomes of some of the clergy at a more rapid rate than the rise in prices. Thus the value of the canonries of Seville Cathedral multiplied sixfold in value during the century from 300 to 2 000 ducats. With the decrease in religious fervour, which accompanied the general decline of the kingdom in the later part of the century, the sense of religious vocation seems to have weakened markedly among the numerous clergy, and contemporary opinion became hostile to them as an unnecessary and useless part of the population.

The sixteenth century inherited from the Middle Ages the greater prosperity enjoyed by the higher clergy compared with the lower. This difference disappeared in Protestant countries, where the ecclesiastical hierarchy was abolished, but another distinction gradually appeared—that between urban and rural clergy. The clergy in the cities were well educated, married into the gentry or even the nobility and received a good stipend. The clergy of the countryside, however, were often peasants and married the daughters of peasants, were appointed by the local landowner and dependent on him, and were often paid so badly that they had to supplement their income by farming. In 1529 the city pastor of Wittenberg had 200 gulden a year, but there were local country pastors who got only twenty gulden.

Plundered endowments and marriage tended to keep the clergy impoverished in some countries. This was particularly true in parts of Germany, where it was not unknown for pastors to undertake other occupations and even to beg in order to maintain themselves. Although Luther's doctrine of the 'priesthood of the laity' inevitably lowered the respect accorded to the Protestant clergy, at the same time they were acquiring a professional status which was partly hereditary as many of their sons became ordained. Both Reformation and Counter-Reformation sought to improve the education of the clergy and encourage them to preach sermons, but the Protestant authorities were probably more successful because the changes that had been made in the ecclesiastical constitution of their Churches made it easier for them to transfer endowments to educational purposes. Their proclaimed intention and determined efforts to produce a better trained and more effective clergy were often among the factors that gained them popular support, but the progress made by both Roman Catholics and Protestants during the sixteenth century towards this end was comparatively slow.

6

SCIENCE
AND
THOUGHT

The medieval outlook

Professor H. Butterfield has written, 'The so-called scientific revolution . . . outshines everything since the rise of Christianity and reduces the Renaissance and Reformation to the rank of mere episodes, mere internal displacements within the system of medieval Christendom. . . . There can hardly be a field in which it is of greater moment for us to see . . . the precise operations that underlay a particular historical transition, a particular chapter of intellectual development.'* To what extent was the change a scientific revolution? It was in the sense that the entire edifice of intellectual assumptions derived from the ancient Greeks and sanctified by medieval theology was overthrown and replaced by a radically new system. A new world-picture replaced the old which had been generally accepted for nearly two thousand years. At the same time, during the outset of the movement in the sixteenth century, it was considered a return to antiquity, a revival of the ideas of other ancient writers which had been lost and neglected during the Middle Ages.

Medieval thought largely accepted the set of ideas devised by Aristotle (384-322 BC), who had been a pupil of Plato at Athens. In his writings, which cover the whole range of knowledge, he sought to produce an orderly account of every aspect of mankind and the world known during his lifetime. Using Plato as a basis, the medieval conception of the universe was qualitative, stable, limited and religious. The achievement of the scientific revolution was to change this into a quantitative, atomic, evolutionary, infinitely extended conception of the world. To do this the limits of medieval scholastic thought had to be transcended and the necessary methods of free enquiry developed.

Though Aristotle had been a disciple of Plato, his outlook was very different. Plato started from the world of 'ideas', regarding them as alone having a real existence and being arranged in increasing importance, headed by the 'Idea of the Good'; but Aristotle insisted that an idea

* The Origins of Modern Science (1957).

existed only as expressed in the individual object. He asserted, therefore, that so far from there being an ideal 'tree', possessing existence in its own right, it was the union of the 'form' (essence, nature) of the tree with 'matter' (the passive and indeterminate capacity of receiving 'form') which made the real individual tree. To explain this conjunction of form and matter, he laid down a 'First Cause', though he did not represent this as being a personal God. All being he regarded as ascending a continuous scale from mere matter (about which, because it was quite without form, nothing could be said) up to the pure actuality or 'thought thinking itself', which was this supreme or first cause.

Aristotle, consequently, took a static view of life and did not allow for the growth of one thing out of another. He refused to consider how the world was made; his philosophy saw no need for any creation. To him the world was marked by permanence. All things were always as they are now because such is their 'nature'. This he explained by his idea of 'final causes', which held that all organisms, even matter, were endowed with a purpose to reach appropriate 'ends'. A bird flew in the air or a fish swam in the water because it was their 'nature' to do so; similarly, the earth and heavenly bodies tended downwards and fire and light bodies upwards through their 'nature'. Aristotle thus explained 'phenomena' by postulating 'ends' for them and did not enquire how such phenomena work. Moreover, he held that everything in nature tended towards perfection, which it achieved in different degrees. Man represented perfection, and all other species fell short of this. Since for Aristotle the world was essentially unchanging, this did not imply evolution, but rather an eternal order of varying grades of perfection. The greatness of his system lay in its comprehensiveness, its orderliness and the rational unity imparted to it by his logic; but its consequences were to encourage acceptance of the world as he explained it. It did not seem that his observations should be checked or results obtained from them by the application of mathematics. His teaching probably contributed to the halting of the earlier Greek scientific movement.

There was no medieval scientific revival, but rather a lack of interest in natural phenomena, a disregard of individual judgment and a supernatural and other-worldly mentality. Since this present existence was regarded entirely as the prelude to man's fate hereafter, the brief span of human life on earth was considered of little importance compared with eternal life in heaven. Thinkers, therefore, were concerned with the true 'end' of human existence on earth, and they sought to justify the truths of Christianity as upholding this belief. The most important knowledge of all was the divine scheme of salvation for mankind, taught by the Church and realized through its sacramental and penitential system. Medieval thought was directed towards the ordering of all knowledge and experience to produce an explanation of nature and the universe which would convey to men what they should know to fulfil the purpose of their existence on earth.

During the early centuries of the Church, Aristotle's ideas were looked upon with suspicion because his teachings were thought to lead to a materialistic view of the world, opposed to Christian belief. Moreover, the Fathers had a high regard for Plato, who was thought to be completely opposed to Aristotle. In the Middle Ages, when first-hand knowledge of Aristotle had been unavailable for several centuries, familiarity with his philosophy was gradually regained from Arabic translations of his writings made by Jews and Arabs, which were translated into Latin during the twelfth century. At first the Church regarded these works with considerable hostility, but gradually his ideas were assimilated into Christian doctrine. His notion that all changes occur in the attempt to attain perfection was seen to imply anticipation, a working towards some future event, which was completely in accordance with the Church's teaching that present good works led to future blessedness. Schoolmen followed his distinction between 'form' and 'matter' to explain the doctrine of trans-substantiation, which held that after consecration in the Mass the 'substance' of the elements changed into those of the Body and Blood of Christ, but their 'accidents' continued to exist.[1]

This doctrine found classic formulation in the teaching of the Dominican friar, St Thomas Aquinas (1225-74), the most important medieval scholastic philosopher, who completed the establishment of a Christian system of thought based upon the ideas of Aristotle. His greatest work, the *Summa Theologica*, was a compilation of human learning, subsumed under a Christian philosophy, to give to the diverse activities of nature and man a pattern which exhibited the fundamental truths of Christianity.[2] To Aquinas there were two sources of truth—reason and Christian revelation. The truths of reason were discovered by the application of Aristotle's logic, which could show that, since everything seeks perfection, the perfection of the 'rational soul', possessed by man alone, must be to strive for the supreme perfection of God. The truths of revelation were to be found in the Bible and the traditions of the Church. By this synthesis Aquinas sought to show that, since God made Himself known by both reason and revelation, the two sorts of truth could never be contradictory. There is both a sphere of natural reason and a sphere of knowledge obtained by faith through revelation. Reason and revelation always agree, but revelation is superior to reason in the sense that reason alone cannot discover everything. Beyond reason, the act of faith is needed to arrive at complete truth through reliance upon revelation,

[1] P. 96.   [2] P. 35.

which presents men with mysteries to be believed when they cannot be understood.

The scholastic system, therefore, confined the sphere of reason to premises based upon authority in theology and all branches of human learning. To Aquinas rational investigation was needed 'for the greater clarification of the content of the divine teaching'. Generally speaking, therefore, experimental science was not possible in the Middle Ages because of the scholastic conception of the finality of the natural order of things as part of God's eternal purpose. Attention was concentrated upon the problems of man's relations with God; comparatively little thought was given to nature.

The changing background

The background to the scholastic system of the universe and the neglect of science and technology was the feudal and largely self-contained social and economic organization of medieval Christendom. During these centuries the people of western Europe lived in almost complete isolation from the rest of the world and had only a slight and fragmentary knowledge of the great Asiatic and North African civilizations. European agriculture was mainly conducted on a subsistence basis, its industry negligible and its commerce relatively slight. Its society was organized in a combined secular and ecclesiastical hierarchy which seemed divinely sanctioned. Such a situation accorded well with a system of thought which regarded the whole universe as permanent and designed to fulfil its 'end' in the divine will. It also accounted for the limitations of medieval science. Not only was the scholastic outlook unfavourable to scientific work, neither was there a desire to promote or benefit from its activities. Of such inventions and discoveries as were made, some were forgotten and rediscovered more than once because there seemed to be no practical need for them. Medieval science was accordingly mainly book-learning and disputation. Not until the break-up of the old economy and society did a new, progressive, experimental science begin to replace the static, rational science of the Middle Ages.

Such a change, which began in Italy during the thirteenth century, gradually and unevenly transformed the feudal economy into the capitalist economy. The growth of towns, trade and industry proved incompatible with the old order in Europe. Towns, in which markets had been established, had for generations occupied a secondary, and even redundant, part in economic life, but by the fifteenth century they were starting to develop a form of production based upon money payments instead of customary services. The need for greater production and the wish for increasing wealth, which marked the rise of capitalism, provided the conditions which made the development of experimental science desirable and possible. Technical advances were necessary for the advancement of agriculture, industry and trade. During this period, therefore, it was the demands of economic progress that brought about the growth of scientific enquiry rather than the practical successes of science contributing markedly to the success of industrial expansion. Often, indeed, the attempts made to solve practical problems could not be put into effect because scientific knowledge was not sufficiently advanced to develop them; the best-known examples of this were the many ingenious ideas of Leonardo da Vinci, which got no further than the paper on which they were sketched.[3]

There were, however, some instances in which the development of scientific ideas accompanied the desire to solve technical questions. An example of this is the work of the humanist, Agricola (George Bauer, 1494-1555), who was for many years a physician to the miners of Saxony, the men whom Martin Luther's father had moved from the family farm to participate in and to prosper from this industry. Agricola also held shares in some of the most profitable mines and studied both mining techniques and geology. He wrote *De re metallica*, a handbook to the mining technology of his time. He also wrote books on geology in which he displayed a high measure of critical observation together with an exceptional mistrust of accepted ideas and the traditional beliefs of the miners. His own notions about the origins of ore deposits and the effects of erosion on the form of mountains were not completely correct, but prepared the way for subsequent developments in geological science.

Another such man was Simon Stevin (1548-1620), a Fleming who lived in the northern Netherlands. He was a practical engineer and in 1568 introduced the decimal system of representing fractions. As a quartermaster in the army of William of Orange, he was particularly interested in the mechanics of warfare and navigation. He designed 'machines' for lifting the Dutch fishing-boats above high-water mark and became an expert in the art of fortification. His achievements included preceding Galileo in experiments on the relative rate of the fall of bodies of different weight,[4] and giving the first mathematical proof of the principle of the lever and of the conditions of equilibrium on inclined planes. He was also the first to discuss the 'hydrostatic paradox'—that is, that the downward pressure of a liquid on the base of its containing vessel depends only on the depth of the vessel and the area of the base and is independent of its shape and size. In addition, he was able to calculate the pressure on any given portion of the side of the containing vessel. In this way he provided the essential basis for the whole of the later science of hydrostatics.

The effect of practical needs upon the development of new scientific

[3] P. 53.   [4] P. 105.

ideas must not, however, be exaggerated. Technology and scientific theory only sometimes influenced each other. At other times, inventions and improvements were made which did not influence theoretical science. This was particularly true of the navigators, shipbuilders and gunners, who made overseas exploration and colonization possible.[5] In medicine, the treatment of gunshot wounds with cool unguents instead of boiling them in oil, advocated by Ambrose Paré in his *Method of Treating Wounds caused by Firearms* (1545), was an important practical advance and saved many lives, but it came about from his observations as an army surgeon and did not influence medical theory. The same applied to another book written by Paré in which he advocated the ligature invented by him in cases of amputation. He also invented artificial limbs. He was, however, in common with men like Agricola and Stevin, ready to ignore accepted tradition in favour of personal observation and experiment, an essential for the development of science.

The effect of the Renaissance

As well as the effect of contemporary practical problems, there was also the influence of the humanist writers of the Renaissance, though this would not, at first sight, appear to be of much consequence. These writers were neither interested in science themselves nor made any important contribution to its development.[6] They were quite prepared to accept the traditional world-picture received from the past, and the authority of Aristotle in scientific matters remained as great during the sixteenth century as it had done previously.

Moreover, those who did take an interest in the physical universe often did so in a way that did not assist the growth of scientific study. Interest in alchemy persisted, and the search for the 'Philosopher's Stone' or 'Elixir' which would change base metals into gold, based upon Aristotle's view that one substance could be changed into another by altering its primary qualities, was continued with intensity. Queen Elizabeth I of England employed an alchemist in Somerset House to make gold for her and imprisoned him in the Tower of London when he did not succeed. Similarly, the other traditional pseudo-science, astrology, found devoted supporters among the humanists. The Renaissance did nothing to diminish their belief in it. On the contrary, the study of ancient cults and superstitions tended to increase such interest and belief. They were ready to accept that the movements of the heavenly bodies could foretell revolution, war, sudden death and other disasters as well as determine the inborn desires and abilities of all mortals and govern the success or failure of medicine. A writer of the later sixteenth century said, 'Above all

[5] P. 48.   [6] P. 48.

things next to grammar, a physician must have surely his astronomy, to know how, when and at what time every medicine ought to be administered.'

It may be said, however, that the preoccupation with alchemy and astrology, while not directly contributing to the development of any branch of natural science, did bring about a change of attitude which was to be of fundamental importance in the future. In the Middle Ages, scholars had accepted the traditional explanations of the material world and had not tried to investigate or exploit it. But now these forms of magic represented an attempt to understand more fully the natural forces and heavenly bodies of the universe, to formulate laws to explain their working and to discover their effect upon both inanimate objects and human life. The methods were wrong and the aims illusory, but the spirit of curiosity, enquiry and experiment was that which in the future would give impetus to scientific investigation.

Again, it was the humanist scholars who brought about the revival of Greek studies. They sought out the original texts of the ancient Greek scientific works, edited them and often translated them into Latin, endeavouring to separate the original expositions from interpretations and commentaries of medieval Arabic translators and writers. As a result of their work during the sixteenth century, most of those Greek texts that had survived were made available for contemporary study.

The effect of this rediscovery must not be exaggerated. The increased availability of ancient scientific literature did not ensure that its accuracy would be tested by personal observation and experiment. Most humanists did not doubt the accuracy of the Greek view of nature; if they criticized the medieval philosophers, it was for deviating from that view rather than for accepting and teaching it. In general, therefore, the effect of Renaissance studies was to strengthen the authority of the traditional explanation of the world rather than to encourage fresh scientific effort to investigate and understand it.

Nevertheless, the reappearance of ancient treatises did result in some scientific advances. It was apparent from the treatises that the classical writers had not agreed among themselves on important scientific questions and, during the sixteenth century, Plato, the Pythagoreans and Archimedes, whose conclusions were in various ways not in accordance with accepted ideas, were more often and more sympathetically mentioned than previously. At some places, therefore, notably the University of Padua, it was possible to challenge the teaching of Aristotle. At the same time, improved texts, such as the full text of Aristotle on biology and the original text of Galen on medicine, were made available for the first time, and thus the possibility of understanding them more accurately was increased.

The most significant result of the improved knowledge of Galen was achieved by a Fleming, Andreas Vesalius (1514-64) who combined it with greater skill in dissection and was, like Galileo, a professor at the University of Padua. His anatomical treatise, *De Humani Corporis Fabrica* (1543), was the most important work of science in the Renaissance period and did much to prepare the way for the development of modern biology. In his description of the bones and joints, muscles and organs of the human frame, he followed Galen, but in a second edition of the book, published twelve years later, he criticized Galen's explanation of the action of the heart, 'though not long ago I would not have dared to turn aside even a hair's breadth from Galen'. In itself his book represented the most accomplished feat in the attainment of scientific accuracy until Tycho Brahé's work in astronomy, some thirty years later, while his attitude to practical investigation made him a true poineer of the scientific revolution.

Generally speaking, however, the European universities took only a small part in the scientific movement—those like Padua were exceptional. Most remained attached to traditional ideas and only slowly tolerated the teaching of Renaissance humanism, still less of science. Scientists, therefore, had to find another form of organization to promote their work and communicate it to others. They made use of bodies already in existence for other purposes. These were the societies or academies of the fifteenth century, originally formed to enable people to assemble together to discuss literary and philosophical subjects at the time of the Renaissance. The members of these societies met informally and read newsletters received from correspondents abroad, describing political happenings, new ideas and recent books, among which would be scientific works and even experiments. Sometimes those members particularly interested in science would seek to make the proceedings predominantly scientific or would leave and form a scientific group of their own. Among the earliest such literary societies were the Florentine academies of 1433 and 1442; the first scientific societies were also Italian, notably the *Accademia Secretorium Naturae*, which was formed at Naples in 1560. Others followed in Italy, France, England and other countries during the seventeenth century, and had an important role in the development of science as an academic discipline.

The Copernican system

Astronomy was first to challenge seriously the medieval system of thought. In fact, it may be said that it was the only branch of science in the sixteenth century marked by achievements and discoveries sufficient to distinguish it from its medieval position. The way for

this advance was prepared by the activities of late medieval practi-
tioners. By the end of the fifteenth century, as Dr J. D. Bernal has
said, 'descriptive astronomy was the only science at that time which
had accumulated enough observations and developed mathematical
methods accurate enough to permit hypotheses to be set out clearly
and tested numerically.'* The reason for this was partly the sustained
interest in astrology, which had gained astronomy princely support
as the only really practical medieval science, and also the beginning
of overseas voyages, which gave it a new and valuable use as an aid
to navigation.

Aristotle had considered that the circle and the sphere were the
most 'perfect figures' and, therefore, those on which the universe
was modelled. He considered the heavens to be a series of concentric
spheres ranged round a central body, the earth. Immediately surrounding the earth was the sphere of the atmosphere and around that spheres
of pure elemental nature, which were—going outwards from the
earth and in order of density—water, air and fire. Beyond them was a
subtle fluid permeating space, the ether, which entered into the composition of the heavenly bodies. Next in succession came the seven
crystalline spheres, each of which carried a planet, and beyond was
the eighth sphere which bore the fixed stars. Finally, beyond all others,
was the sphere whose divine harmony caused the circular nature of
the whole celestial system.

Aristotle's system was criticized, even during his lifetime, as raising
certain difficulties. The most serious was that observation clearly
showed that only the sun and fixed stars moved in circles round the
earth, the stable pivot of the universe, while the moon and the planets
were seen to make contrary movements, at varying speeds, against
the background of the stars. An answer to this was put forward by
the Greek mathematician, Ptolemy, who lived in Alexandria from AD
139 to 161. He explained the more complicated movement of the
moon and the planets by holding that each revolved in its own circle,
the centre of which described another circle round the earth. He took
rapidity of movement as the test of the nearness of the planets. From
the centre, therefore, he held the universe to consist of Earth, Moon,
Mercury, Venus, Sun, Mars, Jupiter, Saturn, the fixed stars and,
beyond, heaven and outer darkness.

The Middle Ages accepted this picture of the universe described
by Aristotle and Ptolemy with the earth as a stationary body, constantly at rest in the centre of the universe, and the sun, moon, planets
and fixed stars revolving around it as attendant satellites, though there
was disagreement whether the earth was a sphere or not. Many
practical astronomers, however, had criticized Ptolemy's system of
concentric spheres because it was not supported by their observations.

* *Science in History* (1954).

The planetary motions were too complicated to be explained in this way without an impossibly cumbersome combination of spheres. The achievement of Copernicus was to put forward a hypothesis that simplified the whole problem, though he was, in fact, the last of the medieval students rather than the first of the modern astronomical observers.

Nicholas Copernicus (1473-1543) was born in Poland, the son of a Germanized Slav merchant, and studied mathematics and astronomy at the University of Cracow and at several Italian universities until he was over thirty years old, when he was appointed a canon of Frauenburg Cathedral, near the Baltic. He used a small tower on the wall of the cathedral close as an observatory, where he lay on his back nightly examining the stars. He had no telescope, but made a few crude instruments, including a large wooden isosceles triangle and square, which he used in favourable weather to measure the height of the celestial bodies. But his ideas were not really based upon astronomical observations. He had learned that several ancient Greek writers had suggested that the five planets might have the sun instead of the earth as the centre of their orbits, and this seemed to him to have the great merit of mathematical simplicity. He postulated that the earth is but one of the planets revolving round the sun and turning on its own axis to make day and night. Otherwise his conception of the nature of the universe remained the same as the traditional one. He retained the Ptolemaic notion of circular planetary orbits and even the Aristotelian plan of celestial spheres. Nevertheless, his new cosmology was plainly contrary to that of Aristotle and, therefore, of medieval scholasticism as well.

Yet, his ideas made very little immediate impression. From about 1530 he privately circulated them in manuscript among his friends, but was not persuaded to publish them until 1543, when the first printed copy of his *De Revolutionibus Orbium Coelestium* was brought from the press to be touched by him on his deathbed. It was dedicated to Pope Paul III, whose interest and protection he claimed, and had a preface by a Lutheran theologian, Andreas Osiander, who described the work as merely a 'mathematical hypothesis'. Dedication and preface may have combined to delay condemnation of Copernicus by the Roman Church until early in the seventeenth century. Luther and Melancthon both opposed the Copernican theory, though by 1550 Melancthon seemed to have regarded it as possible, and the new ideas were taught at the University of Wittenberg.

Perhaps the general lack of controversy aroused by the theory, during the first three or four decades after its publication, was really because the objections to it seemed so strong as to make it impossible. It was opposed to the long-established Aristotelian system. It undermined the conception of the world (and man) as being at the centre of

God's creation. It was unacceptable to common sense. And other astronomers produced hostile arguments, such as if the earth revolved it would cause loose objects to fly away from the ground or deflect the course of falling bodies. The question could not be taken further until accurate astronomical observation could supplement mathematical reasoning.

The work of Tycho Brahé

The first important step towards achieving this was taken by Tycho Brahé (1546-1601), a Danish nobleman, who through the patronage of Frederick II, King of Denmark, had built for him in 1576 a costly observatory at Uraniborg on the island of Hveen.[7] He equipped this with the most accurate instruments possible without lenses. Unlike Copernicus, who spent his time largely in reading the classical astronomers and working out mathematical proofs of his theory, he was a thorough and skilful observer.

In 1572 a new star, a supernova, appeared in the constellation of Cassiopeia, grew in brilliance, but vanished again after sixteen months. Tycho's measurements proved that it lay in the sphere of fixed stars, where the traditional cosmology asserted no change could take place. Even more significantly, a comet, which appeared in 1577, was observed by him to travel across the supposedly impenetrable crystalline spheres. Moreover, previous astronomers, since they assumed that the orbits of the planets were compounded of circles, had only observed them at points in their orbits; but Tycho pursued them in detail across the sky and found that this essential presupposition of the old astronomy did not seem applicable. The combined effect of his observations in these directions was to make impossible belief in uniform circular motion by celestial bodies, in the immutability of the heavens and in the very existence of the celestial spheres.

A violent quarrel with the Danish court interrupted Tycho's work in his last years. He was himself a passionate alchemist and convinced astrologer, and in 1596, at the invitation of the Emperor Rudolf II, he transferred himself and his instruments to the strange alchemical-astrological institute founded in a castle at Prague by the Emperor. Tycho's great contribution to the development of scientific astronomy lay in the method he evolved. His observations were uniquely accurate, systematic and comprehensive, and he was prepared to draw logical conclusions from them, even if they were opposed to long-held beliefs. His early death prevented him developing a numerical planetary theory based on his data.

The work of Tycho represents the limit of the advances made by astronomy during the sixteenth century, and, indeed, there was not

[7] P. 319.

much farther it could go along the lines it had been proceeding. Tycho's assistant and successor in Prague, Johann Kepler (1571-1630), discovered more correct laws about planetary motion, perfected the geometric scheme of the solar system and increased considerably the possibilities of accurate astronomical forecasting, but the physical, dynamic explanation of the discoveries of the sixteenth century and the complete acceptance of the heliocentric universe had to await the revolutionary achievements of Galileo and Newton in the next century. This period did little more than initiate scientific study in the direction it later followed successfully.

The end of the century

By the end of the sixteenth century, however, the scientific revolution had begun. Scientific societies were giving expression to the new curiosity about the nature of the physical universe which was a feature of this period. The general acceptance of the authority of Aristotle's notions about physics and astronomy was gradually being challenged, though more by reasoning and criticism than by observation and experiment. There was thus a conscious return to the rival approach of the ancient world, the method of Plato, emphasizing discussion of the mathematical aspects of the world and providing the basis for that critical enquiry in general which came to be adopted in the natural sciences. During the sixteenth century, however, this approach lacked positive results. These were achieved rather by the advance of technological developments in response to practical needs in navigation and industry.

Scientific activity and results during this period were accomplished, therefore, within the framework of the ancient and medieval system rather than by breaking through to the adoption of a modern outlook. In fact, the coherent, cohesive traditional picture of the universe was being broken up and replaced only by uncertainty and disorder. Astronomers were producing their theories and pragmatical technicians their inventions, but the relation of either to cause and effect in the working of nature was hardly considered. Little had been done so far to devise means of either distinguishing facts from fiction or correlating what were recognized as facts and devising explanations for their existence and properties. All these developments were to come during the seventeenth century, which was really to make the break from medieval traditionalism and credulity to modern scientific insistence upon observation and verification. The sixteenth century fell between these two eras and attitudes, but by the end of the period there were very clear signs of the changes and achievements of the future.

7
POLITICAL
ORGANIZATION

The monarchies

By the beginning of the sixteenth century, hereditary monarchy had become the normal form of government in western Europe. Moreover, these monarchies seemed to be in a stronger position than they had been for some time. In England, France, the Netherlands and Spain they had recovered from the weaknesses from which they had suffered through contests with powerful subjects seeking for power during the fifteenth century. This process had not involved any outstanding constitutional innovations on their part. They remained essentially medieval in character and ruled through the traditional institutions of government. During the sixteenth century, however, and particularly in the second half of it, they had to face the threat of new dangers and difficulties, and they evolved new administrative organs and expedients to deal with them.

When these problems arose, however, several of the leading monarchies were in a better position to meet them because of their success in making their states more effective and coherent political units, a process sometimes known as the 'consolidation of the nation state'. The future seemed to lie with compact, united, well-governed entities inhabited by people sharing the same racial origins, cultural traditions, language and religious beliefs; success lay during the century with those monarchies and their countries which best achieved these criteria.

The outstanding example of this situation is to be found in Spain, the country which was to become the most powerful in Europe during the century and yet was the most recently-united of the leading monarchies.[1] During the reign of the 'Catholic Kings', the authority of the new monarchy was extended over the Iberian peninsula, and the strengthening of racial and religious unity was sought. In 1492, the same year that the conquest of Granada, after an occupation of nearly eight centuries by the Moors, brought the *Reconquista* to a successful

[1] P. 238.

conclusion, the expulsion or forced conversion of the Jews took place; it has been said that some 150 000 Jews left the kingdom, 50 000 were baptized, and 20 000 were killed in race riots. This was also the year Columbus set out on the voyage that was to initiate Spanish imperialism, a development which, whatever its ultimate political and social consequences for Spain, further increased the sense of national purpose and pride of her people. There followed the acquisition of Navarre in 1512, much desired by Ferdinand to strengthen his defensible frontiers and give him more territory with the same culture and language. Such conquests were accompanied by careful control over the military orders of the *Reconquista* and the Spanish Church and a building-up of a centralized system of administration which overrode provincial institutions and privileges.

The neighbouring kingdom of France had been compelled to fight for its survival during the Hundred Years War (1337-1453), the series of wars with England punctuated by periods of peace or truce. Yet both during the years when English military successes seemed almost irresistible and during the turning of the tide which finally drove the invaders from French soil, the Crown had remained the mainstay of national resistance and the focal point of military recovery. It had been immune from disputes about succession largely because Salic Law, applied to the Crown since the fourteenth century, excluded descendants of female members of the royal family from the throne and so limited the number of possible claimants. Moreover, the hazards of war had not deprived the Crown of one of its most important powers: the right of the monarch to impose taxation, imprison offenders, seize property and impress men on his own initiative had been recognized in law. The awakening of national consciousness during the war and the eventual victory over the enemy had contributed to the popularity of the monarchy, while the nobility were disunited and weakened by private struggles among themselves. The Crown emerged from the period of troubles, therefore, in an unexpectedly strong condition and in a position to make further advances in peacetime.

During the reign of Louis XI (1461-83), the monarchy, after suffering many defeats and humiliations at the hands of combinations of powerful vassals, finally triumphed, thus greatly strengthening its rule over the French people. Most of the great feudatories were subdued and their lands brought under the direct rule of the Crown. Louis XI's outstanding triumph was the extinction of the power of the Duchy of Burgundy, whose rulers had long threatened the integrity of the monarchy. He annexed Burgundy and its territories of Picardy, Artois and Franche Comté. He acquired also, as escheated fiefs, the provinces of Anjou and Maine, while Provence, a fief of the Empire, and the Duchy of Bar passed under his rule as well. By the end of his reign, the only important province to remain a semi-independent feudal fief was Brittany, but its duchess, Anne, first married his successor, Charles VIII (1438-98) and later became the second wife of the next king, Louis XII (1498-1515), thus ensuring that Brittany remained attached to the French crown. The French monarchy entered the sixteenth century with the greatest potential power and the most centralized government of all the rulers of Europe; but, in the second half of the century, it encountered during the Wars of Religion more formidable opposition to its ascendancy than it had ever known before. Its survival was an indication of its strong foundations.

The growth of monarchical power in the western kingdoms was not to be found in those of eastern Europe. Poland, Hungary and Bohemia, each ruled by a member of the Lithuanian dynasty of the Jagiellons, were monarchies more or less under the control of the land-owning nobility, whose estates on the great eastern plains prospered by supplying the growing populations of the west with corn.[2] They alone enjoyed constitutional and political rights, both towns and peasantry were increasingly made subservient to their interests, and the numerous provincial diets or assemblies of estates in all three kingdoms were dominated by them. These diets could impose their power over the monarchy because they were elective in each kingdom and, like the Electors in Germany, they commonly chose impotent princes to succeed to the throne. Poland remained weak and divided; overwhelming Turkish defeat led to the replacement of the Jagiellons in Hungary and Bohemia in 1526 by the Habsburgs, who did at last achieve some success in the reduction of aristocratic power and the establishment of centralized administration.[3]

Further east, however, Russia and Turkey both shared the western trend towards monarchical absolutism. The traditional subjection of the people to their ruler in Russia went back to what Karl Marx called the 'bloody time of Mongol slavery' which began in the thirteenth century. For over two centuries the Mongols were the overlords of the country. Even after their oppression was brought to an end in 1480, they continued for another three hundred years to make periodic slaving-raids and invasions. The strain of meeting this menace, on the great Russian plain entirely without natural frontiers, placed continual severe demands on the resources of the state. This, and the ever-present fear of powerful enemies in the west, did much to account for the despotism of Ivan the Terrible (1353-84).

The Ottoman Turks established in Constantinople a powerful and efficient government which made them appropriate successors to the Byzantine Empire they had conquered.[4] At the head of the government was the Sultan, whose office was hereditary, though the right of the eldest male heir to succeed to it was not established until early in the

[2] P. 312.   [3] P. 280.   [4] P. 285.

nineteenth century. Previously, the son who first seized the capital and its treasure gained the throne, and he was legally empowered to kill his brothers and other rivals. The Sultan governed through the Ottoman Ruling Institution, the members of which, like the standing army of janissaries, were slaves taken as children from the Christian subject peoples. He had to heed the advice of the Moslem Institution, however, which could judge all his edicts according to the Sacred Law based upon the Koran. Nevertheless, the Sultan was more powerful than any European monarch, which meant that the effectiveness of the office depended very much upon the character of the holder; it was at its most effective during the reign of Suleiman the Magnificent (1520-66).

Church and state

In western Europe, the growth of the power of the monarchies inevitably brought them into conflict with the Church. Owing to the absolutism that past popes had established for themselves within the Church, this trial of strength was not between a ruler and the clergy of his state, but rather between him and the Papacy. Indeed, in many ways the problem of the relations between Church and state came about through the determination of monarchs to divert to themselves the control over the wealth and administration of the Church which the Papacy had secured for itself. In those countries where the Reformation triumphed and papal authority over the Church was abolished, the rulers achieved this aim to a considerable extent, but even in the states which supported the Counter-Reformation, the Papacy found it necessary to make concessions and divest itself of some of its powers in favour of the monarchy.

When the Archduke Frederick of Saxony was succeeded in 1525 by his brother, John, who openly supported the cause of reform,[5] Luther was able to organize a separate Lutheran Church in his state. He replaced the bishops by superintendents, but they were subject to a disciplinary organization made up of two theologians and two electoral councillors and known as the Consistory, which was empowered to appoint and remove the clergy from their posts and determine the form of worship they used. This was the general form of ecclesiastical government wherever the Lutheran Reformation was adopted in Germany, and in effect the new Churches were state churches because the princes or city councillors appointed and controlled the Consistories. The rulers also took possession of monastic and other ecclesiastical lands but, according to the recent studies of Professor Carsten, they did not gain much financial benefit from the Reformation. In most Protestant states a large part of the former ecclesiastical

[5] P. 162.

revenue was devoted to religious, educational and charitable purposes. The diets everywhere were careful to see that the princes made little profit, and price-rises within a few years forced them back into their former financial dependence upon the diets.

The adoption of Lutheranism in Scandinavia saw the state triumph over the Church there also. In Denmark, King Christian III confiscated the lands of the Church in 1536 and made the clergy salaried officials, and in 1539 he published a Church Order which placed the government and Church worship completely under the Crown acting through consistory courts and clerical administrators.[6] He imposed the same system also in his dependent realms of Norway and Iceland. Much the same sort of arrangement was established in Sweden and her dependent province of Finland, though the reorganization of the Church was not accomplished as abruptly, since it was not finally completed until after the long reign of Gustavus Vasa (1523-60). In 1527 the Diet transferred much ecclesiastical property to the Crown and some to the nobility and in 1544 abolished papal authority over the Church, but only in 1572 was the government of the Church finally settled.[7] The Swedish bishops obtained a degree of independence, since they were to be appointed by the clergy and laity of the dioceses, but they had to be approved by the King, who thus retained ultimate control of the Church.

These examples of the establishment of monarchical control over the Church in Protestant countries were, however, equalled to a surprising extent in the two largest Roman Catholic kingdoms. In Spain, with the *Reconquista* nearly complete, Ferdinand was determined to exert the fullest possible control over the Church in reconquered Granada. Since Innocent VIII needed Spanish support for his political aims in Italy, Ferdinand persuaded the Pope to issue a bull in 1486 giving the Spanish monarchy the right of making all important ecclesiastical appointments in the newly-established kingdom. Ferdinand tried to use this as a precedent for all Spain's dominions. He managed to ensure that appeals from Spanish ecclesiastical courts did not go to the Papal Curia in Rome, and that a considerable part of the wealth of the Church was diverted to the Crown by means of special taxation. In 1523, Charles V obtained from Adrian VI the right of appointment to all Spanish bishoprics. But the Spanish monarchy secured its greatest control over the Church in the New World where, by 1508 as the result of a number of papal bulls, it had the right of presentation to all ecclesiastical posts. The continuing need of the Papacy for Spanish help in Italy enabled the Crown to exercise wide ecclesiastical powers in the peninsula itself. In Sicily, Naples and Milan it could prevent the publication of any papal bull, and when Pope Julius II (1503-13) attempted to ignore this, Ferdinand threatened to sever Spanish

[6] P. 318.   [7] P. 314.

relations with the Papacy; and in Sicily the Spanish kings also claimed (though the popes never accepted this) the position of permanent apostolic legate (or personal representative of the Papacy) for themselves.

Above all, the Spanish monarchy possessed its own Inquisition, which had been set up with papal approval by Ferdinand and Isabella in 1479, at first in Castile and then in Aragon as well. It was originally directed against Jews and Moors who had been baptized but relapsed from Christianity, and later it was used also against Protestants. Its members were appointed by the Crown, and in 1558 Philip II gave it the function of censoring the press. Its jurisdiction was superior to that of any other ecclesiastical court in Spain, and it could proceed against the highest figures in the kingdom and even act independently of the Papacy itself. This was demonstrated when it arrested Cardinal Carranza, Archbishop of Toledo, in 1559 and charged him with Lutheranism. The Papacy insisted that it alone had the right to try bishops, but this was contested by Philip. Not until 1566 was the Archbishop transferred to Rome where he remained, owing to Spanish delaying tactics, a prisoner for a further ten years. At the end of that time he was compelled formally to abjure heresies of which he was declared 'vehemently suspect'. The ecclesiastical power of the Spanish monarchy made it unnecessary for any king to emulate Henry VIII of England or Christian III of Denmark in abolishing papal authority within their kingdom. 'There is no pope in Spain', declared a President of the Council of State.

The French monarchy had clashed sharply with the Papacy during the Middle Ages. Philip the Fair in 1303 had brought about the death of Pope Boniface VIII through the humiliating treatment to which he had subjected him.[8] At the same time, the French Church had long contained within it a Gallican movement which insisted upon the existence of special *libertés de l'église gallicane* in opposition to papal prerogatives. In 1438 the French clergy issued the Pragmatic Sanction of Bourges, which deprived the Papacy of practically all rights of appointment, jurisdiction and taxation in France and asserted the supremacy of a council over the pope. Strenuous efforts by successive popes to secure its repeal were eventually able to do no more than secure an agreement between Pope Leo X and Francis I of France, the Concordat of Bologna in 1516, by which the French monarchy was empowered to make appointments to all cathedral, abbey and priory churches, as well as to bishoprics.[9] Leo X had difficulty in getting his cardinals to agree to it, and Francis I had to coerce the French Church to accept it in place of the Pragmatic Sanction. The Papacy (to the regret of the French clergy) secured the abandonment of the assertion made at Bourges of the supremacy of a general council, while the French

[8] P. 36.   [9] P. 221.

kings henceforward had no more financial interest (as they now had rights to taxation and the use of ecclesiastical benefices) than the Spanish kings in supporting a change of religion in their kingdom.

During the second half of the sixteenth century, attempts made by several popes to recover their lost powers led to difficulties in their relations with both the Spanish and the French monarchies. Indeed, during the pontificate of the strongly anti-Spanish Pope Paul IV (1555-9), Spain and the Papacy actually went to war.[10] The rulers of both countries were determined that the reforms of the Counter-Reformation should not result in an increase in papal authority at the expense of their own. At last in 1565, Philip II agreed to the publication of the decrees of the Council of Trent in the Spanish Empire, but only with a proviso asserting the continuance of the Spanish monarchy's powers in ecclesiastical jurisdiction and episcopal appointments. Successive French kings persisted, despite repeated resolutions by the clerical assemblies of the French Church, in refusing to allow the enforcement of the Council's disciplinary decrees in their realm. Yet neither side could afford to push a dispute to extremes. The Papacy needed monarchical support, and the kings needed ecclesiastical revenues. Moreover, the kings were in a strong position because their control of the Church naturally produced clerics who looked to them for preferment and supported their attitude. Of course, medieval monarchs in the past had, in practice, exercised wide powers over the Church but now the Papacy had been compelled to recognize the legality of their position and abandon its claim to be exalted above them.

Administrative developments

To be effective, monarchical power had to be asserted and, therefore, European rulers during the sixteenth century adopted styles and observances which seemed to emphasise their authority. Both Philip II of Spain and Henry II of France assumed the title of 'Majesty' which had hitherto belonged exclusively to the Emperor. The Spanish court in 1548 adopted the elaborate, formal Burgundian ceremonial, and during the second half of the century the daily life of the French kings became subject to stylized observances in which chosen noblemen participated and privileged spectators were present by invitation. At the same time, the doctrine of the divine right of kings gained general acceptance. Medieval popes had sought to insist that kings derived their authority from them as God's representative on earth but now the kings insisted that they owed their position to God's direct appointment and were responsible only to Him.

Traditionally, kings had looked to the nobility to assist them in

[10] P. 278.

maintaining their power, and in the sixteenth century monarchs might still require their support as, for instance, in Spain to crush the Revolt of the Comuneros.[11] The financial difficulties of the nobility made them as anxious as ever to gain as much power for themselves. In France, there were three great families, each strong in their own part of the country. The oldest were the Montmorencys, who possessed vast lands in the centre of the country; in the south and west were the Bourbons, who were kings of Navarre and related to the ruling house of Valois; and most powerful were the Guises, who had acquired their fortune in the service of the Valois, and whose large estates in the east gave them predominant influence over a third of the country. These were the three families that were to contend for the control of the Crown on the death of Henry II in 1559.[12] In Spain, the noble families were not as powerful, but some were equally ready to vie with each other for ascendancy over the Crown and consequent control of its patronage, such as occurred in the early years of Philip II's reign between the Prince of Eboli and the Duke of Alva.

By the sixteenth century, however, monarchs were themselves becoming strong enough to appoint whom they chose to act as their administrators. Both Charles V and Philip II in Spain were careful to exclude the great noblemen from posts in the central administration and to make them only viceroys, ambassadors and military commanders. Such appointments satisfied many of the ambitious, and a large number of the rest preferred to remain in the provinces on their estates rather than seek office under the Crown, but they did not placate those who struggled to gain profit and power at court. Philip decided that the best way of keeping them under his observation and giving them a means of venting their mutual rivalry was to make them members of the Council of State.

From the reigns of Ferdinand and Isabella, a conciliar system of government was established in Spain, at first for Castile and Aragon and then for the whole country. At the head of the councils was the Council of State, which was supposed to advise the King on matters of general policy 'concerning the government of Spain and Germany', but its pre-eminence was nominal. Both Charles V and Philip II tended to use it mainly as a place to play off against each other the rival noble factions which were contending for influence over the monarchy. Its advice was mainly ignored, and its functions tended to be limited to undertakings of a routine, official nature. More important were nominally subordinate specialist councils, which either (like the Council of War, the Council of Finance and the Council of the Inquisition) advised the monarch on particular aspects of the central government or (like the Council of Castile, the Council of Aragon, the Council of the Indies and the Council of Italy) were responsible for the administration

[11] P. 195.   [12] P. 222.

of particular territories. All these councils functioned both as governmental departments and as courts of law.

For the actual executive work of the government, the Spanish monarchy relied upon its secretaries, whose duties became increasingly important and manifold as the scope of government became more embracing and complex. They were the men who conveyed directives and information between the king and the councils and between the councils and the viceroys, who exercised local rule in Spain, Italy and America; at their head were the king's secretaries, who became secretaries of state with ministerial positions. They were expert administrators, often trained lawyers or financial specialists, appointed from the lesser nobility or the professional and middle classes, but not from the great noble families. An aristocratic Viceroy of Sicily under Charles V bitterly said that the secretaries were ignorant of honour and chivalry and treated the Viceroys of Sicily and Naples as if they were the mayors of Salamanca or Avilla. In Spain the secretaries were not to become as powerful during the sixteenth century as those in other kingdoms because of the close supervision and conscientious industry of Philip II himself, of whom Cardinal Granvelle said, 'No secretary in the world uses more paper than His Majesty'. Philip restricted himself to the services of a single Secretary of State, Gonzalo Perez, until his death in 1566, when the work was divided among two men, one of whom was his better-known son, Antonio.[13]

Similar administrative developments took place in other European countries, partly in imitation of Spanish methods and partly because the conciliar and secretarial system evolved naturally to meet their needs as well. In France, during the last years of the fifteenth century, judicial work was transferred to the *Grand Conseil*, an offshoot of the *Conseil du Roi*, which continued to concern itself with judicial and administrative duties, while Francis I and his successors took to making all important political decisions through a small, inner council, the *Conseil des Affaires*. In 1547 Henry II appointed four special secretaries, who were given the title of Secretaries of State in 1559. As in Spain, they served as the link between the Crown and the councils and between the councils and the thirteen *gouvernements* into which the kingdom was divided. The kings of France, too, did not make appointments to their governmental staff from the old nobility. Instead they created a new nobility, the *noblesse de robe*, and they, and not the old *noblesse d'epée*, held the highest administrative and judicial posts.[14]

Financial problems

All European states during this period were faced with financial difficulties. Government was becoming steadily more expensive in a

[13] P. 120.   [14] P. 85.

way that it never had before. Diplomacy and administration both required ever-larger staffs, war grew more complicated and its weapons more costly, and the continual general rise in prices grew beyond the fixed sources of revenue of the monarchies. In the Middle Ages, a king had been expected, at any rate in normal peacetime circumstances, to be able to 'live of his own', that is to say, to pay for the expenses of government from feudal dues, rents from royal lands, fines levied in the courts of justice and certain customs duties and other payments due to him. By 1500, however, such normal sources of income were no longer adequate for the demands made upon royal treasuries, and as they became increasingly insufficient, ways of obtaining more money had continually to be sought, even in Spain where the Crown drew large quantities of silver from America.

One way of doing this was to revive the payment of feudal dues which had lapsed with the decay of the system itself, although such devices did not usually secure much and caused disproportionate trouble with the nobility.

Another was to obtain money from the Church, either through the confiscation of religious property as in Protestant countries or by taxation and control of ecclesiastical appointments as in Spain and France. The Spanish monarchy was able to draw a considerable financial contribution from the Church. It imposed the *subsidio*, a tax on clerical rents and incomes in all the Spanish kingdoms; the *tercius reales*, a third of all tithes collected by the Church in Castile; and from 1567 the *excusado*, the entire tithe of the most valuable piece of property in every parish, which was a new tax levied to contribute towards the cost of the war in Flanders. The Crown enjoyed also the revenues of vacant sees and in 1523 was granted by Pope Adrian VI control of the vast estates and patronage of the three military orders of Caltrava, Alcantara and Santiago, which had been formed in the twelfth century to fight in the *Reconquista*. Another valuable legacy of the *Reconquista* was the *cruzada*, which had originally been granted by the Papacy to the Crown to assist it in the war against the Moors as a tax payable by both clergy and laity; it became a regular source of royal income during Charles V's reign, paid every three years by all wanting a bull of indulgence and bringing almost as much as the Crown's revenue from the New World.

Another way of raising money was the sale of offices under the Crown. The country where this device was most widely adopted was France. Here many offices were established solely for the purpose of being sold and could be made hereditary for further payments. Such posts, which were particularly attractive to the middle class, ranged from the counsellorships of *parlements* to local customs collectorships. The practice was common also in Spain and in the Italian states and even in the Roman Church, where the reforming Pope Pius V (1566-72) was unable to do much to stop it.

Though not every monarch sold offices, all borrowed money. The Fuggers gained monopoly contracts for mining silver and copper in Hungary, the Tyrol and other parts of central Europe as security for loans made to the Emperors Maximilian and Charles V. Jacob Fugger asserted that Charles V could not have become Emperor without the money he lent him for his election campaign in 1519.[15] Indeed, Charles V, whose annual revenue as King of Spain was usually about a million ducats a year and increased to a million-and-a-half after 1542, succeeded in borrowing from a number of German, Genoese, Flemish and Spanish bankers, between his accession to the Spanish throne in 1516 and the disastrous period after 1552 when his credit collapsed, thirty-nine million ducats against payment from the next treasure-fleet or future Castilian taxation.[16] After 1560 the banking houses of Genoa overtook the Fuggers as the main Spanish financiers and handled the sale of bullion on its arrival from the New World. Another form of loan adopted in Spain was the *juros*, which was a life annuity and was sold widely by Charles V. The system spread rapidly to the Spanish territories in Italy and the Netherlands, as well as to France, where the sale of *rentes* led to the growth of a powerful *rentier* class living on its annuities. The raising of money by loans in these ways by rulers meant that more and more of their income had to go each year in paying interest.

Ultimately, however, neither ecclesiastical wealth nor the sale of offices nor loans could provide the monarchies with the money they needed, and they had, therefore, to resort to increased taxation. In seeking to do so during the sixteenth century, they had to face the traditional obligation imposed upon them of obtaining consent to fresh taxation, usually through some representative assembly, and of overcoming opposition to it by all classes who did not want to strengthen the power of the Crown in this way.[17] During this period, the Spanish monarchy had considerably less difficulty, on the whole, than the French in dealing with this problem.

In Spain, the three Cortes of the States of the Crown of Aragon were so powerful and privileged that each grant of money obtained from them by Charles V was only as the result of concessions which made them still stronger against the monarchy. At the end of his reign Charles V was receiving from them no more than he was at the beginning, though prices had more than doubled during those years. Consequently, Philip II summoned them only in 1563 and 1585 and otherwise confined himself to requests for voluntary contributions.

This inevitably meant that he had to rely increasingly for money on Castile, where the Cortes had steadily declined in power and lacked

[15] P. 187.   [16] P. 151.   [17] P. 119.

control over a number of valuable sources of revenue, including internal and external customs duties, taxes on the Granada silk industry, on the transit of sheep and cattle, on American trade, and, most important, the *alcabala* or sales tax. In the face of a doubling of price-levels, Charles succeeded in doubling the yield from Castilian taxation; but from 1515 the *alcabala* was compounded for a fixed sum, which declined in relative value as prices increased, though in 1561 and 1574 Philip was able to secure a large addition to it. To compensate for the losses incurred by the compounding of the *alcabala*, the Crown succeeded, particularly after the defeat of the Comuneros,[18] in having made regular and increasing the yield of a hitherto occasionally-levied direct tax, the *servicio*, from which, however, all the nobility were exempt. When in 1538 Charles asked the Cortes to establish the *sisa*, a tax on foodstuffs paid by everyone, he was successfully resisted by the bishops and noblemen, who were no longer summoned to the meetings of the Cortes. Philip was successful in 1590 in persuading the Cortes to vote a new tax, the *milliones*, levied on articles of consumption, which applied to all classes of society, though the nobility, in fact, could largely escape paying it by supplying themselves with many of the dutiable articles from their estates. The general social effect of Spanish taxation during this period was, therefore, to fall most heavily on the poor and raise the cost of living in Castile.

Charles V was able also to draw a considerable sum of money from the Netherlands, which gained economic advantages from its inclusion in his empire. A Venetian ambassador stated, 'These are the treasures of the King of Spain, these his mines, these his Indies which have sustained all the Emperor's enterprises.' The Netherlanders complained that they were paying for his conquest of Italy, and from about 1530 economic strain and rising prices led to growing opposition to his taxation. By 1540 Charles wrote to his brother Ferdinand, 'I cannot be sustained except by my kingdoms of Spain.' In 1557 the States-General agreed to make him an annual grant for nine years, but only on condition that its own representatives controlled the raising and spending of the money. Twelve years later it rejected the Duke of Alva's attempt to impose the tenth penny, a permanent tax of ten per cent on articles for export and on the sale of goods, which, once accepted, would have been immune from the States-General's control.[19]

In France, the most important direct tax was the *taille*, which Charles VII (1422-61) had been able, amid foreign and civil war, to make into an annual tax levied at the discretion of the monarch. Since the clergy and nobility were exempt from it, and many members of the middle-classes also managed to secure exemption, it fell mainly on the peasantry. There were two forms of the tax, since it was levied differently in the *Pays d'État* and the *Pays d'Election*.[20] In the *Pays*

[18] P. 195.   [19] P. 257.   [20] P. 121.

d'État it was *réele*, levied on land; in the *Pays d'Election* it was *personnelle*, levied on each individual according to his means.

The *taille personnelle* was most disliked by the peasants because it was more just to levy the amount of taxation a man had to pay upon the value of the land he owned than upon his estimated ability to pay, while once the land was liable to the *taille* it could not be exempted, even if acquired by a nobleman. Moreover, the local estates of the *Pays d'Etat* negotiated a composite sum with the royal treasury and then shared it out among the landowners in the province.

In the *Pays d'Election*, however, which comprised most of France, every time an inhabitant of a parish acquired noble rank and consequent exemption from the *taille personnelle*, the rest had to pay more. There were no estates to bargain with the treasury and arrange the collection of the tax. Instead the *taille* was farmed out by financial agents to middle-men, who compounded with the treasury for a definite sum of money and sought, without check, to get as much as they could from the peasants. Though during the reigns of Francis I (1515-47) and Henry II (1547-59), the *taille* did not apparently increase much more than prices, it remained a heavy imposition on those least able to pay, and in 1542 the Venetian ambassador reported that peasants not uncommonly left their parish to avoid paying it. Later the insolvency of the Crown in time of civil war pushed it up from seven million livres in 1576 to eighteen million in 1588.

Besides certain *aides* or customs duties, another tax which the French monarchy could impose regularly was the *gabelle* or salt-tax, which also was levied differently in various regions. While some provinces were exempt from the tax, it was lowest in the provinces known as the *Pays de Petite Gabelle* and highest in the *Pays de Grande Gabelle*, stretching from Normandy and Picardy southwards to Touraine and Burgundy. Here salt was also a government monopoly, sold by licensed merchants at a high price, and heads of households were required to purchase a fixed annual quantity. This lack of uniformity in levying the *gabelle* meant that the price of salt in some provinces was only a twenty-fifth of what it was in others, and inevitably cheaper salt was smuggled into the *Pays de Grande Gabelle* to supplement the *sel de devoir*, despite the heavy penalties with which the offence was punished.

Despite its powers of taxation, the French monarchy in the later part of the sixteenth century was no more able than other rulers to exist on its customary sources of revenue. In 1560 Francis II sought more money by summoning the Estates-General for the first time since 1484. Though this could neither grant nor withhold taxes, it could recommend the local estates to grant them. But it refused to do even this, saying that it had been given no powers to discuss the financial affairs of the Crown, even though Catherine de Medici not only

offered redress of grievances in return for financial aid, but also suggested that the estates themselves should control the collection of
the taxes. Indeed, the second and third orders suggested that the first
order, the clergy, could contribute more to the national finances. The
clergy, already alarmed at the spread of heresy in the kingdom, took
the warning and made a substantial contribution, which they repeated
throughout the civil war. The Crown proceeded to impose a duty on
wine without the approval of the Estates-General and continued to
collect the *taille*. At further meetings, the Estates-General displayed
the same attitude. In 1576 it rejected the royal demand for a grant of
money, saying, 'The deputies are without the power to act otherwise';
and in 1586 it accompanied its refusal by a demand that the *taille*
should be reduced to the level of 1576. So the Estates-General declined
to become involved at all in the imposition of taxes by the Crown,
but such a firm stand was to be highly detrimental to its active survival
as a constitutional institution.

The estates

Not only taxation, but also the general drive towards the achievement
of greater power brought the great continental monarchies into conflict
with their estates, which were a constitutional feature of all the
countries of western Europe. The system of such assemblies was
feudal in origin. A medieval tenant-in-chief or baron owed his king
the duty of attending and giving advice in the royal court. When
such a court or *curia regis* was held, the king and his barons judged
pleas and took decisions on matters of state. The Middle Ages did not
distinguish between bodies which made laws and those which judged
offences against these laws. The *curia regis*, therefore, acted as both a
legislative assembly and a court of justice. Later, in kingdom after
kingdom, the *curia regis* assumed additional functions, especially the
imposition of taxation, and gained additional members. Though these
extended feudal bodies developed differently in the various kingdoms
in composition, procedure and powers, most came to include or represent the three feudal orders of society—the clergy, nobility and
burgesses.

The English *curia regis* of the Norman kings became Parliament,
composed of the House of Lords and House of Commons. To-day,
its official designation remains the High Court of Parliament, but it
developed into a legislative assembly, though the House of Lords
remained the supreme court of appeal. Long before the English
Parliament assumed its present composition, the idea of elected
representatives of local communities already existed in the ancient
county courts. At first all freemen were supposed to attend these courts;

later the burden of attendance was restricted to some only, but those who went to each court were regarded as speaking for the county. Thus the county courts themselves were something like miniature parliaments.

The growth of the English Parliament was paralleled, each in its own way, in the other kingdoms of western Europe. All came to have estates or systems of estates with varying legislative and judicial prerogatives; but during the sixteenth century the continental assemblies did not develop along the same lines as the English institution. In England, despite the great increase in power gained for the monarchy by the establishment of royal supremacy over the Church, Parliament became more and not less important in the government of the country and by the later years of the reign of Elizabeth I (1558-1603) was beginning to make determined efforts to encroach upon the royal prerogative. On the Continent, however, the kings were ready to dispense with their estates, though they did not achieve in this century the success that was to enable them to establish monarchical despotisms in the next.

In Spain, the strongest of the estates were the Cortes of the States of the Crown of Aragon—Catalona, Aragon and Valencia. Each met separately, though they could be summoned to joint sessions presided over by the King. Charles V held such a general Cortes six times during his reign—almost every five years—but Philip II held them twice only.[21] This was an unwilling tribute to their powers, both financial and legislative. The Kingdom of Aragon itself possessed an official called the Justicia, an Aragonese nobleman appointed by the Crown to preserve and protect its 'liberties and laws', but not removable from office by the Crown. The clash between the Crown and this official came about in an episode involving Antonio Perez.[22] In 1590 he escaped after ten years of imprisonment in Madrid on a charge of political murder involving the King's own name and fled to Aragon where he sought the protection of the Justicia. Determined to recover both his Secretary and the documents in his possession, Philip ordered him to be handed over to the all-powerful Inquisition on a charge of heresy, but a mob released him from the Inquisition building in Saragossa and he escaped to France. Philip sent an army into Aragon, had the Justicia executed and in 1592 summoned a meeting of the Cortes of Aragon at which he required it to accept the appointment of a Castilian viceroy and grant him power to dismiss future Justicias. That he took such moderate measures showed that his policy was integration rather than subjection, and he had already indicated this at the previous Cortes of 1585 when he granted the Aragonese equal rights with the Castilians in holding offices in the Indies.

The Cortes of Castile differed in several significant ways from the

[21] P. 116.   [22] P 243.

Cortes of the States of the Crown of Aragon. The Crown could impose a number of taxes and make new laws without its consent. There was no obligation upon the monarch to summon the clergy and nobility to it, and by the reign of Charles V it consisted normally of representatives of eighteen cities, and only on special occasions, such as coronations, were the two other orders summoned. In 1520 Charles V's persistent demands for money from the Cortes contributed, after his departure for Germany, to the outbreak of the Revolt of the Comuneros in which the cities demanded, as well as the removal of his Flemish officials (including his Regent, the future Pope Adrian VI), regular meetings of the Cortes without royal interference.[23] It was, however, defeated within a year by the Castilian nobility, and the authority of the Crown prevailed. The Cortes met thereafter, in fact, more frequently than in the past, but mostly to ensure that the *servicio* became a regular tax, a development with which it had to comply.[24]

The Estates-General of France consisted of the clergy, nobility and the third order, mainly drawn from the middle-classes of the towns. When it met in 1560, after an interval of nearly eighty years, its refusal then and on subsequent occasions during the century to become involved in the finances of the kingdom stultified its future development. Without the authority to grant taxation, it failed to obtain the power to make political bargains with the Crown or to gain any share in the government. Through its unwillingness to take up the great weapon of finance, it sacrificed the possibility of challenging the royal prerogative in the way that the English Parliament was doing.

In addition to the Estates-General, six French provinces, those most recently added to the kingdom, were still privileged to summon their own estates. These were Normandy, Brittany, Burgundy, Dauphiné, Provence and Languedoc. They formed the *Pays d'États*, the rest of the country, where royal officials levied taxes, being called the *Pays d'Elections*. Though the *Pays d'États* represented one-third of the size and wealth of France, because they taxed themselves, they paid only a tenth of the national taxation.

There were also the French *parlements*. During the sixteenth century they numbered twelve—Paris, Toulouse, Grenoble, Bordeaux, Dijon, Rouen, Aix-en-Provence, Rennes, Pau, Metz, Besançon and Douai. They were not like the English Parliament, being high courts of justice, which heard appeals from inferior courts, and their members were rich magnates who bought their offices. During the fifteenth century the monarchy had weakened their functions by establishing new courts in the provinces with supreme powers, which rendered appeals to the *parlements* unnecessary, and this process was continued during the reigns of Francis I (1515-47) and Henry II (1547-59). The most important of the *parlements* was the Parlement of Paris with an area of

[23] P. 195.   [24] P. 117.

jurisdiction that included half the kingdom. It was, too, the only one of any political consequence since it had the function of authorizing and registering laws made by the King and Council so as to protect them against infringement; since the fifteenth century it had claimed the right of *remonstrance*, which enabled it to refuse to register ediçts to which it was opposed. Sixteenth-century monarchs, however, undermined its resistance to royal legislation by frequently resorting to a constitutional procedure known as a *lit de justice,* a special meeting of the Parlement in the presence of the King, seated on a couch, at which it could be compelled to register an edict.

In the Netherlands there were also a number of provincial estates. There were six of them at the beginning of the sixteenth century— Flanders, Holland, Zeeland, Brabant, Artois and Hainault—and there was a States-General, which had been created by Philip the Good, Duke of Burgundy (1419-67), on the French model. It was essentially an assembly of delegates from the provincial estates and very ready therefore, to uphold their liberties and privileges. Nevertheless, Charles V made considerable use of it as the only means of taking united political action with the provinces; but Philip II disliked having to summon it because of the control it insisted on exercising over finance.[25] When the seven northern provinces accepted the Union of Utrecht in 1579 and formed the 'United Provinces of the Netherlands', their States-General retained fundamentally the same position with regard to the provincial estates and the Stadtholder. But the States-General in the south was not able to prevent increased taxes or to control government finances, although the provincial estates retained enough of their old rights to make the continuance of Spanish rule acceptable to them.

In addition to the Imperial Diet,[26] the German states had their local diets, and it is difficult to generalize about their relations with their princes. It would seem, however, that constitutional developments within them produced much the same strengthening and extension of monarchical authority as took place in Spain and France. The princes reformed their administrations and reorganized their powers, developed systems of conciliar government and employed trained, professional administrators. Nevertheless, as elsewhere, the diets still retained a considerable amount of power and importance. In particular, they continued to exercise effective control over finance, even in those states where the Reformation led to the confiscation of ecclesiastical property. This did not, however, lead to conflicts with the princes because they usually showed themselves, as for instance in Brandenburg, willing to co-operate. As with the great powers of western Europe, the age of princely despotism lay in the next century.

In the three central European kingdoms of Poland, Bohemia and

[25] P. 254.   [26] P. 20.

Hungary, there was a multiplicity of provincial estates or dietines, which seriously handicapped the ability of the national assemblies to govern the whole realm effectively. Thus, Poland had five such provincial estates to which a sixth was added in the sixteenth century. Moreover, they were all dominated by the landowning classes, though the differing interests of the wealthy nobility and the smaller gentry or knights was shown in the existence of separate chambers for each. Only in Bohemia, because of the greater power and wealth of the trading towns in that kingdom, was there a chamber for the burgesses. They were strong enough to survive Ferdinand I's punitive measures after their participation in the rebellion of 1547, but even so the two chambers of the nobility and the knights usually exercised a predominant influence during this period.[27]

Ferdinand tried also to establish an Estates-General for all the Habsburg lands, but the attempt failed owing to jealousy and suspicion among the provincial estates. The existence and constitution of these estates was an expression of the political power possessed by the landed nobility of these kingdoms, and the attitude they adopted was an indication of their determination to maintain their authority by preventing the development of strong monarchies and centralized, efficient administrations as was occurring elsewhere. The result was, particularly in Poland, to prevent the kingdoms attaining during this period the political greatness which might otherwise have been possible.

[27] P. 283.

8
WAR
AND
DIPLOMACY

Militarism and the Renaissance

During the Middle Ages, Christian thinkers sought to define the attitude that should be taken towards war. They realized that, if men were entirely to accept Christian principles, war would be inconceivable as contrary to the mission and message of Jesus. But they recognized also that, since Christians had to live in a secular order in which force was needed to preserve the authority of law, there were inevitably instances in which Christian participation in warfare was morally justifiable. In particular, they came to hold that wars could be fought to secure religious aims. The Crusades, designed to recover the Holy Land from Islam, were an outstanding example of this sort of war, and so was the Spanish *Reconquista* against the Moors. Since the kingdoms of medieval Christendom were, however, constantly at war with each other, theologians were led to distinguish between wars in which Christians could and could not rightfully take part—between 'just' and 'unjust' wars. Typical of the medieval conditions for a just war were those laid down by St Thomas Aquinas, who insisted that it must be waged on the authority of a lawful sovereign, its cause must be just and its participants must have a rightful intention, seeking the advancement of good or the prevention of evil. In the sixteenth century, the Spanish theologian, Francisco de Vitoria (*c* 1485-1546), who was also a humanist, went further than Aquinas and insisted that war should be waged by 'proper means' and that no war could be allowable if it would cause serious evil to Christendom and the world.

By that time, however, the notions of those who wrote within the tradition of the medieval attitude toward war were becoming more and more irrelevant. Erasmus poured scorn on the idea that wars and crusades could be justified in the name of religion when they were really an expression of human aggression and cupidity—'If what we want is really to expand our Empire, if it is the wealth of Turkey we are after, why cover our mundane greed with the name of Christ?'

He asserted that the acceptance of the principle that it was permissible for rulers to wage a just war had, in fact, meant the sanctification of all wars in the past. In the sixteenth century, such distinctions were powerless to prevent the outbreak of war. The great states of western Europe had come into being through wars and had expanded their frontiers or expelled foreign invaders by fighting. They retained their readiness and ability to make war, and during this century they were confronted by the persistent attraction of the wealth and prestige offered by a campaign in the weak and divided Italian peninsula.

Moreover, the nature of the struggle for Italy further weakened the already-declining authority of the two powers which in the past had been invoked as arbiters between nations in the cause of peace—the Emperor and the Pope. Charles V, as King of Spain and Holy Roman Emperor, was seen to act as any other ruler in building up a great alliance against France and seeking to dislodge her from Italy. The international authority of the Papacy similarly ceased to gain recognition. Papal legates had often acted as mediators in the final stages of the Hundred Years War, and Erasmus wrote in 1514, 'It is the proper function of the Roman Pontiff, of the Cardinals, of Bishops and of Abbots to compose the quarrels of Christian princes.' But this role was becoming obsolete. The Italian situation inevitably affected the position of the Papacy and its territory and compelled popes to act as secular princes rather than as spiritual arbiters. An example of this was when Pope Leo X in 1521 made a secret agreement with Charles V undertaking to support his policy and crown him Holy Roman Emperor in return for Imperial protection for the Papacy and the Medici family.[1] Equally ignored was the authority of the Papacy to control the nature of warfare, such as the prohibition by the Second Lateran Council of 1139 of the enslavement of Christian prisoners of war. The Council of Trent, though condemning private duels, had nothing to say about national contests.

Indeed, the revival of Renaissance military studies, which has taken place during the last few years, has emphasized the paradox that it was an age both of culture and of war. Renaissance Italy, like fifth-century Athens, was a society almost obsessed with warfare. Its architects designed fortifications as well as churches, its craftsmen produced arms and armour. Bartolomeo Colleone, Federigo di Montefeltro and Francesco Sforza were patrons of art and scholarship, but gained fame and wealth as brutal, ruthless soldiers. Italian humanist literature described martial deeds and martial virtues with relish and approval; published accounts of battles and sieges in prose and verse became increasingly popular during the sixteenth century. That ideal of Italian humanism, the complete man as depicted in Castiglione's *The Courtier*, expressed his qualities at least as much in

[1] P. 147.

war as in any other activity.[2] One Renaissance writer extolled death in war, 'for which sole purpose we were created,' and another congratulated his age on having had 'the good fortune to witness the revival of the long-lost art of warfare.' It is no exaggeration to say that Renaissance Italy was a society at war.

It was this Italy that produced Niccolo Machiavelli (1469-1527), the most brilliant of the writers on war and diplomacy, whose best-known book, *The Prince* (which he started writing in 1513), established a new science of statecraft which openly discarded the religious morality of the past. This book has been described as the most influential book of the Renaissance, only approached perhaps by Castiglione's *The Courtier*. Machiavelli was born of an old Florentine family and in 1498 was appointed the principal of a group of secretaries dealing with foreign affairs in Florence. The Medici, the virtual rulers of the city since the end of the fourteenth century, had been expelled in 1494 by Charles VIII of France;[3] and during the years that followed, when Florence was under French domination, Machiavelli served on several embassies, though he was never made a permanent ambassador. He became fascinated by diplomacy and also by warfare, being very critical of the *condottieri*, the mercenary troops employed by Italian states, who seemed to him likely to be as great a threat to the independence of a state as a hostile army. He organized a citizen army, which distinguished itself at the capture of Pisa in 1509, but was scattered by the armies of the Holy League three years later.[4] This meant loss of employment and exile for Machiavelli, who took to writing books, including *The Prince*, through which he hoped to regain his post, even from the Medici, by displaying a capable knowledge of political affairs.

The book was dedicated to Lorenzo de' Medici (1492-1519), the ruler of Florence, whom Machiavelli regarded as the prince who might unite the faction-ridden states of Italy and expel the foreign invaders from the peninsula. Such a prince, he insisted, should seem to be honest, trustworthy, religious and forgiving, but should be prepared to resort to force and fraud without limit and scruple whenever the interest of his state demanded such conduct. His exemplars of statecraft were Ferdinand of Aragon, because 'always under the pretext of religion, he had recourse to a pious cruelty, driving out the Moors from his kingdom and despoiling them', and Caesar Borgia, Pope Alexander VI's illegitimate son, 'who did everything that can be done by a prudent and virtuous man, so that no better precepts can be offered to a new prince than those suggested by the example of his actions.' He admired Borgia's perfidy and complete ruthlessness towards his enemies, but at the same time he condemned senseless cruelty since he made a careful distinction between private and public virtue. The public good required individuals to observe ethical

[2] P. 84.   [3] P. 140.   [4] P. 143.

standards of conduct towards each other, but it also required a prince to ignore them whenever public policy so required. 'The manner in which we live and that in which we ought to live are things so wide asunder, that he who quits the one to betake himself to the other is more likely to destroy than to save himself; since anyone who would act up to a perfect standard of goodness in everything must be ruined among so many who are anything but good.' It was better, he considered, for a prince to be feared than to be loved, 'for love is held by a chain of obligation which, men being selfish, is broken whenever it serves their purpose, but fear is maintained by a dread of punishment which never fails.' Accordingly, 'it is necessary for a prince wishing to hold his own to know how to do wrong and to make use of it or not according to necessity.' He may on occasion be callous and pitiless. 'The act may condemn the doer, the end may justify him.' Machiavelli believed that men's actions were prompted solely by self-interest, and so morality could never produce success in politics.

By the later sixteenth century, Machiavelli had become a popular synonym for cunning and unscrupulousness in politics. Nowadays, the originality of his thought is questioned, since the cities of northern Italy were astir with new ideas in his lifetime; he is seen as a realist, who swept aside the veil of pretence and make-believe in politics and showed how men really act and by what motives they are influenced. Emphasis is placed also upon his devotion to Italian unity, republicanism and patriotism. Indeed, Machiavelli suggested that patriotism should be substituted for the universal truths of religion, but here he was at least premature. His knowledge of the Italian Church made him disillusioned and contemptuous of religion, and he believed it would soon cease to exert an important influence over men; but soon after *The Prince* appeared, Luther initiated the movement that was to ensure that religion played a vital part in politics for generations to come. The value of Machiavelli's thought is also questioned nowadays. It does not seem that success and failure in politics depend on the astuteness or ineptitude of the politician who manipulates events to his advantage and takes such independent action as he wishes; rather it would appear that the most realistic outlook is that of Bismarck who, after his successful career in achieving German unity in the nineteenth century, described himself as 'the helpless child of time' and said, 'Man cannot create the current of events. He can only float with it and steer.'

The development of diplomacy

In his concentration on the preservation of the state by the use of power, Machiavelli was indeed a product of the militarism of the

Renaissance period. As a diplomat, he was typical also of the development in this field which took place at the same time as the growth of warfare and was, in fact, a consequence of it. Previously European states had not possessed permanent diplomatic services. Embassies had been appointed to go abroad for some particular purpose, such as the granting of a chivalric honour, the arranging of a marriage contract or the declaration of war or peace. When they had achieved their object, they returned and were disbanded. There was little continuity in diplomatic representation and negotiation. Meetings between ambassadors tended to be ceremonial as much as business occasions, and so did the infrequent meetings between monarchs, such as those between Ferdinand I and Louis XII in 1507 at Savonna or Henry VIII and Francis I in 1520 on the Field of the Cloth of Gold.

The wars of the sixteenth century, however, increasingly made such haphazard, intermittent arrangements inadequate. The long-drawn-out Italian Wars produced a situation in which diplomatic activity played as important a part as the actual fighting. Between the wars, there were periods of peace or truce arranged by negotiated treaties, and when these did not last, new conferences had to be summoned to attempt fresh settlements. During this time, alliances were made and remade, which also required diplomatic negotiations. Moreover, the success of a state in such undertakings often depended upon the knowledge its government might have of the conditions of the army, the progress of a dispute in a ruling family on the other side, or upon the influence it could exert upon political factions or potentially disaffected individuals.

For such reasons, the traditional sort of formal, temporary embassy had to be replaced by permanent representatives at the courts with their attendant agents, spies and couriers. This had already taken place in Italy, where the almost continuous political uncertainty and tension had led the states to exchange such resident ambassadors. The greater European monarchies gradually began to imitate this system for their own purposes during the Italian Wars. Spain, which had acquired through Aragon a close knowledge of Italian diplomacy, was the first and established a resident ambassador in London as early as 1495. France was among the last; she was finally stimulated into action by her disastrous defeat at Pavia in 1525, after which French embassies were established in Rome, Venice, Madrid and Vienna. By the time of the Treaty of Cateau-Cambresis in 1559, it had become the usual practice for monarchs to maintain permanent embassies at each other's courts.

During the years of general peace in Europe after 1559, however, there was a decline rather than a further increase in diplomatic activity. This was because the Reformation and Counter-Reformation divided the states into opposing religious groups whose hostility to each other made diplomatic negotiations and even contacts seem impossible. Successful conferences and settlements between the two sides were out of the question. In the second half of the sixteenth century the Papacy prevented the establishment of permanent embassies by the Protestant countries in any Italian state, and the ambassadors of the Protestant countries left Spain during this period. Even where there was no open war, the schism in Christendom was so irreconcilable that the diplomatic machinery built up during the earlier part of the century fell into disuse. This situation was not ameliorated either by any important new diplomatic activity beyond western Europe since neither of the two large empires on its fringe, Russia and Turkey, showed any willingness to exchange resident ambassadors or consider far-reaching negotiations.

Towards the end of the century, the situation began to change again. As it became clear that neither the forces of the Reformation nor those of the Counter-Reformation could hope to conquer the whole of Europe, a willingness to renew the diplomatic system appeared. Spain in particular had to face the consequences of the defeat of the Armada in 1588, the English reconquest of Ireland and the success of the Dutch revolt; and the Papacy found it impossible to maintain indefinitely a ban against dealings with heretics. The way was thus prepared for the exchange of resident ambassadors with Spain and Italy when James I came to the throne of England in 1603, and similar arrangements were made with other Protestant countries. The Thirty Years War, however, interrupted this process again, and not until the Treaty of Westphalia in 1648 was the style of diplomacy, established in Italy nearly two hundred years earlier, generally adopted by European states.

Military warfare

By the beginning of the sixteenth century, the reliance of monarchs upon the medieval system of the feudal levy was abandoned. This summoning together of lords, their men-at-arms and other dependants and retainers, as the means of raising armies, had been rendered obsolete by the greater length of wars and complexity of weapons. Mercenaries were employed instead, though noblemen, who were trained to war, continued to provide the cavalry. It was the increasing need for experienced, trained infantrymen, who dominated tactics in warfare, that led to this reliance upon mercenary troops. Hiring such troops for particular wars or campaigns solved many problems. Monarchs did not have the money to raise and maintain in peacetime large bodies of armed men, nor the resources to train and equip them when their numbers had to be increased on the outbreak of hostilities.

E

Moreover, rulers found that their subjects, whether urban merchants or prosperous peasants, did not want to serve as soldiers but preferred to pay the taxation necessary to secure the services of professional foreign armies. They feared also the riotous behaviour of soldiers, both in service and when discharged; mercenary troops could be sent back to their own country when they were no longer needed and might be a menace to the social life of the state for which they had fought.

The finest mercenary troops were the Swiss. As a country which could not provide work or grow food for the whole of its increasing population, economic necessity caused Switzerland to offer soldiers for hire abroad. The victories won by the Swiss infantry over the heavy Burgundian cavalry under Charles the Bold at Grandson and Morat in 1476 gained them a reputation for invincibility which enabled them to offer their services to whoever would pay most. Traditionally France was the chief employer of the Swiss, which was to the advantage of Louis XII in Milan in 1500.[5] But the agreement came to an end in 1509,[6] and the Swiss lost both their fame and their freedom of action when their troops, in alliance with the Holy League, were defeated by the French at the Battle of Marignano in 1515. The next year the Swiss Confederacy had to agree that in future its men would only be employed in Francis I's forces, though Zwingli was able in 1521 to induce Zurich not to renew the treaty.[7] The Battles of Bicocca in 1522 and Pavia in 1525 completed the destruction of the paramount importance of the Swiss infantry in the Italian Wars,[8] but both France and the Papacy still engaged regiments of Swiss guards, and the French government made use of Swiss troops during the Wars of Religion.

Other mercenary troops came from Germany and Italy—the *landsknechten* and the *condottieri*. In these parts of Europe, although there was not the same economic need as in Switzerland, there were a number of princes and noblemen ready to hire out themselves and their men to engage in war. In the Italian Wars, the French were helped by Italians and the Spaniards by Germans—Rome was sacked by Charles V's German troops in 1527.[9] Alva besieged Haarlem in 1573 with an army composed, not only of Spaniards and southern Netherlanders, but also of Italians and Germans.

The *condottieri* in Italy were bands of professional soldiers of fortune in the service of the Italian states from the thirteenth century onwards. Several of their leaders obtained much power and position, among them Francesco Sforza, for instance, who became Duke of Milan in 1450. Contemporary Italian writers, particularly Machiavelli, disparaged the *condottieri* as incompetent, treacherous and deliberately avoiding battle whenever possible, but their criticisms were very much exaggerated. For instance, Machiavelli wrote of the Battle of Molinella in 1467 that 'some horses were wounded and some prisoners were

[5] P. 142.   [6] P. 144.   [7] P. 172.   [8] P. 133.   [9] P. 148.

taken, but no deaths occurred', whereas it appears that some six hundred men died, and contemporary chroniclers described how the whole surrounding countryside smelt of death for days as the bodies rotted in the ditches. Italians were dismayed by the seemingly easy successes gained by the French forces in the peninsula during the campaign of 1494, but the fault did not lie with the *condottieri*, who fought faithfully and well for the states which employed them. The *condottieri* could not withstand the invaders because they were neither as numerous nor as well-equipped as their enemies, and, above all, because the Italian states could not achieve political unity in the face of danger.

Contemporary European writers compared their own troops unfavourably also with the only regular standing army in the continent, the corps of janissaries of the Ottoman Empire.[10] These were not composed of feudal levies or mercenaries, but of renegade prisoners and the 'tribute of children' taken from Christian subjects, especially Serbians and Albanians; they were not allowed to marry and numbered about 14 000 men. In fact, they were not equal in fighting skill to the best western European infantry, and their artillery and technical skill were also inferior. Moreover, during the sixteenth century they did not prove as capable as European armies of adapting themselves to contemporary developments and improvements in warfare. Their fighting quality and exclusive loyalty to the Sultan declined when they were permitted to marry, and when, in the later years of the reign of Suleiman the Magnificent (1520-66), their sons were admitted to the corps. They did, however, enjoy certain important advantages. They were well disciplined and regularly paid, all ranks spoke one language, and their regiments were permanently up to strength. It was, indeed, their large numbers, together with the political disunity of their opponents, that probably accounted most for their successes in this period.

Machiavelli strongly criticized the use of the *condottieri* in Italy, urging that the best defence of a state was its citizens imbued with a strong desire to defend their homes, wives and personal freedom. 'Men not money are the sinews of war,' he insisted, and no state should hire foreign soldiers to undertake a task it should be doing itself. His military ideas received growing respect, and the need for national, standing armies was continually advocated, though their actual establishment was far from generally successful. Among the western European countries, France possessed the nearest approach to a standing army, but it consisted entirely of the royal household cavalry to which was added in the reign of Louis XII (1498-1515) an artillery force that accounted mainly for the French victories in Italy. Louis XII tried also to free himself from dependence upon Swiss troops by

[10] P. 288.

organizing a national infantry, but it proved impossible to get suitable men to serve, and France had to continue to rely upon Swiss and German mercenaries. Similarly, the only permanent part of the Spanish army was the cavalry, though during the sixteenth century it proved possible to obtain from the impoverished mountainous regions of Castile valuable volunteers to form an infantry which increasingly supplemented the foreign mercenaries.[11]

In military warfare, the sixteenth century opened upon a period of transition. In the fourteenth century, the feudal knights in armour, whose irresistible charges had usually carried the day in battle, were overcome by the infantry, which after a thousand years again came into its own in warfare. Prominent among those that destroyed the effectiveness of the cavalry of the age of chivalry were the English bowmen, who threw the French knights into confusion at the Battle of Crécy in 1346; but still more prominent were the Swiss pikemen, whose reputation was established in the later part of the fifteenth century.[12] Hence the high wages they could command as mercenaries—'point d'argent, point de Suisse' was a saying of the time—and their tactics were imitated by the German landsknechten and the Italian condottieri. They did not wait for the cavalry to charge them, but always attacked first, advancing into battle with surprising speed and cohesion and usually proceeding in three parallel divisions, the soldiers in each rank not directly behind the man in front in order to allow plenty of room for manoeuvre while presenting a tight front to the enemy. Wearing only light armour to ensure their mobility, each column marched forward with its eighteen-foot (about five and a half metres) long, steel-headed pikes, those of the first four ranks projecting forward and the rest held upright in reserve amid the banners. In front of them skirmished crossbowmen—continental archers preferred the cross-bow to the long-bow because, though it took longer to load and fire and had a shorter range, its square-headed, armour-tearing bolt was more effective against cavalry than the arrow. In this way, to quote Sir Charles Oman, 'the solid masses glided forward in perfect order and in deep silence until the war-cry burst out in one simultaneous roar and the column dashed itself against the solid front.'* Held in reserve to deliver the final slashing attack were the halberdiers, each armed with an eight-foot weapon combining a spear and a battle-axe, such as laid open from crown to chin the head of Charles the Bold in 1477 at the siege of Nancy.

The development of firearms, however, changed all this. During the early years of the sixteenth century, artillery reached very much the form it was to maintain during the next three centuries. The French in particular had light field-guns mounted on wheeled carriages, which could be transported with moving armies and repositioned during

[11] P. 195.   [12] P. 130.   * The Art of War in the Middle Ages (1898).

battles. Nevertheless, the evolution of really effective light artillery did not come until the Thirty Years' War in the next century, and hand-guns were more important in open fighting. During the 1520s the cross-bow was largely superseded in battle by the arquebus, a portable gun supported on a tripod. By then the matchlock had been invented whereby the match or fuse was applied to the gunpowder by the mechanism of the lock activated by the trigger. The soldier no longer had to steady the arquebus with one hand, therefore, and apply the match to the touch-hole with the other, but could concentrate on aiming with both hands. During the century the wheel-lock appeared; it consisted of a small wheel of steel wound up with a spring, the friction of which against a piece of flint produced sparks which fired the gunpowder. This made the arquebus more effective against cavalry and prepared the way for the development of the pistol before the end of the century.

Between 1494 and 1559 the Italian Wars provided military testing-grounds for the new weapons. The Battle of Ravenna in 1512 saw the first decisive use of artillery in the field when the French guns dislodged the Spanish cavalry from its fortified position and forced it to attack. At the Battle of Marignano in 1515, the massed artillery of Francis I tore gaps in the close ranks of the Swiss pikemen fighting in alliance with the Emperor and the Pope, but this was followed up by mounted knights in the medieval fashion, who only forced the pikemen to give way after thirty charges and twenty-eight hours of fighting. The Battles of Bicocca in 1522 and Pavia in 1525 demonstrated the superiority of gunfire first over pikemen and then cavalry. At Bicocca the Swiss pikemen, advancing against arquebusiers firing from a rampart behind a sunken road, suffered such heavy casualties that they were unable to storm the Imperialist position; and at Pavia the Spaniards defeated a charge of heavy French cavalry by harassing them with arquebusiers hiding behind trees and hedges on the battlefield.

These battles indicated the need for new tactics. The practice generally adopted was to employ both pikemen and arquebusiers in an army. The pikemen protected the arquebusiers from a cavalry charge, particularly when they were engaged in reloading, while the arquebusiers broke up enemy attacks before they could approach close enough to cut gaps through the pikemen. These were the tactics adopted in the first half of the sixteenth century by the Spanish infantry, which became renowned for its fighting qualities, both against the Turks and in Mexico and South America. Spain's enemies also adopted similar tactics. During the revolt of the Netherlands, Maurice of Nassau formed small, flexible companies of equal numbers of pikemen and arquebusiers, who were stationed three feet (about a metre) apart from each other. In the French Wars of Religion, the Huguenots, since they generally lacked artillery and pikemen to protect their arquebusiers, adopted the practice of placing a number of arquebusiers, called 'enfants perdus', in advance of the main body to check the enemy onslaught. The French Wars of Religion saw also the reappearance of cavalry on the battlefield, made possible by the invention of the pistol. The Huguenots used cavalry in long columns, armed with pistol and sword, for raiding and shock tactics, but the better-trained horsemen of the Catholic League practised the more difficult and more effective 'caracole', in which line after line rode up to the enemy, fired their pistols and then wheeled back to the rear to reload.

The general result of these changes on the battlefield was that defence was able to assert itself over offence, and the same applied to fortification and sieges. During the fifteenth century, the French artillery had been used successfully against castles and towns because the tall curtain-walls, designed to be secure against wooden siege-engines and scaling-ladders, were too thin to withstand gunfire, particularly when stone balls were replaced by iron ones. Some castles were rebuilt with thicker walls, but the most important answer to the challenge of artillery was the angle bastion, which was developed by the Knights of St John in 1496 at the Boulevard of Auvergne on Rhodes to meet the threat of Turkish attacks on the island. This was a solid construction projecting from the curtain-wall and of about the same height, but presenting an angle to the field so that attacks on the adjacent wall could be met with flanking fire. New ideas about fortification continued to appear during the century, culminating in the work of the Italian engineer, Nicholas Tartaglia in 1546. Early forms of the new type of fort which he perfected had already been erected by Henry VIII on the south coast of England. They had deep, wide ditches, walls completed by bastions and small, thick, round towers. Though expense prevented the wide-scale adoption of such forts, where they were built they were very effective. Sieges became protracted, since mining and sapping and, still more, hunger and disease seemed to be more likely than the heaviest cannon to reduce the defenders to surrender.

The result of these changes of weapons and tactics was to make land warfare slower and longer. Firearms prevented opposing armies fighting effectively at close quarters, and fortifications could not be taken by storm. Lengthy campaigns and drawn-out sieges became inevitable. Set battles became rarer, and strongpoints were often bypassed rather than invested. These developments also made warfare more expensive. Larger armies, new weapons and continual and increasing supplies and munitions for them, all these cost more and more as the century progressed, so that the waging of war became a serious financial burden for even the wealthiest and most powerful states. In France, the powers of taxation possessed by the Crown enabled it to raise considerable sums, but resulted in impoverishing the country; and Spain, despite the wealth she gained from her overseas trade and possessions, could not avoid defaulting on her debts.

Naval warfare

At the beginning of the sixteenth century, not much attention was paid to naval warfare. Ships were regarded as useful for transporting and supplying armies, and naval operations were generally limited to raiding the coast and blockading the ports of the enemy. Such actions as did occur at sea were fought by boarding-parties of soldiers, who engaged each other on deck in the manner of land fighting.[13] Moreover, there was little distinction in design between warships and merchant-ships. Royal navies hardly existed, and in time of war merchant-ships were hired, mainly from the Italian sea-states, to make up fleets. It was not until the later part of the century that specialized naval design and tactics were considered, and naval warfare became more important.

From the time of the Roman Empire until the sixteenth century, the maintenance of sea-power in the great European artery of the Mediterranean depended upon the galley, the low, flat, single-decked vessel propelled by sails and oars. By this time the old Roman square sail had been discarded in favour of the Moorish lateen rig, a loose-footed triangular sail suspended from a long spar which reached diagonally almost from deck level to a high peak aft, far above the masthead, a sail-plan which enabled the galleys to sail much closer to windward. 'The perfect galley,' a writer said in the middle of the century, 'should in every way resemble a graceful girl whose each gesture reveals alertness, vivacity and agility, while at the same time preserving a seemly gravity.'

In battle, fleets of galleys opposed each other in line-abreast formation. Since their oars and sail-plan made them quite easily manoeuvrable, it was possible to keep the ships pointing at the enemy, and each would try to strike an opponent in some vulnerable spot with the great beak or ram built over its bow, or to disable it by shearing off a bank of oars. By the sixteenth century, this method of attack had been made more effective by the addition of heavy bow guns to the galleys. After this opening move, the galleys drew alongside each other, and hand-to-hand fighting took place on the decks between armed boarding-parties in the usual medieval manner.

The last great battle between fleets of galleys took place in 1571 off the Greek shore at Lepanto near the Gulf of Patras, when the combined fleets of Christendom under Don John of Austria, the

half-brother of Philip II of Spain, met the Turkish fleet.[14] The Christian
fleet consisted of some three hundred ships and eighty thousand men,
of whom fifty thousand were sailors and oarsmen, and the Turkish
fleet was about the same size; they were the largest opposing fleets of
galleys that had ever met in battle. Don John drew up his fleet in a
line extending five miles across the mouth of the Gulf. The two wings
of the Turkish fleet attempted an outflanking movement, which
achieved considerable success, but the decisive contest took place in
the centre. The gunfire of the Christian ships proved to be more
effective than that of the Turks, and Don John was able to fasten his
galleys with grappling-irons to the Turkish ships and get his soldiers
on board. The Turks lost 117 ships and some thirty thousand men.
Among those killed was Ali Pasha, the Turkish commander, whose
head was mounted on a pike set up on the prow of his captured
flagship. The Christians lost fifteen or twenty ships and perhaps eight
thousand men, together with some fifteen thousand wounded. The
considerable extent of the damage and loss on both sides indicated the
fierceness of the engagement when these large ships and their military
contingents fought each other.

Though their sail-plan enabled galleys to sail close to windward,
they were not well suited for longer, rougher ocean voyages. Of the
four great galleys which set sail with the Spanish Armada in 1588, not
one reached the English Channel. In the closed waters of the Mediterranean, the galleys remained the most valuable warships, enjoying their
great technical advantage of freedom of movement uninhibited by
wind or tide, but as trade beyond the oceans grew, the maritime
powers needed vessels that did not suffer from their instability in the
open sea and lack of broadside fire-power. Beyond the Mediterranean,
therefore, ocean-going warships were required, and important changes
in naval design and sea warfare came about.

One result was the development of the 'round ship', so-called
originally by the French because at its longest its length was hardly
more than twice the measure of its beam (width). At first these were
all single-masted ships, but by 1450 the Portuguese had produced the
three-masted, and sometimes four-masted, carrack which was capable
of sailing round the world and in which soon afterwards guns were
mounted, at first on deck and then between decks.[15] Ocean-going
ships were at first designed primarily to carry cargo because they were
merchantmen and only became warships when hired by governments
on the outbreak of hostilities, but in the sixteenth century governments began to provide themselves with a nucleus of permanent
warships with consequent effects upon naval design. The aim was to
have a ship that would combine the manoeuvrability of the galley with
the seaworthiness and strength of the round ship. The final result in

[14] P. 247.   [15] P. 65.

the middle of the century was the galleon, which was longer in proportion to its beam than the round ship and without fore and aft castles; it was also higher and bulkier than the galley, fully-rigged and supplemented the round ship's guns mounted along the sides with the galley's guns fore and aft. These ships were faster than merchantmen, though they had to be as strongly built for oceanic voyages and have sufficient space for provisions, munitions and loot.

The obvious tactic to adopt in battle with heavily-gunned ships was, as the Portuguese first realized, the broadside.[16] Delivered by galleons aiming near to the enemy's water-line and postponing their fire until within close range, this transformed the nature of naval warfare. The English seem to have been the first to have used it in European waters, possibly in 1545 against the French off Shoreham, and in 1547 Philip II of Spain was warned that the English ships had been firing broadsides at the hulls of ships to sink them for some thirty years. Yet this development was not accompanied by any planned manoeuvring during an engagement between fleets; instead each captain sought an opponent, and the battle became a series of individual combats between ships each seeking to sink its opponent by gunfire. The obvious tactic that would most effectively exploit the broadside, the fleet line-ahead (that is, all the ships drawn up in a continuous line and following each other) was not adopted, however, until the middle of the next century during the Anglo-Dutch wars.

The Spaniards were slow to appreciate the change in naval fighting made possible by the use of guns in ships. They preferred to arm their galleons with heavy-shotted but short-ranged cannon, which were designed to cripple and halt enemy vessels so that they could be boarded and captured with the result that, in 1588 the Armada could not get near enough to the English fleet to damage the ships. On the other hand, the shot fired by the long-range guns, preferred by the English for their ships, proved to be too light to pierce the Spanish galleons. The running fight up the English Channel was, therefore, very much of a stalemate. The Spanish ships were able to move up in unbroken formation, but they hardly hurt the English ships, though they fired over a hundred thousand rounds of cannon-shot at them.

In opposing the Armada, the English ships, despite their weaknesses, showed themselves greatly superior in mobility and sailing quality. They were better built too. Later, in 1591, Sir Richard Grenville in the *Revenge* was able to beat off fifteen Spanish galleons in turn, sinking two and disabling two; and no Elizabethan warship ever sank in a wreck. Though the outcome of the war against Spain was inconclusive, England emerged from it with the enhanced prestige and self-confidence that were to make her a great sea-power.

---

[16] P. 65.

9
THE
ITALIAN
WARS
1494-1559

The invasion of Charles VIII

Charles VIII, the son of Louis XI, came to the French throne in 1483, but as he was only thirteen years old, his capable sister, Anne of Beaujeu, became Regent of France. The French monarchy still enjoyed the prestige it had gained from the defeat of England in the Hundred Years War (1337-1453), and Louis XI had succeeded in strengthening its power at the expense of the feudal nobles.[1] When his firm rule came to an end, however, the nobility, as it was to do again and again in the future, sought to take advantage of a young king and a woman ruler and reassert its influence in the government of the country. They found a leader in Francis II, Duke of Brittany, who supported the cause of Louis of Orleans, the heir presumptive to the throne and an aspirer for the regency. Despite help from Maximilian of Austria and Henry VII of England, the rebellion was defeated. Louis was captured and submitted to the Regent.

Anne faced a more serious threat in 1488, when Francis died, leaving a daughter of twelve years, also named Anne, who was immediately married by proxy to Maximilian. Since Maximilian already controlled the Netherlands and was very likely to become Holy Roman Emperor, his possession of Brittany would place the French kingdom in a very dangerous position. The Regent, therefore, sent troops into Brittany and compelled the Duchess Anne to marry Charles VIII, a move which was eventually to bring this last great feudal province under the direct rule of the French monarchy. Though this was a serious slight for Maximilian, he was too much engaged with the problems of Germany that continually beset the Habsburgs to take any further action. France had triumphed, although the result was that, when the regency of Anne of Beaujeu came to an end in 1492, Charles VIII was free to embark upon his dreams of Italian conquest.

Charles, whom a Florentine historian said was 'more like a monster than a man', was addicted to reading romances of chivalry and longed

[1] P. 107.

to distinguish himself in military adventure. He felt himself to be in a strong position to do so. The power and prestige of the French monarchy were high, and the feudal nobility had been subdued. He ruled a large and prosperous country which had a considerable army and a warlike spirit engendered by the almost continual warfare of the previous century. The obvious battleground for the French was Italy. It was disunited and defenceless, offered valuable works of art and prosperous cities to loot, could be entered without great difficulty by French forces in possession of the Alps, and offered territory which would strengthen France's position in Europe and provide her with further Mediterranean ports.

These circumstances, however, which encouraged a French campaign, probably did not influence Charles himself as much as the claim to the Kingdom of Naples, which he had inherited from the house of Anjou.[2] Possession of this would not only establish him powerfully in Italy, but might also be·a base from which he could launch a campaign for the recovery of the Holy Land from the Turks. Since he had also inherited from the house of Anjou a claim to the short-lived Christian Kingdom of Jerusalem, this crusading notion appealed particularly to his chivalrous obsessions.

Charles was provided in 1492 with a pretext to start his Italian campaign. Certain nobles who had been exiled since 1485 after revolting against the oppressive ruler of Naples, Ferrante I,[3] offered Charles support for his claim to that kingdom. This was followed the next year by Lodovico Sforza, Duke of Milan, offering Charles the help of Milanese troops for the same purpose. Lodovico Sforza had made himself Duke of Milan in 1480 in place of his nephew, Gran Galeazzo Sforza, who in 1489 married the daughter of Alfonso, the heir to the throne of Naples. Alfonso determinedly pressed his son-in-law's claim to Milan and in this was supported by the Medicis of Florence. Sforza, however, was supported by Cardinal Guiliano della Rovere, an enemy of the newly-elected pope, Alexander VI. In this way Italian disunity and mutual enmity encouraged a campaign which was the prelude to years of foreign invasion and warfare in the peninsula.

In order to accomplish his campaign, Charles was prepared to make territorial sacrifices, even though some were on France's vulnerable north-eastern frontier, which had been strengthened through the acquisition of the Burgundian dominions in the previous century. After obtaining a promise of perpetual peace with Henry VII of England in return for the payment of a subsidy through the Treaty of Etaples in 1492, he went on the next year to cede the Pyrenean counties of Roussillon and Cerdagne to Ferdinand of Aragon through the Treaty of Barcelona, and Artois and Franche-Comté to Maximilian through the Treaty of Senlis. As a result the security

[2] P. 274.   [3] P. 273.

of the French kingdom was endangered for the next two centuries.

Charles crossed the Alps by the pass of Mount Genève and occupied for a time both Pisa and Florence. Piero de Medici fled, and Savonarola sought friendship with France in order to establish a reformed republican constitution and bring about a religious revival.[4] Charles advanced on the Papal States and entered Rome, compelling Pope Alexander VI to recognize his title to Naples and allow free passage for his troops through papal territory. As the French troops entered his kingdom, Ferrante I died, but Alfonso was so unpopular that his subjects deserted him, and by February 1495 Charles was in possession of Naples.

His triumph, however, was short-lived. The success of his invasion of the peninsula had aroused alarm both among the Italian states and the outside powers. Only a month after his entry into Naples, the League of Venice was formed, ostensibly to undertake a crusade against the Turks, but in reality to drive the French out of Italy. It was joined by most of the Italian states, except Florence, but including the Papacy, and was supported by Ferdinand and Maximilian. The length of the French communications compelled Charles to retreat and he was only able to escape to France by checking the Venetians at the Battle of Fornovo in July 1495.

Charles had gained nothing from his campaign. Except in Florence, the Italian ruling families remained in possession of their states. Nevertheless, the events had ominous implications for the future of the peninsula. The wealth and weakness of Italy and the importance of her territory had been made clear to France and Spain, who had been able to intervene in Italian affairs through the disunity of the states. Further expeditions into Italy had become inevitable. Moreover, not only had Charles VIII's campaign brought about the formation of the League of Venice in which Ferdinand and Maximilian had participated, but the same year saw also the marriage of Maximilian's son, Philip the Fair, Archduke of Burgundy, to Joanna of Spain, heiress to Aragon and Castile, which prepared the way for the union of the house of Habsburg with the Spanish dynasty. These events at the end of the fifteenth century thus foreshadowed the struggle in the next between France and Spain, Valois and Habsburg, which was fought in Italy and resulted in Spanish domination over Europe. Charles VIII, however, did not see the omens. Only his death in 1498 prevented him preparing for another invasion of Italy.

The invasion of Louis XII

Charles was succeeded by his cousin, Louis XII, who had been Duke of Orleans and had a claim to Milan as a descendant of the Viscontis.

[4] P. 271.

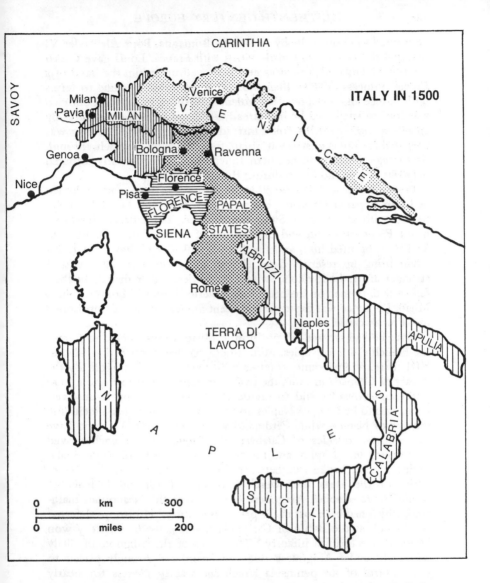

ITALY IN 1500

CARINTHIA

SAVOY

Nice

Genoa

Milan
Pavia
MILAN

Venice
V E N I C E

Bologna
Ravenna

Florence
Pisa
FLORENCE

SIENA

PAPAL
STATES

ABRUZZI

Rome

TERRA DI
LAVORO

Naples
N A P L E S

APULIA

CALABRIA

SICILY

0 km 300
0 miles 200

He showed his determination to renew the French campaign in Italy by taking the titles of both King of Naples and Duke of Milan upon his accession. He was assisted in his preparations by the continuing disunity in Italy. The League of Venice had already been dissolved as the result of rivalries and suspicions among its members. Angry that Federigo, the new King of Naples, would not agree to the marriage of his daughter to his own illegitimate son, Caesar Borgia, for whom he wanted to create a duchy out of the Romagna, Pope Alexander VI deserted the League and made terms with France. Louis gave Caesar the title of Duke of Valentois and bestowed upon him the hand of a French princess. Venice then thought it advisable to come to terms with France and was promised Milanese territory by Louis. Lodovico was thus isolated, and he had already rendered himself defenceless by spending money on his court instead of on his army. The way was prepared for Louis to strike at Milan, the possession of which, through its strategic position in northern Italy, was to be constantly disputed between France and Spain during the Italian Wars.

French troops entered Milan in the autumn of 1499, and Lodovico fled into Imperial territory. Early in 1500, however, Lodovico reappeared with an army of Swiss mercenaries. The citizens, resenting heavy French taxation and the transfer of some of their territory to Venice, supported him, and the French had to withdraw; but Louis could bring up reserves from France and soon came back with a stronger army. Lodovico's Swiss mercenaries, rather than fight their fellow-countrymen on the other side, deserted him, and Louis regained Milan. Lodovico was captured and spent the rest of his life imprisoned in a French castle.

Once he had secured his position in Milan, Louis wanted to pursue the French claim to Naples. Mindful of what had happened to Charles VIII there, he first came to terms with Ferdinand of Aragon. By the Treaty of Granada in 1500, the two monarchs agreed to make a joint attack upon Naples and to divide the kingdom among themselves; Louis was to be King of Naples and have the northern part, including the city of Naples, while Ferdinand was to be Grand Duke and have the southern duchies of Calabria and Apulia. The French moved southwards into Naples, and the Spaniards crossed over from Sicily. Fighting soon broke out between them, however, over the boundaries of the areas they were to occupy. Ferdinand had always wanted to re-establish Aragonese control over the Neapolitan mainland, which had been lost in the previous century.[5] His troops defeated the French at the Battle of Cerignola in 1503, the first victory won by the native Spanish infantry.[6] The whole of the Kingdom of Sicily was again under Aragonese rule and Spain was strongly placed to gain control of the peninsula which she was to possess for nearly two centuries.

The League of Cambrai

In Italy, despite Louis XII's defeat, his two allies, Venice and the Papacy, had both benefited from his campaign. French help had enabled Caesar Borgia to reconquer the Romagna, but his career was

5 P. 273.   6 P. 195.

cut short by his father's death in 1503. Alexander VI was succeeded, after the brief pontificate of Pius III, by Guilano della Rovere as Julius II, who got back for the Papacy the lands which Caesar had conquered for himself. Venice, however, took advantage of Caesar's fall to seize three towns in the Romagna and refused to return them when called upon to do so by the pope. Julius, therefore, skilfully set about forming the League of Cambrai, an alliance against Venice. The lands which Venice had taken from other Italian states during the previous century had gained her enemies with territorial claims against her, and Louis, Ferdinand and Maximilian were all ready to support them. Louis demanded lands in the Po valley which had formerly been Milanese, Maximilian required the restoration of Trieste and Fiume to his Duchy of Carinthia, and Ferdinand wanted the ports in Apulia that had been taken by Venice during Charles VIII's short occupation of Naples. Together with several Italian states, including Florence, these rulers joined the League, which was ratified with a religious ceremony in Cambrai Cathedral towards the end of 1508.

The alliance, however, had little actual strength. Only France and the Papacy were willing and able to fight in Italy. The only important fighting occurred in the spring of 1509. Florence was able to capture Pisa, which had revolted when the French had occupied the Republic;[7] and Louis XII defeated the Venetians at Agnadello, which was in the Milanese territory ceded to Venice by France ten years earlier. The Venetians, however, were able to withdraw their forces from the mainland and hold their lagoons, which the French could not push on to attack, and months of stalemate followed. This gave time for suspicion and dissension to grow among the allies. The success of the French alarmed Julius, who now considered that they were a more serious threat to the Papacy than the Venetians. By 1510 he had made terms with Venice and was at war with France. Having recovered the cities in the Romagna from Venetian occupation, he no longer needed French support, and he regarded as an insult the calling by Louis of a schismatic general council at Pisa—later removed to Milan—to consider the question of papal authority.

The Holy League

Julius laboured to unite the enemies of France and brought about a diplomatic reversal of alliances. In the autumn of 1511 the Holy League was formed, supposedly to protect the Papacy from attack, but really to expel the French from Italy. Venice joined, and so did Ferdinand of Aragon, who had recovered his Apulian ports without having to fight for them and was to secure Navarre in 1512.[8] Ferdinand

[7] P. 272.   [8] P. 239.

obtained the adhesion of his son-in-law, Henry VIII, who wanted to regain the former English possession of Gascony and also to take a more prominent part in international affairs. Maximilian also joined in 1512, and so did Switzerland. The French occupation of Milan had alarmed the Swiss since it was important for their trade and was their main source of corn and wine. The agreement providing France with Swiss mercenary troops was not renewed in 1509, and Julius induced Switzerland to join the Holy League by suggesting the possibility that her troops might provide a papal guard.

A French army advanced into the Papal States and on Easter Day 1512 defeated a Spanish force at Ravenna, one of the towns recently obtained from Venice by the Pope. Maximilian then allowed the Swiss to enter Italy through the Brenner Pass, and they advanced towards Milan. The French, who had lost their commander at the Battle of Ravenna, were taken by surprise and retreated, taking with them the general council, which had to abandon its consideration of the election of an anti-pope and soon came to an end at Lyons. The next year, when a French army sought to regain Milan, it was overwhelmed by the Swiss at Novara.

The Holy League had succeeded in driving the French from Italy, and after eighteen years of fighting the Italian states had regained their freedom, with the exception of Naples in the south of the peninsula which remained Spanish. In 1512, the Sforzas were returned to Milan and the Medici to Florence, France's only ally; and early the next year, on the death of Julius, Cardinal Giovanni de Medici became pope as Leo X. The Holy League, however, was unable to preserve a united, free Italy. The new pope was more concerned to live as a Renaissance prince than to lead the Italian states in opposition to the foreigner, and neither of the other Medici princes was able to do so. Leo made peace with France in 1513, and Italy was as disunited and defenceless as ever when the contest between Habsburg and Valois was renewed within two years.

The invasion of Francis I

Louis XII died in 1515 and was succeded by his nephew and son-in-law, Francis I, who was a young man of twenty, eager and ambitious for military fame. To display his prowess in battle and avenge the French defeat at Novara, he immediately invaded Italy. He had obtained the neutrality of Henry VIII (who had attacked the French coast during 1512 and 1513) and an alliance with Venice. He was opposed by Milan and the members of the Holy League, but they again failed to act together.

Francis routed the Milanese at Villafranca and was met by the

Swiss at Marignano, a few miles south-east of Milan. After a desperate battle, lasting two days, the French cavalry and artillery with Venetian assistance defeated the Swiss infantry. The battle established the young French King's reputation as a soldier and destroyed the fame of the Swiss mercenaries.[9] It restored a French domination in northern Italy, which was not to be challenged for five years. One by one the members of the Holy League had to accept the consequences of defeat and make their terms with France, which seemed at last to have reaped the harvest of her invasions of Italy by three successive monarchs.

Francis became Duke of Milan, where the brief renewal of Sforza rule was brought to an end. Leo X made peace with him immediately and was able to obtain French acceptance of his family's possession of Florence, but he had to cede Parma to Milan. Most important, however, he also had to agree to the Concordat of Bologna, which substantially confirmed the relationship of the monarchy with the French Church established by the Pragmatic Sanction of Bourges.[10] The Swiss withdrew from their conquests in Lombardy and by the Perpetual Peace of Fribourg agreed to provide troops only for France in the future.[11] Ferdinand died in 1516, and Spain and her territories passed to his grandson, Charles V, who was already the ruler of the Netherlands. Neither Charles nor his chief adviser wished at this stage to become involved in Italian affairs.[12] By the Treaty of Noyon the two monarchs recognized French possession of Milan and Spanish possession of Naples, while Charles agreed to restore to France southern Navarre, which had been taken by his grandfather, Ferdinand, and to marry Francis I's infant daughter. The Emperor Maximilian was left isolated by the collapse of the Holy League. His attempt to capture Milan in 1516 was a complete failure. He had to adhere to the Treaty of Noyon, restoring Verona to Venice, which was rewarded for her alliance with France by regaining the boundaries she had possessed in 1494.

The effect of Francis I's invasion of Italy was not only to deprive the Swiss of their reputation as outstanding mercenary soldiers, but also to eliminate them from any independent role in Italian affairs. No longer could they hope to hold Milan, and they increasingly adopted an attitude of neutrality in international politics. Milan was to be contested between the two powerful European countries, France and Spain, as part of their struggle with each other for predominance. During this contest, the Italian states could do no more than seek to preserve some independence by joining first one and then the other of the contestants, whichever seemed to suit their interests best. This was all they could do because by now little freedom remained to them after the three successive French campaigns in the peninsula. The Italian states had been unable to withstand invasion partly because

[9] P. 133.   [10] P. 121.   [11] P. 130.   [12] P. 191.

of military inferiority, but far more because of the absence of any common national Italian patriotism. The attachment of its citizens to each state fostered mutual rivalries and inhibited joint action against the enemy, and so control of the future of the peninsula passed out of their hands.

The triumph of Charles V

The renewal of war between France and Spain in Italy under Francis I and Charles V was largely due to the contest between Habsburg and Valois in its widest aspects. Since their countries were rivals for the control of western Europe and the Mediterranean, the situations and policies which both kings inherited, together with their own ambitions and objectives, meant that conflict was almost inevitable.

Charles V had inherited the traditional, recurrently revived disputes with France of both the Burgundian and Spanish ruling families. As a Burgundian prince he wished to recover the ancient Duchy of Burgundy from French possession, as a Spanish king he asserted his right to Navarre and Rousillon, while as Holy Roman Emperor he could claim Milan as an Imperial fief. He recognized, indeed, that the capture of Milan was of vital importance in his chain of communication with Spain's strategic outposts and the Habsburg territory which he now ruled also. Troops from Spain and bullion from the New World could be landed at Genoa, moved across to Milan and then through Savoy to southern Germany and Austria, Franche Comté and the Netherlands. If this route could not be secured, the only other one was the long and dangerous voyage to the Netherlands and possibly along the Rhine. Milan, therefore, through its domination of the Alpine passes was of crucial significance to him in the unification and preservation of his European dominions.

Francis I, on the other hand, was determined to maintain the integrity of his kingdom and even to regain possession of Naples, which both Charles VIII and Louis XII had briefly occupied. He was bound to regard Charles as a dangerous rival. The unification under his personal rule of Spanish and Habsburg territory enabled Charles to threaten France on her east, north-east and south-west frontiers, and only by holding on to Milan could Francis hope to save his kingdom from encirclement. In addition, the Electors' choice of Charles as Emperor instead of himself was regarded by Francis as a personal affront.

In military strength and strategic advantage, the two monarchs were fairly evenly matched. Charles had large territories in Europe, including control of the southern part of Italy, and a great revenue supplied by the New World, but at the same time he had to face revolt in Spain, the support of the German princes for the Lutheran movement and the continual Turkish threat to his Austrian lands coupled with the activity of the Corsairs (Moslem pirates from the northern coast of Africa) in the western Mediterranean. Francis, on the other hand, ruled over a compact kingdom in which the power of the monarchy had been strengthened, had a large, well-equipped army which he had already used in an effective manner, could attack almost any of his rival's territories from a strong central position and held the strategic Duchy of Milan.

In such a situation, much of the diplomatic activity of the two countries from 1519, when both seem to have considered the renewal of war likely in the near future, was directed towards securing the support or at least the neutrality of England. In the summer of 1520, Henry VIII and Francis I met amid the pageantry and festivities of the Field of the Cloth of Gold near Calais and pledged their lasting friendship. But Charles had already been to England and arrived at a secret understanding with Henry's minister, Cardinal Wolsey, which late in 1521 became the Treaty of Windsor, an alliance between the two rulers for a common war against France. Traditional English enmity towards France, the cloth trade with Flanders, the lead given by Leo X who feared French supremacy in Italy and Henry's personal desire for glory all combined to bring Charles this English alliance.

By then there had been a resumption of the war in Italy, which was to last, with short intervals, for nearly ten years. In the early summer of 1521, because Charles had not restored southern Navarre to France under the terms of the Treaty of Noyon, Francis took advantage of the revolt of the Comuneros in Spain to launch an attack across the Pyrenees; but this was unsuccessful, and the ensuing war was fought mainly in Italy. The following November, after a secret agreement made with Leo X, Imperial forces defeated the French, occupied Milan, sacked Genoa, restored the Sforzas to rule the duchy as Imperial lieges and ceded Parma and Piacenza to the Papacy in accordance with the terms of the agreement.[13] By the end of the year, however, Leo was dead and was succeeded by Adrian VI, Charles V's old Burgundian tutor, Adrian of Utrecht, who wished to bring the war to an end so that the rival monarchs might unite in a crusade against the Turks. The French tried to take advantage of this papal defection from Charles V by advancing on Milan in the spring of the next year, but were overwhelmed by the Imperial forces at the Battle of Bicocca, near Monza.[14]

Charles now seemed assured of a lasting triumph, especially when, late in 1522, the Duke of Bourbon defected to Charles. But the next summer, a twofold attack on France mounted by the English from Calais and by the Spaniards across the Pyrenees failed completely; so

[13] P. 125.   [14] P. 130.

also, the following year did an attempt at invasion of eastern France by the Duke of Bourbon, whom Charles had placed in command of the Imperial army in Italy. Clement VII, the Medici Pope who succeeded Adrian VI on his death in September 1523, sought to exploit this challenge to Spanish supremacy in Italy by allying himself with France. Francis entered Italy once more and captured Milan, but on 24th February 1525 he was defeated at the Battle of Pavia; he himself was made prisoner and taken to Madrid.

Europe was amazed at this sudden and complete reversal of fortune, but Charles V's triumph was not as complete as might appear. French territory was intact, and it was not likely that Charles would be strong enough to invade it. His chances of enforcing any terms he might impose on Francis were not, therefore, very good, especially as fear of Habsburg domination was already turning other rulers against him. Early in 1526 Francis agreed by the Treaty of Madrid to renounce his claims to Milan and Naples, surrender the Duchy of Burgundy, marry the Emperor's sister, Eleanor, and go on a crusade with him against the Turks. Although Francis swore on the Gospels after Mass to observe this settlement and left his two sons as hostages in Spain, he repudiated his concessions as soon as he returned to France and was absolved from his oath by the pope.

This made the renewal of war inevitable. In May 1526 the Holy League of Cognac was formed by France, the Papacy, Florence, Venice and Francesco Sforza of Milan (who had been ejected by the Spaniards). Charles V's position had already been weakened in the previous month by the Turkish victory in the Battle of Mohacs which resulted in the loss of the whole of Hungary.[15] Charles was particularly enraged against Clement VII. He ordered his forces in Italy to march on Rome. Though the Duke of Bourbon died in the first assault, the city was stormed on 6th May 1527, and the troops, many of whom were Lutheran mercenaries from Germany, plundered, pillaged, raped and slaughtered for a week. The pope took refuge in his own castle of St Angelo and in June surrendered as an Imperial prisoner.

The Sack of Rome shocked Europe, but the Papacy was now firmly under Charles V's domination, and the French attempt to oust him from Italy failed. One French force besieged Milan and another marched southwards to threaten Naples, but both failed. Then Genoa, which had joined France in 1527, changed sides again the next year and rejoined Spain with her fleets of galleys—an important event which secured the Spanish maritime link with Italy.[16] By 1529 Italy was once again securely under Charles V's control, and he was able to impose a settlement upon both the Papacy and France in that year. By the Treaty of Barcelona, Clement recognized Charles as King of Naples (which was a papal fief) and promised to crown him as Emperor, while

[15] P. 280.   [16] P. 146.

Charles agreed to restore the Sforza to Milan and the Medici to Florence. This was followed by the Treaty of Cambrai between France and Spain, commonly called the Ladies' Peace because it was negotiated by Louise of Savoy, the mother of Francis, and Margaret of Savoy, the aunt of Charles. Its terms were much the same as those of the Treaty of Madrid, but now that the Duke of Bourbon was dead, Charles no longer demanded the cession of the Duchy. Francis had to pay a ransom of two million gold crowns for the sons he had left as hostages in captivity in Spain. The treaty was sealed by the marriage of Francis to the Emperor's sister. Early in 1530 Clement crowned Charles Holy Roman Emperor in Bologna Cathedral; this was the last time an Emperor was crowned by the pope.

The Treaty of Cambrai not only ended the contest between Francis and Charles which had begun in 1521, but also marked a new stage in the Italian Wars and European international relations. Spain now controlled the Papacy and the whole of Italy, and efforts to dislodge her were not to succeed. There was to be more fighting in Italy, but the peninsula now ceased to be the main battlefield of Europe and the contest between Habsburg and Valois moved westwards. Moreover, during the following years that conflict became less continuous and intense. This was partly due to the changes in the nature of warfare telling against the wars of movement which had previously altered the fortunes of the contestants so frequently and rapidly.[17] It was also affected by Francis I's financial problems and by the menace presented to Charles V by the Turkish offensive in Europe and the religious struggle in Germany which occupied the remainder of his reign.[18]

The renewal of war

Charles, indeed, wanted to take advantage of his triumph by devoting himself to dealing with the Turkish invaders and the Lutheran princes, and though success in solving his German difficulties eluded him, Vienna was saved from the Turks in 1529, while in 1535 the Algerian pirates were defeated and Tunis was captured.[19] Francis was prevented from an immediate renewal of the war by his financial difficulties;[20] but he was ready to harass Charles as much as possible by intriguing with those who were alarmed by the powerful Habsburg position in Europe. Clement VII was too cautious to commit himself openly, but showed his French sympathies by going to Marseilles in 1533 and arranging a marriage between his niece, Catherine de Medici, and Francis I's son, Henry, Duke of Orleans, who later became Henry II. Francis entered also into commercial negotiations with the Sultan and opened discussions with the German princes and with Henry VIII of England, who was seeking to end his marriage with Charles V's aunt, Catherine of Aragon.

[17] P. 134.   [18] P. 189.   [19] P. 200.   [20] P. 199.

In 1535 the last Sforza died without heirs. Charles took possession of Milan as an escheated fief. Francis regarded this as a challenge to himself and revived his claim to the Duchy. Having made a formal treaty with the Sultan, he sent his troops into the Duchy of Savoy, which was under Imperial control, occupied Turin and prepared again to move towards Milan. Charles replied by sending an army into south-eastern France in the summer of 1536, an expedition which was, however, unsuccessful. The French army did not achieve further progress in Italy either, and both Henry VIII and the German princes remained neutral. Clement VII had died in 1534 and was succeeded by Paul III who, wishing to establish a lasting peace between the Emperor and the King of France, also remained neutral. Papal intervention, in fact, brought the fighting to an end with the Truce of Nice, which confirmed the Treaty of Cambrai and allowed Francis to keep his conquests in Savoy. The two monarchs met at Aigues Mortes, near Nice, and agreed to unite in taking action against the Turks, Lutherans and English, all of whom menaced the established order on the Continent.

This co-operation came to nothing, though in the winter of 1538-9 Francis allowed Charles to send troops across France to put down the rebellion at Ghent.[21] In 1540, however, Charles formally invested his son, Philip, with the Duchy of Milan. Francis could not accept this move which strengthened Spanish possession of the vital Duchy. His opportunity seemed to come in 1542 when Charles V's expedition against Algiers failed disastrously, and the German army sent into Hungary against the Turks was equally unsuccessful.[22] And so war broke out again. Francis attacked Luxembourg in alliance with the Duke of Cleves, who had given support to the Lutherans and sought a fresh ally after the failure of the marriage of his daughter, Anne, with Henry VIII of England. Francis also joined his ships to the Turkish and Corsair fleets, which raided the coasts of Italy and captured for him the town of Nice, one of the last few remaining possessions of the Duke of Savoy; then they wintered at Toulon and there sold as slaves the thousands of prisoners they had taken in Italy.[23] Francis, however, was discredited in Europe by this Turkish alliance and found himself without allies ready to assist him in exploiting his success. Charles acted with unwonted alacrity and determination. He defeated the Duke of Cleves in the late summer of 1543 and, by playing upon Henry VIII's old desire to display his power in Europe, was able to combine an attack by Spanish troops across the Maine with an invasion by an English force from Calais towards Paris. Though Francis defeated an Imperial army at Ceresole in Piedmont, he had not the resources to go on to attack Milan and had to ask for peace. Charles, too, was running short of money to pay his mercenaries and wanted to be able

[21] P. 194.   [22] Pp. 200, 291.   [23] P. 291.

to give his attention to Germany again. The result was the Peace of Crespy in 1544 by which each monarch restored the territory he had lost since the Truce of Nice. For Charles the most valuable part of the agreement was the undertaking given by Francis to stop aiding the German princes. He was prepared to make a moderate settlement with Francis so that he could campaign in Germany, where he considered it more important to assert his power—with the result that he obtained a victory at Mühlberg in April 1547.[24]

Meanwhile, Francis I had died in March 1547, and his son, Henry II, was not able to answer the appeal of the leaders of the Schmalkaldic League for assistance, though he wished to renew the contest with Charles and felt a personal resentment towards him because of the three years' captivity he had undergone in Spain as a hostage for his father. By 1552, however, he was ready and made the Treaty of Chambord with the Protestant princes.[25] This fresh outbreak of warfare, however, showed that a new phase in the struggle between Habsburg and Valois had developed for there was little fighting this time in Italy. The result of the fighting in Germany was that Charles finally decided to abdicate.[26]

The continuing war against France, which Philip inherited from his father, produced one more spasmodic outbreak of fighting in Italy as Henry made a final, unfruitful attempt to challenge Spanish supremacy in the peninsula. In 1555 Cardinal Caraffa, who vainly wanted to rescue the Papacy from Spanish domination, became Pope Paul IV. He persuaded Henry to revive the French claim to Naples and to send an army into Italy under the Duke of Guise, who had held Metz against Charles.[27] The issue, however, was not to be decided in Italy. In June 1557 England declared war on France, and a strong force of Spanish, German and English troops invaded France from the Netherlands. The Duke of Guise, who had entered Naples, hurried back, but was too late to prevent the complete defeat of a French force at St Quentin in August. Philip, however, could not exploit his victory and was unable to prevent Guise taking Calais from the English in January 1558 and going on to invade the Netherlands, where he was, however, defeated at Gravelines in August. Both France and Spain had repudiated their debts and declared themselves bankrupt in 1557. Only the arrival of a cargo of silver from America had enabled Philip to conduct his last campaign against Guise. Neither country could continue the war, and negotiations began for the conclusion of peace.

The Treaty of Cateau-Cambrésis (1559)

The treaty was signed in 1559 at Cateau-Cambrésis, a small town in northern France. Its terms were arranged in a derelict castle there

[24] P. 166.   [25] P. 167.   [26] P. 201.   [27] P. 213.

belonging to the Bishop of Cambrai; windows of paper set in wooden frames had been hastily installed and a little furniture hurriedly placed in the empty building. Its terms restored the two countries' frontiers to what they had been thirty years previously by the Treaty of Cambrai. France had to relinquish the gains she had made at the Truce of Nice, but she kept Calais and the bishoprics of Metz, Toul and Verdun. Philip, newly-widowed by the death of Mary Tudor, was to marry Henry II's daughter, Elizabeth, and the two monarchs agreed to co-operate in the extinction of heresy in Europe.

The long-drawn-out Italian Wars, started by Charles VIII's invasion of the peninsula, had not in themselves altered the relative position of the two contestants, France and Spain, nor changed the territorial boundaries of these kingdoms. They had, however, imposed very severe financial strains upon them both. The continued imports of bullion from the New World saved Spain from disaster until the end of the century, but France was severely weakened by her huge debt and the heavy taxation which undermined the power of the Crown and encouraged the outbreak of internal anarchy and civil war during this period. The Italian Renaissance, deprived of the wealth and independence of the states which had enabled it to flourish, was replaced by the austerity and intolerance of the Counter-Reformation everywhere except in Venice.[28] The Turks had been able to advance across the Balkans into Hungary and Austria and to increase their maritime strength in the western Mediterranean. In Germany, the power of the princes and the spread of Protestantism had been able to destroy both Imperial authority and religious unity partly, at least, through the distractions imposed upon Charles V by the Italian campaigns.

The Treaty of Cateau-Cambrésis marked the beginning of the age of Spanish domination in Europe which was to last until the Treaty of Westphalia in 1648. Possibly this may have been because France was, for almost a generation, in no position to challenge Spanish supremacy after Henry II had died of a wound accidentally received in a tourna-ment organized to celebrate the signing of the Treaty and so plunged his kingdom into the debilitating religious strife of the following years. Spain, however, would have been strong in any event but, ironically enough, not as the result of her supremacy in Italy which she retained after the wars. Italy and the Mediterranean were fast losing their importance; greatness was to go to Spain (and later France) because they were countries which could turn away from this area which had been so long contested between them, and look across their other sea, the Atlantic, to the trade routes and new lands which were changing the centre of power and prosperity in Europe.

[28] P. 57.

10

THE
LUTHERAN
REFORMATION

Luther's early years

Though the date of Martin Luther's birth is not certain, most historians have agreed with Melancthon in accepting 1483 as the year. He was born at Eisleben in south-western Saxony. His family had been small farmers for generations, but his father, Hans Luther, had left the land to work in the newly-opened copper mines. After a hard struggle in the early years, he leased several mines and furnaces of his own and became a member of the town council of Mansfeld. Luther's references to his own childhood are so few that attempts to relate his later career to his early relationships with his parents, such as have been made by recent psychoanalysts, notably Erik H. Erikson in *Young Man Luther* (1959), inevitably fail because of an inadequate factual basis.

His father gave him a good education, including a year at a school conducted by the Brethren of the Common Life, which introduced him to contemporary mystical and monastic movements.[1] He went on to the University of Erfurt and graduated in law. His socially ambitious father hoped he would become a counsellor to a prince or town council. He also had an eye on a rich wife for him.

In 1505, however, Luther amazed his friends and angered his father by entering the Priory of the Augustinian friars at Erfurt, which was one of a group of thirty houses, mostly in Saxony, which had been reformed in the fifteenth century to conform more strictly to the rule of the order. He adopted the monastic life, as men commonly did in the Middle Ages, to secure the forgiveness of his sins; he was, he said, constrained 'by the terror and agony of sudden death' for which he was spiritually unprepared. There is a story that, when caught in a violent thunderstorm as a student, he vowed to St Anne, the patron saint of miners, that if he survived this sign of God's judgment upon him, he would join a religious order.

Luther became a novice at Erfurt in 1505, professed his vows in

[1] P. 44.

1506, was ordained and said his first Mass in 1507. During these years of preparation and training, he submitted himself to the life and discipline of the order in a way that gained him the reputation of a saint among his fellow-friars. 'I was a good friar,' he recalled in 1533, 'and kept strictly to my order, so that I could say that if the monastic life could get a man to heaven, I should have entered. . . . If I had kept on any longer, I should have killed myself with vigils, prayers, reading and other works.'

He also studied industriously and gained an equal reputation as a scholar. In 1508 he was sent to the Augustinian house at Wittenberg to teach at the university recently founded there by Frederick of Saxony. At that time, Saxony was divided into two states, an arch-dukedom (which was also an electorate) and a dukedom. Frederick ruled the archdukedom, his nephew, George, the dukedom with the great capital city of Leipzig. Frederick was trying to increase the reputation of his state and of Wittenberg. One way was through his collection of relics.[2] The other was his university. Luther was to spend nearly all the rest of his life at Wittenberg. He became a Doctor of Theology in 1512 and was appointed Chaplain of the Castle Church and Professor of Biblical Theology. For the next six years he lectured in Biblical subjects and brought the university the reputation desired by its founder.

During this time, however, he was sadly troubled in his mind and conscience. He had become a friar to save his soul and believed that God had called him to this way of life, but as the years passed he could find no spiritual satisfaction in the religious observances he tried hard to carry out. 'Who knows', he asked himself, 'whether these things please God?' They seemed, in fact, to bring him no nearer to God and salvation. 'The more I tried these remedies,' he said later, 'the more troubled and uneasy my conscience grew.' As a religious man, he was constantly and urgently aware of the contrast between God's supreme goodness and man's desperate wickedness. 'God's ever-present judgment clutches man in the loneliness of his conscience,' he wrote, 'and with his every breath conveys him to the Almighty and Holy One to prosper or destroy.' He feared God's judgment and was overwhelmed by his sense of sin; confession and penance did not bring him the longed-for sense of forgiveness and reconciliation. At the same time, he was becoming increasingly dissatisfied with the condition of the contemporary Church and particularly critical of the considerable incomes obtained by priests for saying Masses for the release of souls from purgatory. In 1510, when his doubts were beginning to shape themselves, he was sent to Rome to represent his order on a matter of business. There he joined the pilgrims at the Scala Santa, the twenty-eight steps close to the Lateran Church which

[2] P. 33.

were believed once to have stood in Jerusalem in front of the court-house of Pontius Pilate, who had shown Christ to the mob at the top of them. With the pilgrims, Luther crawled up on hands and knees, repeating the Lord's Prayer at each step in the belief that this would release a soul from purgatory. Luther's prayers were for his grand-father—'but when I got to the top, I thought, who knows if it is true?' He returned to Wittenberg still tormented by his fears and doubts and shocked by the scandalous tales he had heard about the Renaissance popes and by what he had seen of the immorality, irreverence and laziness of the Roman clergy. Years later he said he would have been sorry if he had not gone to Rome, 'for then I might have been afraid of being unjust to the Pope.'

Luther's friend, John Staupitz, Vicar-General of the Saxon province of the Augustinians and his predecessor as professor at Wittenberg, advised him to read the writings of the German mystics. He did so, being particularly attracted by the books of John Tauler (c 1300-61), who was a disciple of Master Eckhart and proclaimed, 'Life does not consist in repose, but in progress from good to better.'[3] At the same time, Luther was now lecturing on St Paul's Epistle to the Romans, and one day in 1515 he found there, in the text 'the just shall live by faith', a promise that seemed at last to provide an answer to his problems. Now he believed that none could gain salvation by his own works—the prayers, fastings and penances to which he had devoted himself—but rather that God freely grants forgiveness of sin and eternal life to all who earnestly repent, believe in the message of the Gospel and have faith in Him through Jesus Christ. Once a man puts his trust in God and discovers His grace, he is justified through his faith. The human heart is too wicked to save itself; forgiveness is God's gift which cannot be earned by personal efforts. This was Luther's doctrine of 'justification by faith alone', which was to become the watchword of the Reformation. 'God our Father has made all things depend on faith,' he said, 'so that whoever has faith will have everything, and whoever does not have faith will have nothing.'

He expounded his ideas in his lectures at Wittenberg and gained general support in the university, particularly from Philip Melancthon (1497-1560), the professor of Greek. Luther insisted that his teaching was not novel. He had found it in St Paul's epistles, and later he was delighted to find that St Augustine, among the early Christian Fathers, had emphasized it; but it had long been overlaid by other teaching, and its implications were far-reaching. Indeed, it threatened the whole position of the medieval Church, which over the centuries had developed a system designed to enable men, through participating in its sacra-ments and observances, to save their souls. But if men could only be saved by turning themselves directly to God and receiving His grace,

[3] P. 44.

the entire system became useless and even harmful. The clergy were no longer the vital mediators between God and man; the sacraments were no longer absolutely necessary channels of divine grace. All were replaced by the need for a personal relationship between God and the individual believing Christian, whose faith was the means by which he received the spiritual gift.

At first, however, the implications of Luther's teaching were not realized and he was not accused of heresy. He himself, indeed, had not even begun to work out these implications himself when he was caught up in the consequences of an event which was to transform him from a little-known university teacher into a figure famous throughout Germany and beyond.

The break with the Papacy

This event was the arrival in Germany of John Tetzel, a Dominican friar, to sell indulgences.[4] He was employed by Archbishop Albert of Mainz, who had been commissioned in 1517 by Pope Leo X to proclaim throughout Germany an indulgence on behalf of the rebuilding of St Peter's, Rome, and had also been allowed to keep half the proceeds himself. He needed these badly, because he was in debt to the Fuggers from whom he had borrowed money to pay for the dispensations he had obtained from the Papacy to enable him to hold three bishoprics at once. Frederick did not allow Tetzel to enter Saxony, because he did not want competition with the indulgences that could be bought by pilgrims visiting his relics, a practice which Luther had already criticized. It has been estimated that the indulgences attached by the Papacy to these relics carried with them a possible total remission of 127 799 years and 116 days from purgatory, but Tetzel was offering complete and immediate release. Tetzel did come near enough to Saxony to sell indulgences to parishioners of Luther, who felt bound to condemn them as a flagrant instance of the false notions about the forgiveness of sins upheld by the Church.

The way he did this was to nail to the door of the Castle Church at Wittenberg a list of *Ninety-Five Theses* or arguments in Latin against indulgences and pilgrimages. There was nothing defiant or revolutionary in this action. It was the usual way for a medieval scholar to announce that he wanted to discuss some subject with other scholars. None came to debate with Luther, and it seemed as if his pronouncements would have as little effect as those of many other earlier scholars. So they might have done if he had lived in a previous age, but an enterprising local printer translated the *Theses* into German and published them throughout the Empire.

Probably Luther was as surprised as any one by the excitement

[4] P. 40.

created by his *Theses*, but they raised issues upon which German opinion was becoming increasingly sensitive. Sixteenth-century Germany was a religious country. Thousands of little books of religious instruction in German had been printed for use in homes, and many versions of the Bible in German had also been printed. There was much criticism of the abuses of the Church, and the religion of the mystics was not in accordance with the idea of indulgences.[5] Moreover, while the achievements of the Italian Renaissance had been welcomed by educated and cultured men in Germany, others had been scandalized, like Luther himself, by the irreligious and immoral character of the papal court in Rome. The extension of papal authority and financial exactions and the inability of the Emperor and princes to resist them had caused resentment.[6] Charles V even stated that the Papacy drew more money from Germany than the Emperor himself did. To many Germans, therefore, the Papacy seemed a foreign power exercising an unwelcome, harmful authority in their country.

Luther had the support of his fellow-friars and teachers at Wittenberg and also of Frederick, who seemed less concerned about the criticism of his relics than about the academic renown of his university to which Luther had brought distinction; but Archbishop Albert was alarmed and referred the matter to the Pope. Leo X thought it was a trivial matter and ordered the Augustinian authorities to interview Luther, which they did, inconclusively, at Heidelberg in 1518. Support for Luther in Germany continued to grow. Leo reluctantly decided that he must act himself. He summoned Luther to Rome, but was opposed by the Emperor Maximilian, who needed the support of the Electors (among whom was Frederick of Saxony) for his arrangements to have his grandson, Charles, crowned King of the Romans. Luther, therefore, met Cardinal Cajetan, the papal legate in Germany, at Augsburg, to argue the case; Cajetan vainly insisted that Luther should submit to the Church. Luther then appealed beyond the authority of the pope to a general council of the Church; he was still anxious for an agreement about his position, even though Leo had now issued a bull upholding indulgences.

Leo also did not want to become embroiled in German affairs, and his power in the Empire remained weak because early in 1519 Maximilian died, and for six months, until Charles V was elected, the Elector Frederick was able to protect Luther unchallenged. All that time Luther's popularity with the German people was growing. In the summer of 1519 he accepted an invitation to go to Leipzig for a public disputation with a notable German theologian, John Eck, who skilfully drove Luther to admit that even a general council might be wrong and that Scripture was the only final authority, and so to admit that he shared the outlook of John Huss.[7] The effect of the controversy

[5] P. 44.   [6] P. 41.   [7] P. 44.

was thus to make Luther's conception of ecclesiastical authority undergo a steady change. He began by asserting that the pope must be subordinate to a general council, then admitted that both popes and councils could and had erred and that Scripture must prevail, and finally concluded that the pope's intractability showed him to be the very Antichrist.

Political circumstances continued to make it possible for Luther to survive the proper punishment for such a heretical stand, and his cause now became a movement that was to grow into a separate ecclesiastical communion in Germany. This development moved forward as Luther went on to think out his ideas still further and consider their implications in a number of widely-read pamphlets. The most important of these were the 'Three Treatises' written in 1520. The first, *To the Christian Nobility of the German Nation*, called upon the German princes, since the clergy had not reformed the Church, to do it themselves. This was their duty, he insisted, since laymen are as important in the life of the Church as the clergy, who have only been set apart for the performance of certain functions and have no special privileges. He was here expounding another Reformation doctrine, which followed from the first, that of 'the priesthood of all believers', the assertion that all Christians have an equal priestly calling in the Church. All have responsibilities towards God, and the princes particularly, as rulers of the people, must consider both their material and their spiritual welfare. The second treatise, *On the Babylonian Captivity of the Church*, questioned the sacramental system of the Church. Luther declared that there were only two sacraments— Baptism and the Eucharist—and denied the validity of the other five recognized by the Church—Penance, Confirmation, Extreme Unction, Holy Orders and Marriage. He also rejected the doctrine of transsubstantiation in the Eucharist.[8] His third treatise, *Of the Liberty of the Christian Man*, developed the religious and ethical implications of his doctrine of justification by faith. He held that this makes the Christian free from slavish obedience to the insistence of the Church upon compliance with its laws; he secures salvation through his faith and not the performance of works. Nevertheless, he insisted, this does not mean that he is free to behave as he chooses. Rather he shows his love of God in his love for men—'Good works do not make a good man, but a good man does good works.'

Luther's proclamation of his views and the widespread popular acclaim he received for them forced Leo at last to act decisively. In the summer of 1520 he issued the bull *Exsurge Domine*, condemning a number of Luther's beliefs, ordering the public burning of his books and threatening him with excommunication unless he recanted. Luther's reply was to burn at Wittenberg, amid cheering students, the papal

[8] P. 34.

bull and, symbolically, the books of canon law as well. Early in 1521, therefore, Leo formally excommunicated him and called upon Charles V to take action against him as a heretic; but the Emperor, though he would have liked to have curtailed Luther's career, did not wish to provoke the German princes and people whose sympathies were so strongly with the reformer. He agreed to give Luther a safe conduct to go to the small town of Worms on the Rhine so that he could defend himself before the Imperial Diet which was to meet there.

At the Diet of Worms, Luther was summoned to recant the heresy contained in his writings, but he refused, saying, 'Unless I am convicted by Scripture and plain reason (for I do not accept the authority of popes and councils, since they have often erred and contradicted each other) . . . I neither can nor will recant anything since it is neither safe nor right to act against conscience.' Charles then outlawed him by placing him under the ban of the Empire, but on his way from Worms he was taken by officers of the Elector of Saxony and lodged in Wartburg Castle near Eisenach. Frederick's action was determined by his wish not to have to defy the Emperor openly. He could keep Luther in his hands without having to admit that he knew anything about him. For Luther, a stage in his religious career was over. His search for personal spiritual peace had led him to defy and then break with the Papacy and so with the whole system of the medieval Church.

Luther and the German people

Luther spent the time of his incarceration by beginning his translation of the Bible into German. He was to finish it by 1534, and it went through three hundred editions in his lifetime. It appealed to contemporary German piety, which was already based upon the Scriptures, but it completed his break with Rome because it emphasized his insistence that the Word of God was the supreme authority in religion.

While Luther was in Wartburg Castle, it proved impossible to enforce the Imperial ban against him in Germany, though severe measures were taken against Lutheran adherents in the Netherlands.[9] In several parts of Saxony monks and nuns began to desert their monasteries, and crowds demonstrated against the Papacy and demanded reforms in the Church. At Wittenberg, another professor at the university, Andrew Carlstadt, who shared Luther's belief in justification by faith, began to initiate changes there. He celebrated the Mass without wearing vestments, omitted the passages making it a sacrifice and the elevation of the elements at the consecration and administered both the bread and the wine to the congregation. Crowds of students and townspeople overthrew altars and smashed images in the churches. The Augustinian friars left the priory there, and many

[9] P. 182.

married, some to former nuns. Then the Zwickau prophets arrived in the town from the borders of Bohemia, and claimed to have received direct visions from God which made the Bible unnecessary.

The town council urgently appealed to Luther to return to Wittenberg which he did in 1522, taking up residence in the deserted priory where he lived for the rest of his life. He secured the expulsion of Carlstadt and preached a series of sermons urging moderation. He accepted the closing of the monasteries, the marriage of the clergy and other changes (and he himself married in 1525), but he restored the altars and ornaments in the churches and the use of vestments. He was afraid that if changes took place too rapidly and were accompanied by violence, the cause of reform would be discredited and opposed by the princes, who would be alarmed by the threat of anarchy in their states. His own ideas of worship were moderate, as he showed when he introduced his reformed services in the parish church in 1523. The Mass was in German instead of Latin, and there was now communion in both kinds; transsubstantiation was denied, but belief in a real presence retained,[10] preaching was accorded an important place in the services, as was the singing by the congregation of German hymns—some of them written by Luther himself—an innovation which proved popular. 'The people sang themselves into heresy,' one of his opponents bitterly complained. On the whole, however, the manner of worship and the arrangement of the churches continued much as before.

Even more alarming to Luther than religious extremism were some of the social consequences of the Reformation. His movement took place in Germany at a time of widespread popular discontent, and there were those who welcomed his message, not because it brought them spiritual satisfaction, but rather because it seemed to support their desire for social and political change. His mission coincided with a period of economic difficulty which affected several classes, but Luther was anxious that their grievances should not become identified with his message because he saw, again, that this would threaten its acceptance by the German rulers.

Among those who suffered from the current circumstances were the Imperial Knights.[11] Under the leadership of Franz von Sickingen, who declared himself a Lutheran, the Rhineland knights proceeded in 1522 to attack the wealthy ecclesiastical principalities of the district; but the local princes combined against them and quickly brought the so-called Knights' War to an end. This episode strengthened the authority of the princes, as against that of the Emperor who had been powerless to take any action himself, but it did not affect the Reformation since Luther had refused to be associated with the movement.

More serious was the Peasants' Revolt, which also was a consequence

[10] P. 173.   [11] P. 21.

of the prevailing situation.[12] It began with a series of isolated risings in south-western Germany in 1524 and by the spring of the next year had spread to many central and southern parts of the country. Castles, manor houses and monasteries were sacked and set alight, and their occupants were slaughtered. Support often came from urban artisans, who were also facing economic distress.[13] Religious extremists put themselves at the head of the movement in many districts, chief among them being Thomas Müntzer, a former follower of Luther, who had come under the influence of the Zwickau prophets. Belonging to a family of peasants himself, Luther at first sympathized with them and believed that many of their grievances were justified. When the risings broke out, he told the lords that they were themselves to blame for the situation, but as the violence and bloodshed increased, his attitude changed. He feared that the peasants had distorted his plea that men should possess their spiritual rights into a demand for political and social rights. He had never intended that his teaching should lead to revolt and bloodshed. Already people were calling the insurgent peasants 'Lutherans', and if it were thought that he supported them all religious reform would be impossible. After the princes had put down the revolt, they would suppress his movement as a threat to law and order.

He went round the country preaching against violence and wrote his bitter pamphlet, *Against the Murdering, Thieving Hordes of the Peasants*, in which he gave his full support to the princes and called upon them to 'smite, slay and stab, secretly or openly, remembering that nothing can be more poisonous, hurtful or devilish than a rebel.' When he wrote these words, the rising was at its height and seemed as if it might plunge all Germany into civil war, but the Electors of Saxony and Hesse and the Duke of Brunswick rapidly united to raise an army, and early in the summer of 1525 they routed a large gathering of peasants at Frankenhausen, and soon resistance was at an end everywhere. Thousands of peasants were slaughtered or hanged.

Luther had been carried away by his excitable temperament, and as a result his vocabulary was often extreme; when his tract was published, therefore, it appeared to be a summons to the princes to treat the defeated rebels without mercy. Yet it is difficult to see that Luther's attitude had much influence on the situation. The peasants would have revolted, and the princes would have repressed them ruthlessly, whatever he had done or said. One effect certainly was that many of the poorer classes now turned to the new revolutionary sects, especially the Anabaptists, which spread in Germany and neighbouring countries, but were almost obliterated by governments which feared their attacks on privilege and property.[14] On the other hand, many

[12] P. 80.   [13] P. 83.   [14] P. 86.   F

Germans had been terrified by the Peasants' Revolt, and Luther gained strong support from the upper and middle classes, who were educated enough to realize the need for religious reform, disliked the power of the Papacy and wished to limit the rights and wealth of the Church. Without them Lutheranism could not have defied both pope and Emperor, and it was with their powerful assistance that it now made progress; at about the same time Luther lost the support of a number of scholars, including Staupitz and Erasmus, because of his attitude towards the Roman Church.[15]

In the same summer that the Peasants' Revolt was being suppressed, Archduke Frederick of Saxony, who had protected Luther, died and was succeeded by his brother, John, who had more sympathy with Luther's religious outlook. In Saxony, therefore, Luther was able to take a step which he had never considered when he made his first criticisms of papal policy. He organized a Lutheran Church, separate from the old Church which was under papal supremacy.[16] His hope that a council would meet to reform the Church had not been fulfilled, and he now believed that the Church should be reformed in Germany wherever possible in defiance of pope and Emperor. Thus Lutheranism began to spread beyond Wittenberg and Saxony into many other parts of Germany.

The general initial popularity of Lutheranism was displayed by the way in which from the 1520s the people of the free cities, often partly for economic reasons, were the first to turn against the Papacy and induce the town councils, sometimes unwillingly, to reform the churches within their walls.[17] By 1524 Nuremberg, the most powerful of these cities, had put Luther's ideas into effect. Its example was quickly followed by Strasburg, Ulm, Augsburg and many smaller cities. Between 1528 and 1531 the leading northern cities, including Hamburg, Bremen and Magdeburg, did the same. By then 213 or some two-thirds of the free cities had adopted the cause of the Reformation. Of the larger cities, only Regensburg, which was dominated by the conservative Dukes of Bavaria, and Cologne, which was restrained by its Archbishop, remained consistently faithful to the Papacy. In those cities which became Lutheran, a popular Reformation was accomplished by being undertaken by the town council or the craft guilds which dissolved the monasteries, reformed worship and placed new pastors in the churches.

In the 1520s most of the German princes, though very critical of the Papacy, were opposed to Lutheranism. Nevertheless, some came sincerely to accept it, while others appreciated the apparent advantages to be gained by supporting it, though the gains they made from the Reformation in fact were not very great.[18] The first to adopt the cause of the Reformation was Albert of Brandenburg, Grand Master of the

[15] P. 62.   [16] P. 109.   [17] P. 83.   [18] P. 110.

Teutonic Knights, a military order which governed East Prussia. In 1525 he declared himself a Lutheran and made himself the first Duke of Prussia.[19] His action caused a sensation, but his lead was followed by several other rulers in Germany itself. Among the first were the Landgrave of Hesse in 1526 and Margrave of Brandenburg-Ansbach, the Dukes of Schleswig and Brunswick and the Count of Mansfeld in 1528. In these states the rulers adopted the new faith and declared it to be the religion of their subjects; they made the necessary changes in religious organization along the lines of those in Saxony.

The Reformation in Germany was thus both a religious and a political, a popular and a princely movement. It was not really a single, great development, but rather consisted of a number of separate, localised reformations, each of which was organized by the city council or the prince, who were able to make the religious changes within their territory. This arrangement was entirely acceptable to Luther, who held that the responsibility of rulers towards their subjects made it their duty to reform the churches under their care. Moreover, Luther was dependent upon local authorities and especially upon the princes. Their power had preserved him in the first stages of the movement, and now the prevailing political situation in Germany made it inevitable that this alone could promote religious reform in the country.

The development of Lutheranism

So far Charles V had not been able to do anything to check the growth of Lutheranism and princely power, though he strongly regretted the way these developments prevented him gaining German support for a campaign to meet the Turkish threat to the Habsburg territories.[20] Soon after the Diet of Worms he left for Spain, and the ban against Luther remained unenforced. In 1525, however, Charles added greatly to his prestige by his victory at Pavia;[21] and when the Diet met at Speyer the next year, he instructed his brother, the Archduke Ferdinand, to demand that those who defied the laws of the Empire should be made to submit. But the princes, both Roman Catholic and Lutheran, were not prepared to take any action against each other which would weaken them and strengthen the Emperor. They unanimously agreed, therefore, to the Recess of 1526, which asserted that each prince 'should so live, govern and conduct himself as he hopes and trusts to answer for his behaviour to God and to the Emperor.' The growing power of Lutheranism and its divisive effect on Germany were clearly revealed. In return for his acceptance of the Recess, the Lutheran princes granted Charles financial and military aid for his wars, including the troops which sacked Rome in 1527.[22]

When the Diet met again at Speyer in 1529, Charles was in a much stronger position. The Turkish threat to Vienna had been averted, and his success in Italy was to bring him the Ladies' Peace of Cambrai with France and the Treaty of Barcelona with the Papacy.[23] He was prepared to take a firmer stand against the Lutheran princes, and Ferdinand was able to persuade the Diet to replace the Recess of 1526 by another which stated that, while Roman Catholics should be tolerated throughout the Empire, Lutherans would not be accepted in Roman Catholic territory, and that there should be no more changes in religion and no further secularization of ecclesiastical property. The Lutheran minority, consisting of six princes and fourteen cities, thereupon issued a Protestation asserting that 'they must protest and testify before God that they could consent to nothing contrary to His Word'. From this Protestantism came to take its name.

The Lutherans were further weakened by the failure of the Colloquy of Marburg later that year.[24] In 1530 Charles, having consolidated his triumphs, came in person to the Diet of Augsburg, wishing to settle the religious problem and prepare an expedition against the Turks. His hope was to be able to obtain the summoning of a Council of the Church, which would initiate reforms acceptable to the Lutherans. He had secured papal approval of this in principle, but only on condition that the Lutherans were first reconciled to the Church, a reconciliation he sought to secure at Augsburg. He asked the Lutherans to state their position. Luther himself, being still formally under the Imperial ban, could not come to Augsburg, but his friend and fellow-theologian, Philip Melancthon, drew up the Confession of Augsburg. This was a moderate, conciliatory statement of Lutheran beliefs—so much so that it alarmed Luther—but neither Roman Catholic nor Lutheran princes were really in the mood for conciliation, and the Papal legate, Cardinal Campeggio, insisted that the Lutherans must accept full papal supremacy. By the autumn, the Lutheran princes considered the situation so hopeless that they withdrew from the Diet, which proceeded to assert that all sequestered property should be returned to the Church and the Lutherans must accept its authority within six months.

The Confession of Augsburg, produced by Melancthon with the intention of bringing about agreement and unity, instead became an important stage in the development of a separate Lutheran Church by providing it with a broad statement of belief. The failure of the attempts at religious pacification in Germany meant that the country was now divided between rival faiths, and the Lutheran Church had gained an assured position among its people and princes.

Religious disunity now led to inevitable political disunity. In the face of the threat to their position, the Protestant princes, led by the Elector John of Saxony and the Landgrave Philip of Hesse, formed a

[23] P. 148.   [24] P. 173.

league for mutual defence in the town hall of the small town of Schmalkalden on the borders of Saxony and Hesse at the end of 1530. Its eight princes and eleven cities demanded security for all Protestants, including Evangelicals (as the supporters of Zwingli and later of Calvin were termed) and the settlement of religious differences by a Council of the Church to be held in Germany so as to be beyond papal domination. They pledged themselves that, 'wherever any one of us is attacked on account of the Word of God and the doctrine of the Gospel', they would all 'immediately come to his assistance.'

Renewed war against France and the continuous threat to his lands from the Turks in the Balkans again compelled Charles to compromise rather than meet the threat of force offered by the League of Schmalkalden. In 1532 he agreed, therefore, that the Diet of Nuremberg should publish the Peace of Nuremberg, which suspended all action against heretics until a Council of the Church should meet. The League of Schmalkalden promised him assistance against the Turks, and was able also to increase in size and assert itself. Augsburg, Frankfurt, Hamburg and Hanover became members, and in 1534 it sent troops to restore the exiled Duke of Würtemburg to the territories from which he had been expelled by Charles V some fifteen years earlier. A precarious religious peace was maintained in Germany for some fifteen years after the formation of the League of Schmalkalden, during which Lutheranism continued to consolidate and extend its position in the country. By 1545 all north-eastern and north-western Germany was Lutheran, and so was much of the south-west; Bavaria, and the bishoprics along the Main alone stood out.

The religious struggle

During that time, a last attempt at reunion was made. Charles convened the Conference of Ratisbon (Regensburg) in 1541 between three Roman Catholic and three Lutheran theologians. The pope sent a legate, Cardinal Contarini, a noted moderate and Erasmian reformer. Doctrinal agreement was reached on most of the controversial subjects, including the crucial question of justification. But Contarini, in his search for a common formula on this subject, was accused in many quarters of having expressed heretical views, and the subsequent hostility of Luther combined with political rivalries, prevented anything coming of the conference.

In 1544 the Treaty of Crespy again freed Charles from warfare against France and enabled him to transfer the Spanish army from Italy to Germany; and the Papacy had at last agreed to summon a general council, which met at Trent in 1545. Moreover, divisions had appeared among the Protestant princes. When young, Philip of Hesse had been married, for political reasons, to Duke George of Saxony's daughter, but the marriage soon broke down, and until his conversion to Lutheranism he had a number of mistresses. In 1540 he wished to divorce his wife and marry again, but Luther firmly upheld the permanence of marriage and in the end had to agree to Philip taking a second 'wife'. When the bigamy became known, the scandal troubled the last months of Luther's life (he died in 1546) and caused Philip to withdraw temporarily from the League of Schmalkalden. The Protestant ranks were also weakened when Charles won over Maurice, the new Duke of Saxony, by promising him his cousin's electoral lands and dignity, and when Duke William of Bavaria pledged his help wholeheartedly to the Imperial cause.

Charles decided the time had come for him to strike. In 1546 he imposed the Imperial ban against John of Saxony and Philip of Hesse (who had now rejoined the League of Schmalkalden), and while Spanish troops crossed the Alps into southern Germany, Maurice invaded electoral Saxony. In the resulting Schmalkaldic War, Charles decisively defeated the Protestant forces at the Battle of Mühlberg in Saxony on the Elbe in April 1547. John of Saxony and Philip of Hesse fell into his hands and were put in prison. Maurice was given the electoral title and the greater part of the lands that went with it. The victory of Charles seemed complete.

Its very extent, however, deprived him of its fruits. The princes, Roman Catholic and Protestant alike, resented the imprisonment of John of Saxony and Philip of Hesse as arbitrary and striking at the dignity of their order. Still more, when Charles summoned the Diet to Augsburg in 1547 and required it to finance an Imperial standing army to enforce the laws of the Empire, they realized that his victory threatened their power and independence. Pope Paul III, too, was alarmed by Charles V's triumph and deserted him. The Council of Trent ignored his wishes by first considering dogma instead of ecclesiastical reform, which might have placated the Protestants, and in the spring of 1547 it was removed to Bologna to secure it from Imperial control. The Protestants at the Diet of Augsburg, therefore, refused to submit to the Council; the most that the princes would accept was the Interim of Augsburg which made minor concessions to the Protestants, such as clerical marriage and communion in both kinds, but otherwise insisted upon the general observance of Roman Catholicism. Such a compromise proved unacceptable to either side, and the pope rejected it.

In 1550, a new pope, Julius III, reconvened the Council at Trent, but it had already condemned the beliefs of the Protestants as heretical and now refused to consider negotiating with them. Charles V's hope of a religious settlement in Germany was now seen to have failed, and the Protestants became more restive. Their revolt was led by Maurice of Saxony who, once he had become Elector, considered that his position was now threatened both by the increase in Imperial power and by the hatred of the Protestant princes for him because of his desertion of their cause. In 1551, after assisting an Imperial army to recover the secularized bishopric of Magdeburg, he kept it for himself. He was now so powerful in northern Germany that the Protestant princes had to seek to come to terms with him. With him they formed a defensive alliance, the League of Torgau, and in 1552 negotiated at Chambord an agreement with Henry II, the new King of France, who promised to give them military asistance in return for the cession of the bishoprics of Metz, Toul and Verdun in Lorraine, which were strategic fortresses near the French frontier.

When fighting was renewed, Charles was caught defenceless and had to flee across the Alps into Carinthia. None of the Roman Catholic princes, not even the Duke of Bavaria, came to his aid; they too had realized the political significance for them of an Imperial victory. With the Emperor out of Germany, Ferdinand had to negotiate with the triumphant Maurice of Saxony. This resulted in the Convention of Passau, a truce which agreed to the release of the two Protestant princes and the suspension of the Interim until the summoning of yet another Diet. Charles secured a loan from the Fuggers and once more attempted to return to Germany, but he failed to regain Metz, which the French had occupied, and in January 1553 left the country forever.

During the following years Maurice was killed in a skirmish with the Margrave of Brandenburg-Kulmbach, with whom he had a dispute; both the Habsburgs and the Valois faced imminent bankruptcy; and Charles announced his intention of abdicating as Emperor in favour of Ferdinand.[25] As a result of these developments the Diet of Augsburg, which was presided over by Ferdinand, was able in 1555 to reach a compromise settlement of the German question.

Lengthy negotiations produced the Religious Peace of Augsburg, which maintained an uneasy settlement in the country for sixty-three years. This recognized Roman Catholicism and Lutheranism as the two official confessions of the Empire, though not Calvinism which had by now begun to establish itself in Germany.[26] Each prince was to be able to decide which of the two he would adopt for his state, and his subjects must accept it, but dissidents should be allowed to move elsewhere after disposing of their property at a reasonable price. The free cities, in which Roman Catholicism had made some gains as a result of Charles V's recovery of power and the Interim, were to accord equal treatment to both Roman Catholics and Lutherans. Ferdinand was determined that there should not be a majority of

[25] P. 201.   [26] P. 182.

Lutheran princes in the Empire and, particularly, that the prince-bishoprics of Mainz, Cologne and Trier should not become Protestant as this would mean Protestant control of the college of Electors which chose a new Emperor. He insisted, therefore, that Church property should remain as it had been in 1552 and that no more should be secularized, so that if a prince-bishop became a Lutheran he would have to resign his office and be replaced by a Roman Catholic prelate. This provision, called the Ecclesiastical Reservation, was not included as a clause in the formal treaty accepted by the Diet, but was issued as an Imperial edict and accepted only reluctantly by the princes.

The Peace of Augsburg not only accepted the fact of religious disunity in Germany, but of political disunity as well. The failure of Charles V's attempt to solve the religious question had also resulted in a failure to assert Imperial authority in Germany. The country continued divided with effective power remaining in the hands of the various princes at a time when other European nations were being made into strong, united national states under sovereign rulers. Even a long and destructive war in the next century did not change this situation, which lasted for over three hundred years.

Lutheranism and the Counter-Reformation

With the signing of the Peace of Augsburg, the first phase of the Reformation in Germany had come to an end. Luther's struggle for personal spiritual peace and detestation of contemporary ecclesiastical abuses had culminated in an unexpected result. It had destroyed the unity of the Church, a situation that neither Luther nor Charles V nor, indeed, anyone else had orginally wanted to bring about. So strongly had his ideas appealed to the German people that at one time it seemed as if the whole country might become Lutheran, but this had not been achieved by the middle of the sixteenth century when the great age of the Reformation came to an end. Lutheranism had secured a large part of Germany, but it did not gain a hold over other European countries, except for the Scandinavian states, and future Protestant expansion lay with the greater international appeal of Calvinism.

Nevertheless, Protestantism continued to gain strength in Germany for some years after the Peace of Augsburg. The prohibition of further secularization of ecclesiastical property was not effective. Protestant princes interpreted the Ecclesiastical Reservation to mean that only when a prince-bishop, elected by a Roman Catholic chapter, became a Lutheran must he vacate his office and its property; if the chapter itself became Protestant and elected a Protestant prince-bishop, he could retain that dignity and secularize its property. Indeed, the

Protestant princes temporarily obtained from the Emperor the Imperial Declaration, a personal decree which set aside the Ecclesiastical Reservation in their favour. More princes, including prince-bishops, became Protestants and secularized ecclesiastical property, and by 1577 Hildesheim was the only northern German bishopric not under Protestant control. Contemporary Venetian envoys in Germany agree that it was likely to be only a question of time before the whole country became Protestant.

In the later part of the sixteenth century, however, Protestantism in Germany was faced by the rivalry of the Counter-Reformation movement. The Jesuits, who had founded a German college in Rome in 1552, obtained possession of the University of Ingoldstadt in 1563, and it became as important for the Counter-Reformation as Wittenberg had previously been for Luther's work; Loyola called it his 'little Benjamin'. From it, the Jesuits established throughout Germany schools and colleges which combined sound general education with the inculcation or revival of Roman Catholicism.[27] The gains of the Counter-Reformation were mainly in southern Germany, where—in contrast to northern Germany which remained almost entirely Lutheran —Calvinism was strong, and its lack of recognition by the Peace of Augsburg served to disunite the Protestant forces. In the south-east of Germany, Roman Catholicism gained the support of the Habsburgs, who crushed Protestantism in their family lands; in the southern centre the rulers of Bavaria (especially William V from 1564 to 1576) took the lead; while the Prince-Bishop of Würzburg combined reform of the clergy in his great diocese with the expulsion of Protestants, and other southern bishops followed his example. Even in the north-west it had a centre in Cologne, where the entry of Bavarian troops in 1582 was not opposed by the Lutheran princes largely because the Archbishop-Elector had become a Calvinist.

Trials of strength with Protestants resulted in Roman Catholic successes. In 1573 the Prince-Abbot of Dernbach in Fulda forced the Protestant knights of his domains to become Roman Catholic, and the Archbishop-Elector of Mainz did the same the next year. By the end of the sixteenth century, the Roman Catholic Church had made great gains in Germany. Though the Peace of Augsburg remained in force, it seemed in danger of being undermined by the greater energy, unity and initiative of the Roman Catholic compared with the Protestant princes. The resentment and alarm this development caused among Protestants produced a situation which contributed towards the outbreak of the Thirty Years War in the next century.

[27] P. 206.

II

THE CALVINIST REFORMATION

Zwingli and Zurich

Although Luther was the first religious reformer to bring about a movement which renounced papal obedience and adopted its own changes in doctrine, worship and ecclesiastical government, he was not the only one. The abuses of the Church in Germany were much the same as elsewhere, and the desire for reform was widespread in Europe. Successful reform depended, however, on local circumstances. Germany was a region in which political and social conditions favoured religious change, and the same applied to Switzerland.

Switzerland, like the German states, was part of the Holy Roman Empire, though its inclusion within the Imperial boundaries was by now only nominal. From the end of the thirteenth century, the several small Swiss sovereign states or cantons, some German-speaking and some French-speaking, had resisted attempts to strengthen Imperial rule over them and formed themselves into the Confederation. The ensuing struggle in the fourteenth and fifteenth centuries culminated in the victory over the Empire at Dornach in 1499, which marked the real establishment of Swiss independence since the Confederation was released from the payment of the Imperial tax. The Confederation remained no more than a loose association of mostly self-governing states; it had a Diet, but in practice the laws it passed were resolutions which the individual cantons might or might not accept and enforce. There was, therefore, as in Germany during the sixteenth century no central power able to impose a uniform religious settlement upon the local authorities.

Economically and socially there were considerable differences between the Swiss cantons. Some were inhabited mainly by peasants engaged in small-scale farming and had no settlements larger than little market-towns. Zurich, Berne and Basle, however, were quite rich and powerful city-states, which had benefited from their position on important European trade routes and shared in the profits gained by supplying mercenary troops to the armies of the greater powers. Such foreign contacts had enabled them to share also in the Christian humanist movement of the times which had encouraged the wish for religious reform. The desire for change was further encouraged by the fact that all the cantons were under the religious control of arch-bishops in Germany or France, who were widely disliked as foreigners although they exercised little supervision over the Swiss clergy, whose standards of morality and education were much the same as those in the rest of western Europe.

The Swiss Reformation began at the time Luther was making his protest at Wittenberg, though it was almost independent of him and was to take a very different course. In the early days of this Reformation, the most important figure was Ulrich Zwingli (1484-1531), who was born less than two months after Luther in the German-speaking part of the country. His father was a poor farmer, but he followed the usual means of advancement through the university and ordination. He studied at Basle, Berne and Vienna, but received a different education from that which Luther had experienced as a university student. He had a much greater knowledge of the new learning than the German reformer. He came in contact with the works of the Christian humanists, especially Erasmus, which gave him a new understanding of the Bible and the part it should play in upholding Christian belief and life. He never experienced the same harrowing spiritual doubts as Luther and although he always insisted that he attained his religious outlook independently of him, it is likely that he was affected by the impact of Lutheran ideas upon the Swiss cities which preceded his reforming activities.

After his ordination in 1506, Zwingli became a parish priest and twice went to Italy as a chaplain to the men from his parish who had been hired as mercenaries in the papal cause during the Italian Wars. He became known as a good preacher and in 1518 was appointed to a minor preaching post at Zurich Cathedral. At first he preached against such ecclesiastical abuses as had aroused Luther's protests, including the selling of indulgences, but then he went on to attack images in churches, the veneration of relics and, finally, the doctrine of transub-stantiation and the supremacy of the pope. Indeed, he showed himself to be more radical and uncompromising than Luther, who was prepared to retain many traditional practices and ceremonies from the past. Zwingli wanted to abolish whatever could not be justified from the Bible, and he insisted that religion was essentially a personal, spiritual experience which did not require sacraments and ceremonies to sustain it. His ideas seem to have been closer to those of Carlstadt, who visited him in Zurich.

The city council was impressed by Zwingli's preaching, and between

1522 and 1525 he was able to carry out his religious changes in Zurich with its support. In the cathedral and the other churches in the city he removed all the outward signs and symbols of medieval religion—images and pictures, shrines and relics and even organs—as hindrances to the true worship of God. He introduced sermons, lectures on the Bible and services in German. The monasteries were dissolved and clerical marriage was allowed. Finally, in 1525, the Mass was abolished and replaced by a simple communion service in which the people no longer knelt at the altar to communicate, but received the bread and wine from the minister in their seats.

Since Zurich had a population of only 5 400, the city council were anxious not to provoke either the Papacy or the Bishop of Constance, within whose diocese the canton was situated. On the other hand, it seems that the Papacy did not wish to be drawn into a dispute in Switzerland at a time when it still needed Swiss mercenaries, although Zwingli was, in fact, able to prevent Zurich hiring them out for patriotic and religious reasons.[1] At any rate, by the end of 1525 the authority of both pope and bishop had been abolished in the city and the exercise of ecclesiastical authority transferred to the city council, which set up for this purpose a law-court composed of the clergy, the magistrates and lay representatives from the congregations. An important part of the bishop's former jurisdiction, which it took over, was concerned with matrimonial matters, and from this it developed a more extensive moral jurisdiction, punishing couples who stood together in doorways or behind barns, women who received male visitors, and even innkeepers who neglected to report any immoral behaviour by their guests. When church attendance was made compulsory in 1529, the court punished also those who were not present regularly at public worship, and became concerned with the general enforcement of ecclesiastical discipline over the people. Such systematic oversight of morals, which had not been attempted by Luther (and probably would not have been possible in Germany) was an important contribution by Zwingli to the development of the Reformation.

In Zurich, lay people were not only given a place in the disciplinary activity of the Church, but also in its teaching function. In place of the daily choir services in the Cathedral, Zwingli instituted *lectiones publicae*, which he called 'prophesyings'. These were devoted to the study and interpretation of the Bible—the Old Testament in the morning and the New Testament in the evening—and laymen were encouraged to attend and take part in the discussions. These 'prophesyings' were later adopted by the English Puritans, who held them during the reign of Queen Elizabeth I in an attempt to spread their beliefs in the Church of England.

As a reformer, Zwingli was more revolutionary than Luther, not

[1] P. 130.

only in practice, but also in belief, including his doctrine of the sacraments. This was shown at the Colloquy of Marburg in 1529.[2] Philip of Hesse wished to bring Luther and Zwingli together in the hope that union could be achieved between the two reformed faiths. They met in his castle at Marburg, and though they reached agreement on a number of matters, they found themselves completely opposed over the sacramental issue. Luther could not accept the scholastic doctrine of transsubstantiation. He was never himself quite clear what he did believe happened to the bread and wine in the Mass at the consecration, but he always insisted that Christ was really and truly present at every celebration. Zwingli, on the other hand, held that the communion service was essentially a commemoration of Christ's sacrifice for mankind and regarded the elements as unchanged symbols of His body and blood. At Marburg Castle, Luther pulled back the heavy velvet cloth on the table at which they sat and chalked on it the Latin version of the words of Jesus at the Last Supper—'*Hoc est corpus meum*' (This is my body)—and would not accept Zwingli's interpretation of them as a figure of speech meaning 'this signifies my body'. After four days of discussion, the two reformers parted without having come to an agreement, and the alliance between the German and Swiss movements, wanted by others as well as by Philip of Hesse, was never achieved.

Though Zwinglianism was rebuffed in Germany, its influence spread in Switzerland. Other cities, notably Basle and Berne, reformed the churches within their limits and repudiated papal authority; but five cantons resisted the movement, partly because of fear of domination by Zurich, and remained Roman Catholic. They formed, with Habsburg support, an alliance aimed at the suppression of heresy in Switzerland. In the war that followed, Zwingli considering that it was the duty of Christian ministers and laymen alike to take part in a just conflict, joined Zurich's army and was killed at the Battle of Kappel in 1531. The Swiss Reformation, however, was not destroyed. After the war, it was agreed that each canton should be allowed to determine its own religious settlement. Zwingli was succeeded in Zurich by his son-in-law, Henry Bullinger, who was later able to secure an agreement which united the Reformed Churches, Zwinglian and Calvinist, and so preserved the unity of the Swiss Reformation.

The influence of Zwingli was limited compared with that of Luther and, later, Calvin as reformers. Zurich was too small a place to be important in itself, and the union of ecclesiastical and municipal authority, which worked effectively there, was not suitable for adoption elsewhere. The expansion of Zwinglianism, therefore, was inhibited in much the same way as that of Lutheranism, and in addition it did not have as large an original base as Lutheranism did in Germany. Without change, Zwinglianism could not take root in other places

[2] P. 164.

where reformed ideas were adopted. This was particularly shown in the Imperial free city of Strasburg, which in 1527 came under the influence of Martin Bucer (1491-1551), who on Zwingli's death became the leader of the Reformed Churches in Switzerland and southern Germany. His views on the Eucharist and other matters of doctrine were substantially the same as those of Zwingli, but he insisted that Church and state should be completely separate, though co-operating, authorities and that the Church alone should have the power to impose a moral discipline. This made possible a form of reformed religion that could exist without reliance upon the state, and under him Strasburg became an important centre of refuge for Protestant exiles and reformers; but the city lacked both the natural defences and military strength of Switzerland, and this region was not to become a flourishing stronghold of Protestantism.

A further limitation of Zwinglianism was its close identification with the new urban and educated classes in Switzerland. Zwingli's ecclesiastical reforms were not inspired or followed by any wish to effect social changes. The city council of Zurich, which put his ideas into effect and controlled his Church, was dominated by the wealthier commercial and manufacturing classes. The urban artisans and the peasants in the surrounding area of countryside ruled by the city, who had at first been strongly in favour of him, came to lose their enthusiasm as he failed to concede to their wishes and agreed to the imposition of the death-penalty on Anabaptists. Indeed, it may be that his indifference to these classes was a cause of the numerical inferiority of his side which contributed towards his military defeat and death.

Calvin and Geneva

While Luther and Zwingli were both pioneers of the first phase of the Reformation, they were succeeded in its later phase by John Calvin (1509-64). His career as a reformer took place when Christian unity under the direction of the Papacy had already been successfully challenged in Europe and new religious movements firmly established and organized. He did not have to struggle to bring himself to accept the idea of personal dissidence when he became dissatisfied with the religion in which he had been brought up. A new way had already been made to which he could turn and which he could open up further. It was a situation which well suited his logical, systematic manner of thought and his great organizing ability.

He was born at Noyon in Picardy. His father, like Luther's, was a self-made, socially-ambitious man, who had become a lawyer of some importance in the town, but the family background was not that of rural, popular piety, but rather of sophisticated, humanistic urbanism.

Calvin's entry upon an ecclesiastical career came about, not through sudden personal conversion, but because it was the traditional way of life of one who wished to devote himself to scholarship and literature. His father secured for him in 1523 a small chaplaincy attached to Noyon Cathedral to provide for his maintenance while studying theology at the University of Paris. He was admitted on this occasion to minor orders, but never proceeded to the priesthood as was expected of him. In 1528 he went to Orleans and Bourges to study law at the wish of his father, who died, however, in 1531, leaving him free to resume his studies in Paris. At all three universities he met groups of French humanists, who had been influenced by Erasmus and were advocates of the reform of abuses in the French Church, and also some who openly favoured the ideas of Luther. Soon after his return to Paris he underwent a spiritual experience, 'God subdued my soul to docility by a sudden conversion'. This took him unhesitatingly to the acceptance of Protestantism, and he became a close associate of those who were suspected of holding heretical beliefs.

He made his decision at a perilous time. In 1534 the 'day of the placards' was followed by Francis I's enforcement of the laws against heresy.[3] With other humanists and Protestants, Calvin had to flee for safety from France and went to Basle, the home of Erasmus and by then an important centre of the Swiss Reformation.

In Basle he published in 1536 the first edition of his *Institutes of the Christian Religion*, which Lord Acton described as 'the finest work of Reformation literature'. Its purpose was to combine a theological exposition of the Bible and an assertion of the principles of the true Christian faith which should be based upon it. Though he continued to produce longer and fuller versions of it for the rest of his life, from the first it was a clear and careful explanation of his fundamental religious beliefs; the later versions were important mainly for the development of his ideas about the organization of the Church. It had an immense effect when it appeared; it seemed to the sixteenth century to provide a complete and orderly system of belief derived from the truth of the Scriptures.

For Calvin, the central reality of Christianity was the absolute power and supremacy of God, who created the world in order that man might come to know Him. He believed that the medieval Church had dangerously obscured this by allowing the popular veneration of the Virgin Mary and the saints. He held, however, that man, because of his sinfulness, could not approach Him by his own efforts in the form of masses, penances, pilgrimages or any such undertakings, but only through faith in Christ, the God-made-man and true revealer of Him. The two sacraments of the New Testament, Baptism and the Eucharist, had been ordained to provide man with the continual assurance of

[3] P. 221.

divine guidance in seeking this faith, and Calvin did not accept Zwingli's idea of the purely commemorative nature of the Eucharist.

To him, God was not only the creator and ruler of the world but also the judge and lawgiver of men, and because He was omnipotent, He was not to be influenced by good works or other human attempts to gain salvation. Calvin's belief in the uselessness of mere human effort led him to accept Luther's doctrine of justification by faith alone, and he brought it to its logical conclusion by his insistence on the doctrine of predestination. The faith in Jesus Christ, which both brought man to the knowledge of God and was the sole way in which he could be justified, was the gift of God and, therefore, was not given to everyone but only to those whom God had predestined to eternal life. 'We call predestination,' he wrote in the *Institutes*, 'God's eternal decree, by which He determined what He willed to become of each man. For all are not created in equal condition; rather, eternal life is ordained for some, eternal damnation for others;' and again, 'God hath once for all determined both whom He would admit to salvation and whom He would condemn to destruction. We affirm that this counsel, as far as it concerns the elect, is founded on his gratuitous mercy, totally irrespective of human merit, but that to those whom He devotes to condemnation, the gate of life is closed by a just and irreprehensible and incomprehensible judgment.' Thus, the decision had been made by God at the beginning of time, and man could do nothing to change God's decree of predestination. If man was destined to eternal salvation, he was among the elect and could never fall from grace in the future. And like Luther, Calvin claimed that his teachings were to be found in the New Testament and the writings of St Augustine.

In the year that Calvin's *Institutes* were first published, he paid a visit to the Swiss French-speaking city of Geneva, arriving at a momentous period in its history. With the assistance of Berne, which after Zwingli's death aspired to become the leading Protestant canton, Geneva had risen against the two authorities who had long tried to exercise control over it—the Bishop of Geneva and the Duke of Savoy. The bishop fled from Geneva in 1533, and the duke's army was defeated in 1535. Protestant preachers from Berne, led by a Frenchman, William Farel (1489-1565), persuaded the city council, which had declared its independence, to adopt the reformed religion. The monasteries were dissolved, the Mass was abolished and papal authority was formally renounced. But the Reformation here was superficial, and Farel had great difficulty in enforcing the decrees of the city council imposing moral discipline and church attendance upon the citizens.

Calvin intended to spend only a night at Geneva, but his *Institutes* had already made him well-known among Protestants, and Farel asked him to stay and complete the work of reform which was proving too much for him. Calvin wanted to be a scholar and writer rather than engage in public life, but Farel convinced him that it was God's will that he should undertake the work. The two men set out together to bring about the changes they wanted in Geneva, but many of the citizens were not prepared to submit to their authority. In 1538 their opponents secured control of the city council, and the two reformers were ordered to leave the city.

Calvin went to Strasburg, where Bucer's ideas of ecclesiastical organization had an important influence upon him, and he married there the widow of an Anabaptist. In 1540, however, the reform party in Geneva, which had regained control of the city council, asked him to return. He accepted their invitation on condition that in future no obstacle would be placed in the way of his changes. He went back to the city in 1541 and spent the rest of his life there. During that time he held no other office than that of a preacher, but although he became the most powerful man there, it was only after fourteen years that he was able to triumph fully over all opposition.

In the ordering of public worship in the Genevan churches, Calvin followed the same principle of austerity as Zwingli. His services, too, were marked by plainness and simplicity, and there was a similar emphasis upon the importance of the sermon and instruction of the people. He himself enjoyed music, but he mistrusted its use in worship. He thought that, like the rites and ceremonies of medieval worship, it diverted people from truly seeking the knowledge of God. He banned musical instruments from church services, but he introduced congregational singing, and this became a very popular and, therefore, powerful aspect of the Calvinist movement. At the same time, he believed that everything in worship must come from the Scriptures, and so metrical psalms took the place of Luther's hymns in his services. Though in his doctrine of the sacraments, he did not believe with Zwingli that the communion service was a mere commemoration, neither did he accept Luther's retention of a bodily presence of Christ in the elements. He taught that Christ was spiritually present in the sacrament and would bestow the power of His grace on all true believers at the service. It was a spiritual presence linked with a bodily ceremony—'the spirit of God is the means of our partaking, which is therefore said to be a spiritual partaking.'

One of Calvin's first actions on his return to Geneva was to draw up, with the support of the city council, the Ecclesiastical Ordinances of 1541 laying down his ideas of Church government. Rejecting the whole organization of the medieval Church as contrary to the outlook of the New Testament, he modelled his arrangements on what he believed had been the practice in the early Church in Apostolic times. There were no bishops, but all ministers or presbyters were equal, and so his system became known in Britain as Presbyterianism. The duty of the ministers was to preach, administer the sacraments and attend to the spiritual welfare of the people. They were assisted in upholding moral discipline in their congregations by elders, who were laymen chosen with Calvin's reluctant agreement by the city council, and by deacons, also laymen, who were responsible for the relief of the poor. In this way Calvin gave the laity a prominent part in religious affairs, and leading members of the long-established families of the city became important in the management of his Church.

Supreme control over the Church was exercised by the consistory, which comprised the Genevan clergy and twelve elders chosen annually by the congregations. One of its main functions was to act as a court to supervise the religion and morals of the people and enforce the strict ecclesiastical discipline enjoined by the Ecclesiastical Ordinances. Although Calvin did not believe that men could gain their salvation by what they did in this world, he insisted that all must honour God by acting according to His will. At first, however, the consistory was not a very effective body. Only when it came to contain more ministers than elders among its members, and when the city council in 1555 conceded it the right to pronounce excommunication against offenders, did it succeed in imposing upon the city a strict moral code which made every sin a crime. It met every Thursday, and its surviving minutes show it forbidding any work or pleasure on Sundays, cursing and swearing, gambling and dancing, extravagance in dress and excessive meals. Of course, the idea of such ecclesiastical discipline was not new. Medieval ecclesiastical courts had often tried to control people's behaviour in this way, but they had rarely been able to act as effectively as Zwingli had done in Zurich and Calvin could in Geneva.

Though Calvin followed Zwingli in insisting upon obedience to the moral law by all the people, he shared Bucer's insistence upon the separation of Church and state. The consistory not only tried moral offenders, but also sought them out; in every parish, two of its members, accompanied by the local minister, went regularly round the streets so that 'their eyes might be on the people.' At the same time, Calvin held that the state must obey the teaching of the Church, and when he had succeeded in getting the city council to recognize the full authority of the consistory, he was able to ensure that its decisions were enforced by the magistrates as the agents of the Church. Excommunication meant outlawry and banishment from the city, and punishments of varying severity followed condemnation by the synod. Thus, in one day, a man was sentenced to be executed for blasphemy, two men to be pierced in the tongue for lewd singing, a woman to be fined for curling her hair and a girl of thirteen to be publicly birched for absence from church on the previous Sunday. In 1546 Calvin persuaded the city council to replace the taverns by evangelical refreshment places, where drinking was to be accompanied by readings from the Bible and meals to be preceded by the saying of grace, but these all failed to attract customers, and the taverns had to be reopened.

Of course, there were those in Geneva who opposed Calvin's control over the city, and his position was not secure until he had got the support of its most important families, about 1 500 men who had the right to elect the city council which governed the population of 13 000. Many of the citizens were not prepared to submit to ecclesiastical jurisdiction over their private lives and were able to resist his authority on a number of occasions. The crisis came when Michael Servetus (1511-53), a Spanish scholar who denied the divinity of Christ, escaped from a bishop's court in Lyons and fled to Geneva. He had already written a thorough-going attack on Calvin's *Institutes*, and Calvin, since he was at this time having particular difficulties with his opponents, suspected that they had invited Servetus to come to Geneva to challenge his regime. Servetus was arrested, found guilty of heresy and executed by burning, Calvin having failed to get the sentence changed to the more merciful one of beheading. Calvin's opponents were discredited, and in 1555 the most prominent of them fled abroad, leaving the city council virtually subservient to Calvin for the remaining nine years of his life. Servetus was not alone in being put to death in Calvin's Geneva, particularly during the last years; by then Calvin's moral code had gained general acceptance, and his constitution and principles, though not so rigidly enforced, survived unaltered in the city for a century and a half.

Indeed, Calvin had increasing success in moulding Geneva according to his beliefs. Most of the citizens were prepared to obey his precepts, and the most determined of the dissidents were either banished or left the city. They were more than replaced by Protestants from other countries, who came there either because they fled to the city for safety from persecution or because they wished to learn from and work with Calvin. He was very ready to secure the granting of citizenship to foreigners, particularly to French religious refugees, and their support made his position even stronger in the city. His opponents naturally disliked this development, but during the last nine years of his life, when he was so powerful, more than 5 000 foreigners were allowed to settle in the city.

The effect of Calvinism

During Calvin's lifetime, Geneva rapidly overtook Zurich, Berne and Wittenberg as the most influential city of the Protestant movement. To many throughout Europe it seemed to be the place where religion had been most truly reformed and taught and put into effect; John Knox of Scotland called it 'the most perfect school of Christ that ever was in earth since the days of the Apostles.' Its impact upon the rest of the continent was immense, and this was largely due to Calvin's deliberate policy. He never wanted Geneva merely to be an example to other Protestants and a place of refuge for the persecuted. He never regarded his mission as being confined to establishing a reformed Church in a single Swiss canton, but rather to initiating and fostering a universal cause which would purify religion everywhere.

This purpose was based upon the educational system which he established in the city. It comprised primary and secondary schools and culminated in the University of Geneva which he succeeded in founding in 1559. Its purpose was not only to strengthen the cause of true religion in the city, but also (and this was particularly the intention of the university) to train evangelists to go forth into other countries to spread the new faith. He secured the necessary money for the university from his supporters. Fortunately for him, a dispute broke out just at that time between the city of Lausanne and the lecturers at the Protestant college there, most of whom then came to be the first teachers at his new university. In its first year it had 162 students, but by the time of his death the number had risen to more than 1500, most of whom were foreigners.

Since Calvin was a Frenchman and Geneva was a French-speaking city, it was to be expected that many French Protestants would come to the university to be trained as missionaries. When they had completed their course, they usually took charge of French-speaking congregations in Switzerland, particularly in Lausanne, and then went to France. The first of them reached France in 1553, and during the next ten years the Huguenots (or French Calvinists) received from Geneva nearly ninety ministers, of whom John Knox was one. Calvinism spread with a rapidity in France that surprised even Calvin himself, and it was not checked by the persecution of the *chambre ardente* set up by Henry II in 1547.[4] The first congregation to have a permanent minister was formed in Paris in 1555; at first it met secretly, but three years later several thousand Huguenots openly worshipped in the capital protected by armed sympathizers. By 1559 so many congregations had been established in other towns that the first synod (or national assembly) was held in Paris, and was attended by ministers and elders from seventy-two local congregations. It was not possible, however, for every congregation to have its own minister; there had to be a system of travelling ministers preaching and administering the sacraments to groups of congregations, each of which, however, displayed the strength of the Calvinist system by being able to organize itself with elders on the Genevan pattern.

[4] P. 222.

The Calvinist missionaries could work better in the towns than among the scattered villages of the countryside. Calvin's writings and their preaching appealed most strongly to the better educated urban merchants and craftsmen, who found in them a more satisfying form of religion than that offered by the contemporary French Church. These were the classes first attracted to Lutheranism in France, but Calvinism also won adherents from the nobility. Some of the missionaries were themselves of noble birth, and among their early converts were noble ladies who had their children educated as Calvinists at home or in Geneva. In particular, Theodore Beza (1519-1605), who came of an old family in Burgundy and was later to organize the new University of Geneva and after Calvin's death succeed to his position in the city, achieved considerable successes among the Burgundian nobility. Among those who were converted was, in 1555, Anthony of Bourbon, head of the house of Vendôme and King Consort of Navarre; another notable Huguenot of high birth and position was Gaspard de Coligny, Admiral of France and a member of the Châtillon family of the house of Montmorency.[5]

It was, indeed, the support it received from such noble families, and not the appeal it had for the middle classes, that really determined the fortunes and spread of Calvinism in France. The north and east of the kingdom, including the provinces of Champagne and Burgundy and the cities of Troyes, Tours, Bourges and Lyons, had accepted the influence first of Lutheranism and then of early Calvinism. It then came under the control of Roman Catholic families, particularly the Guises and, together with the family's Duchy of Lorraine, formed part of the large stretch of Counter-Reformation territory extending from Italy to the southern Netherlands. But in the maritime provinces of the west and south-east the Huguenots were able, after 1569, to establish their cities of refuge and their notable cavalry force which gained them victories in the Wars of Religion. In these areas, whole populations, including the peasants, became Huguenots, no longer facing the danger of being arrested as heretics and put to death. Instead of having to meet in private houses and barns, fields and woods and other secret places, they could form themselves into settled congregations with places of worship of their own. As early as 1561 Admiral Coligny asserted that they had 2150 churches, while Calvin estimated their numbers at about a million in 1559 or perhaps a tenth of the total population of the kingdom. At that point their hopes of expansion in France were high, but Calvin's belief that their faith would be accepted by the majority of the French people was not realized, and the century ended with their toleration as a minority religion unlikely to achieve further growth.

The other part of the continent in which Calvinism made important

5 P. 222.

progress was the Netherlands. It was first brought there in the 1550s by ministers sent from Geneva, who were later joined by refugees from persecution in France and England, but its progress was much slower than in France. This was probably partly due to the fact that both Lutheranism and Anabaptism had already succeeded in penetrating into the country, particularly through Antwerp and other ports which had trading links with Germany, and partly because of the persecution inflicted upon Protestantism in general. In 1523 two former Augustinian friars were burned at Brussels and became the first Protestant martyrs. In 1524 Charles V introduced his own Inquisition, and in 1529 and 1531 issued Placards or edicts ordering the death penalty for all who became Lutherans, sheltered them or spread their views. When city magistrates showed themselves sympathetic towards accused heretics, Charles in 1550 removed jurisdiction in such cases from the city councils to provincial courts over which he could exert some control. This policy checked the growth of Protestantism, particularly since neither Lutheranism with its lack of an independent ecclesiastical organization, nor Anabaptism with its emphasis upon individual spiritual regeneration, could effectively oppose such hostile action. Calvinism, which had a system of government that could operate regardless of the attitude of the secular authorities, was much better able to survive and spread in such a situation.

At first the development of Calvinism in the Netherlands remained slow. By 1560, when it was established and organized throughout France, the total number of Protestants in the country was probably hardly more than five per cent of the population of which the Calvinists were a small minority. They were unable, as they did in France, to make many converts among the gentry and nobility of the Netherlands, who were moderate in their views and more concerned with political than religious issues. Though they were anti-clerical and had listened readily to the criticisms of the Church made by Erasmus, who had lived in Louvain for a time, they found Calvinism too intolerant and authoritarian for them and only later accepted it owing to pressure of events and then often unwillingly. The Calvinists made most of their gains among the populations of Antwerp, Ghent and other Walloon towns in the south and among the peasantry of the north-east. Only later did one or two of the greater nobility, notably William of Orange, and some of the lesser nobility embrace the faith which was beginning to gain support in the country. The most important and determined of these Calvinist converts among the lesser nobility were the Gueux or Beggars, whose actions were of considerable significance in the early stages of the Revolt.[6]

The influence of Calvinism in the Netherlands spread to neighbouring north-western Rhineland and Westphalia, and these were the only

[6] P. 255.

areas in Germany in which it developed as a popular movement. In 1562 Frederick III, Elector of the Palatinate, remodelled the churches in his territory along Calvinist lines in direct opposition to the terms of the Peace of Augsburg.[7] This gave the faith a firm foothold within the Empire, and Heidelberg became its chief German intellectual centre. It made some other gains in Germany. It was adopted by the Count of Nassau-Dillingen in 1578 and by the free city of Bremen a few years later; and afterwards there were a few princely converts, such as John Sigismund of Brandenburg. On the whole, however, Calvinism made only limited progress in Germany, where it tended to disunite Protestantism and thereby assist the Counter-Reformation.[8]

In Poland circumstances were much more favourable for Calvinism. Lutheranism spread rapidly in the German-speaking areas, but its Germanic influence offended nationalist susceptibilities and its attachment to princely authority did not appeal to the nobility who were seeking to assert their 'liberties' against their monarch. By 1550, however, Calvinist ideas were becoming known in Poland, and the large part given to the laity in the management of the churches appealed strongly to the nobility, who saw also that its synodical organization would provide them with a means of extending their influence throughout the country. Calvinism was spread not by foreign missionaries, but by Polish noblemen such as Prince Radziwill the Black and native divines like John à Lasco (1499-1560), who worked in England and Germany and returned to spend the last years of his life organizing a Polish Church on Calvinist lines. Soon the Protestant noblemen were in a majority in the Polish Diet, and both Sigismund Augustus (1548-72) and Stephen Bathory (Prince of Transylvania from 1571 and King of Poland 1575-86) followed tolerant policies. Calvinism did not, however, have a monopoly of Polish Protestantism. The Bohemian Brethren, Anabaptists and Unitarians all gained footholds with the support of sympathetic noblemen. Since it was apparent that the maintenance of their political privileges was closely bound up with religious toleration in 1573 the Protestants, Roman Catholic and Orthodox noblemen agreed through the Confederation of Warsaw to make toleration part of the Polish constitution, to be sworn by each king on his accession. This toleration, however, together with the continuing Protestant disunity, was to enable the Counter-Reformation to succeed in making Poland a thoroughly Roman Catholic country.[9]

In Hungary, Lutheranism made rapid progress among the German-speaking areas, but the nobility preferred Calvinism for the same reasons as the Polish nobility. It was adopted on their estates over a large part of the country, and an important Calvinist centre was the town of Debrecen, the 'Hungarian Geneva', which was governed for a quarter of a century by its redoubtable bishop, Peter Juhasz, who made

7 P. 167.   8 P. 169.   9 P. 324.

it an example of the strictest Calvinism. The years of encouragement for the Counter-Reformation in the Habsburg lands under the Emperor Rudolf II (1576-1612) did not succeed in eradicating Protestantism in Hungary, and the Calvinists continued to form about twenty-one per cent of the population and the Lutherans six per cent.

In some ways, the country where Calvin's ideas were most fully put into practice was Scotland. Here it gained support, at first among the nobility, who were opposed to French domination of the country through the Guise family, and the small city-state of Geneva was accepted as the model for the entire kingdom. In the neighbouring kingdom of England, Calvinism was not so successful, but it provided the theology of the Puritan movement, especially of its early leaders who had been exiles in Geneva during the persecution of Mary's reign. The Puritans brought spiritual inspiration to the English Reformation, after the first political changes of Henry VIII's reign, and became strong in Parliament although they were opposed by Elizabeth I who was determined to retain the episcopal, hierarchical Church of which she was Supreme Governor. Neither did the English Puritans exert, in European affairs, as much influence as many of them wished. Their sympathies lay with the Protestants on the Continent. They would have liked more open intervention on behalf of the French Huguenots and the Dutch Protestants and a more determined stand against Spain than the Queen was prepared to allow in her foreign policy. Their influence in European history was, therefore, largely thwarted, but they contributed towards that national Protestant feeling which inspired England to take such an important part in Europe and overseas during the later sixteenth century.

Why did Calvinism spread much more widely than Lutheranism? The answer is to be found in Calvinism itself, which was a religion that appealed to more than one class of the population and to more than one nation and was particularly suited to the later, more difficult phase of the Reformation. The idea that its expansion was due particularly to commercialism and the middle classes can no longer be upheld.[10] In fact, it appealed to all classes of people—noblemen in France, merchants in the Netherlands and peasants in Scotland. It was primarily Calvinism's religious message that attracted all these people. The doctrine of predestination encouraged them to believe that they were among the elect and that their salvation was assured, and so they were able to resist their opponents because they were assured that God was with them. Also, they came to believe that, though the elect could not win their salvation by their good works, they were known by the lives they led. The adoption of Calvinism led to greater earnestness and seriousness and an emphasis on piety and morality, which strengthened their endurance and won them respect.

[10] P. 87.

Calvinism also gained support because of its well organized system of ecclesiastical government in which the laity took an active part, that appealed particularly to educated, ambitious classes. It proved to be a system which could be adapted to suit the needs of larger countries by the introduction of assemblies of representatives of the congregations, such as the synods in France and presbyteries in Scotland. Moreover, this made it possible for Calvinism to expand in countries, such as the Netherlands and France, where the government was hostile to Protestantism, which Lutheranism could not do because it depended, as in Germany and Scandinavia, on the support of the rulers, who settled the religion of their territories. Calvin's organization made it a fighting faith. Its self-governing groups of ministers could resist French persecution and seize power in Dutch towns. It was well suited to be the Protestantism of the second part of the century when it needed to be active and aggressive if it were to continue and survive.

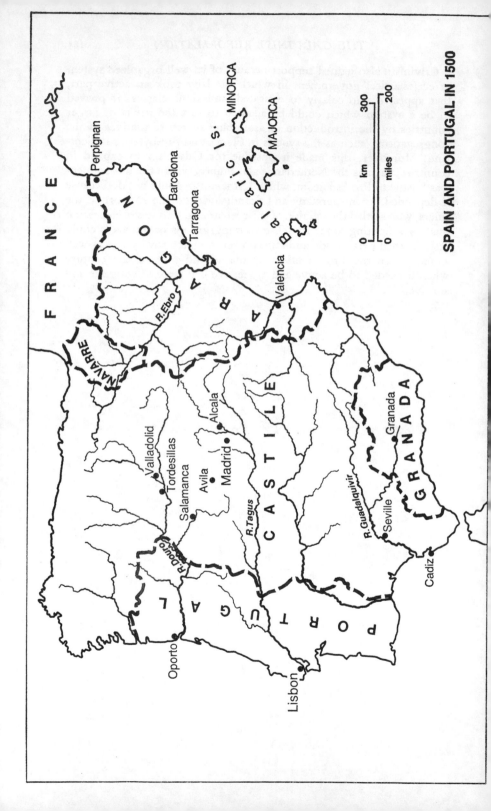

SPAIN AND PORTUGAL IN 1500

12

THE
PROBLEMS
OF
CHARLES V

The inheritance of Charles V

When only a youth of nineteen, Charles V had become ruler by inheritance of an empire which comprised a large part of western and central Europe and was acquiring possession of nearly the whole of the recently-discovered New World. It was inevitable, therefore, that he should play a dominating role in the affairs of Europe during the period of his reign which lasted over thirty years.

He was born in 1500 in Ghent in the Netherlands. His father was Philip of Habsburg (known as Philip the Fair), the son of Maximilian I, who was Holy Roman Emperor from 1493 to 1519 and by his marriage with Mary, heiress of Charles the Bold, Duke of Burgundy, added the Netherlands, Luxembourg and Franche Comté to his own Habsburg family lands in Austria. Philip married Joanna, daughter of Ferdinand of Aragon and Isabella of Castile, and the marriage produced two sons, Charles and Ferdinand. The deaths of Isabella in 1504, of Philip in 1506 and of Ferdinand of Aragon in 1516 made Charles the ruler of the Burgundian and Spanish territories, and the death of Maximilian brought him the Habsburg estates. During the last years of his life Maximilian had been determined that his eldest son should become Holy Roman Emperor, and in 1519 Charles was chosen by the Electors, who preferred his claims, as the Habsburg candidate, to those of Francis I of France. Charles followed Maximilian I's break with tradition by disregarding the customary title of King of the Romans and calling himself Emperor-elect without waiting for papal sanction. He was crowned Emperor at Aix-la-Chapelle the next year, and in 1530 he secured the title of King of the Romans for his younger brother, Ferdinand, giving him the care of the Habsburg lands. Ferdinand, through his marriage in 1521 to the daughter of Ladislaus of Hungary and Bohemia, had already secured the reversion of these kingdoms to the house of Habsburg.[1]

To contemporaries, this vast collection of territories which Charles had accumulated under his personal rule was naturally impressive. Many of them thought, during his early years of authority, that the long-held dream of a revived, universal Roman Empire in Europe in a Christian form was now nearer than ever to being realized since the time of Charlemagne. 'God has been very merciful to you,' his chief adviser, Gattinara, wrote to him after he had been elected Emperor in 1519. 'He has raised you above all the kings and princes of Christendom to a power no sovereign has enjoyed since your ancestor, Charles the Great. He has set you on the way towards a world monarchy, towards the unity of all Christendom under a single shepherd.' As represented on the map, Charles V's position certainly looked impressive, but in reality his territories hardly presented their ruler with a base on which to initiate such a programme of consolidation and expansion.

As Holy Roman Emperor, the successor of Charlemagne, his power was practically limited to an overlordship depending on the acceptance of religious and feudal ideals which were increasingly ceasing to be applicable to the period. To enforce it, he was without an organized administration, a standing army, financial resources and popular support. The heart of the Empire was Germany. If he could not assert his authority there, he could not hope to succeed in giving substance to his position. But the German princes were determined to obtain independence from every form of Imperial control, and the rise of Lutheranism added to his constitutional difficulties. Moreover, never at any time was he certain that he had the full support of the Papacy, the spiritual counterpart of the secular loyalty he was supposed to be able to command in Christendom.

Nor was his position as ruler of the various inherited territories, in which he possessed actual authority, really as impressive as might at first appear. There was no bond of union between them other than that of his own person. The only connection they had with each other was that he was their ruler, and, constitutionally, his authority was different in each country and far from being generally accepted. Thus, when he became the first joint ruler of Aragon and Castile, he also became King of Spain, the unifier of a country in which he had up until then never set foot and whose language he could not speak, and this also brought him territory in Italy as King of Naples. Again, as Duke of Burgundy he governed the Netherlands, which consisted of several provinces where feudal privilege and separatist feeling were opposed to any attempt to establish effective central control and unity of administration. Even in the Habsburg hereditary lands in Central Europe he ruled as Archduke of Austria, Duke of Styria, Carinthia and Carniola and Count of Tyrol.

Moreover, the very extent of his dominions brought him problems which inevitably weakened his authority further. The several countries over which he ruled were not sympathetic towards the needs which were the result of a policy concerned with wider considerations than their own individual interests. Spain never showed herself willing to provide him with the resources for his Imperial conflicts; his reign began with risings there, and it was some time before his authority was established over that kingdom. In the Netherlands, revolt against his rule at Ghent in 1537 was to show the mistrust felt for his Imperial and Spanish policy among its inhabitants.[2] The Germans were always suspicious of his foreign connections, and their fear that he wished to arrange for the 'Spanish succession' of his son, Philip, to the Imperial title contributed to his loss of authority among them during the last part of his reign.

In addition, Charles inherited not only his territories, but also several international issues which were made more difficult by the magnitude of his rule. As the foremost sovereign in Christendom, he was bound to uphold the cause of Roman Catholicism, threatened in his reign by the Reformation which had begun in the most important part of his Imperial territory. He was bound also to be concerned about the ever-present menace of the Turks upon the borders of the Empire in the Mediterranean and in Hungary and Austria. He had inherited, too, the struggle between Habsburg and Valois—Francis I was helped in his campaigns and diplomacy by other rulers who were afraid of the conglomeration of titles and territories which Charles had brought together through inheritance.

Such circumstances also deprived him of the support of the Papacy which seemed to him his right and which he always hoped to receive. The Papacy, however, was an Italian state as well, and Clement VII and Paul III shared with the medieval popes a fear of the consequences for them of Naples and Milan united under a single powerful ruler. Consequently they were always ready to support France against Charles and struggled to avoid the Spanish domination which eventually overtook the Papacy after the Sack of Rome in 1527. Charles found himself opposed by the Papacy in Germany too. His attempts to reach agreement with the Protestants on matters of doctrine which should be binding on all Christians and his continual threat to summon a general council to produce an ecclesiastical settlement were bound to be regarded by the Papacy as a threat to its authority and, therefore, quite unacceptable. The Sack of Rome was the only instance of actual violence inflicted on the Papacy by Charles. They were usually kept together in some measure of uncertain agreement owing to the threat to their positions from the Protestants and the Turks, but the failure of the Emperor to get complete papal support for his policies was one of his greatest weaknesses.

In 1519, however, all these difficulties and weaknesses which were

[2] P. 194.

to beset Charles during his reign lay, of course, in the future. It was natural that his advisers should then speak of the possibility of his deliberately setting out to dominate Europe, but there is no evidence to suggest that he himself was ever attracted by such an imperial vision. 'Never did I aspire to universal monarchy,' he is said to have stated in 1556, 'though it seemed well within my power to attain it.' He had no overriding plan for his dominions, but rather sought to solve his difficulties as they presented themselves—to strengthen his authority in Spain and the Netherlands, to defeat the princes and check the spread of heresy in Germany, to maintain Spanish rights in Italy against France and to restrain the Turkish advance into Europe. Had he conquered and founded his empire himself, his position might have been different, but he had lawfully inherited each of his dominions and was pledged to preserve their laws and constitutions. While he was ready to attempt all legal means to strengthen his rule in these individual states, he never sought to deprive any of his subjects anywhere of their rightful liberties and traditions. This made it impossible for him to create a single imperial administration or to develop a common economic policy for his dominions such as might have united them under an effective central control.

The policy of Charles V

By descent Charles was as cosmopolitan as his dominions. He had a Spanish mother and maternal grandmother, a Burgundian father and paternal grandmother and a German grandfather who was the son of an Austrian prince and a Portuguese princess. Though he had, therefore, little Habsburg blood, he inherited the Habsburg looks, particularly the typically long jaw. His abilities were not outstanding, but he was courageous, could benefit from experience and had a good memory all his life. His favourite recreations were hunting and jousting, and he ate and drank heavily, never consuming less than a quart of wine at a meal. He spent the first nineteen years of his life in the Netherlands before going to Spain, and thereafter he spent a total of about another eleven years in the Netherlands, eighteen in Spain, eight in the Empire and three in Italy. Yet he was not a good linguist. His native language was French. He did not begin to learn Flemish until he was thirteen and Spanish until he became King of Spain, and he was never fluent in either; nor did he become proficient in Latin or German. Nevertheless, he had the gift of gaining the friendship of many sorts of people, and he was always dignified. He was very conscientious and devoted himself to his work with a strong sense of duty.

He was guided throughout his reign by his attachment to his religion and his dynasty, the two were in his mind bound together inseparably.

He told Luther, when the reformer appeared before him at the Diet of Worms, that he was descended from 'true sons of the Roman Church, defenders of the Catholic faith', and he felt himself bound to uphold his spiritual and territorial heritage. The Reformation came as a bitter shock to him, and he devoted much of his time and energy to restoring unity in the Church, undeterred by the lack of support he seemed to get from the Papacy. He saw both religion and his family holding his dominions together. Apart from his Italian possessions, which were usually administered by Spanish viceroys, he relied to a great extent upon the services of members of his family for the government of his dominions. Not only did he place his brother, Ferdinand, in control of the hereditary Habsburg lands, but he made his son, Philip, Regent of Spain as soon as the boy came of age, and he appointed as Regent of the Netherlands first his aunt, Margaret, Duchess of Savoy, and then his sister, Mary, formerly Queen of Hungary, both of whom served him with great ability and loyalty.

Charles had a Council of State, the members of which were drawn from his various dominions, but he did not use it for policy-making decisions. He relied for assistance in these matters upon a small number of advisers, the most important being at first a Burgundian nobleman, Guillaume de Croy, Lord of Chièvres, whom he made his Imperial Chancellor. Chièvres was naturally concerned mainly with the defence of the Netherlands. He believed that if France were allowed to control northern Italy, she would be content to respect the Habsburg connection with the Netherlands, and he was largely responsible for negotiating the Treaty of Noyon, which recognized French possession of Milan and preserved the peace during the period which covered the election of Charles as Holy Roman Emperor.[3] On his death in 1521, Chièvres was succeeded as Imperial Chancellor by a Piedmontese, Mercurino Gattinara, who pursued a policy of imperial mission for Charles.[4] He wished to establish an Imperial treasury which, together with the Council of State, could unite all his dominions into a political and economic unit. His concern was not concentrated upon the defence of the Netherlands, and he wanted to eliminate France from Italy because he thought that a revived Empire under Charles must be in control of Rome. He was responsible for the agreement with Pope Leo X in 1521 which led to the expulsion of the French from Milan.[5] The short pontificate of Adrian VI and the accession of Clement VII were a setback for him, and not until 1530 did the papal coronation of Charles as Emperor signify the success of his policy, but he died in that year, and the ideal of a great Christian empire under Habsburg rule came to nothing.

After Gattinara's death, Charles appointed no more Imperial Chancellors. Instead he relied on his secretaries.[6] They were men of

[3] P. 145.   [4] P. 188.   [5] P. 147.   [6] P. 114.

considerable ability, but they enjoyed little real authority or independence because Charles insisted upon keeping power in his own
hands and taking all important decisions himself. He was notoriously
unable to do this quickly, however, and his movements from territory
to territory often further delayed matters. Viceroys, generals and
governors all had to await decisions from him and follow his instructions closely. The most crucial instance of this occurred early in his
reign during the Revolt of the Comuneros in Spain, when the
difficulty the Regent had in obtaining instructions from Charles,
who was in the Netherlands, added to the danger of the situation.[7]
He insisted also on retaining control over public appointments and
all other forms of patronage, refusing even to allow Margaret to reward
those who served her in the Netherlands. This led to the desire of the
people of each of his dominions to have him living among them.
Although the effect of such concentration of authority in his own
hands emphasized the unity of the empire in his person, ultimately
it contributed towards his failure to solve its problems and achieve its
consolidation and showed this to be a task beyond the capability of
any ruler.

The Netherlands

Charles V's Burgundian inheritance, the Netherlands, which came to
him at the age of six, presented him with as complicated problems as
any territory, yet he had to retain the support of its people because of
its wealth.[8] Flanders was in decline because of competition from the
growing English cloth industry and heavy taxation by the Dukes of
Burgundy, but Brabant could import the unfinished English cloth,
work it up and export it to central Europe through its great Scheldt
port of Antwerp, which had become the commercial and financial
centre of Europe. From the Netherlands, Charles looked for taxes
and loans to provide him with the money that he needed to maintain
his rule over his territories and, still more, to fight his wars.

He had to do this, however, in the face of considerable political
problems resulting largely from the past history of the country.[9]
Only the person of the ruler united the Netherlands. Each of the
provinces had its own constitution, traditions and rights based upon
a series of charters granted by various rulers in the past. To the
differences of race and language were added social and economic
variations between the provinces and even within them. In the south
the rural areas were dominated by a feudal aristocracy and the
important manufacturing towns by oligarchies of wealthy burghers,
while in the north agriculture and fishing were the main occupations.
The States-General, established on the French model by Philip the

[7] P. 195.   [8] P. 117.   [9] P. 24.

Good in the fifteenth century, consisted of delegates from the provincial estates of the Netherlands, and after 1530 it met occasionally in Brussels. Its powers were limited. On the one hand, it was subordinate to the Duke who alone had the right to initiate legislation, and on the other anything decided by it had to be ratified by the provincial estates. It was largely a negative body, able to frustrate important measures, but unwilling and unable to take over the government of the country itself.[10]

Charles followed the ducal policy of promoting centralization and unity in the Netherlands. Under him the unification of all the provinces was almost completed. He conquered, during his Italian Wars, Tournai from the French in 1521 and Cambrai in 1543 and forced the French monarchy to relinquish its claim to the suzerainty of Flanders. Much more difficult, however, was his struggle with Charles Egmont, Duke of Guelders, whose lands lay on either side of the frontier between the Netherlands and Germany. The Dukes of Guelders had a long enmity with the Dukes of Burgundy. Receiving French help, Egmont in 1528 sacked the Hague and in 1542 nearly captured Antwerp and Louvain. In the end, the northern provinces of Holland and Brabant came to prefer co-operation with the government in Brussels to Egmont's depradations and petitioned that action should be taken against him. When this was in vain, these two provinces eventually conquered Egmont's provinces one by one—Friesland in 1523, Overijssel and Utrecht in 1528 and Groningen in 1536. When Egmont died in 1568, his successor, William of Cleves, tried to continue his aggressive policy, but Charles was able to take action against him and in 1543 annexed the Duchy of Guelders as the seventeenth province of the Netherlands. Only the Prince-Bishopric of Liege remained a separate entity. The delay in taking effective action against Guelders, however, showed the Netherlanders the disadvantages of having a ruler who was absent from the country and had wider and more urgent interests than their own.

To promote stronger central government in the Netherlands, Charles established three councils to assist the Regent in 1531—the Council of State, the Council of Finance and the Council of Justice. These bodies achieved some success, but they met with opposition from the States-General and the provincial estates, particularly in finance, since all taxation had first to be approved by the States-General and then accepted by the individual estates before it could be levied. In 1534 Charles suggested to the States-General that a defensive union of the provinces should be set up with regular, fixed financial contributions to a common fund for the maintenance of a standing army, but the notion was immediately rejected.

As a Fleming by birth, who continued to visit the Netherlands,

[10] P. 122.   G

Charles retained, nevertheless, considerable popularity among its people. He was generally supported by the high nobility, from whom he appointed the Stadtholders or governors of the provinces, and who found employment in his great empire and numerous wars. From the towns, however, he met rising opposition, especially to his heavy and increasing taxation. In 1537 the city of Ghent, already suffering through the economic decline of Flanders, revolted and refused to pay its share of the taxes approved by the States-General. Other towns might have supported it, but power fell into the hands of the city's unemployed craftsmen and artisan guilds, which alarmed the urban oligarchies elsewhere. Ghent, therefore, was isolated, but it held out until Charles himself arrived with a large army to reduce it. During the last years of his reign he was able to raise in the Netherlands the ever-larger sums he needed for his wars against France, but in consequence there was mounting resentment in the country and a declaration of bankruptcy by the government two years after his abdication.

The situation was further complicated by the appearance of Protestantism in the Netherlands.[11] During Charles V's reign it was mainly Lutheranism and Anabaptism, which found support among the working classes of the old industrial towns. Since the dioceses were partly in France and Germany, there were no resident bishops to suppress heresy, and Charles was able to take his own measures.[12] Moreover, he had the support of the nobility and the wealthy urban classes whose fears of the political and social consequences of these movements were again greater than their dislike of his intervention in the affairs of the country.

When Charles announced, in 1555, his abdication to the States-General in the great hall of the palace of Brussels, its members expressed their distress and some wept. He had kept his hold on the ruling classes of the country, but left behind him problems and fears that Philip was not able to prevent from leading to rebellion and war.

Spain

Charles V's accession in 1516 to the throne of Spain, which was destined to be the most important of his territories and gave him most of his money and troops, took place in difficult circumstances. The union of Castile and Aragon was only personal; to the people he was only 'Charles of Ghent', an unknown foreigner, and he tactlessly sent Flemings to assume important posts in the country. Cardinal Ximenes, the reforming Archbishop of Toledo who had been appointed Regent by Ferdinand on his death bed, was effectively superseded by a Dutch bishop, Adrian of Utrecht, the new King's former tutor. When

[11] P. 182.   [12] P. 182.

Charles arrived in Spain a year later, he was accompanied by more Flemings, and on the death of Ximenes, a nephew of Chievres was made Archbishop of Toledo.

The Cortes of Castile and Aragon both recognized his kingship and voted him sums of money, but only after lengthy debates and the presentation of petitions calling for the safeguarding of Spanish interests. His sudden departure on the death of Maximilian, to secure his election as Emperor, caused further discontent, particularly as it did not seem that his assumption of this title would be to Spain's advantage. It resulted in the Revolt of the Comuneros in 1520.[13] For a time this threatened royal rule in Spain, particularly as Adrian had difficulty in getting Charles to send instructions from the Netherlands, and city after city in Castile joined Toledo in its resistance, refusing to pay taxes and expelling royal officials; but the movement fell under the control of poorer and radical elements and was defeated by the Castilian nobility. Meanwhile, the artisan guilds of the towns of Valencia had formed, in 1519, a Germania or armed brotherhood, which also gained widespread support but was eventually destroyed by the Aragonese nobility in 1521. The two movements had made no contact with each other and, when they both alienated the nobility, had no chance of success.

When Charles returned to Spain in 1522, he found the kingdoms very nearly pacified and his position already secure. Though the Cortes of Aragon remained powerful, the Cortes of Castile could not put up any resistance and had to agree to vote him taxes before presenting him with their petitions.[14] Consequently, Castile joined the Netherlands as the main source of his financial supplies, and the revenue he drew from it by taxation grew by about fifty per cent during his reign. This enabled him to build up an effective Spanish army. Mercenary troops had still to be hired from Germany and the Netherlands, but the Spaniards came to rely more and more on their native infantry. Created by Gonzalo de Cordoba (1453-1515), the Great Captain, its first victory had been at the Battle of Cerignola in 1503.[15] Now it was to enjoy over a century of supremacy on continental battlefields until defeated by the French at the Battle of Rocroi in 1643. This record was only achieved at great cost to Castile, which during the 1530s and 1540s had to contribute the greater part of the cost of Charles V's armies and campaigns, since the Netherlands was reaching the limit of its ability to pay more; only towards the end of his reign did bullion come from the New World in sufficient quantity to contribute appreciably towards Charles' demands.

Management of the Cortes of Castile and possession of an army placed Charles in a strong position over the nobility, despite its victory over the Comuneros. He was able to exclude the grandees

[13] P. 85.   [14] P. 117.   [15] P. 142.

from important roles in the government of the country, though they were compensated in other ways.[16] Charles, indeed, came to see that the support of the Spanish nobility was important to him and from 1538 granted the Castilian nobility immunity from taxation, while at the same time using the Council of State to nullify their attempts to gain influence over the Crown.[17] After the Comuneros and the Germania had been defeated, the independence of the towns was destroyed, and further power over the internal government of the country was obtained through royal control of the all-powerful Spanish Inquisition.[18] This was later used by Philip II to limit the powers of the Cortes of Aragon in his continuance of the policy of Castilianization begun by Charles.

Indeed, his work in Spain must be regarded as Charles V's greatest achievement. Despite constant absences and distractions elsewhere, he gave Spain and her empire a strong, effective government under the monarchy which was not to be challenged during the rest of the century. Towards the end of his reign, he came to see that his real power rested not upon his office as Holy Roman Emperor nor upon him as ruler of the family lands or of the Netherlands, but as King of Spain and her overseas possessions; he showed this at his abdication when he arranged for his Spanish and Burgundian territories to be separated under his son from the Imperial title and the Habsburg lands. That the sixteenth century was to be the great age of Spain was really due to Charles rather than Philip. During his reign, Spain's strength was not being sapped by economic weakness and exhausting international commitments, but her wealth was increasing and her empire expanding. Amid the failures and setbacks he suffered elsewhere, his solid success in Spain stands out in high contrast.

The Habsburg succession

Charles V took over from his grandfather, Maximilian I, in 1519 a twofold position. He inherited rulership of the Habsburg lands in the Austrian provinces and around the Upper Rhine between Switzerland and Burgundy, and he was elected Holy Roman Emperor. Maximilian was a reckless and unstable adventurer, whose most successful achievements were through his dynastic alliances, but he did try to establish for his family lands a greater degree of unification and improved institutions and had some success. He set up a central treasury at Innsbruck, which continued to work successfully after his reign; but in the last year of his life, when he summoned an assembly representing all the estates in his territories, he failed to secure their agreement to the establishment of a central court of justice, and so each duchy retained its separate jurisdiction with its own courts and

[16] P. 113.   [17] P. 113.   [18] P. 111.

laws and procedures. Nevertheless, he has been recognized as the founder of the unity of the Habsburg territories, and his policy was followed by his successors.

He was less successful as Holy Roman Emperor. He wished to make German kingship into a strong monarchy, able to impose taxation and maintain a standing army. But he was opposed by a party among the German princes, led by Berthold, Archbishop-Elector of Mainz, who also wanted a supreme central authority to establish peace and order in the country, but one that would be controlled by the greater princes and retain the management of any troops it might raise. Maximilian summoned a Diet at Worms in 1495 at which he sought financial assistance for his campaign against Charles VIII of France in Italy.[19] The reformers persuaded him to set up a Supreme Court of Justice (*Reichskammergericht*), which was to have the majority of its judges appointed by the German states and was to be financed by a poll tax, the 'Common Penny'. Since part of the tax was to go to the Emperor for military purposes, however, many princes refused to pay it in their states, and so the *Reichskammergericht* was handicapped from the start by lack of funds. By 1500 the French had triumphed again in Italy, and the Swiss had gained their independence from the Empire.[20] Maximilian's need for money was so great that at the Diet of Augsburg he had to agree to the establishment of an Imperial Council (*Reichsregiment*). This council was composed of twenty-one Electors, princes and representatives from the Empire and was to take over virtually all the functions of the Emperor, but it failed largely because the Electors would not renounce any of their power to it, and was dissolved in 1502.

No sooner, therefore, did Charles V go to Aix-la-Chapelle for his coronation in 1520 and to Worms the next year for his first Diet, than he was faced with a number of pressing problems arising from his new situation. Most urgent seemed to be the government of Germany and the Habsburg lands. Charles showed his concern for his dynasty and family possessions when he formally made over to his brother, Ferdinand, the direct control of these lands. Ferdinand married Anne of Hungary, and his younger sister, Mary, married Anne's brother, King Louis II of Hungary and Bohemia. Five years later the Turks under Suleiman the Magnificent defeated the Hungarian forces at the Battle of Mohacs in which Louis II died together with 2 archbishops, 3 bishops, 500 nobles and 9 000 men. The Turks occupied Budapest and most of lowland Hungary. As Louis and Mary were childless, Ferdinand inherited the kingdoms of both Hungary and Bohemia, but though this strengthened the position of the Habsburg dynasty, it brought him serious new problems. The Turks now directly menaced him, threatening Vienna in 1529 and pushing into Styria in 1532; and he

[19] P. 140.   [20] Pp. 142, 170.

had to contend with John Zapolya, Prince of Transylvania, who was declared king of Hungary by many of the Magyar nobility with Turkish support.[21]

As regards the government of Germany, Charles showed that he considered it of less importance than his hereditary lands. He made no attempt to improve the administrative arrangements or strengthen the Imperial institutions. In order to become Emperor, he had to agree to certain concessions to the Electors. These included promises to respect existing laws and traditions in ruling the Empire, to consult the Diet on all important occasions, to refrain from employing foreign administrators and troops in Germany and to establish a new *Reichsregiment*. The Diet of Worms in 1521 instituted the *Reichsregiment*, but Charles insisted that its authority must be restricted and that it should only act independently when he was absent abroad. The next year he formally appointed Ferdinand to be its head; in fact, his absence from Germany lasted nine years. Ferdinand, however, was too preoccupied with dynastic interests and the defence of his lands against the Turks to pay much attention to Germany. The new *Reichsregiment* received no more support from the Electors than the old and had a very short term of existence, meeting for the last time at the Diet of Nuremburg in 1524.

Under Charles, therefore, initiative in German affairs increasingly passed to the princes, and effective action could only take place when groups of them united for some common purpose. This was shown by the Knights' War and the Peasants' Revolt, both of which were suppressed by the princes and not by the Emperor.[22] The formation of the League of Schmalkalden by the Protestant princes in 1530 was a further example both of the power of princely combinations and of the weakening effect they had upon Imperial authority.[23] Indeed, such a situation hastened the collapse of any hope of establishing the Empire as an effective administrative authority. The consequences of this were fully illustrated by the League of Torgau formed by Maurice of Saxony, the Treaty of Chambord between the Protestant princes and Henry II of France, the Convention of Passau whereby the Emperor had to submit to their demands, and the lengthy negotiations (as between equal rulers rather than dependent princes and their suzerain) which finally resulted in the Religious Peace of Augsburg.[24] They represent a struggle which the Emperor finally and completely lost.

Indeed, Charles V's reign produced in Germany a brief interlude in which an attempt was made to reverse the process towards disunity which had already been taking place for a long time, but without the Reformation that interlude would probably never have occurred. If it had not been for Lutheranism, Charles would almost certainly have been content to leave German affairs to Ferdinand, who would probably

[21] P. 282.   [22] P. 160.   [23] P. 164.   [24] P. 167.

have done no more than Maximilian did. As it was, he was bound to attempt to bring the heretical movement to an end, though for political reasons (particularly his wish for support against the Turks) he consistently and sincerely sought for the compromise and reform which would have brought religious peace in Germany. Despite his efforts, the Reformation produced further disunity in Germany because religious differences were added to personal and political ones. The Protestant princes refused to accept the decisions of the *Reichskammergericht* as it had a majority of Roman Catholic judges and declined to recognize the Recess of 1529 of the Diet of Speyer.[25] The already-doubtful position of both these institutions was further undermined by their actions.

His wish to restore religious unity in Germany led Charles to engage in an effort to secure strong authority for the German kingship, an effort which only came to an unsuccessful end in 1555. Whether he would have been more successful if he had not been so preoccupied with the rest of his territories, particularly the Italian Wars, can never be known. In a way, the Reformation strengthened his potential position in Germany by dividing the princes and identifying the cause of the Roman Catholic princes with the Imperial cause, but this proved insufficient to make them forgo their wish for individual independence. When Charles, freed at last from warfare against France, won a decisive victory at Mühlberg in 1547 over the Protestant forces, the very completeness of his triumph served to reunite Protestant and Roman Catholic princes against him for political reasons so that he was unable to exploit his success.[26] Habsburg power had not been revived in Germany and religious unity had not been restored, a situation which the Thirty Years War of the next century failed to change.

The Italian and Turkish Wars

Together with Lutheranism in Germany, the most serious and persistent difficulties experienced by Charles V were occasioned by war with two separate enemies, who were, at one time, however, in alliance against him. There was the war with France in order to retain the territory acquired by Spain in Italy in previous campaigns;[27] and the war against the Ottoman Turks, whose power was continually increasing in Europe, was made more formidable by their alliances with the piratical races of North Africa.[28]

The outbreak of war between France and Spain in 1521 was in many ways a renewal of the conflict that had been waged in Italy between 1494 and 1516, though it was fought on a larger scale and, therefore, cost much more—so much more, in fact, that it placed a very severe financial strain on both combatants. This, together with the

[25] P. 164.   [26] P. 166.   [27] Pp. 146 ff.   [28] Pp. 291 ff.

way it prevented him for years from concentrating upon either his German difficulties or the Turkish menace was a high price for Charles to pay for the retention of Spanish supremacy in Italy, particularly as by the end of his reign control of the peninsula was ceasing to be as important as it had been earlier in the century. Nevertheless, the long-drawn-out fighting had weakened France more than Spain. She was in no position to challenge Spain again, as her brief attempt to do so in 1555 was to show. Spanish domination in Europe was assured and was to last for nearly a century after Charles V's abdication.

Charles from the outset of his reign believed it to be his Christian duty to take the offensive against the Moslem Turks as firmly as he later believed he should oppose the Lutheran heretics, and was naturally particularly apprehensive about their threat to the Habsburg lands. He thought that the rulers of Christendom should join him in mounting a crusade against Turkish power and encroachments, but their unwillingness and his own difficulties made this impossible. In his negotiations with the German princes he sought constantly to reach a settlement which would enable him to obtain financial and military assistance from the Diet so that Ferdinand might be able to check the Turkish threat to the Habsburg lands, but neither Lutheran nor Roman Catholic princes were prepared to share his outlook. In the critical year of 1529 Vienna received no German support. He had to adopt a conciliatory attitude towards the League of Schmalkalden in order to get help to meet the threat of a renewed Turkish advance up the Danube,[29] though the Sultan abandoned his campaign and withdrew before Charles V's advancing army could engage his forces. The Emperor's great triumph against the Moslem peril came in the summer of 1535 when his fleet captured Tunis and destroyed most of the ships of the Corsair pirates led by Khair ad-Din Barbarossa, who had been made an admiral of the Turkish navy which controlled the eastern Mediterranean.[30] It did not check the activities of the pirates in the Mediterranean, and an attempt by Charles to capture Algiers in 1541 failed, while a Turkish fleet co-operated with the French in raiding the Italian coast in 1543; but it was a dramatic victory which brought Charles greatly-needed prestige.

On the whole, Charles V's contest with the Turks ended in stalemate. At the best their advance into central Europe was checked, and though they threatened Vienna again in 1683, their danger to Christendom was never really serious again. The most effective action Charles took against them was probably to defeat France and so deprive them of an ally and a base in the western Mediterranean. Italy was not raided by them again, though even the Battle of Lepanto in 1571 did not destroy their power in the Mediterranean.

[29] P. 165.   [30] P. 291.

The abdication of Charles V

In the summer of 1547 Charles seemed to be in a position of triumph. In Germany he had defeated the League of Schmalkalden, and in Europe neither France nor England, after the deaths of Francis I and Henry VIII, were in a position to oppose him. Within a few years, however, the situation had changed, and by 1553 he had left Germany with his authority shattered. The country was divided and Lutheranism triumphant. France, which had assisted both the German princes and the Ottoman Turks against him, was still defiant.

Charles decided to abdicate. The burden of office had made him an old man, and his health was bad. In the course of the coming months he divested himself of his territories and titles. In 1554 he granted Milan and Naples to his son, Philip, on his marriage to Queen Mary of England. In the autumn of 1555, after an impressive and emotional ceremony at Brussels, he resigned the Netherlands to Philip, and early in 1556 relinquished Spain to him as well. Later in the year he completed the process by assigning the Imperial office to Ferdinand. Then he went to Spain and spent the last two years of his life in the house he had built for himself near to the monastery of San Jerimo de Yuste in Estremadura preparing for his death, but still taking a close interest in the affairs of the countries to which he had devoted himself for so many years.

Charles abdicated amid the wreck of his policy in Germany to which he had given the last twelve years of his life, but in other ways he had not failed. France had been defeated and was now encircled by Habsburg territories. The Turks had neither advanced into Austria nor made conquests in the Western Mediterranean. The Netherlands accepted his rule and its territory had been enlarged. Above all, Spain controlled Italy and was predominant in western Europe; its government had been strengthened and its rule over the New World enlarged. This situation was recognized by Charles in the disposition of his territories at his abdication. The Imperial cause had perished in Germany, and he wished to cut his other possessions away from it. In place of the unwieldy, insecure group of territories he had inherited, he planned to give Philip an empire which united three areas under his rule—England and the Netherlands, Spain and Italy, and America. Soon after Charles V's death, however, Mary Tudor died childless and England was lost to Philip; and during his reign the Netherlands were to revolt against their inclusion in the Spanish realm. Yet Spain, supreme in Europe and with her overseas empire, still remained the real symbol of the success of Charles V's labours.

13
THE
COUNTER-
REFORMATION

The nature of the movement

The Counter-Reformation was essentially a movement that had two stages in its development. It began as an expression of the same desire for spiritual regeneration that inspired the Reformation. The need for reform within the Church had been realized even before the end of the fifteenth century. The Brethren of the Common Life emphasized the desire for greater spiritual piety.[1] Erasmus and his fellow Christian humanists hoped that the New Learning of the Renaissance would bring about a purging of ecclesiastical abuses so that the Church could meet the demands of the changing times.[2] In Spain, Cardinal Francisco Ximenes de Cisseros, who was Archbishop of Toledo from 1436 to 1517, lived an austere life, applying the revenues of his princely see to religion and charity. With the assistance of Queen Isabella of Castile, he imposed strict observance of their rule on the religious orders of Spain and founded the University of Alcala for the promotion of theological studies. These were instances of developments that prepared the way for the Counter-Reformation. Indeed, it could be argued that the Counter-Reformation began before the Reformation because the Oratory of Divine Love, an early manifestation of the movement, was founded a few months before Martin Luther nailed his Ninety-Five Theses to the church-door at Wittenberg; and years later Ignatius Loyola created his Society without at first clearly considering it to have an anti-heretical mission. The Counter-Reformation must, therefore, be regarded in its first phase as a movement for religious reform, parallel to the Reformation and arising out of the same general background of discontent and unease, but developing on different lines and taking a different direction. To some extent, they both represent a triumph over the worldliness and paganism of the Renaissance.

While it is true, however, that the Counter-Reformation would have taken place had Protestantism not developed, it would certainly have

[1] P. 44. [2] P. 59.

been a very different movement. The crisis presented by Protestant renunciation of papal authority and attacks on medieval doctrines inevitably affected the later course of the Counter-Reformation. After 1542 the guidance of the Counter-Reformation passed from the liberal, reforming Gasparo Contarini to the intransigent, violent Pietro Caraffa;[3] it then became more specifically anti-Protestant and ultimately more political. The result was the transformation of the medieval Catholic Church into the modern Roman Catholic Church. Moreover, the Council of Trent, instead of seeking to resolve differences with the Protestants as the reformers had hoped, increasingly asserted doctrines in a definite and uncompromising manner that left no room for discussion or concession.

This had the lasting effect of leading the Roman Catholic Church always to confront its opponents and seek refuge from its difficulties through discipline and order, administrative efficiency, orthodoxy and uniformity. In doing this, the Church adapted itself to the spirit and to the needs of the post-medieval world, but such a sacrifice of flexibility and comprehensiveness created fresh problems for it.

The religious orders

An early aspect of the Counter-Reformation, which began about the same time as Savonarola's revival in Florence,[4] was the establishment of new and reformed religious orders which followed the later active, practical outlook of the friars, though they did not neglect the contemplative ideal of enclosed monasticism.[5] The first were brotherhoods or oratories of clergy and laity, who met to pray together and perform works of charity. Among the earliest were those founded at Vincenza in 1494 and at Genoa in 1497, but the best-known was the Oratory of Divine Love, established in Rome in 1517 by some fifty Italian priests and laymen, among whom were both Contarini and Caraffa. Its members followed their normal occupations, but assembled to pray and study, went frequently to confession and communion and relieved the poor and the sick. This Roman Oratory did not survive the Sack of Rome in 1527, but another new order, already founded by some of the members of the Oratory, did and was able to establish itself in Venice. This was the order of Theatines, which followed the pattern of the medieval orders more closely, though it was a community not of monks but of secular priests, and they wore no special habit. They lived together under the three monastic vows of chastity, poverty and obedience, but preached, heard confessions, administered the sacraments and performed other pastoral work. Their numbers were never large, and they came mostly from rich families (whose wealth maintained the order), but they exercised a great influence in the Italian

[3] Pp. 165, 213.   [4] P. 271.   [5] P. 37.

Church, and many of the bishops of the Counter-Reformation came from them. The granting of papal approval to them in 1524 marked official recognition of this sort of community in the Church.

The Theatines were followed by other orders organized on similar lines. Among them were the Barnabites, founded at Milan in 1530. Established at first to relieve the sufferings caused by the Italian Wars, they later came to undertake general pastoral work and conducted open-air missions among the people. There were also the Capuchins, who sought to return to the early ideals of the Franciscan friars, and their rule, drawn up in 1529, strongly emphasized the principles of poverty and austerity. Their enthusiastic preaching and missionary work soon gained them popular support, at first in Italy and then in other continental countries.

One of the most significant of the new orders was the Ursuline, founded at Brescia in 1535 and designed to give women a new place in the work of the Church. Its members, who were to be unmarried or widowed, were to live with their families, worship in their own parish churches except for a monthly corporate communion and wear no habit, but they were to assist the clergy, especially in works of charity. In 1595, however, some of them formed themselves into a community, which led a monastic life and conducted a school for girls, and others followed their example. In this way, they departed from their original scheme, becoming an organized religious order and the first teaching order of women in the Roman Catholic Church.

The Society of Jesus

The earliest religious orders of the Counter-Reformation were established in Italy, but the order which was destined to be by far the most important and successful of all, the Society of Jesus, originated in Spain, the country that in many ways took over the lead of the revival of religion in the Roman Catholic Church during its later stages. It founder was Ignatius Loyola (1491 or 1495-1556), a Spanish nobleman who was born in the castle of Loyola not far south of the Pyrenees. He was a soldier and a courtier until 1521 when he was crippled by a cannon ball while fighting in Charles V's army against the French in Italy. While recovering from his wound, he read a life of Christ and biographies of the saints, which inspired him, in accordance with the Spanish knightly tradition, to become a soldier of Christ. After his recovery, he made a pilgrimage to the shrine of Our Lady at Montserrat in Aragon, where he hung up his sword at the altar, dedicated himself to a new life of service and exchanged his clothes with a beggar. But he also underwent a religious crisis like that experienced by Luther some fifteen years earlier; he felt the same sense of sin and desire to be reconciled to God. For nearly a year in 1522, he lived as a solitary hermit in a cave outside Manresa, some forty miles north-west of Barcelona. Like Luther, he sought there to achieve an assurance of salvation by rigorous austerity and mortification, and he, too, found relief in a personal conversion. He did not find it in Scripture, however, but in a direct mystical experience which assured him that he knew God's truth for himself. James Laynez, who was to succeed him as the General of the Jesuits, wrote of him, 'He thought to himself that, even if no Scriptures had been given us to teach the truths of faith, he would nevertheless have determined to give up life itself for them solely on account of what he had seen with the soul.'

This did not, however, lead him to dispense with all external religious authority and observance. Rather, as a soldier, he found fulfilment in giving himself in complete obedience to the Church and its faith. 'To make sure of being right in all things,' he later said, 'we ought always to hold by the principle that the white I see I should believe to be black if the Church were so to rule it.' He realized that to be of service to the Church he would have to become better educated. He went to study first at the University of Alcala, which Ximenes had founded, and then at the College of Montaigu in Paris, where both Erasmus and Calvin had been students. At both places he attracted a number of fellow-students who were inspired by his idealism to attach themselves to him.

At first they thought, again in the Spanish tradition, of going on a crusade against the infidel, but when they set out in 1534 for the Holy Land, Turkish activity in the eastern Mediterranean prevented them getting further than Venice. While waiting in Italy, Loyola got to know several of the leading Counter-Reformation reformers, and his ideal of service to the Church was widened. He and several of his companions were ordained priests, and they went to Rome to place themselves completely at the disposal of the Papacy. They were welcomed by Pope Paul III, who in 1540 allowed them to form the Society of Jesus, which was to exist for the care of souls in life and doctrine and for the preaching and teaching of the faith. Ten years later Loyola drew up the constitution of the Society, which laid down that its services should be at the disposal of the pope; that its members should take the three traditional monastic vows and, in addition, a fourth: to go without question, delay or the provision of journey-money wherever the pope might order for the salvation of souls; and that none of them was to accept any bishopric or ecclesiastical dignity except upon the express command of the pope. This distinguished the Society from all other religious orders.

Those who aspired to become Jesuits were required to undertake the *Spiritual Exercises* compiled by Loyola, which were a series of meditations designed to direct the mind towards a complete union with Christ and so to thorough obedience to His commands as fulfilled in the Society. All had to submit to an unquestioning, military obedience such as Loyola had accepted for himself. The Jesuit, he said, must always obey commands 'like a corpse which can be turned this way or that, or a rod that follows every impulse, or a ball of wax that might be moulded in every form.'

Loyola had thought of the Jesuits primarily as missionaries, taking Christianity to the pagan peoples of the new countries overseas which were being brought into contact with Europe. Indeed, by the time of his death the Society was engaged in worldwide missionary work in India, China, Japan, Africa and America. Outstanding among the Jesuit missionaries was Francis Xavier (1506-52), one of the Society's original members, known as the 'Apostle of the Indies' and the 'Apostle of Japan'.[6]

Europe had not been considered by Loyola as an area for missionary work, but the Society was formed at the time when the Counter-Reformation was beginning to mount an attack on the rising tide of Protestantism, and Pope Paul III entrusted it with the duty of seeking to win heretics back to the Church. It was particularly active in Germany where, by the end of the century, over a thousand of its members were at work as teachers and preachers in the Roman Catholic states.[7] The lead was taken there by the Jesuit theologian, Peter Canisius (1521-97), who was a Dutch convert. After establishing a Jesuit settlement at Cologne, he travelled from 1549 on preaching missions in Bavaria, Vienna and Prague with the support of the Archduke (afterwards Emperor) Ferdinand and was very largely responsible for the establishment of colleges at Augsburg, Munich and Innsbruck. Another Protestant country to which Jesuits were sent was England, where from 1580 they sought to strengthen the faith of the Roman Catholic minority.

The Society's missionary activity, both in Europe and overseas, led Loyola to develop its educational work, which he had at first limited to the training of its members. The Gregorian or Roman College was first established in the city in 1550 as a seminary for Jesuit novices, but he was later persuaded to admit lay students. During the sixteenth century the Society established a network of houses, colleges and schools in Italy, Spain and Portugal, and some also in France, Austria and southern Germany. Their methods of education were thorough and achieved high standards, bringing them pupils from wealthy and important families, so that they controlled the education of a large proportion of the influential upper classes in Roman Catholic countries. Later they directed a number of seminaries and took an important role in the training of secular priests. In this way, they raised the

[6] P. 216.   [7] P. 169.

standard of education and devotion in Roman Catholic countries and did much to remedy the ignorance of religion among both clergy and people which had been such a grave weakness of the medieval church.

The extent of their success varied from country to country. In Italy the support of the Papacy ensured them ready triumphs, and they had more communities in the peninsula at the time of Loyola's death than anywhere else in Europe. In Portugal they were patronized by the Crown and founded some of their earliest schools. At first the Spanish Crown suspected them of being papal agents and they were resented by the Dominicans, who were powerful in the Inquisition and the universities, but they steadily gained support through the quality of their preaching and pastoral work, and in the Spanish Netherlands they were prominent in encouraging religious reform. In France they made little progress because of the influence of Gallicanism;[8] but on the outbreak of the Wars of Religion, the Roman Catholics discovered their value as allies in the struggle against Protestantism. Similarly, they played a vital part in the spread of the Counter-Reformation in Poland.[9]

The success of the Jesuits was remarkable within the lifetime of their founder. In 1556, the year of Loyola's death, the Society had over fifteen hundred members distributed among a hundred houses, colleges, schools and other institutions, and grouped into a dozen provinces of which seven were in Spain and Portugal and their colonies, three in Italy and two in Germany. It trained its novices thoroughly and attracted able men as members, men who were prepared to accept its command of complete obedience to the Church and were encouraged by the belief that they were the spearhead of the Counter-Reformation. The earlier monks and friars had renounced worldly and social ways, but the Jesuits were learned, cultured and accomplished and able to make their impression on society. The vigorous and aggressive Roman Catholic Church, which developed during the sixteenth century, was largely the product of the Jesuits.

The Council of Trent (1545-63)

The controversy over the summoning of a general council to undertake religious reform had begun in the early years of the Reformation. Reformers within the Church wanted it, and so did the Protestants, though with some doubts, for Luther had declared in his disputation with Eck that even Councils could err.[10] Charles V was insistent in his demands for one as a means of uniting Germany. Successive popes, mindful of the Councils of Constance and Basle, feared it would mean a reduction of papal power,[11] and they did not feel any enthusiasm for the abolition of abuses which were lucrative for the Papacy. Paul III

[8] P. 111.   [9] P. 324.   [10] P. 157.   [11] P. 41.

reluctantly agreed to call a Council at his election in 1534, but the prolongation of the Italian Wars enabled him to postpone it. The coming of peace in 1545, however, meant that he could no longer ignore Charles V's insistence.

The Council met at the small cathedral city of Trent, which was just within the Holy Roman Empire, but was also in northern Italy, to meet Charles V's wishes. At the outset, of the seven hundred bishops eligible to attend, only 31 were present. By the time it ended, eighteen years later, some 270 bishops had attended its meetings; 187 of them were Italian, 32 were Spanish, 28 French and two German. It was unlikely that such an assembly would deal sympathetically, as Charles wished, with the ideas of Lutheranism; and the pope, indeed, who took no part in the proceedings himself, relied for support for his wishes upon the Italian bishops, whose incomes were small and whose promotion prospects depended on him. At the very beginning, the bishops asserted their power by deciding that bishops and heads of religious orders alone should vote and that the voting should be, not by nations (as at Constance and Basle), but individually.

This was an important papal victory, and so also was the decision about procedure taken at the opening of the Council. The papal bull summoning the Council had declared that its task was to consider both doctrine and ecclesiastical reform. Charles V was very anxious that abuses should be reformed first, so that the Lutherans would be appeased and prepared to come to the Council to discuss doctrinal questions, but Paul III wanted neither reforms that would affect his income nor concessions to the Lutherans that would diminish his authority. The matter was settled by the compromise that doctrine and reform should be considered concurrently by separate sections of the Council. In fact, however, the first sessions of the Council were occupied mainly with doctrine, and no attempt was made to grant concessions to the Lutherans. Instead, definite statements were made which showed clearly where Roman Catholicism differed from Protestantism and prevented all doubts in the future.

The Council began by considering the Confession of Augsburg of 1530;[12] but only to express its differences with it. The first decision, that Scripture and tradition were of equal authority, was the most important because, right at the start, it denied the fundamental Protestant acceptance of the Bible alone as the basis of Christian belief. Other decisions flowed inevitably from this. The sole right of the Church to interpret the Bible and the authority of the text of the Vulgate were asserted. Justification by good works was upheld, and the seven sacraments were declared to be absolutely necessary channels of divine salvation. These decisions struck at the root of the Protestant system and destroyed any hope of reconciliation.

[12] P. 164.

In return for this triumph, the pope accepted some reforms, none of which affected his position. Bishops and priests were ordered to preach regularly and the holding of bishoprics in plurality was forbidden, but no decision was reached about the problem of non-resident bishops, many of whom were attendant upon the papal court in Rome. These measures did not satisfy Charles V at all, and Paul III was alarmed by his military triumph over the Lutherans at Mühlberg.[13] On the pretext of an outbreak of plague at Trent, he moved the Council to Bologna, beyond the possibility of Imperial control. Charles refused to allow the Spanish bishops to attend, and the Council was virtually suspended.

Pope Paul's successor, Julius III, recalled the Council to Trent in 1551. Lutheran representatives attended, at Charles V's insistence, but they demanded that discussion should be resumed upon the subjects previously defined, that bishops should be released from their oath of obedience to the Papacy and that the authority of Councils should be declared superior to the Papacy. It was evident that neither side was in the mood to make such concessions as might make an agreement possible. The Council upheld penances and pilgrimages and affirmed the doctrine of transubstantiation, before being suspended again in 1552 after Charles V's flight from Germany.[14]

While Paul IV was pope between 1555 and 1559, there was no chance of the Council re-assembling.[15] Not until he was succeeded by the more tolerant Pius IV did it meet again in 1562. By then all hope of reconciliation with the Protestants had gone, and the Jesuits were exercising a powerful influence in the Council. The political situation, however, had changed. Charles V had abdicated, but Ferdinand I wanted to follow his brother's policy of reconciliation with the Lutherans, and he was supported by Charles IX of France (represented by the Cardinal of Lorraine), who was faced with growing religious strife in his kingdom and had threatened to call a national council of the French Church.[16] At the same time, the Spanish bishops, supported by Philip II, wanted the authority of the bishops in the Council to be declared superior to that of the pope. With the support of the Italian bishops, however, the papal cause again triumphed. The Council declared that the residence of bishops in their sees was by papal appointment and not by divine command, and this was a defeat for the Spaniards. Further decisions were taken on the same lines as before. The celibacy of the clergy, communion in one kind for the laity, the invocation of the saints and the veneration of relics and images were upheld. Finally, a number of practical reforms were promulgated. Bishops were to ordain only suitable men to holy orders and to supervise their moral life, the clergy were to reside in their parishes and perform their duties regularly, and a seminary was to

[13] P. 166.   [14] P. 167.   [15] P. 278.   [16] P. 227.

be established in every diocese for the training of those seeking ordination.

When the Council finally adjourned for the last time in 1563, its eighteen years of existence had actually only comprised four-and-a-half years of working sessions. It transferred to the pope several tasks which it had not considered—the revision of the Index, the compilation of a catechism and the revision of the Missal and Breviary—so giving him a further means of extending his influence. Indeed, the most important aspect of the Council was the way in which the pope emerged from it victorious. Already, above all particular doctrines and practices, was appearing the principle that the pope was supreme in the Church. Its complete expression was not possible at this Council, but it took a significant step forward. Papal confirmation was necessary for its decrees, and the Roman Pontiff was recognized as the Vicar of Christ on earth. The subordination by the Vatican Council in 1870 of all the labours of the Church, whether in doctrine or law, to an infallible pope was really the logical outcome of the Council of Trent.

The decisions of the Council were very conservative. It paid little attention to such developments of the time as humanistic Biblical studies, the participation of the laity in ecclesiastical administration and the mystical approach to religion. To Lord Acton, it 'impressed on the Church the stamp of an intolerant age and perpetuated by its decrees the spirit of an austere immorality.'* It created a structure and doctrinal system for the Roman Catholic Church which lasted until recently. Although it restricted the degree of latitude and freedom that had existed in the Middle Ages, the increased centralization of government and strict definition of doctrine made Roman Catholicism, in the conditions of the sixteenth century, a more effective force, able to retain the adherence of its members and confront its opponents with a degree of unity and certainty that they could not achieve. On the theological side, the Council's traditional approach defined the results of medieval scholasticism and drew from it all that could be of service to the Church of the Counter-Reformation. By defining doctrinal points on which hitherto there had been uncertainty, it made agreement and unity with other Christians impossible, but it also presented a bold intellectual front to all outside its ranks and a system which both the instructed and the ignorant could accept.

The Inquisition and the Index

The Inquisition was of medieval origin.[17] During the sixteenth century, however, it was revived in new forms—the Spanish Inquisition and the Roman Inquisition—to play an important part in combating

* *Lectures in Modern History* (1906).   [17] P. 37.

heresy. In many ways the Spanish Inquisition was more an instrument of the state than of the Church. It was set up by the Crown at the end of the fifteenth century and always remained under its control as a weapon against both heresy and sedition.[18] Religious and national unity were so closely bound together in Spain that Protestantism, in fact, gained little acceptance in the country and was soon destroyed. During the sixteenth century less than two thousand people were punished in Spain as Protestants, and some four-fifths of them were foreigners; these numbers probably exaggerate the influence of the Reformation, because any suspicion of religious error or political disloyalty was liable to bring condemnation upon the individual as a Lutheran. The Spanish Inquisition was established also in Sicily and in the New World; a similar Inquisition was introduced in the Netherlands in 1524. A Portuguese Inquisition was set up in 1536.[19]

The success of the Spanish Inquisition led Cardinal Caraffa, who had been a papal representative in Spain, to induce Paul III to revive the Roman Inquisition in 1542 with the Holy Office, composed of six cardinals, as the final court of appeal in trials of heresy. Its methods were similar to those of the Spanish Inquisition. The six cardinals, known as Inquisitors General, had authority over all clergy, monks and lay-people. Its trials were in secret, both witnesses and accused could be tortured and the accused was considered guilty until proved innocent. Its punishments included confiscation of goods, various degrees of imprisonment either temporary or perpetual and handing over to the secular arm which meant death by burning at the stake. Paul III intended that it should function not only in the Papal States but in all the countries of Christendom. In fact, however, rulers were not ready to allow it to be introduced into their kingdoms as a rival to their power, and its work was confined to Italy where, by a series of heresy trials, it eliminated the small Protestant movement before it could gain an effective foothold in the peninsula.

Closely connected with the Inquisition was the censorship of the press. The invention of printing was soon seen as a means by which heresy might be spread, and the Fifth Lateran Council decreed in 1517 that no book should be printed in any city or diocese of Christendom without a licence from the bishop. Caraffa, who was appointed the first Inquisitor-General of the Roman Inquisition, insisted as early as 1543 that no book should be published without permission from the Holy Office and that it should be able to destroy heretical books. This it was able to do in Italy, where some ten thousand books are said to have been burnt on a single Sunday morning in Venice. When Caraffa became pope, the Inquisition published in 1559 the first *Index* or official list of books which members of the Roman Catholic Church were forbidden, except in special circumstances, to read or possess.

[18] P. 111.   [19] P. 69.

By decree of the Council of Trent, this was given its final form in 1564 by Pope Paul IV, and in 1571 Pius V established a special Congregation of the *Index* to be in charge of the list and revise it as needed. There was also an *Index Expurgatorius*, which listed books that might be read or published freely as long as certain passages were deleted from them. There was, in addition, a Spanish *Index* established in 1551 and a Spanish *Index Expurgatorius* established in 1571, which did not necessarily list the same books as their Roman counterparts. The Spanish government also banned the importation of foreign books in 1558 and the next year forbade Spanish students to study outside the kingdom.

The Counter-Reformation popes

None of the changes and reforms of the Counter-Reformation would have been of any avail if the Church had remained inert and corrupt at the centre. The reform of the Papacy itself was of great importance since its weaknesses had contributed so much to the decay of the Church during the later Middle Ages and the Renaissance. By then, however, the popes were changing their character. Spanish domination in Italy and the decline of Rome as the centre of the High Renaissance brought to an end the series of popes who sought to fulfil territorial and family ambitions and rival the princes as patrons of artists and scholars and as builders on a large scale. The Counter-Reformation brought new popes, who exercised their authority over the Church and were imbued with its spirit. The Papacy and the Rome of the Renaissance, which had shocked the visiting Luther, underwent a remarkable change in the second half of the century.

Among the popes who contributed to this transformation, mention must first be made of Paul III (1534-49), born Alexander Farnese in 1468. Educated at the Court of Lorenzo the Magnificent in Florence and sharing the outlook and virtues as well as the ambitions and vices of the Renaissance popes, at the same time he sympathised with the movement for reform, partly from fear of Protestantism, and gave it his support. On the one hand, he was made a cardinal at the age of twenty-five even before becoming a priest, had four illegitimate children before his election to the Papacy and commissioned Michelangelo to paint the *Last Judgment* in the Sistine Chapel. On the other hand, he appointed a commission of nine cardinals to investigate the condition of the Church, the report of which (called by him the *aureum consilium*—'golden counsel') was of a frankness which had never before come from the Papacy. It condemned unworthy appointments to ecclesiastical office, the traffic in benefices, dispensations and indulgences and 'the reckless exaggeration of the papal authority'.

He also gave the Papacy a new role of leadership by encouraging the Barnabites and Ursulines in Italy, approving the Society of Jesus in 1540, reviving the Roman Inquisition in 1542 and convening the council of Trent in 1545.

The first true Counter-Reformation pope was Paul IV (1555-59), who had, as Cardinal Caraffa, established the authority of the Roman Inquisition and said, 'Even if my father were a heretic, I would gather wood to burn him.' At the time of his election to the Papacy he was seventy-nine years old. He was still a man of great energy, however, and during his brief pontificate put into effect a number of reforms, including reduction of the extravagant expenditure of the papal court and ordering the bishops there to leave it and return to their sees. He had no sympathy with Humanism, and his *Index* contained the works of Erasmus. He also displayed the austerity of the Counter-Reformation, expelling travelling entertainers from the city, forbidding dancing and hunting and ordering the figures in the *Last Judgment* to be draped.[20] To his energy he added, however, a violent character and prejudiced hatreds. He particularly hated Spain, which had conquered his native Naples. He threatened to dissolve the Jesuits, quarrelled with Mary Tudor and brought about a last vain renewal of the Italian Wars.[21] His reforms initiated the new manner of the Papacy, but his politics wasted its resources and even endangered its existence.

Paul IV's death brought about a reaction in Rome. A mob sacked the headquarters of the Inquisition and threw the pope's statue into the Tiber; and the college of cardinals elected a man of different character, Pius IV (1559-65). He reversed the anti-Spanish policy of his predecessor, four of whose relatives he tried and executed because they had been advanced by papal influence. The Council of Trent came to a conclusion during his pontificate, and during the last two years of his life he began to put its decrees into effect. He also published the new *Index* and prepared for the issue in 1566 of the Roman Catechism, a doctrinal exposition of the creed, the sacraments, the decalogue and prayer for the use of priests; he also opened a seminary for the diocese of Rome as an encouragement to other bishops. One of his most important reforms was to issue regulations for the college of cardinals and insist on their right to elect a pope as against the claims of a council. In some ways, however, he was like the old Renaissance popes. He knew little theology and continued the practice of nepotism, though the nephew he entrusted with the administration of his affairs was Charles Borromeo.[22]

His successor, Pius V (1566-72), the first pope to be elected after the Council of Trent, was a more severe man, like Paul IV in many ways, but with none of his violence and political obsessions. A

[20] P. 57.   [21] P. 151.   [22] P. 215.

Dominican friar and an Inquisitor, who led a strict and abstemious life, he was nicknamed 'Friar Wooden Shoe' by the people of Rome because of his monkish narrowness. He enforced clerical residence and monastic discipline throughout Italy, forbade the sale of indulgences and reduced the expenses of his administration—the heavy taxation in the Papal States imposed to maintain it having led to an unsuccessful attempt to assassinate his predecessor during the last year of his pontificate—but he did not succeed in stopping the sale of offices in the Roman Church.[23] As the Council had directed, he reformed the Breviary in 1568 and the Missal in 1570, and in 1570 he also ordered a new complete edition of the works of St Thomas Aquinas to emphasize their importance as the basis of Roman Catholic theology. His encouragement of the Inquisition in Italy and Spain was a sign that under him the Counter-Reformation really took the offensive. But he was a poor diplomat; his excommunication of Queen Elizabeth of England in 1570 and support for Mary, Queen of Scots, his encouragement of Philip II's policy of religious persecution in the Netherlands and his exhortation to Charles IX of France to take action against the Huguenots, all had disastrous consequences. On the other hand, he put aside his differences with Spain and Venice to form the Holy League, which made possible the defeat of the Turks at Lepanto in 1571.[24]

Pius V was succeeded by Gregory XIII (1572-85), who gave his particular attention to two causes—the relationship of the Papacy with those countries which recognized its authority and the place of education in the Church. He developed the system of sending papal nuncios or ambassadors to reside at the courts of Roman Catholic rulers to represent the interests of the Papacy and influence governments in their attitude towards the Church. In the cause of education, he established many colleges and seminaries in Rome and elsewhere in Italy, most of which he placed under the control of the Jesuits; among them was the English College in Rome which he founded in 1579 as a seminary to train missionary priests for England. He approved the Congregation of the Oratory and the Barefooted Carmelites in 1580.[25] The inadequacy of the finances of the Papacy as the centre of the revived Roman Catholic Church was shown, however, towards the end of his pontificate when the large sums he had spent on education and building threw papal finances into chaos and again produced disorder in the Papal States.

This problem was tackled by Gregory XIII's successor, Sixtus V (1585-90), who was a Franciscan friar and an Inquisitor and in the tradition of Paul IV and Pius V. He put the papal finances in order by selling dispensations and privileges, imposing more taxes and increasing the number of *Montes Pietatis*, charitable institutions first

[23] P. 116.   [24] P. 143.   [25] Pp. 216, 217.

established in the later Middle Ages, for lending money in cases of need. Equally important, he set about modernizing the administration of the Papacy. He limited the number of cardinals to seventy and in 1587 divided them among fifteen executive departments or Congregations. Some of them were concerned with the government of the city of Rome, but others with important aspects of the life of the Roman Catholic Church, such as the appointment of bishops, the control of missions and the supervision of religious orders. Thus he provided the Church with an effective central organization by making the cardinals ecclesiastical civil servants. Under him the transformation of the Papacy into the spiritual leader and director of the Church in many ways reached its climax, and yet this last of the Counter-Reformation popes was also a patron of art and scholarship. He embellished Rome in a manner worthy of the Renaissance popes, building the Lateran Palace and the Vatican Library, completing the cupola of St Peter's and providing the city with new water supplies and roads.

The Counter-Reformation reformers

Important though the popes' contribution, through administrative action and moral example, to the success of the Counter-Reformation undoubtedly was, the movement depended still more upon the intense and widespread religious revival in the Roman Catholic Church whereby thousands of men and women, clergy, religious and laity, in various ways brought new strength and inspiration to it. Of course, most of those who contributed towards this spiritual transformation are not known to history, but an insight into this development can be gathered from the recorded lives and achievements of some of the important figures who attracted and led the rest.

Prominent in the revival of pastoral standards in the Church was Charles Borromeo (1538-84), who was born of a noble family at Arona on Lake Maggiore. He was early destined for the priesthood and, an example of the abuses in the Church of Rome, he was made a monk at the age of eight and titular abbot of a wealthy monastery five years later. In 1559 his uncle, the newly-elected Pope Pius IV, summoned him to Rome and created him a cardinal and Archbishop of Milan, though he was then only twenty-one and not at first even ordained, in order to make him, as was traditional, his chief secretary. The main task of a nephew in that position had been to protect the pope against the intriguers surrounding the papal throne, but at this time Borromeo underwent a spiritual conversion which changed his life into one of complete devotion to the Church. He played an important part in the final session of the Council of Trent and assisted in the drafting of the new Roman Catechism.[26] After his uncle's death, he went in 1566 to his diocese, where there had been no resident archbishop for nearly eighty years. He set about reforming the parishes and the monasteries and improving clerical education. He patronized the Jesuits, founding three seminaries in the city of Milan and another three elsewhere in the diocese. He also established the Confraternity of Christian Doctrine for instructing children, from which the Sunday School movement later originated. His own life was very simple, and he gave most of his money to the poor. When Milan suffered from famine in 1570 and from plague in 1576, he worked unsparingly for the relief of the sufferers, and his life was shortened by his labours and harsh existence. He was a hard man, and some resented his methods, so much so that in 1569 a number of monks hired an assassin to shoot him at the altar, but the shot only grazed his skin. Nevertheless, his reforms made his diocese a model for the rest of the Church, and his influence was extensive, particularly in Switzerland.

Indeed, the main impact of the Counter-Reformation continued to be on the revival of practical pastoral and charitable work. This was exemplified in Philip Neri (1515-95), the founder of one of the later religious orders of the movement. Born in Florence, he refused the offer of a rich relative to make him a merchant and resolved to devote himself completely to God. At the age of eighteen, he went to Rome where he helped and taught the poor and spent hours in solitary prayer in the catacombs, but he was also gay and cheerful and scandalized some by encouraging the young to join in games and dances. He was persuaded to become ordained in 1551 and gathered round him a community of priests at the Church of San Girolamo. They met in the oratory or chapel of the church, and from this probably came the name of the Congregation of the Oratory which achieved papal approval in 1575. This was an order of secular priests living in community without vows, dedicated to leading men to God by prayer, frequent popular preaching and the regular administration of the sacraments. Learning from the congregational singing of popular worship, Philip Neri encouraged the holding of popular musical services by his Oratorians, from which the word 'oratorio' came. By the time of his death, there were oratories in Italy, Spain and southern Germany with preaching and services for the people, as well as the organizations and societies which were to become part of the life of all churches and parishes.

The overseas missionary work of the Counter-Reformation was represented by Francis Xavier (1506-52), an original member of the Jesuits and one of the greatest missionaries since the days of St Paul. He met Ignatius Loyola at the University of Paris and was ordained

[26] P. 213.

priest with him. In 1541 he was invited by King John III of Portugal to evangelize the East Indies. The ship on which he sailed from Lisbon was filthy and fever broke out on board; Xavier, who came from an aristocratic Spanish family, washed the linen and cooked the food of the sufferers. He settled in the Portuguese colony of Goa in India, where he laboured with equal success among the European and native population, but he stayed there only a year. Although he was always seasick, he travelled continuously, going in his tattered gown and old black hood to Travancore, Malacca, the Molucca Islands and Ceylon. In Travancore alone he baptized 10 000 natives in a month and founded thirty-five Christian settlements; in Ceylon he converted the King of Kandy with many of his people. In 1549 he landed in Japan, whose language he had studied, and there founded a Church which endured through terrible persecution. He longed to go to China; but he had worn out his strength and died on an island near Hong Kong, attended by a faithful Chinese servant, before he could enter the country. His body was taken to the Church of the Good Jesus in Goa, where it was placed in a magnificent shrine. Wherever he had preached, he left organized Christian communities, and the Jesuits said he had converted more than 700 000 people.

Though its emphasis upon practical activity and the need for man to find God through the institutions of the Church overshadowed the mystical approach, the Counter-Reformation was not without its spiritual, contemplative side, exemplified by the Spanish mystics, Teresa of Avila (1515-82) and John of the Cross (1549-91). Teresa was descended from an old Spanish family and at the age of eighteen entered a Carmelite convent, where the life was easy and the discipline relaxed. She longed to revive all the original rules of the Carmelites and in 1562 founded her first reformed convent. Her Carmelites were called the Barefooted, because they wore rough sandals, and the older, relaxed order was sometimes nicknamed the Barefaced. She founded sixteen convents and fourteen monasteries, being helped in this by John of the Cross, whom she met in 1567. Teresa and John were both organizers and mystics, whose spiritual writings became widely influential. Together they represent a great strength of the Counter-Reformation—its combination of administrative reform with deep religious commitment.

The political aspect

To a considerable extent the Counter-Reformation inevitably depended for much of its success upon the attitude of the political rulers of Europe. This was particularly true of some of the decrees of the

Council of Trent. The decrees concerning dogma were gradually accepted everywhere, but national rulers disliked the disciplinary decrees because they were likely to encroach upon their own ecclesiastical authority. They were soon accepted in Italy and the Roman Catholic states of Germany and cantons of Switzerland, but the kings of Spain and France were very hesitant to do so. In Spain they were finally accepted with the express reservation of the rights of the Crown, particularly with regard to ecclesiastical appointments; while in France they were never formally confirmed by the Crown, though a number of provincial church councils accepted them in the 1580s.[27] In both these countries, the Papacy could not do much to improve the standards of the clergy as long as appointments were controlled by the monarchs. In France, for instance, the diocese of Paris was without a seminary until the late seventeenth century.

Nevertheless, the Counter-Reformation was able in the last resort to achieve its successes because of the support it received from lay rulers. Foremost among these was Philip II of Spain, who was the most powerful European monarch in the second half of the sixteenth century. Though the Papacy did not always find him an easy ally,[28] he was a vigorous supporter of Roman Catholicism. His power in Spain and the Netherlands alone ensured that the Counter-Reformation was able to exercise a strong influence over the rest of Europe. In addition, Spain's possessions and influence in Italy enabled him to play an important role in preserving the peninsula entirely for Roman Catholicism. Overseas, the Spanish Empire provided it with peoples to convert in new parts of the world, as also did the Portuguese Empire.[29] Indeed, the Counter-Reformation in its later stages was in many ways a movement guided by Spaniards and promoted by Spanish power. Of Loyola's first six followers, four were Spaniards and one Portuguese, while the first three Generals of the Society were Spaniards; and the Council of Trent was so much dominated, especially in its last session, by Spanish ecclesiastics that it has been called the 'Spanish Council'.

Among other European rulers who assisted the Counter-Reformation were the Holy Roman Emperors, beginning with Charles V, who re-established the dominance of Roman Catholicism in Austria, Bohemia and Hungary. The kings of Poland made it possible for the Jesuits to recover the country for their faith, while the ultimate defeat of the Huguenots in France was due, above all else, to the French kings. The Elector of Bavaria and other Roman Catholic princes in Germany prevented the whole of this important part of Europe becoming Protestant. It had seemed that the old medieval Church, corrupt and disorganized under the influence of the Renaissance, would be unable to resist the new religious movements, but when the

[27] P. 112.   [28] P. 245.   [29] P. 69.

Counter-Reformation renewed the Church, the political forces which favoured it were able to check the growth of Protestantism and drive it back in several places. The Counter-Reformation was thus able to ensure, in a way that earlier in the century would have seemed very unlikely, that half of Europe was retained for papal authority.

Calais
Valenciennes
PICARDY
Amiens
Rouen
NORMANDY
Paris
CHAMPAGNE
Verdun
Metz
BRITTANY
R. Seine
Orleans
Blois
Tours
Amboise
BURGUNDY
R. Loire
Poitiers
La Rochelle
Lyons
Coutras
GUYENNE
LANGUEDOC
DAUPHINÉ
Bayonne
NAVARRE
Montpellier
Nimes
PROVENCE

| 0 | km | 200 |
| 0 | miles | 100 |

SIXTEENTH-CENTURY
FRANCE

14
THE
FRENCH WARS
OF
RELIGION

The background to the wars

One of the causes of the outbreak of the French Wars of Religion was the condition of the French Church in the sixteenth century. The Concordat of Bologna in 1516 had retained for the French monarch control over all important appointments in the Church.[1] This inevitably meant that the Crown used its ecclesiastical authority to provide for its diplomatic service and reward its favourites out of the endowments of the Church. Such appointments produced worldly bishops and abbots, who were swayed by court factions and cared little for their dioceses or monasteries. It also produced pluralism and absenteeism on a large scale, a glaring example of such abuses being provided by the Cardinal of Lorraine, a member of the important Guise family.[2]

Such men were not capable of being reformers, who could deal with the ignorance, worldliness, immorality and other abuses which the French Church shared with the rest of Christendom at the beginning of the century. The impulse for reform came from without, particularly from among the humanists whom Calvin met at the universities.[3] Their first leader was Jacques Lefèvre (c 1455-1536), who published in 1512 a Latin commentary on St Paul's Epistles and became one of a group of scholars who settled for a time at Meaux, under the protection of Guillaume Briçonnet, the bishop of the diocese, but they were not very influential, and the French reform movement during this time made slow progress. Later the French humanists came to favour the ideas of Luther, whose books were first brought into the country by traders from Germany. At first they suffered only occasional persecution until the 'day of the placards' in 1534 when Lutheran placards condemning the Mass were posted up in Paris and other towns; one was even fixed to the door of Francis I's bedchamber at Amboise. The King's anger resulted in the arrest of some two hundred people, mostly humble individuals, of whom twenty-four were burnt at the stake.

[1] P. 111.   [2] P. 91.   [3] P. 175.

During the following years, the reform movement practically disappeared in France, and the Reformation would probably never have revived in the country had it not been for the growth of Huguenotism or French Calvinism. The growth in the number of Huguenots led to more rigorous persecution by the government, culminating in the setting up by Henry II of the *chambre ardente*, a special court of the Parlement of Paris which tried cases of heresy between 1547 and 1550. Persecution, however, did not stop the growth in their numbers, and by the end of the 1550s they had become a formidable minority, which was consolidated by the Colloquy of Poissy.[4] Nevertheless, persecution compelled the Huguenots to consider their means of survival.[5] In some parts of the kingdom they were able to develop their own military organization, but still more had they to rely upon the protection of noblemen, some of whom became genuine converts to Calvinism, while others were more concerned with their own political ambitions and financial needs. The sixteenth century was a difficult time for many French noblemen. In the past they had always been recognized as warlike, uninterested in culture or court life and preferring to live in their provincial castles where life was often violent and unsettled. Originally land had been their great source of wealth, but now they were facing serious financial problems, which had been caused in a number of ways. Their estates were split up among their sons, owing to the absence of primogeniture and the belief that it was wrong for them to engage in trade or the professions; the real value of rents fell because of the inflation of the period; there was the expense of the wars in which they engaged and their extravagant imitation of the luxury of the Italian Renaissance.[6]

So the religious issue in France became involved in the contest between rival noble factions for control of the Crown and access to its patronage. During the reign of Henry II, these factions were gathered behind three great families.[7] The Bourbons were a younger branch of the reigning house of Valois and were next in succession to the throne after Henry II's sons. The head of the family, Anthony of Bourbon, had become a Calvinist, and so had his younger brother, Louis, Prince of Condé, who was to lead a Huguenot army for a time. The oldest family of France, the Montmorencys, were divided in their religious allegiance. The head of the family, Anne de Montmorency, Constable of France, remained a Roman Catholic, but his nephews, the Châtillons, became Huguenots, the chief among them being Gaspard de Coligny, Admiral of France, who spent much of his life at the court and in the service of the Crown. He was converted to Calvinism in 1560 and on Condé's death in 1569 became the recognized leader of the Huguenot cause. The leading Roman Catholic family, the Guises, were not related to the royal family, but possessed great

4 P. 224.   5 P. 180.   6 P. 90.   7 P. 113.

wealth and influence. Francis, Duke of Guise, was a prominent soldier and captured Calais from England; his brother, Charles, Cardinal of Lorraine, was a distinguished diplomat, and played an important part at the final session of the Council of Trent; and their niece, Mary, Queen of Scots, in 1558 married the Dauphin, Francis. Each of these families had their tenants, dependents and relatives, who supported them and relied upon them for favour and patronage, as did the religious groups whose leadership they had undertaken, and their conflicting ambitions brought civil strife ever nearer.

Catherine de Medici (1559-73)

In 1559 two events occurred that brought the threat of internal strife still closer. The bankrupt French monarchy signed the Treaty of Cateau-Cambrésis, bringing the Italian Wars to an end, but leaving many French noblemen without employment or resources. Secondly, Henry II died accidentally of a wound received in a tournament held to celebrate the signing of the Treaty, leaving four sons, the eldest of whom, the Dauphin, became King as Francis II at the age of fifteen. Henry also left a widow, Catherine de Medici, who was descended from the rulers of Florence. During her husband's reign she had not been at all prominent in state affairs, but now, at the age of forty, she came forward determined to save the heritage of her sons and defend their future. Her immediate plan was a policy of religious toleration in the hope that she could use the Huguenots as a check upon the Guises without allowing them to gain any control over state affairs. She was a woman of immense energy, and she devoted it all to her self-imposed task; she even came to have a desire to rule the kingdom.

At first, however, she had little opportunity to do anything because the Guises were able to secure control of the weakly Francis II and the Council, though the Chancellor, Michel de l'Hôpital (1504-73), stood for moderation. Condé and a group of Huguenot noblemen decided to strike at the Guise supremacy. They plotted to seize the King, when he was at Amboise in March 1560, capture or kill the Guises and establish a government of their own, but the plan failed, and several of the conspirators were killed. The Conspiracy of Amboise was the first attempt at force by the Huguenots, and it alarmed the Guises. They had Condé arrested, tried for treason and sentenced to death in November 1560; his life was only saved by the death of Francis II the next month.

Charles IX, who was only nine-and-a-half years old, succeeded to the throne, and this gave Catherine her opportunity. She showed her determination to be in control by moving from the Tournelles, the traditional residence in Paris of the Queen Mother, into the King's palace, the Louvre, and even slept with her son in his bedchamber. She got herself made Regent, appointed Anthony of Bourbon Lieutenant-General of the kingdom, retained L'Hôpital as Chancellor, released Condé from prison and excluded the Guises from power. She also summoned a meeting of the Estates-General, for the first time since 1484, at Orleans in December 1560 with the hope of obtaining a grant of taxes to meet the Crown's serious financial situation and a solution of the country's religious difficulties. But the Third Estate, in which the Huguenots were strongly represented, refused to consider either proposal.

Nevertheless, she persisted in her attempt to put into effect a policy of reconciliation and mediation and a programme of religious toleration and ecclesiastical reform that would preserve peace in the kingdom and save the Crown from factional domination. In May 1560, L'Hôpital had secured the publication of the Edict of Romarintin, which provided for the trial of heretics by the ecclesiastical courts under the French bishops (whom he hoped to be able to influence), in order to thwart the wish of the Guises to introduce the Inquisition into the country. Other attempts at propitiation were made by the government during 1561. The Ordinance of Orleans proposed certain Gallican reforms such as the election of bishops by a mixed body of laymen and ecclesiastics, who were to submit three names to the King for his final choice. The Colloquy of Poissy, a conference between bishops and Calvinist divines at Poissy on the Seine near Paris, was arranged. Though this was indecisive, it was followed in January 1562 by the Edict of Saint Germain, which for the first time gave official recognition to the Huguenots and allowed them to hold their synods, to worship freely in private and to hold public services in the suburbs of towns (where they were less likely to provoke disorder) and in the countryside.

Such concessions to the Huguenots united Catherine's opponents. In the spring of 1561 Guise and Montmorency abandoned their rivalry and, together with Marshal Saint-André, a distinguished soldier and friend of Montmorency, formed the 'Triumvirate' with the intention of gaining control of the government. They made approaches to the Parlement of Paris and to Spain, and they were joined by Anthony of Bourbon, who resented that he had not been made Regent. They opposed the Edict of Saint Germain, which was, indeed, generally unpopular in the kingdom and was only registered by the Parlement of Paris after a long debate. The intermingling of religious and factious differences was now producing an increasingly dangerous situation, and in March 1562 the incident occurred that precipitated the outbreak of the First Civil War. This was the Massacre of Vassy, which took place when some armed retainers of the Duke of Guise, passing through the town of Vassy in Champagne, came across a Huguenot congregation worshipping illegally in a barn within the town walls. In the riot that followed, some thirty Huguenots were killed. Guise immediately went to Paris and secured control of the capital and the government, the Huguenot pastors called on their congregations to resist, and fighting began in several parts of the country.

Though the First Civil War was marked by skirmishes rather than battles, there were also savage incidents which showed the bitterness of the feelings that had been aroused. For instance, in the village of St Gilles in Provence the Huguenots in 1562 cut the throats of the parish priests and threw their bodies down a well in the crypt of the church; in another village the local lord had the Huguenots drowned in a river near his house. Moreover, both sides suffered losses among their leaders during the encounters. Anthony of Bourbon and Marshal Saint-André were killed fighting, Guise was murdered, and Condé and Montmorency were each taken prisoner by their opponents. These events were to the advantage of Catherine de Medici. She was freed from Guise control and was able to negotiate an end to the fighting, with the aid of L'Hôpital. The two prisoners were exchanged, and the Pacification of Amboise was signed in March 1563. This allowed Huguenot worship in the houses of noblemen, in places where it was already established and in the suburbs of one town in each administrative district, but none was to be permitted in Paris.

At first it looked as if Catherine's policy of appeasement and compromise had succeeded, but in reality the country was not in the mood for mutual toleration. The First Civil War and the Pacification of Amboise had intensified and not calmed the opposing feuds and hatreds. Each faction was still determined to gain power, and the murder of the Duke of Guise was not forgotten by his family. The Huguenots resented the continuing limitations placed upon their freedom of worship, but the Roman Catholics were indignant that concessions should have been made to heretics. Moreover, it was clear that the greater part of the French people remained Roman Catholic, and that the Counter-Reformation revival was beginning to have an effect in the country. The Parlement of Paris refused to register the Pacification of Amboise, thus increasing the dissatisfaction and alarm of the Huguenots.

Catherine began to see that her plan to calm the situation by making concessions to the Huguenots was showing signs of failure. She decided to make an effort to rally public opinion behind the Crown. Between 1564 and 1566 she and the King undertook a solemn royal progress around France, and in the course of it she met the Duke of Alva and her favourite daughter, Elizabeth, who had been married

H

to Philip II as part of the Treaty of Cateau-Cambrésis. This meeting in June 1565 aroused, almost certainly wrongly, Huguenot suspicions that she was seeking Spanish help against them; and their apprehension seemed justified in the summer of 1567 when Alva marched his army from Milan along the eastern frontier of France into the Netherlands.[8] In September, therefore, they staged the Surprise of Meaux, an unsuccessful attempt to seize the King in this town to the north-east of Paris, an event which set off the Second Civil War.

This was a short war, and the only notable casualty was Montmorency, the last of the Triumvirate. His death seemed to strengthen Catherine's position further, and she and L'Hôpital were able to restore peace in March 1568 by the Edict of Longjumeau (the 'Patched-up Peace' as it was called), which ratified the Pacification of Amboise and so satisfied no one and did nothing to calm the situation. The Parlement again refused to register it, and clearly only a brief truce had been procured. Moreover, Catherine had been enraged by the Surprise of Meaux. She now believed that her policy had been a mistake and that the Huguenots could not be induced to support the Crown. She dismissed L'Hôpital and issued edicts withdrawing all previous grants of freedom of worship to the Huguenots and ordering their ministers to leave the country. For a time she even planned to seize Coligny and Condé. By October 1568 the Huguenots had risen, and the Third Civil War broke out.

This was the longest of the wars hitherto and marked by increasingly cruel acts of slaughter. Early in 1569 Henry, Duke of Anjou, the King's brother, who was now Lieutenant-General of the kingdom, won the Battle of Jarnac, defeating Condé and executing him after he had surrendered; and in October he defeated Coligny at the Battle of Moncontour. The Huguenots seemed to have been decisively beaten, but Coligny reformed his army and marched it across the south of France to the Rhône, adding to its numbers all the time. Catherine had not enough money to renew the fighting, and she wished to free herself from the power of the Cardinal of Lorraine, who had now come to dominate the Council. She opened negotiations with the Huguenots, which resulted in the Peace of Saint Germain in August 1570. Despite the Huguenot defeats, its terms were still similar to those of the Pacification of Amboise. They were now to have freedom of worship in two towns in each administrative district and were assured civil and judicial equality. In addition, they were allowed to garrison and fortify four towns—La Rochelle, Montauban, La Charité and Cognac—for two years as guarantees of the fulfilment of the treaty. The Huguenots remained as strong as ever in the country, and they had now won for themselves political security as well as religious toleration.

[8] P. 256.

The settlement placed Coligny in a very powerful position. In the summer of 1571 he appeared at court and rejoined the Council. There he gained the support of Charles IX, who resented his younger brother's military triumphs and saw himself able, with the Admiral's assistance, to assert himself as King and follow a policy that would gain him national support and renown. Coligny had a forceful character and was capable of a single-minded determination to achieve anything to which he set his mind; he was inspired as strongly by his patriotism as by his religion. His plan now aimed equally at uniting his country, serving its national interests and promoting the cause of international Protestantism. It was essentially an anti-Spanish policy; Spain had defeated France in Italy and threatened her position in Europe, and Spain was also the upholder of the Inquisition and the oppressor of the Calvinists in the Netherlands. Since 1568 he had been in close contact with William of Orange and Louis of Nassau and discussed with them the possibility of France receiving the southern half of the Netherlands in return for military assistance against Spain.[9] At first Catherine supported his plan and was pleased that it was proposed that it should be accompanied by dynastic marriages. Negotiations were begun for the marriage of her favourite son, Henry of Anjou, with Queen Elizabeth I to secure England as an ally, and her daughter, Margaret of Valois, was betrothed to the young Henry of Navarre, son of Anthony, a match which it was hoped would end the civil strife in France.

Coligny's plan, however, was not as likely to succeed as he believed. There were strong factors opposed to its fulfilment both at home and abroad. France, as a fundamentally Roman Catholic country, did not relish a role that would make it an ally of Protestant states and an opponent of the Counter-Reformation. The hatred aroused by three civil wars was still as bitter as ever, and the Guises had always suspected Coligny of complicity in the Duke's murder. Papal and Spanish influence was increasingly directed against his policy, and the Battle of Lepanto in October 1571 was a reminder of Spain's power and prestige.[10] Elizabeth of England had no real intention of either marrying Henry of Anjou or becoming deeply involved against Spain in the Netherlands. Above all, Catherine turned against the plan. She disliked Coligny's growing dominance over the King, and she feared that France would be dragged into a war against Spain, the outcome of which would be detrimental to her position whatever happened, because success would be likely to aid the Huguenots and defeat would strengthen the Guises.

Her hand was forced, however, when in April 1572 Elizabeth I withdrew the permission she had given the Sea Beggars to use English ports as bases from which to prey on Spanish shipping, with the result

[9] P. 258.   [10] P. 135.

that the next month they seized the ports of Brill and Flushing.[11] Louis of Nassau followed this up by advancing from Germany and capturing Mons. William invaded Brabant and Flanders, and a volunteer force of Huguenots took Valenciennes. Another Huguenot force, sent to relieve Louis who was now besieged in Mons by Alva, was surprised and defeated by the Spaniards, but Charles and Coligny agreed in August (without consulting Catherine) to send an army of 15 000 men into the Netherlands to assist the revolt. Catherine could think of only one thing to do. She suggested to Henry, Duke of Guise, that he should avenge his father's death by arranging the assassination of Coligny.

The occasion for this was presented by the wedding between Margaret of Valois and Henry of Navarre in Paris in August 1572. Thousands of Huguenot noblemen and gentlemen had come to the city for the event. While returning home one day from a visit to the court, Coligny was shot by an arquebus from the window of a house, but he was merely wounded in the arm. Angry and alarmed, the Huguenots demanded an enquiry into the event, and Charles IX publicly promised that he would see that justice was done. Catherine was now in a much more dangerous position than ever before. Her complicity and that of the Guises in the deed would certainly be discovered and revealed. She acted quickly and desperately. Within twenty-four hours she had persuaded the King to sign an order for the assassination of Coligny and other banned Huguenot leaders, who were, she succeeded in assuring him, about to seize control of the government and threaten his life.

Early in the morning of the next day, St Bartholomew's Day, 24th August 1572, the Duke of Guise and Roman Catholic noblemen began the killing of the designated Huguenot leaders. Guise himself supervised the murder of Coligny, waiting outside the Admiral's house until his bleeding body was thrown by the assassins from the window on to the street. Within a few hours, however, the slaughter had spread beyond its instigators' intentions. Parisians, who were always staunchly Roman Catholic, resented the presence of so large a number of Huguenots in the city for such an important event. Mobs roamed the streets killing indiscriminately every Huguenot they could find, and many private enmities that had arisen during the years of strife were avenged too. The massacres spread to the provinces, and similar scenes were repeated in other cities. How many perished during those days is not known. Estimates put it between five and ten thousand, about half the killings probably taking place in Paris itself. Among prominent Huguenots, only Henry of Navarre and the new Prince of Condé were spared; they were kept prisoner at court and forced to abjure their Protestant faith.

[11] P. 258.

Pope Gregory XIII greeted the news of the Massacre of St Bartholomew as a triumph for the Counter-Reformation. He ordered a solemn
Te Deum to be sing in Rome as a thanksgiving, and a commemorative
medal was struck; and, later, scenes of the slaughter were depicted on
the wall of the Sistine Chapel. Philip II welcomed it too and, indeed,
he gained most from the deed, for without French military help Louis
of Nassau had to surrender Mons to Alva, who restored Spanish
authority in the southern Netherlands and captured and sacked Malines,
Zutphen and Naarden and laid siege to Haarlem in the north.[12] In
England and the German Lutheran states, the news was received with
horror as a brutal blow at the cause of Protestantism; Queen Elizabeth
I dressed herself in mourning when she received the French ambassador
in London.

At first it seemed as if Catherine had emerged triumphant from the
Massacre. The danger of war against Spain was averted; the Huguenots
had lost their leaders among the nobility, and many of their followers
had been terrorized into returning to Roman Catholicism or fleeing
to Geneva or Strasburg. She had reason to hope that they had been
eliminated as a militant party. Certainly the numbers and influence of
the movement had been greatly reduced. Its members were now
confined largely to areas in southern and western France, and their
survival depended more than ever upon the inability of the Crown to
assert itself over the other parties which opposed it. Nevertheless,
within these areas and especially in the towns, its ordinary members
remained faithful to their faith, found leaders among their ministers
and were able to organize their armed forces and defend their
cities.

The continuance of Huguenot resistance was made evident in
September 1572 when a royal governor was sent to take possession
of the seaport of La Rochelle, which had become a Huguenot stronghold. The ministers and people refused to admit him and successfully
defied a royal army sent to intimidate them, thereby starting the Fourth
Civil War. After a siege of seven months, La Rochelle still held out,
and Catherine made peace because Anjou had to abandon the campaign and go to Poland, where he had been elected King.[13] In July
1573 the Peace of La Rochelle granted liberty of conscience to Huguenots everywhere and freedom of worship in all noble households and
to the citizens of La Rochelle and also of Montauban and Nîmes,
which had also revolted against the government. These terms were
less favourable to the Huguenots than those they had obtained in
previous settlements, but they represented the failure of the Guises
and the Roman Catholics to refuse them any tolerated position in the
kingdom. The Huguenots had survived, though they had passed their
period of greatest strength and political capability.

[12] P. 259.   [13] P. 323.

The emergence of the Politiques (1573-85)

The Massacre of St Bartholomew had led many Roman Catholics to give their support to the Politiques, a group which had appeared in France in the middle 1560s and now became more important in French politics. Never a well-organized movement, they held that, while religion was an individual matter, the state had a supreme claim upon the allegiance of all its members. To them the kingship was an institution that should be above all parties and the government of the kingdom should be put first beyond belief in any other movement. They stood for a strong monarchy and religious toleration so that France could put aside her fratricidal strife and unite all her citizens in the common cause of her greatness. The policy adopted by Catherine, which meant the continuance of national disunity, the political supremacy of the Guises and monarchical dependence on Spain, led the Politiques, though they were monarchists and many of them devout Roman Catholics, to ally themselves with the Huguenots. They also, like the other movements, attracted leaders of their own from the court factions. Catherine's restless, ambitious youngest son, Francis of Alençon, joined them as a move against his brother, Henry; but their most important new member was Henry of Montmorency-Damville, the former Constable's younger son, who was a Roman Catholic and Governor of Languedoc in the south of France, where the family had large estates. The Politiques were supported also by lawyers and administrative officials, who wanted strong government, and by merchants and financiers, whose businesses had suffered from the internal strife.

Together the Huguenots and Politiques set up in the part of France where they were strongest a state within a state comprising the southern provinces of Languedoc, Provence, Dauphiné and Guyenne. Under the control of Damville, it had its own republican form of government with its Council of State, meetings of estates and law courts. It also collected its own taxes and customs duties, which worsened the Crown's financial difficulties. All France south of the Loire was under Damville's rule, and Catherine was unable to take any effective action against him. This was shown when his action brought about the outbreak of the Fifth Civil War in February 1574.

A few weeks after the renewal of fighting, Charles IX died at the age of twenty-four. Anjou hastened back from Poland and succeeded him as Henry III. He and Catherine found that they could make no impression upon the firmly-entrenched Huguenots and Politiques, particularly since both Condé and Henry of Navarre escaped from the court, renounced their forced conversion to Roman Catholicism and joined the revolt. After some months of indeterminate fighting, the Crown had to agree in May 1576 to the Peace of Monsieur, which granted the Huguenots the maximum rights they ever achieved. They were to have complete freedom of worship everywhere except in Paris and places of residence of the royal family, courts composed of an equal number of judges of each religion were to be set up to try cases in which Huguenots were involved, and the Huguenots were to garrison eight fortified towns to guarantee the observance of the treaty. Henry of Navarre was made Governor of Guienne, and Condé was made Governor of Picardy.

The settlement was very acceptable to the Huguenots since it brought them complete religious toleration. The Politiques welcomed it also because they hoped it would free the Crown from control by the Guises and so enable it to take its rightful place in the government of the kingdom. Their view was expressed in this same year in *Les Six Livres de la République* by Jean Bodin (1530-96) who held that peace could only be restored if the authority of the Crown were made supreme above all factions. But the Huguenots and Politiques had only been able to obtain this settlement because the Crown was weak, and it proved itself unable to maintain peace by being unable to resist the demands of others who sought to take advantage of the situation for their own ends.

Henry III lacked mental and physical stamina, but even a much stronger ruler could hardly have prevented the developments which followed the Peace of Monsieur. The Roman Catholics were enraged by its terms. For some years they had been forming local unions or leagues, headed by noblemen and bishops, to protect their cause. Now these united into a national Catholic League, centred upon Paris and headed by Henry, Duke of Guise, who assumed the leadership of the movement after the death of the Cardinal of Lorraine in 1574. The League showed its power by dominating the Estates General, when it met at Blois in December 1576, and attacking the powers of the Crown. Much as he mistrusted the League, Henry III could only give it his support, which meant renewed war with the Huguenots. By now Damville had gone over to the side of the court, and the Huguenots were defeated in the Sixth Civil War. By the Peace of Bergerac in September 1577 their freedom of worship was restricted to the suburbs of one town in each administrative district and in those towns where it had already existed before the renewal of fighting.

Henry III now declared all religious leagues dissolved, and the aged Catherine tried hard to bring about a permanent settlement, but both the weakness of the King's character and the continuing factious divisions in the country undermined her efforts. Henry of Guise was now faced as a rival by Henry of Navarre, who had assumed the leadership of the Huguenot cause and, since both Henry III and his brother were childless, was likely to succeed to the throne. Nevertheless, Catherine succeeded in maintaining an uneasy peace, which was broken by the short and indecisive Seventh Civil War in 1580. It was at this time, too, that the publication of *Vindiciae contra tyrannos*, edited by Philip Mornay, asserting the right of the people to rise against and depose a tyrant, showed that the Huguenots were being driven to abandon the idea of a divinely-appointed kingly rule in favour of one based upon popular choice, and also that they were becoming more definitely opposed to the French monarchy and likely to move away from the position of the Politiques.

The uneasy truce was upset by the death of Henry's brother, Francis, in June 1584. Henry of Navarre, who was descended from a brother of St Louis, was now the legal heir to the throne, but Henry of Guise, who claimed descent further back from Charlemagne, did not hesitate to contest this claim in favour of himself. Moreover, the prospect of a heretic on the French throne led to a revival of the Catholic League, which declared its support for Henry of Guise's claim. The Guises had long been in close contact with Spain, and in December 1584 Henry of Guise made the secret Treaty of Joinville with Philip II. By this treaty Philip agreed to give financial assistance to help the League destroy Protestantism in France and to declare (as a temporary solution) the heir to the throne to be Henry of Navarre's aged uncle, the Cardinal of Bourbon. Henry III once again, particularly since the Crown was still chronically short of money, could only give his support to the League. In July 1585 he and Catherine made the Treaty of Nemours with Henry of Guise by which he revoked all previous edicts of religious toleration, exiled all Protestant ministers from the kingdom and gave their congregations six months in which either to adopt Roman Catholicism or to go into exile themselves. This was followed by an edict debarring Henry of Navarre from the throne, and in September 1585 Pope Sixtus V was persuaded to excommunicate him.[14] Henry and the Huguenots had no choice but to renew the fighting.

The War of the Three Henries (1585-89)

The Eighth Civil War is known as the War of the Three Henries since it involved three groups—the Politiques and the Huguenots led by Henry of Navarre, the Catholic League and Spain which supported Henry of Guise, and the Monarchists, who adhered to the reigning monarch, Henry III. Religion had now come to play little part in the contest. It had become a struggle between Henry of Navarre and Henry of Guise for the succession to the throne while Henry III was determined to do all that he could to save the Crown from domination by the Guises.

[14] P. 246.

Henry of Navarre and Henry of Guise were quite well-matched against each other. Navarre received German help in 1587, and Guise had Spanish help, though Philip II's preoccupation with the Revolt of the Netherlands and with the Spanish Armada, as well as his mistrust of the Guises, restricted the amount he received. Both men won victories—Navarre routed a royal army at Coutras in 1587, while Guise defeated the Germans at Vimory and again at Auneau. National support, however, was increasing for the League. The Counter-Reformation was gaining influence in France, and the northern provinces resented the heavy taxation they had been compelled to pay since the establishment of the independent Huguenot enclave in the south. Nowhere was the feeling for the League stronger than in Paris, where a group of about fifty citizens, called the Council of Sixteen from the sixteen districts of the city, took over control. Henry III found his authority virtually defied, but there was little he dared do. The crisis came in May 1588, when the League urged the Duke of Guise to go to Paris to consolidate his power there, but the King ordered him not to do so. The Duke defied the King and made a triumphal entry into the city. The King was able to summon royal troops to his aid, but the people, roused by the preachers, erected barricades in the streets, isolated the troops into small groups and compelled them to surrender. The Day of the Barricades was a complete defeat for the King. He fled from Paris, but then had to return and receive Guise at court, and in July 1588 he issued the Act of Union appointing Guise Lieutenant-General of the kingdom. The League was now effectively in control of the royal government, and when the Estates-General met at Blois in October 1588 its representatives dominated the proceedings and put forward proposals to limit the power of the Crown.

Henry III, however, was determined to free himself from such humiliating domination. Realizing that the defeat of the Armada in August 1588 had crippled Spain for the time being, he ordered Guise to attend a meeting of the Council at the Château of Blois in the early morning of 23rd December and had him murdered by the royal bodyguard; his brother, the Cardinal of Guise, was killed the next day. The King brought the good news to his mother, who was on her death-bed, but she is said to have been unable to share his delight about its results; indeed, when she died a fortnight later, the consequences were said to be the same as those that had followed the Massacre of St Bartholomew. Then the Huguenots had renounced their allegiance to the Crown; now the League became an openly revolutionary party. Guise's brother, the Duke of Mayenne, and the Council of Sixteen ruled Paris, and town after town in the provinces rose in support of the League. The King was without money, and his authority hardly extended beyond the towns of the Loire valley. There was nothing he could do except ally himself with Henry of Navarre, and in April 1589 the two Henries laid siege to Paris. When they were in sight of success on the first day of August, Henry III was stabbed to death by a young Dominican friar, who regarded him as a traitor to God and His Church.

Henry IV and the Edict of Nantes (1589-98)

Henry of Navarre was now Henry IV, the lawful ruler of France—had been recognized by Henry III as his successor before he died—but because Henry IV was a Protestant, many noblemen and towns refused to recognize him, and his army dwindled to half its size. The League recognized the Cardinal of Bourbon as Charles IX, but he was in his nephew's hands and died in 1590. Philip II proposed, therefore, that his daughter, the Infanta Isabella Clara Eugenia, should succeed to the throne. Moreover, he was now prepared to send direct military help to the League. It was essential for Spain that France should remain Roman Catholic, and a monarchy established with her assistance and linked with her by family ties would acquiesce in her supremacy in Europe.

Henry IV's position, however, was far from hopeless. Besides the Huguenots he had the support of the Politiques and of those Roman Catholics who wished to uphold the legal, hereditary succession to the throne and resented the idea of Spanish predominance in French affairs; in addition members of the League began to desert it through uncertainty about their appointments.[15] Moreover, he showed himself to be a very able soldier and pursued the Ninth Civil War with vigour and determination. Though forced to abandon the siege of Paris and withdraw his army into Normandy, he defeated a much larger force under Mayenne at the Battle of Arques, near Rouen, in September 1589. This enabled him to resume the siege of Paris the next year, but he had to retreat when the Duke of Parma advanced from the Netherlands with his veteran army, and again in 1592 when Henry besieged Rouen and Parma intervened to save this city, though he died before the end of the year. An increasing number of Frenchmen were attracted by Henry's courage and military skill and repelled by Spanish intervention, but it was also clear that the country as a whole would never be willing to accept a Protestant monarch.

The crisis came in 1593 when the Estates-General met in Paris to determine the succession to the throne and, in effect, to what extent religion was involved. Philip II based his daughter's claim on the fact that she represented the house of Valois on the female line through her mother; but the Estates-General rejected this as being contrary

15 P. 90.

to Salic Law which had come to be regarded as a vital part of French law.[16] The law of succession was thus declared to be superior to ecclesiastical or any other law and Henry was declared to be the King of France. This decision was particularly welcome to the Politiques because it upheld their belief in the position of the French monarchy as an institution superior to the claims of all parties and creeds in the State. The insuperable obstacle of religion, however, still remained. Paris held out against him, and he could not conquer the country by force. The war seemed interminable.

Henry had hitherto maintained his Protestantism rather than seem to desert and betray those who had suffered and fought with him, but he was now convinced that the time had come when he must accept the religion of most of his subjects if he were to save the country. 'Paris is well worth a Mass,' he said. In 1593 he announced his return to the faith which previously he had been compelled to accept after the Massacre of St Bartholomew; in July he was formally received into the Roman Catholic Church, and absolved and recognized as King by the Pope in September 1595. His action destroyed that fear of a heretical ruler which had united his opponents, and he readily bribed into acceptance of his authority the noblemen and other leaders of the League. He was able to enter Paris unopposed in March 1594. 'That which is Caesar's has been given to Caesar,' said one of his companions as they rode into the city. 'Given' said Henry, looking at the Governor of the city. 'No, sold, and at a good price.' In offices, estates and money he probably made over to the leaders of the League more than his first year's income.

To emphasize that the civil strife was now over and that he was henceforward fighting a foreign invader, Henry formally declared war on Spain in January, 1595. At first the war went badly for him. The Spaniards captured Calais in 1596 and Amiens the next year, but he knew that the campaign was imposing a serious strain on their resources and that they would not be able to conquer France. He held out, and by a supreme effort managed to retake Amiens. Both sides by now wanted peace, and, by the negotiations that ended with the Treaty of Vervins in May 1598, Spain gave up Calais and withdrew her troops from Picardy. So France recovered her former boundaries; Spain had not been able to dismember or subjugate her during the Wars of Religion. Both countries were exhausted and in no condition to renew hostilities against each other. Yet, weak though France was when the Treaty was signed, she was left in a position that would enable her, when strong enough, to challenge the Spanish supremacy in Europe which Charles V and Philip II had maintained during the sixteenth century.

In April 1598, shortly before the signing of the Treaty of Vervins,

[16] P. 107.

Henry issued the Edict of Nantes which was designed to conciliate the Huguenots, many of whom bitterly resented what they regarded as his treacherous desertion of their cause. No longer could they hope to challenge the government of the country or convert the French people to their faith. The two thousand congregations they had possessed in 1562 had now declined to less than eight hundred. The League had deprived them almost completely of the northern and eastern provinces of the kingdom, but they still occupied a compact region in the south where they retained their political and military organization. They threatened to renew the war, which helped Henry to overcome Roman Catholic opposition to a settlement with them. The Edict of Nantes followed the lines of the settlements which had been made during the Wars of Religion. It granted the Huguenots freedom of conscience throughout the kingdom and allowed them the right of public worship in all places where they had exercised it during the preceding two years, except in Paris and five leagues (about 20 kilometres) around the city and places where the court resided. Noblemen, ministers of state, courtiers and officials, even if in attendance at the court, might have Protestant services in their homes or lodgings, provided these were behind closed doors and the psalm-singing was not heard outside. Huguenots were to have all civil rights belonging to subjects of the Crown and be eligible for official posts and degrees, though they might only open schools and print books where they had the right to worship in public; their clergy were to have the same exemptions from military service as Roman Catholic clergy. The special mixed law-courts, previously set up for them, were to be retained; they were granted the right to hold political and religious assemblies and synods; and they were to garrison for eight years with Protestant soldiers and under Protestant governors (but maintained by the Crown) 142 walled towns as guarantees, of which the fortresses of La Rochelle, Montauban and Montpellier were the most important. Finally, the Edict was declared irrevocable and perpetual.

Like most settlements, the Edict of Nantes was a compromise and, therefore, did not satisfy either side. The Roman Catholic clergy denounced it, and the Parlement of Paris refused at first to ratify it, but had to give way before Henry's insistence. A historian has described it as 'a treaty between two powers comparatively equal.' In fact, the Huguenots now amounted to only about a tenth of the population, and its terms, in an age which still mistrusted religious toleration and was moving away from local political independence towards centralized government, represented Henry's determination to avoid a renewal of civil war. He himself showed that he shared the Politique outlook when he said, 'There must be no more distinction between Catholics and Huguenots. Everyone must be good Frenchmen.' It could hardly be a permanent settlement of the religious question. Many Frenchmen only accepted it for the sake of peace and hoped that clemency might convert the Huguenots where force had failed. If this should not happen, it was unlikely that any government strong enough to assert its will would allow the Huguenots to retain their privileged position indefinitely, and this was to happen with the Revocation of the Edict of Nantes by Louis XIV less than a century later.

The consequences of the long-drawn-out Wars of Religion were serious for France, particularly in the field of politics. From the slaughter and suffering, the dislocation of trade and material destruction, France recovered, as countries do after wars, with comparative rapidity, but other consequences remained. The breakdown of royal government and the intransigence of the noble factions had created a readiness in France for strong government. This made possible the powerful monarchy of the seventeenth century, culminating in the rule of Louis XIV and the practical elimination of the feudal nobility from participation in government, but in other ways the Wars of Religion mitigated against the completeness and efficiency of monarchical power. Many of the old nobility had been killed in battle or forced to sell their estates, a development which assisted the rise of the new nobility.[17] The members of this nobility were more tenacious of their feudal rights and privileges, thus preventing, while the monarchy remained in existence, the proper reform of the financial system so essential for the Crown, particularly as it started the seventeenth century burdened by a debt inherited from the Wars of Religion and subsequently made worse by later wars. In effect, therefore, the Wars of Religion contributed towards the undermining of the monarchy less than two centuries later.

[17] P 85

15
THE
ASCENDANCY
OF
SPAIN

The unification of Spain

At the outset of the sixteenth century, Spain was still divided into two kingdoms, Aragon and Castile, though the first steps towards the creation of a united kingdom had already been taken, through the marriage of Ferdinand of Aragon and Isabella of Castile in 1469 and the conquest of Granada in 1492.[1] The union of Aragon and Castile, therefore, existed in the persons of their monarchs, the 'Catholic Kings', and it was, in fact, a loose confederation. Each kingdom kept its own cortes, political institutions and officials, laws, courts, armed forces, taxation and coinage. There were customs barriers between the two kingdoms, and for long they had no mutual system of extradition of criminals. The overseas empire, which came into being during this period, was regarded as belonging to Castile and was administered for her benefit.[2] When the kingdoms were united under the rule of a single monarch later in the sixteenth century, although he was commonly called the 'King of Spain', such a title did not, in fact, exist even then.

Despite the existence, however, of so much division in the government of Spain, an increasing measure of centralization and unity came to be achieved through the actual preponderance of Castile in so many ways. That the King resided in Castile and was surrounded by Castilian courtiers and advisers, that the empire was governed from Castile and trade conducted through it and that the army was largely raised in Castile, all this tended to give Castile a preponderance in the government of the country. Moreover, since the Crown was stronger in Castile than in Aragon,[3] both Charles V and Philip II were to follow a policy of Castilianization aimed at making the Crown equally powerful throughout the country by reducing it all 'to the same order and legal system as Castile[4]. Not until their time was a conciliar system evolved for the whole country, and even then the Council of Aragon and the Council of Castile each retained administrative importance.[5] The most

[1] Pp. 106, 187.   [2] P. 73.   [3] P. 195.   [4] P. 196.   [5] P. 520.

powerful institution to contribute towards the centralization of the country was undoubtedly the Spanish Inquisition, which proved to be a very effective political weapon in the hands of the monarchy.[6]

Ferdinand and Isabella had, by the beginning of the sixteenth century, done much to assert the power of the monarchy in Castile. In 1480 the Council of Castile had been reorganized so that it no longer consisted entirely of noblemen and bishops, but was augmented by the appointment of lawyers who could serve the Crown as trustworthy and efficient officials. The semi-autonomous military orders, formed during the *Reconquista* to fight against the Moors, had been brought under royal control as Ferdinand secured election to the Grand Masterships of all the important ones which, during the reign of Charles V, became permanently attached to the Crown. Another result of the *Reconquista* was the formation by towns of their own *hermandad* or brotherhood of archers for defence against Moorish attacks. These had been reorganized in 1476 into a single *Santa Hermandad* under the control of the Council of Castile, and it had proved a useful means of checking noble factionalism and disorder until, in 1498, it had been incorporated into the ordinary armed forces of the Crown. The nobility had been further subdued in 1480 when they were forbidden to build new castles and engage in private wars and were compelled to restore lands which they had taken from the Crown in previous years of weakness. In 1480 also, the towns had been brought under royal control when *corregidors* or royal officials were appointed to supervise their administration. The Spanish Inquisition was established in 1478, and the Papacy had to make important concessions to the Crown in Granada in 1486.[7] During this time, Cardinal Ximenes carried out his important ecclesiastical reforms.[8]

In Aragon, such an extension of royal power had not been possible because of the different institutions and traditions of the kingdom.[9] However, the Spanish Inquisition had been introduced, and the Council of Aragon was reorganized in 1494 to act as the advisory body to the King. Ferdinand could do no more and probably did not wish to do so. In any event, he did not spend much time in his own kingdom, being occupied with Castilian affairs and the Italian Wars. It was due to the latter and his membership of the Holy League that he obtained in 1512, and in the last years of his life, the return to Castile of Navarre after nearly three centuries of French rule.[10]

The fact that Castile and Aragon remained separate kingdoms presented difficulties when Queen Isabella died in 1504 because, of the family of the 'Catholic Kings', their son, John, had died in 1497, and their daughter, Isabella, married to King Emmanual of Portugal, had died in childbirth together with her son who would have united the whole Iberian peninsula under his rule. Queen Isabella left Castile

[6] P. 111.   [7] P. 110.   [8] P. 202.   [9] P. 116.   [10] P. 143.

to their daughter, Joanna, who was married to Philip of Burgundy.[11] Philip assumed the title of King of Castile and expected to inherit the title of King of Aragon as well on Ferdinand's death. However, he died suddenly in September 1506, and Joanna became insane. A Council of Regency was set up in Castile headed by Ferdinand, who was thus able, when he died in January 1516, to leave both Castile and Aragon to his grandson, Charles, who was the first to unite them under a single ruler and who brought the Habsburg dynasty to the throne of Spain.

Ferdinand and Isabella had done much to forward the creation of a united Spain, though it was still incomplete when their kingdoms passed to the sole direction of their grandson. They had made the Spanish Church a national institution and placed it under the control of the Crown. They had given the Crown also a firm base of authority in Castile, where both the nobility and the towns had been brought beneath royal domination. An international future for the new kingdom had been planned through the contemporary method of matrimonial alliances. Two of their daughters had been married into Portugal, a third and their son to the Habsburgs and a fourth, Catherine, to England. At the same time, the extent of Spanish rule had been enlarged not only in Spain itself and in Italy, but also in the New World where the great Spanish Empire was being established. When, therefore, Charles V came to rule over their kingdoms, he was able, despite his personal difficulties, to continue their work and carry the unification of Spain under the new monarchy much further.[12]

The only threats to his rule in Spain came in the early 1520s. The first was the Revolt of the Comuneros in 1520.[13] The cities of Castile disliked the reduction of their power by the appointment of the *corregidors*, and now they resented the heavy taxation imposed upon them before Charles' sudden departure to Germany, which in itself seemed contrary to Spanish interests. Representatives from the various communes, mostly from noble families, met at Avila and put forward moderate demands, which included the removal of Flemish officials, limits on taxation and the independence of the Cortes. It was essentially a conservative, traditional movement, seeking to preserve the old liberties of Castile against monarchical encroachment rather than to set up a new revolutionary system of government. For a time it seemed dangerous to Charles V's authority, but the movement began to disintegrate, fell under the influence of extremist leaders and was put down with the help of the Castilian nobility at Villalar in 1521, and the power of the Crown was soon restored everywhere. It had been too limited in area, support and aims to be successful. The almost simultaneous revolt of the Germania in Valencia was an equal failure.[14]

[11] P. 187.   [12] P. 196.   [13] Pp. 85, 117.   [14] P. 195.

Henceforward Charles succeeded in making Spain a powerful, firmly-governed kingdom which, during the reign of his son, enjoyed the time of its greatest power and prestige.

The inheritance of Philip II

The accession of Philip II in 1556, following Charles V's abdication and the signing of the Treaty of Cateau-Cambrésis in 1559, made him the strongest ruler in Europe. Charles had carefully allocated to his son territories which formed a powerful, prosperous empire.[15] Philip now ruled over Spain, Naples and Sicily, Milan, the Netherlands and the Spanish possessions overseas, which brought him a seemingly inexhaustible supply of bullion. Spain dominated the western Mediterranean, hemmed in her most serious rival, France, and could hope to dominate the Continent militarily with her unsurpassed infantry. Her government-controlled Church and lack of religious dissension preserved her from a weakness which hampered other countries—she was assuming the leadership of the Counter-Reformation.[16]

Philip II was the only son of Charles V, who had married his cousin, Isabella, the daughter of Emmanuel I of Portugal. He was descended, therefore, from the 'Catholic Kings' of Spain through both his father and his mother, though in appearance he had the fair hair, blue eyes and fresh complexion of his north European ancestors. All through his reign he worked hard at the business of government, reading reports, interviewing ministers and presiding over councils. It was probably not until Louis XIV of France that there was a European monarch who equalled him in industry and persistence. Yet his application did not produce firm and efficient government because he lacked confidence in himself. Each of his decisions was only made after long reflection and consultation with others, and administrative delays became particularly notorious in the later years of his reign. 'If death came from Spain,' commented a Viceroy of Naples, 'we should live a long time.' Once he had come to a decision, however, Philip rarely changed his mind, largely because he was convinced that he was fulfilling God's purpose.

This belief was part of the traditional Spanish outlook which Philip, despite his Germanic appearance, held throughout his life. That strong unity of piety and politics acquired by the Spaniards during the long struggle to free the peninsula from the rule of the infidel, with its accompanying nationalist presupposition in religion and belief in racial purity, was ever with him. Religion and patriotism, heresy and treason, Church and State, God and King, all were to him inseparably linked, and he never doubted that as a monarch his life had to be

[15] P. 201.   [16] P. 218.

dedicated to upholding the cause they represented and overcoming its enemies. Following his predecessors on the throne, he saw himself bound to strengthen royal and Castilian authority in Spain, a task which included the limitation of the liberties of Aragon and the destruction of Protestantism and Mohammedanism in his dominions. He felt he had to assert the power of Spain and the Counter-Reformation abroad, which in turn involved subduing the pretensions of France and England, and checking the threats offered by Turkish attacks in the Mediterranean and the Revolt of the Netherlands.

Philip's choice of a capital and a residence was typical of much of his character. Castile had never had a fixed capital. The court had travelled, though during the previous two reigns it had spent a good deal of time at Toledo and Valladolid. This did not suit an efficient, administrative monarchy; and in 1561 Philip fixed his capital at Madrid, which is located at the exact geographical centre of the peninsula. There he settled in the castle-fortress, which had previously been the prison of Francis I, and gathered his courtiers and officials and established his government departments and councils. It was a new city without traditions from the past or provincial attachments, and dedicated to the organizing and planning activities of the new monarchy.[17]

Two years after the move to Madrid, Philip began the building of the Escorial in an isolated spot among the solitary foot-hills of the Sierra de Guadarrama some twenty miles north-west of the city, and until it was finished in 1584 it attracted his constant interest and attention. Designed in the form of the grid-iron on which St Lawrence was said to have been martyred, it was partly a monastery for Hieronymite monks, partly a mausoleum for the body of his father and partly a summer-palace to which Philip retreated from the heat of the city. Outwardly, it was designed in an austere, restrained classical style, but within it was constructed on a magnificent scale and enriched with jasper and splendid marbles. It contained an imposing chapel furnished with holy relics, a large library possessing fine books, rare manuscripts and a picture-collection in which paintings by Titian and Tintoretto predominated. It was a symbol of the greatness of Spain's religion, royal family and culture; it was the place in which Philip worked and prayed. He spent long hours alone with his papers—his bedroom was so placed overlooking the high altar of the chapel that he could hear the monks chanting the services—and here he was to die in 1598.

Administration and the liberties of Castile

In the administration of Castile, Philip was able to continue the policy of his predecessors and govern through the conciliar system which he

[17] P. 27.

further developed.[18] The Council of State retained its nominal pre-eminence and aristocratic membership, but the real work was accomplished through the various specialist councils, which consisted largely of administrators and officials and permanently advised him and carried out his policy. Yet he rarely attended their meetings himself. He preferred to receive their decisions, consider them and compare them with the advice he received from ministers and the despatches he was sent by governors and viceroys. Sometimes he would remain for several days on end in his private apartments in the Escorial engaged on his work and admitting only his confessor and a few administrators. The secretaries were men of great and growing importance in this system,[19] though their influence remained largely unofficial and indirect because of Philip's unwillingness to delegate authority to them.

The defeat of the Revolt of the Comuneros had left the Cortes of Castile in no position to assert itself against the Crown and, since it was ready to co-operate by voting *servicios*, Philip summoned it frequently and came to rely upon it increasingly during his reign to grant him a large part of his finance.[20] Neither this, however, nor the silver from America was sufficient for the expenses of his reign, and he had to obtain more money from the Church and other sources.[21] He also, as his father had done, borrowed a great deal of money, mainly from Genoese bankers. Within twenty years the total national debt was said to be five times the annual revenue, and the entire income of the government for any one year had to be used in paying interest and repayment of capital. Philip was driven in 1575 to repeat what he had been compelled to do in 1557 and repudiate his debts.[22] This resulted in an inability to pay the troops in the Netherlands and the Sack of Antwerp in 1576.[23] The Spanish government was able to reach an agreement with the Genoese bankers by which the repayment of capital was rephased and all loans were consolidated at an interest of five per cent. But in 1596 the Crown went bankrupt yet again, and its debts were rephased once more.

Philip II's financial problems were partly due to the powers possessed by the Cortes of Aragon and their unwillingness to grant taxes.[24] Indeed, he found the liberties of the Crown of Aragon constantly frustrated his government and hindered the authority of the viceroys. In 1590 he decided to challenge the resistance of the upper class of the kingdom by sending there the Marquis of Almenara, a non-Aragonese nobleman, as a royal official. Unfortunately for him, this coincided with the flight of Antonio Perez into Aragon.[25] This brought to a head Aragonese resentment at Philip's policy of Castilianization of the government and the Castilian officials he employed. Perez, as the symbol of the defence of the liberties of Aragon, became a popular hero, and Philip was faced with a revolt in the kingdom. He suppressed

[18] P. 113. [19] P. 114. [20] P. 121. [21] P. 115.
[22] P. 251. [23] P. 260. [24] P. 116. [25] P. 120.

this with severity, but his settlement substantially preserved the liberties of Aragon. Having made sure that there would be no aristocratic defiance of his rule, he showed himself anxious to follow his father's policy of respecting the laws and traditions of the different parts of his realm.

Religion and the Papacy

Protestantism presented Philip with no great trouble in Spain.[26] It was destroyed almost as soon as it appeared and was never able to gain any strength. At the beginning of his reign Calvinist congregations were discovered at Seville and Valladolid, but were at once crushed by the Inquisition. Philip did not have to fear that religion would, as in France, strengthen aristocratic or sectional resistance to the Crown. By 1565 native Protestantism was virtually extinct. The Spanish Inquisition, however, continued to exercise a strict spiritual discipline within the country, not dissimilar from that of Calvin's consistory in Geneva; its punishments including whipping on the bare back with a leather strap for children who neglected their religious observances. Spain became, outwardly at any rate, the country most faithful to Roman Catholicism.

If the Protestants were never a serious problem, the Moors, however, were. There was still a large Moorish population in Granada and Valencia. These were the Moriscos or New Christians, who had been allowed to remain after the *Reconquista* on condition that they were baptized. They were mostly poor and unimportant, and the notion that they were the most industrious part of the population, whose later expulsion contributed towards the decline of Spain, is without foundation. Most of them had probably been only nominally converted, but their religion was not the real problem. It was rather that they were an unassimilated racial minority and potential allies of the Turks and Corsairs. At various times decrees had been issued in an attempt to compel them to abandon their Islamic past. Such decrees had forbidden the speaking of Arabic, the use of Moorish names and the wearing of Moorish dress, but they had hardly been enforced, and the Moriscos had continued to follow their traditional way of life. The negligence of the clergy allowed this to continue for a long time, but during Philip's reign the religious revival of the Counter-Reformation and the campaign against heresy made the Spanish Church less ready to tolerate the practices of the Moriscos, and in 1567 the decrees were renewed with indications that they would this time be enforced. On Christmas Day 1568 the Moriscos revolted. It happened when Spain was without experienced troops because of Alva's march to Brussels.[27] Fortunately for Philip, the Moriscos did not seize the city of Granada nor did the

[26] P. 211.   [27] P. 256.

Turks come to their assistance, but it was not until 1570 that Don John was at last able to crush the rising. Once the last Moriscos had surrendered, Philip decided to move them from the coastal areas of Granada and disperse them northwards throughout Castile. A considerable proportion of them, estimated at 60 000 or more, undoubtedly managed to remain in Granada, but most, perhaps 150 000 altogether, were moved and were replaced by about 50 000 Spanish settlers from elsewhere. In this way, the danger of Morisco assistance to the Barbary pirates or co-operation with the Turks was lessened, but the problem was far from being solved. Spanish ideas and institutions continued to make their assimiliation impossible, however, and though they were now spread more widely among the population their customary early marriages increased their numbers. The way was prepared for their expulsion from Spain in the next reign.

An important consequence of the campaigns against Protestants and Moriscos was the further strengthening of the Spanish Inquisition, making it an important part of the assistance given by Spain to the Counter-Reformation; its power was shown by the case of Archbishop Carranza.[28] Yet Philip's concern for Roman Catholicism was based firmly upon a determination to uphold the extensive ecclesiastical authority of the Spanish monarchy, which brought it large powers and revenues from the Church and largely excluded the Papacy from the management even of spiritual affairs in Spain.[29] As Dr J. Lynsh* has said, 'The domination of the Church by the Crown was probably more complete in the sixteenth century than in any other part of Europe including Protestant countries.' Philip was not prepared to uphold the reforms of the Counter-Reformation if he considered that they might conflict with his authority and interests, and he showed this by his attitude towards the Council of Trent and the subsequent publication of its decrees.[30]

In the later years of his reign, Philip became involved also in differences with the Papacy over matters of foreign policy. Of course, there were occasions when papal and Spanish policy coincided, and this was particularly true in the Netherlands, where Philip considered that political unity depended upon the preservation of religious unity and was resolved, therefore, never to tolerate heresy, while the Papacy realized that the continuance of Roman Catholicism there depended upon the survival of Spanish authority. And so, on the whole, there was no important divergence between the two in the Netherlands, and successive popes gave Philip both moral and financial support. There was disagreement, however, over Philip II's policy towards England. Twice in 1561 and 1563, Philip stopped the excommunication of Elizabeth I because good relations with England were essential for the success of his policies towards France and in the Netherlands; and

[28] P. 111.   [29] P. 115.   [30] P. 218.
* 'Philip II and the Papacy', *Transactions of the Royal Historical Society*, 5th series, **XI**, 1961.

when Pius V finally excommunicated her in 1570, without consultation with Spain, Philip forbade the publication of the bull in the Spanish Empire and tried hard to prevent it reaching England. Throughout the 1570s Philip resisted also Gregory XIII's wish for a military crusade against England and when he decided to send the Armada against her it was for political and economic, not religious, reasons. By then, however, the pope was the energetic and independent Sixtus V, who mistrusted Spanish power; he only gave his support to the Armada after the execution of Mary, Queen of Scots, and when it failed, he refused to pay Philip the subsidy he had promised. It was over France, however, that papal and Spanish policy most seriously diverged. Sixtus V soon regretted his excommunication of Henry of Navarre and made it clear, in defiance of Philip II, that Henry's return to Roman Catholicism would make him an acceptable candidate for the French throne; and his successor, Clement VIII, absolved and recognized this monarch with whom Philip was at war.[31] These incidents well illustrate the difference in attitude between Philip and the Papacy. The popes believed that he was confusing the cause of religion with Spanish interests, but Philip was convinced that they were the same.

Corsairs and Turks

The threat from the Turks was another instance in which Philip was sure that the interests of religion and Spain were identical. During the first half of his reign, the Turkish advance was continuing in the Mediterranean and constituted a serious danger to Spain. The Corsair pirates, who preyed on Christian shipping from their strongholds on the North African coast, were still allied with the Turks and might threaten the link between Barcelona and Genoa, the first stage in the vital route along which the Spanish forces in the Netherlands were maintained and supplied. At first Philip adopted his father's tactics against them.[32] In 1560 some 18 000 Spanish troops were landed near Tripoli, but the Turkish fleet sailed from Constantinople, destroyed many of the Spanish ships and drove the rest back to their Neapolitan ports, compelling the Spanish army to surrender.

It was clear, therefore, that Spanish naval power would have to be established in the Mediterranean, and by 1563 Philip had operated in the Mediterranean several hundred galleys, which defeated an attack by the Corsairs from Algiers upon the Spanish ports of Oran and Mazarquivir. Two years later, a large Turkish fleet attacked Malta, which had been fortified by a crusading order, the Knights of St John of Jerusalem. Philip was placed in a difficult position. The island was certainly of great strategic importance, and its occupation by the

---

[31] P. 235.   [32] P. 200.

Turks would provide them with a base that might enable them to establish their naval supremacy as firmly in the western Mediterranean as in the Levant, but Philip did not want to risk losing his fleet and so leaving the coasts of Spain open to Turkish attack. Eventually, after Malta had withstood four months' siege, he sent ships which, while avoiding contact with the enemy, took supplies to the island and compelled the Turks to withdraw.

Philip continued to add to his fleet and five years later was able to engage the Turks in their part of the Mediterranean. In 1570 Venice asked the Papacy and Spain for help in defending her colony of Cyprus against a threatened Turkish attack. Pope Pius V promised Philip that, if Spain would assist the Venetians, he would contribute towards the cost of the expedition himself and allow the King to levy further taxes upon the Spanish Church. Philip was ready to send his fleet against the Turks this time because the revolt of the Moriscos had aroused fears that they might attack Spain herself, and he felt able to divert his forces because Alva seemed to have succeeded in suppressing the Revolt of the Netherlands.[33] He appointed his half-brother, Don John, to command the fleet of the Holy League formed by Pius V. It was not able to save Cyprus, but in October 1571 it overwhelmed the Turkish fleet and destroyed or captured most of its ships at the Battle of Lepanto.[34]

The Battle of Lepanto added greatly to Spain's prestige, but its immediate results were disappointing, and not even Cyprus was recovered. Philip did not wish to engage in a lengthy conflict in the Mediterranean at a time when he was having to meet a new threat to his power in northern Europe; and the Ottoman Empire was being threatened in the east by Persia. Nevertheless, the victory had destroyed the legend of Turkish invincibility at sea, and they did not in future risk sending their fleets far from Constantinople. In the end the Mediterranean remained a divided sea, the Turks dominating the eastern section, while the centre remained subject to the depredations of both Corsair and Christian pirates.

The European situation

Realizing that his extensive dominions had made the other rulers of Europe uneasy, Charles V is said to have advised Philip, when placing him in control of the Spanish Empire, to follow a policy of 'sturdy defensiveness'. This he did during the first half of his reign, and his foreign policy was comparatively uneventful. The action taken against the Turks in the Mediterranean (which culminated in the Battle of Lepanto) and the campaigns fought in the Netherlands (which have been described as comprising 'the first half of the Eighty Years War

[33] P. 256.   [34] P. 135.

of 1568-1648) were both, if envisaged historically, defensive undertakings. In those years he wanted to maintain peace in Europe by
preserving the existing situation. He signed the Treaty of Cateau-
Cambrésis in 1559, which brought to an end the long war against
France which he had inherited from his father and, following the death
of Mary Tudor in 1558, he married Elizabeth of Valois, the eldest
daughter of Henry II, to signify a new relationship between France and
Spain. Towards England he sought at this time to uphold friendly
relations, refusing to associate himself with papal hostility towards
Elizabeth I and deprecating the early Roman Catholic plots against her
life. In France, when the religious troubles began, fear of Guise
ambitions caused him to refrain from assisting the Roman Catholic
cause against the Huguenots.

The growing commitment of England to the Protestant cause and
the prolongation of Huguenot resistance in France militated against the
continuance of such a policy, but the real turning-point came with the
Spanish conquest of Portugal. In 1578 Sebastian, the young King of
Portugal, was killed in a campaign against the Moors in Morocco; he
was succeeded by his great-uncle, the aged Cardinal Henry, who had
no immediate heir. Philip probably had the strongest claim to the
throne through his mother, Isabella, the daughter of Emmanuel of
Portugal. It was natural that he should wish to assert this claim and
unite the Iberian peninsula under his rule. When Henry died in 1580,
he sent an army into Portugal and occupied the kingdom within four
months. The next year the Portuguese Cortes recognized him as King,
and he promised to respect the country's laws and liberties.

The acquisition of the Portuguese throne placed him in a much more
powerful position. It gave him Atlantic sea-ports with an ocean-going
fleet to operate from them. It gave him also the Portuguese colonies
which now brought the Spanish Empire to its greatest extent in that it
covered more than a half of the habitable area of the world. It gave
him the opportunity to subdue all his opponents together, but it also
made it inevitable that they should feel bound to act with greater
hostility towards him, both in Europe and in the New World. In the
end, the Spanish Empire was not able to stand the strain of such a
situation, and so the event may be said to mark the beginning of its
decline.

After the conquest of Portugal, Philip changed his defensive policy
to a major campaign aimed at securing his domination over England
and France and so over the whole of western Europe. Again, however,
it could be argued that such action was forced upon him to such an
extent that it might almost appear defensive. English seamen raided
Spanish ships and territories in the New World with Elizabeth's
tacit support, and English troops were sent in 1585 to assist the rebels

in the Netherlands. In France, the Huguenots had not been eliminated by the Massacre of St Bartholomew, and from 1584 there was a Protestant heir to the throne in the person of Henry of Navarre. In these circumstances, both countries might well challenge the position in Europe designed for Spain by Charles V and enjoyed by her since the Treaty of Cateau-Cambrésis, so Philip was bound to do what he could to frustrate them.

A Spanish alliance with England had been established by the marriage of Catherine of Aragon with Arthur, Prince of Wales, in 1501 and continued when Philip married Queen Mary in 1554. When Philip was widowed, there was talk of his marrying Queen Elizabeth. This did not happen, but relations remained friendly for years to come. The cloth trade between England and the Netherlands and mutual fear of France kept them together, so that Elizabeth had to endure the ill-treatment of English seamen by the Spanish Inquisition in Spain and the New World, and Philip had to accept the presence of English volunteers in the rebel forces in the Netherlands; but the cloth trade was ruined by the Revolt of the Netherlands and the Sack of Antwerp in 1576, while the flight of Mary Stuart to England in 1568 ended Philip's fear of a great Guise empire centred upon Paris and Edinburgh. Yet neither side hurried into war, but fought each other indirectly in Ireland, the Netherlands and the New World. It became clear to Philip, however, that Spain and the Counter-Reformation could not triumph in Europe as long as England opposed him. When he was able to do so he decided, perhaps as early as 1585, to subdue her, and with the execution of Mary Stuart in 1587 Philip was free, in the absence of any other Roman Catholic claimant, to dispose of the English throne as he wished.

He therefore dispatched the Spanish Armada, which was defeated in 1588 by fireships and the weather.[35] This was a blow to Spanish prestige but not a severe setback. By the 1590s her naval power had recovered, and Spain could protect her trade in the New World, raid the Cornish coast and assist the rebels in Ireland. The war went on, and only Philip's death prevented him from making another attempt to subdue the country but for which, his ablest ambassador told him, he could 'have kept the rebel provinces and made himself King of France, too, or at least split it up into great fiefs obedient to him.'

In fact, however, Philip hardly showed more signs of being successful with France than with England. When Henry of Navarre became the heir to the French throne, he made the Treaty of Joinville with the Guises in 1585[36], but he still mistrusted them. He did not intervene directly in the civil war until after the deaths of Henry of Guise and Henry III and the accession of Henry IV, and then it was to little avail. Parma's troops outfought Henry IV's forces in France, but they

[35] P. 137.   [36] P. 232.

would probably have been better employed in the Netherlands. Philip's support for the Catholic League, his attempt to gain the French throne for his family and his refusal to accept Henry IV after he had become a Roman Catholic lost him the support of French opinion, and he had no alternative but to withdraw. It may be said that his foreign policy was half-successful, since England was still denied access to the New World, Spain retained the southern Netherlands, and France remained a Roman Catholic country with a Roman Catholic monarchy; but all three at the end of his reign were able to defy his attempts to subject them to Spanish domination.

The end of the reign

Philip II's death in 1598 ended a reign which had made Spain dominant among the nations of the world. As a European power, she seemed invincible. Her infantry was unmatched and her resources unparalleled. Philip had maintained the empire he had inherited in Italy and America and had added to it Portugal and her overseas colonies, though he had deliberately halted further expansion in the New World.[37] He had checked the Turks in the Mediterranean and assisted the triumph of the Counter-Reformation in Europe. Spain under him enjoyed the exports of both the East and West Indies and continued to receive from the mines of South and Central America treasure such as no nation had ever known before. Her fleets sailed in every sea and endeavoured, not without success, to prevent the ships of other nations trading with her possessions. So great was Spain's self-confidence during Philip's reign that a Spanish bishop declared enthusiastically that with twelve galleons and eight thousand men the King could have conquered the Chinese Empire as well. Compared with these achievements, the few occasions on which Philip had not succeeded—the defeat of the Armada, the retreat from France and the resistance of the northern Netherlands—seemed to be of much less consequence.

Nor had such political successes alone made Philip's reign the Golden Age of Spain. It had been a great period of Spanish artistic, literary and religious achievement. It was the age of Cervantes (1547-1616), who wrote the first modern novel, *Don Quixote*, which set out to ridicule the chivalrous romances of the Middle Ages where wandering knights rescued damsels in distress and performed other deeds of valour, and of El Greco (1541-1614), whose pictures display an emotional, religious feeling that expresses the influence of the Counter-Reformation. It was also the age of the Spanish mystics, Teresa of Avila and John of the Cross, and of Ignatius Loyola and the Society of Jesus—Spain's greatest contribution to the religious revival within the Roman Catholic Church.[38] Economic and political greatness were accompanied

[37] P. 76.   [38] Pp. 216, 207.

by a deep religious fervour, closely bound up with nationalism and
patriotism, which gave the country further strength and unity such as
were not possessed by other European countries.

Philip could not bring himself to make peace with England or with
the Dutch rebels. Only his signing of the Treaty of Vervins in May
1598 recognized the setbacks to his foreign policy during the later
years of his reign, and by then he had been a sick man for nearly three
years. In June he made his last journey from Madrid to the Escorial
where he prepared for death. He died there, after months of agonizing
illness, in September 1598 at the age of seventy-one.

Yet failure in his foreign undertakings was not the most ominous
indication that all was not well amid the triumphs and conquests that
Spain had achieved during the sixteenth century. Far more serious
were the financial difficulties that had persisted during Philip's reign
and showed no signs of being alleviated. Spain's conquests in the New
World brought her imports of bullion which rose from £71 000 a
year to a peak of £4 000 000 a year. Without this neither Charles V
nor Philip II could have undertaken their international ventures, but
it was not enough to maintain the expenditure involved. The Armada
cost £5 000 000 and the Revolt of the Netherlands £1 000 000 a year.
England, France and other countries also had financial problems at
this time, but Spain was uniquely afflicted by an inability to meet the
new financial requirements of contemporary warfare. The treasure
from America did not save Castile from a crippling burden of taxation.[39]
Moreover, the high rates of interest the Crown had to pay on its
loans diverted investment from agriculture and industry and inhibited
the rise of a native middle-class. Though Philip II, in the words
of Professor Earl J. Hamilton, 'opposed unsound money no less
tenaciously than he fought the cult of Luther and Mohammed,'*
he was compelled to repudiate his debts and settle them by compulsory
conversions. He went bankrupt in 1557, 1575 and 1596, and yet when
he died, the Crown still owed £50 000 000 to its creditors.

These financial difficulties were but the outward sign of the serious
weaknesses from which Spain was suffering by the end of Philip's
reign and were due fundamentally to the country's sudden rise to
power and wealth. Early in the sixteenth century she experienced the
sudden discovery and conquest of an overseas empire and, simultane-
ously, the equally sudden inheritance of one in Europe. Although the
overseas empire brought her immense wealth—not in the form of
trade and industry, but in a sudden and rapid flow of bullion—she
had to spend an increasing proportion of her wealth on the aggressive
foreign policy necessary to maintain her domination in Europe and
America. Even a growing supply of bullion was not sufficient to meet
the needs of national expenditure. Before the end of Philip's reign,

[39] P. 117.   * *American Treasure and the Price Revolution in Spain* (1957).

indeed, there were signs that this supply was beginning to decline and that the crisis predicted by far-seeing Italian observers was at hand. There was not enough commercial and industrial enterprise to replace the dwindling supply of bullion and provide an alternative means of national income. Inevitably, the Spanish Empire, which could barely maintain itself on an increasing stream of bullion, was bound to falter and decline. Philip's successes bore in them the seeds of ultimate failure because the Spanish financial system was inadequate to sustain them.

16
THE
REVOLT
OF THE
NETHERLANDS

The resistance of the high nobility (1562-66)

The abdication of Charles V was received with sorrow in the Nether-lands.[1] It was also to prove to be an important stage in the history of the country. When Charles had assigned the Netherlands to Philip II, he had thought of them as being held by him in conjunction with England, but the death of Mary Tudor meant that they became a northern outpost of the Spanish Empire, a part which Philip, neverthe-less, was determined to hold, partly because they were a portion of his divinely-ordained inheritance and partly because of their wealth which he badly needed. Yet the Netherlands had never hitherto been regarded as belonging to the Spanish domain, and this was bound to produce unfavourable foreign reactions, particularly from France, who now had Spanish territory on both her eastern and western frontiers, and from England, who found this territory, so favourable as a base from which to invade her coast, occupied by a strong military power. Moreover, relations between Spain and the Netherlands were likely to be difficult. The Netherlanders had always been a manufacturing people, and now they were becoming traders and seafarers, they were independent by nature and different in their way of life and outlook from the Spaniards. Nor was Philip himself as likely to establish good relations with the Netherlanders as his father had done. He was not a Fleming and could speak only Spanish. It is true that he lived in the Netherlands, except for occasional visits to England during the first four years of his reign while Queen Mary of England was his wife, but when he left for Spain in 1559 he never returned, and his aloof and cold manner had not endeared him to them. Henceforward, he sent Spaniards to rule them; they knew him only through the orders he sent them, and they seemed to receive nothing from him but high taxation and religious persecution.

Yet Philip's relations with the Netherlanders and the policy he adopted towards the country were fundamentally the same as those of

[1] P. 194.

his father.[2] He faced the same need to raise money for the Italian Wars, but his request for a nine-year subsidy from the States-General was only granted after he had agreed to receive a remonstrance setting out the liberties of the Netherlands and had recalled the Spanish troops stationed in the Netherlands. When he left the Netherlands in 1559, Philip followed his father's policy by appointing as Regent his illegitimate half-sister, Margaret, Duchess of Parma (1522-86), who was a native of the Netherlands, and of giving the high nobility important posts in the government of the country. They were made Stadtholders of the provinces, and three of the most distinguished became members of the Council of State: William of Orange (1533-84), known as 'the Silent' because of his discretion, who was Stadtholder of Holland, Zeeland and Utrecht and the wealthiest man in the country, being the owner of important estates in Germany, Prince of Orange, a small independent territory in southern France, and Lord of Breda and Gertruidenberg in Holland; Count Egmont (1522-68), who had served as a soldier under Charles V; and their friend, Count Hoorne (1518-68). The most important man in the Council, however, was Cardinal Granvelle (1517-86), a Burgundian by birth who had already served Charles V as a diplomat; he received his instructions from Philip, who had told Margaret to act only on his advice. At the outset this alienated the high nobility upon whose support Charles V had generally been able to reply.

Their hostility was further aroused by Philip's ecclesiastical policy in the Netherlands. By the late 1550s Calvinism was beginning to spread in the country.[3] Philip was determined to crush it before it should gain as strong a foothold as in France. In order to improve ecclesiastical administration and make stronger measures against heresy possible, he decided to undertake a much-needed reorganization of the dioceses.[4] In 1561 he obtained bulls from the Papacy by which fourteen new bishoprics were added to the existing four, together with three new archbishoprics at Cambrai, Utrecht and Malines, of which Malines was to be the metropolitan and to which Granvelle was appointed. The money for the new scheme was to be obtained by appropriating the revenues of the richest monasteries, and the appointment of bishops was transferred from the cathedral chapters to the Crown. The high nobility disliked the way this would increase the power of the Crown and resented the loss of ecclesiastical patronage which they had hitherto been able to use for their younger sons. They joined the Calvinists in alleging that the scheme was a prelude to the introduction of the Spanish Inquisition. In 1563 William, Egmont and Hoorne resigned from the Council of State. Without troops, Margaret needed the support of the high nobility. Philip, preoccupied with his naval campaign in the Mediterranean, did not want trouble in the Netherlands, and so he allowed Margaret to comply with the demands

[2] P. 193.   [3] P. 182.   [4] P. 194.

of the opposition by dismissing Granvelle and promising to govern with the Council of State if William and his friends rejoined it.

Philip, however, was still resolved to destroy Calvinism in the country. He ordered the rigorous enforcement of the Placards and the continuance of the work of the Netherlands Inquisition; he also introduced the Jesuits into the country and ordered the publication of the decrees of the Council of Trent. Few of the nobility sympathized with the Calvinists, but they were anti-clerical and feared that religious persecution would provoke open rebellion as in France. William, Egmont and Hoorne again withdrew from the Council of State, but were unwilling to challenge the Crown further. Meanwhile, Calvinism was spreading and organizing itself much as in France. It was assisted by the weakness of the government and by the bitterness caused by the economic situation in the Netherlands during the winter of 1565-6 when food prices rose rapidly because of the failure of the harvest and the disruption of shipping in the Baltic through the Seven Years War between Denmark and Sweden (1563-70).[5] The starving, unemployed workers in the textile towns of the southern Netherlands were only too ready to consider Spain responsible for their sufferings and to listen to the Calvinist preachers.

The revolt of the lesser nobility and the lower classes (1566-7)

'It is folly to enforce the Placards when corn is dear,' said William, but the high nobility contented themselves with their constitutional resistance and did not want to indulge in treason against the Crown. More drastic action was taken by some of the lesser nobility, who had suffered a loss of income from their small estates through the price rise and could not emulate the high nobility by compensating themselves in the service of the Crown. In 1566 they presented a petition called the Compromise, which urged Philip to abolish the Inquisition and abolish the Placards. Some of them had become Calvinists and others were Roman Catholics. They found a few leaders from the high nobility, notably Henry, Count of Brederode, who had Calvinist sympathies, and William's brother, Louis of Nassau, who was a Lutheran. In April 1566 Brederode led some two hundred of them on horseback into Brussels to present a petition to Margaret. One of the Regent's advisers, who was unimpressed by them, commented scornfully, '*Quoi, madame, peur de ces gueux?*' The petitioners henceforward called themselves the Gueux or Beggars and left Brussels with begging-bowls hanging proudly from their necks.

Though most of the lower nobility, particularly in the southern provinces, gave the Gueux no support, Margaret was sufficiently alarmed to make some concessions, and she virtually suspended the

[5] P. 315.

Placards. By then the artisans in the towns were in open revolt, and the Calvinists were holding their services in public protected by armed men. In July 1566 the radicals of the Compromise agreed to co-operate with the Calvinists, and the next month in Antwerp and other towns there occurred the Iconoclastic Riots when mobs attacked monasteries and churches and smashed ornaments, images and altars. Margaret hastily made the Accord with the leaders of the Gueux by which they agreed to withdraw the Compromise on condition that Calvinism was tolerated where it had now established itself.

Soon the inevitable reaction set in. The religious extremism of the mobs and their attacks on property alarmed many people. Egmont and most of the high nobility obeyed Margaret when she required them to take a new oath of loyalty to the King. Philip sent her some money with which she was able to raise troops. By the winter of 1566 the armed bands of the Calvinists had been dispersed, and Brederode and many others fled to Germany. William, who had not taken the new oath to the King, also went abroad. He sympathized with those who opposed Spanish rule, but he was unable to identify himself with the Calvinist minority. He knew that the government would be unlikely to spare his life, but at the same time he was mistrusted by the Calvinists and their supporters. He exemplified the disunity which led to the failure of the revolt at this early stage.

Alva in the Netherlands (1567-73)

The episode, however, alarmed Philip who decided that the opposition must be suppressed at once before it spread and gained strength. In the summer of 1566 he sent his best general, the Duke of Alva (1508-82), with some nine thousand Spanish and Italian troops from Milan to Brussels; Alva was to be Governor and reassert Spanish authority in the Netherlands. Margaret and the native nobility urged him to adopt a conciliatory policy, but he believed that the Calvinists might well succeed in taking over the whole country, particularly as its long frontier with France would enable the Huguenots to give them assistance and so extend the French religious conflict.

On his arrival, Alva effectively took over the government of the Netherlands from Margaret, who resigned within a month in protest at his assumption of power. First, he sought to intimidate the opposition by taking action against its leaders. Egmont and Hoorne and some others were arrested as hostages for the good behaviour of the nobility. A special court, the Council of Troubles, which became known as the Council of Blood, was set up, and between 1567 and 1573 it tried and condemned some twelve thousand Calvinists who had taken up arms against the King. In the beginning, it seemed as if his policy of terror would succeed. With Spanish garrisons placed in the main towns, no one could do anything; and in 1568, when first William of Orange and then Louis of Nassau invaded the country with troops they had raised in Germany, there were no risings to support them and Alva was able to defeat them without difficulty. Egmont and Hoorne and other hostages were beheaded on Whitsunday 1568 in the market-square of Brussels.

Having apparently established his power, Alva now wished to secure a permanent revenue for the upkeep of his government. He planned to impose the hundredth penny (a once-for-all tax of one per cent on all property), the twentieth penny (a five per cent permanent tax on all sales of landed property) and the tenth penny (a ten per cent permanent tax on articles for export and on the sale of goods). For these taxes, however, he required the agreement of the States-General, which he summoned in March 1569. The States-General was intimidated into approving the taxes, but the tenth penny aroused such violent opposition in the country that little of it was ever collected. It was hated because it was a permanent tax, which would undermine the authority of the States-General, and because it seemed likely to ruin trade. Calvinism had been crippled by Alva's measures, but the tenth penny replaced it as a means of uniting popular opposition to foreign oppression; and the cost of Alva's administration had now to be borne by the Spanish government at the time when Philip was building up his fleet in the Mediterranean for action against the Turks.[6] Alva's influence in the Netherlands was undermined, and he requested Philip to recall him. Philip agreed towards the end of 1570, but before his successor arrived, events occurred which kept him in the country, and he did not finally leave until 1573.

The revolt of Holland and Zeeland (1572-6)

The death of Brederode in 1568 had left William the undisputed leader of the resistance movement. After his failure to invade the Netherlands, he fought with the Huguenots in France, and Coligny suggested that he should associate himself with a group of refugees from the northern provinces of the Netherlands—Calvinists, noblemen, fishermen and artisans—who had provided themselves with ships and raided indiscriminately the ships of all nations in the English Channel. William saw that they could help him by endangering the Spanish maritime links with the Netherlands and provide him with finance from their prize-money. In 1570, therefore, he issued letters of marque to these Sea Beggars, as they came to be called, by virtue of his authority as Prince of Orange. Then they had eighteen ships; a year later they had eighty-four. They were the only Netherlanders able to strike at the Spaniards.

[6] P. 246.   I

So far the Sea Beggars had operated from the ports of south-eastern England, but in April 1572, since she wanted to remain on good terms with Philip, Elizabeth ordered them to withdraw. On leaving English waters, their ships were driven by Channel winds towards the little port of Brill in Holland, where they found to their surprise that the Spanish garrison had left to put down disorder in Utrecht. They sacked the undefended port and then decided to occupy it in the name of the Prince of Orange. Soon afterwards they captured Flushing, on the island of Walcheren in the mouth of the Scheldt. By the summer of 1572 they had taken possession of most of the towns of Holland and Zeeland. In this they were led by the Calvinists, who were only a small minority of the population, even smaller in the northern provinces than in the south. They formed, however, the only armed groups, organized and able to seize control of the municipal machinery of government and, suffering from no conflicting loyalties like the Roman Catholics, they were able to get many to submit to their leadership through hatred of the Spaniards. When armed bands of the Sea Beggars approached a town, they made contact with the Calvinists inside, who often persuaded the municipal council to let them in without resistance. Then the prominent citizens were required to take an oath of loyalty to the Prince of Orange, and Roman Catholics were replaced by Calvinists in the administration of the town. Churches were taken over for Calvinist worship and stripped of their images and ornaments. And so the Calvinist minority gained control of the northern Netherlands.

At first neither William of Orange nor Louis of Nassau thought much of the Sea Beggars' triumphs. Their hopes rested upon the scheme for an alliance with the Huguenots which they had been considering with Coligny.[7] They decided, however, to take advantage of the revolt in the north by striking at the south with Huguenot assistance; but the Massacre of St Bartholomew destroyed all hope of French participation in any scheme for the liberation of the Nether-lands, and Alva was able to frustrate their efforts in Flanders and Brabant. Meanwhile, in July 1572, the estates of Holland had met at Dordrecht and recognized William as their Stadtholder, and he then decided that he must join up with the north. From sharing in the constitutional resistance of the high nobility to the ecclesiastical reforms and anti-heresy edicts of Philip, he had moved to lead the movement in defence of the rights and independence of the whole country as represented by the provincial estates. In this movement, the Sea Beggars took the most effective part, and William had to recognize this, much as he disliked their religious intolerance. Accordingly in April 1573 he made the politically important move of becoming a Calvinist.

[7] P. 227.

The Massacre of St Bartholomew, by removing the threat of a French invasion in the southern Netherlands, made it possible also for Alva to move his troops to the north, where the Sea Beggars remained behind the protection of the waterways of Holland and Zeeland. He had to wage a difficult campaign of sieges of towns protected by flooded marshes and supplied by rivers, and he captured Malines, Zutphen and Naarden amid scenes of slaughter. Haarlem held out for seven months before surrendering in July 1573. Yet despite his military successes on land, Alva was denied complete victory because the Sea Beggars still controlled the sea and stiffened the resistance of the towns. His failure to recover the north led at last to his recall in November 1573.

Philip then wished to attempt a policy of conciliation, and Alva's successor as Governor in the Netherlands was Don Louis de Requesens, a friend of Charles Borromeo and Governor of Milan, who was an administrator and diplomat, not a soldier. Philip had given him permission to abandon the Tenth Penny, abolish the Council of Troubles and proclaim a general amnesty to all who surrendered to the Spanish authorities, but he would not consider any toleration of heresy. 'I would rather lose the Low Counties than reign over them if they ceased to be Catholic,' he wrote in the summer of 1573. In any event, the Sea Beggars wanted independence, not more concessions and toleration. Early in 1574 they captured Middelburg on the island of Walcheren, which completed their blockade of the coast and cut the sea routes between the Netherlands and Spain. Requesens was compelled to renew the war in the north. He defeated and killed Louis of Nassau in April 1574 at the Battle of Mook, near Nijmegen, but then his troops mutinied through lack of pay and marched on Antwerp, pillaging as they went. When money was found to pay them, they laid siege to Leyden, but William and the estates of Holland eventually took the desperate decision to flood the surrounding countryside by cutting the dykes, and the siege was lifted in October. In 1575 the Spanish government went bankrupt.[8] The Spanish armies in the Netherlands were again unpaid and renewed their mutinies. Spanish military operations came to an end. Requesens died under the strain in March 1576, and the mutinies spread. The King's authority in the Netherlands had practically collapsed.

The unification of the Netherlands (1576-78)

Until the arrival of a new Governor from Spain, the administration of the Netherlands devolved upon the Council of State. William saw this as an opportunity to unite all the seventeen provinces in the revolt. He secured the ejection of the pro-Spanish members from the Council

[8] P. 243.

and persuaded it to summon the States-General, including representatives from Holland and Zealand. He was supported by the powerful Duke of Aerschot, his old rival who had refused to support him
in the campaign against Granvelle, but the difficulties in achieving
agreement between the popular, Calvinist revolt in the north and the
aristocratic, Roman Catholic movement in the south seemed considerable. In November 1576, however, the Spanish troops sacked Antwerp,
burning down about a third of the city and killing some seven thousand
citizens.[9] The effect was to unite some sixteen of the seventeen provinces
in a revulsion of feeling against the Spaniards. Their representatives
concluded the Pacification of Ghent by which they agreed to unite to
expel all foreign troops from the country and to insist that it should be
governed only by the States-General. A compromise over the religious
problem was reached by the declaration that all laws against heresy
were to be suspended until an ecclesiastical settlement was reached by
the States-General. Moreover, no mention was made of the question of
independence.

The new Governor was Don John of Austria (1547-78), the hero of
the Battle of Lepanto, whose prestige Philip hoped would assist in the
making of a settlement. The financial situation made conciliation still
very necessary, but Don John, though he realized the need for it, was
not suited by nature for compromise and moderation. Soon after his
arrival in Brussels early in 1577, he signed the Perpetual Edict with the
States-General. This promised that Spanish troops would be withdrawn
and the constitutional liberties of the country observed, but it stated
also that Roman Catholicism would be maintained and enforced
everywhere. The estates of Holland and Zeeland refused, therefore, to
accept it, and William was bound to support them. Don John was
exasperated; he seized Namur with his own bodyguard and recalled
the Spanish troops, who had set out for Spain. Immediately there were
risings by the guilds of artisans, supported by Calvinists, in Antwerp,
Brussels, Ghent and other southern cities, which followed the same
course as that previously taken in the north. Don John was able to
defeat the rebels at Gembloux in January 1578, but not to take Brussels.
In October he died of typhus at the age of thirty-three.

By now, a number of Roman Catholic noblemen of the south, who
styled themselves the Malcontents, had been sufficiently alarmed by
the popular revolts to turn against William. Both sides now began to
look for foreign help against each other, the Malcontents from France
and the Calvinists from Germany. The Calvinists, who had taken
Aerschot prisoner and sent him off to Germany, now won over the city
of Amsterdam and the province of Gelderland. It looked as if William's
wish 'to restore the entire fatherland in its old liberty and prosperity',
which had seemed so near to realization, was now likely to fail. Such

[9] P. 243.

was the situation when Alexander Farnese, Duke of Parma (1546-92), was appointed Governor.

The Unions of Arras and Utrecht (1579-81)

Shortly before Parma arrived in the Netherlands, the leaders of the southern provinces signed the Union of Arras in January 1579 whereby they accepted the Perpetual Edict and swore to uphold it. Parma showed himself to be both an able soldier and a good negotiator. He promised to recognize their privileges and send the Spanish troops away in return for their acceptance of his authority. The seven northern provinces replied by forming the Union of Utrecht in which they united in a confederation to defend their civil and religious liberty, which was to be under the control of its States-General and the house of Orange, though the balance of power between them was not clearly defined. This brought about a cleavage between north and south which was to be final.

William disliked the Union of Utrecht because he had still not given up hope of reuniting all the provinces in a contest against Spain, and he realized that its dominant Calvinism was detrimental to this aim, but circumstances compelled him to accept the settlement. He had now become the acknowledged leader of the rebellion, and as long as he lived, he gave it unity. The Spaniards recognized this, and in June 1580 Philip declared him an outlaw and put a price on his head. William replied by publishing his *Apology* in which he defended his political career and denounced the Spaniards for their cruelty, intolerance and tyranny throughout their empire. His proscription rallied the north to him as the man who stood for the defence of their liberties against the foreigner, and it also removed his last feelings of loyalty to Philip. So far he had never urged that the Netherlands should cut completely its links with Spain, but now he believed that this must be done and that the Union of Utrecht must become an independent entity. The Calvinists had long wanted to do this and were prepared to accept him as the ruler of the new state.

William, however, was convinced that the provinces could not hope to preserve their independence against the might of Spain without foreign help. This would have to come from England or France, but Elizabeth I still did not wish to provoke an open conflict with Philip, and so the States-General was persuaded reluctantly to offer the kingship of the 'United Provinces of the Netherlands', as the confederation now called itself, in 1581 to Henry III's brother, Francis, Duke of Alençon. When he accepted it, the representatives of the estates solemnly ratified the Edict of Abjuration, which deposed Philip II because he had failed in his duty to the people, who thus had the right to replace him by another ruler of their choice. The Dutch were thus the first to put into practice the views the Huguenots had adopted to justify their resistance to the French monarchy.[10]

The acceptance of Alençon as the ruler of the United Provinces seemed to promise a number of advantages. He could bring them both the prestige of his royal family and badly-needed French troops. As a Roman Catholic, he might yet appeal to the southern provinces which William still hoped were not to be separated forever. Also, Elizabeth was engaged in a diplomatic courtship with Alençon, which seemed to show signs of being successful. It would unite the new Dutch state with England to form a Protestant union under French protection which could hope to be strong enough to withstand Spain. Such considerations were now relevant because increasingly the Revolt of the Netherlands was developing from a civil war into an international struggle. It was caught up in the religious and political issues which were dividing western Europe; and it was as much in the interests of France and England that the revolt should succeed as it was in the interests of Spain that it should be subdued. Moreover, it was the only opportunity that these two countries had of challenging Spain and one where they could do it indirectly without causing a general war.

Parma in the Netherlands (1579-92)

Parma's acceptance of the Union of Arras had given him a firm base in the south from which to attempt the reconquest of the Netherlands, and he was quick to take advantage of it. From Artois and Hainault, he first proceeded to win back the other southern provinces. Also, he combined military prowess with diplomatic ability. He did not repeat the mistake made by Alva, in 1568, whose intimidation of the Netherlands nobility had deprived Spain of their support. Instead, they were bribed and promoted and assured of the retention of their privileges; and their experience of the popular, Calvinist-led risings in the southern towns during 1577 and 1578 helped their gradual acceptance of his rule. In addition he did not commit any massacres to terrorize the population. His method was to approach a town in strength, accept its surrender if it promised to obey the Spanish government and conform to Roman Catholicism, spare the lives and property of the citizens, execute a few rebel leaders and grant the Calvinists the opportunity to escape northwards or abroad. This approach secured the surrender of town after town; and the reformed religion of the Counter-Reformation could be made generally acceptable without recourse to the Inquisition. So well did he succeed in gaining the support of the southern nobility that in 1582, when he summoned the representatives of the estates of the provinces forming the Union of Arras to Tournai, they agreed to

10 P. 232.

his request that Spanish troops might be brought back to supplement his Flemish and German army.

For the United Provinces the coming of Alençon proved to be a disastrous failure. Catherine de Medici and Henry III had no wish to provoke Philip by providing him with French troops. He raised an army himself in France and with it captured Cambrai in the summer of 1581, but then went over to England to pursue his courtship with Elizabeth. It was not until 1582 that he was persuaded to take up his residence in Antwerp where he became more and more frustrated by the determination of the States-General not to allow him any real authority. In January 1583 he attempted to seize Antwerp for himself, but he was repulsed by its citizens, and such little reputation as he had enjoyed in the Netherlands was destroyed. William still believed that a Dutch victory depended upon French support, but in the autumn of 1583 Alençon retired to France and died there in the summer of the next year.

In June 1584, a month after Alençon's death, William of Orange was assassinated. He had clearly not been the originator of the revolt. The religious and other causes, which produced it, had existed before he became at all prominent. He had, however, come to the fore in the original aristocratic resistance to the Spanish administration and had not hesitated to support the revolt as it widened and sharpened in its implications. Although he had not succeeded in controlling all the forces that the revolt released nor in achieving his ideal of an independent united Netherlands, free and tolerant, he had remained true to this hope to the end; in the next century, the independent Netherlands were to be conspicuous for that personal freedom and religious toleration which he valued so highly. When the United Provinces were formed, he alone held them together, and his unique accomplishment was recognized by his outlawry and then his murder by his enemies. Yet he had organized the co-operation of the urban leaders and the provincial estates so effectively in the government of the state that after his death it was able to endure; but at the same time the successes gained by Parma after William's death showed that those who continued the development of the government of the state and enabled it to regain its lost territory must rank with him as its founder and saviour.[11]

Parma, indeed, took advantage of the confusion caused by William's death to advance steadily into Brabant and Flanders and capture a number of towns which still held out against him in the south. Ghent fell to him in August 1584, Brussels in March 1585 and, most serious of all, Antwerp in August 1585. Dutch resistance was practically limited to Holland, Zeeland and a part of Gelderland; their greatest protection against Parma's formidable troops were the great rivers of the country and his lack of naval power. The unexpected Spanish

[11] P. 265.

recovery in the Netherlands occurred at the time when Philip, after the conquest of the Portuguese Empire, was in a more powerful position than before to dominate his opponents;[12] but the wider demands of that international conflict were to contribute towards the frustration of Parma's complete success.

The murder of William of Orange was not the only crisis facing the United Provinces in 1584. The death of Alençon meant that the sovereignty of the state was now vacant, and foreign help still seemed vital for its survival. The States-General first approached Henry III of France, but he was already facing Spanish intervention in the conflict within his kingdom and could not disperse his strength by embarking upon a new adventure in the Netherlands. The States-General turned, therefore, to Elizabeth of England. So far she had wished to avoid direct participation in the Netherlands, but Parma's successes, combined with Philip's alliance with the Guises in France, meant that England now would have to take an open part in the war if Spain were to be checked and Protestantism saved. After months of negotiations, the Queen refused the sovereignty of the United Provinces as being needlessly provocative to Philip, but accepted the title of Protector and in August 1585 made an alliance with the States-General by which she agreed to maintain an army in the country at her own expense until the end of the war in return for the cession of Brill and Flushing as cautionary towns to England.

The English troops arrived in the Netherlands in December 1585 under the command of Elizabeth's favourite, the Earl of Leicester, but he was to be no more successful than Alençon in his relations with the northern provinces. He proved himself to be an incompetent soldier and a tactless politician. His first action was to infuriate Elizabeth by assuming the title of Governor of the Netherlands without her permission. Then he became involved in the political and religious problems of the provinces. He antagonized the merchant oligarchy of Amsterdam and other towns by supporting the Calvinist preachers, whose stronghold was Utrecht. These two sides were divided partly over religious and constitutional issues, since the oligarchy wanted religious toleration and greater centralization of government which the Calvinists opposed, and also over economic matters. In particular, Leicester came into conflict with the estates of Holland, which was paying about two-thirds of the cost of the war, and their advocate, John van Oldenbarneveldt (1547-1619), over the wish of the Calvinists to prohibit Dutch participation in the carrying trade between the Baltic and Spain, a prohibition which would have ruined the Dutch merchants.[13] Since Leicester could not gain any successes which might have preserved his reputation in the Netherlands, his position became untenable and he finally left the country before the end of 1587.

[12] P. 248.   [13] P. 312.

By now Parma had reached the network of rivers and canals, lakes and marshes, which formed the Dutch natural defences. These would have been bound to make his advance more difficult, but other circumstances prevented him continuing with his campaign. Philip was planning his invasion of England and ordered Parma to bring his troops back to Dunkirk and Nieuport to await embarkation on the Armada. When this enterprise failed, Parma's plans for the resumption of his campaign in the Netherlands were this time frustrated by Philip's decision to send him into northern France to fight against Henry IV with his troops. He did not return to the Netherlands and in 1592 died of wounds received at Rouen. His memorial was the division of the Netherlands, with the southern provinces now firmly on the side of Spain and the Counter-Reformation.

The deliverance of the north

After the failure of Leicester in the Netherlands, the policy of offering the sovereignty of the United Provinces to a foreign prince was discarded as a failure and not repeated. The urban oligarchy, with the support of the Dutch army, also triumphed over the popular Calvinist movement. The States-General was now determined to exercise its authority and accept foreign assistance only through alliances. Oldenbarneveldt played a particularly important part in securing a greater measure of centralization in the government of the United Provinces. He persuaded the separate provinces, despite their tradition of jealous insistence upon their own rights, to recognize the decisions of the States-General, and he ensured that there was always enough money to pay the Dutch army. He sought also to unite the provinces further through the house of Orange. William's son, Maurice of Nassau (1567 1625), had already been elected Stadtholder of Holland and Zeeland in succession to his father in 1585. Oldenbarneveldt in 1589 persuaded the estates of Utrecht, Gelderland and Overijssel also to elect him as their Stadtholder. His cousin, William Louis, was already Stadtholder of the one remaining province, Friesland. So Maurice, who had in addition received his father's posts of Captain-General and Admiral-General of the Union, was now placed in a strong political and military position in the country.

Despite his youth, Maurice soon showed himself a very able and successful soldier. The lull, which followed Philip's preoccupation first with the Armada and then with intervention in France, enabled him to take the offensive without having to encounter strong Spanish military power. During the 1590s, mainly in a campaign of sieges, he captured many important towns. He took Breda in 1590 and the next year Zutphen, Deventer and Nijmegen, following this up by expelling

Spanish troops from Gelderland and Overijssel in 1592 and capturing Groningen in 1594. This gave the Dutch control of all the country north of the river line of the Rhine and the Meuse. Maurice then went on to invade Flanders and Brabant, but the Flemings did not rise to support him, and despite a spectacular victory at Turnhout in 1597, his advance was checked. Philip refused to include the Netherlands within the terms of the Treaty of Vervins in 1598, but after his death in the same year, a period of military stalemate followed. Both sides were secure on their side of the river line, and neither could wage war effectively beyond it. The final bankruptcy of Philip's reign made it impossible for Spain to continue a long-drawn-out war, and reality was eventually recognized by the Twelve Years' Truce signed with the Dutch in 1609.

The deliverance of the north by Maurice had resulted in the establishment of the United Provinces as a separate, independent state, contrary to both the hopes of his father and the original object of the revolt which had sought to free the whole of the Netherlands from Spanish control. The causes of this division are not to be found, as is often supposed, in differences of race and religion separating the peoples of the northern and southern parts of the country. The final boundary did not mark the dividing line between the French and Flemish-speaking peoples, since it ran much further south through the Flemish-speaking area separating the Walloons of Flanders and Brabant from the Dutch and associating them with the French-speaking people in the south. Neither was this division brought about by religious factors. In fact, Calvinism spread in both the northern and southern provinces in the first part of the sixteenth century and was initially strongest in such southern towns as Antwerp, Brussels and Louvain. When the fighting began, the Calvinists were less than a third of the population of the entire country; and they remained a minority in the north for some years after the establishment of the United Provinces by the Union of Utrecht in 1572.

The fortuitous capture of Brill and Flushing in 1572 by the Sea Beggars and the risings in other northern towns under the leadership of the Calvinists began the developments that culminated in the division of the Netherlands. Once the Spaniards had been ejected from the north and Calvinist rule established, the independence of these provinces was practically secured, particularly as the Sea Beggars had control of the adjacent waters. The attempt to unite the whole of the Netherlands in 1576 failed because the southern aristocrats did not wish popular Calvinist control to spread to their provinces, and Alva was, therefore, able to crush resistance in this part of the country, but he could not proceed further so easily. The more active rebels, many of whom were Calvinists, retired to Holland and Zeeland, where the nature of the country made possible the waging of a type of war in which they could hope for success. In its many sea inlets and extensive inland waters, a people well-provided with small craft and lightly-equipped troops were able to engage in novel mobile fighting very successfully against the Spanish infantry who were well-trained and armed, but heavy and slow-moving.

Thereafter, the division of the country was determined by geographical and strategic considerations, especially its great rivers which acted as natural strategic frontiers. In the later years of fighting, Parma could not reconquer the north for Spain, while the Dutch under Prince Maurice could not wage war beyond these rivers to liberate the south. Of course, by the end of Philip II's reign thirty years of warfare and separate rule had already brought about political and religious, social and economic differences between the two parts of the country. The Calvinists had strengthened their position in Holland and Zeeland, while in the south the Counter-Reformation was succeeding in transforming those provinces which, in the words of Ranke, like the northern provinces 'had previously been half-Protestant, into one of the most-decidedly Catholic countries in the world.'* The native aristocracy in the south was secure in its privileges and wealth under Spanish favour and protection, but the urban oligarchy of Holland flourished in their freedom from feudal control. Amsterdam was beginning to supplant Antwerp as an international commercial and financial centre. The southern provinces remained strictly excluded from the trade of the Spanish Empire, but Dutch merchant ships, already trading with every country in Europe, were now sailing in the Indian Ocean as pioneers of that empire which was to be established in the next century. Nevertheless, developing differences between the northern and southern Netherlands were the result of the division of the country in the sixteenth century and not the cause of it.

* *History of the Popes* (1846).

17
ITALY
AND
THE
PAPACY

The Republic of Venice

Northern Italy by the beginning of the sixteenth century was dominated by the three city-states of Venice, Milan and Florence, which owed their pre-eminence to the position of Italy in the centre of the great European commercial artery between east and west. Trade, finance and industry had made them important, and they had each extended their boundaries into the surrounding countryside in the interests of political security and obtaining food supplies.

The best-known of these city-states was the Republic of Venice, ruled by merchants' oligarchs and possessing extensive territories on the Italian mainland and in the Mediterranean. She lay across the most important European trade route of the Middle Ages, which went from the Levant, up the Adriatic, through the Alps and down the Rhine to western and northern Europe. Her merchants traded cotton and spices from Egypt, the Levant and the Black Sea for metals, particularly copper, from central Europe. She also sent galleys through the Straits of Gibraltar to England and the Netherlands, trading wine, olives, fish, silk and other Mediterranean products for grain, timber and wool. In addition, she was an important glass-making centre, wove silk and woollen cloth and built ships. At first she established a maritime empire comprising settlements of strategic or commercial value along the most important trade routes. Then she conquered territory on the mainland both to provide herself with grain and meat and to protect the Alpine passes leading to her northern markets. Always, however, the city of Venice with its wharves and warehouses, its commercial and financial institutions, remained the centre of her existence. She lived for trade and by trade. At the beginning of the sixteenth century it was still the greatest of the Italian cities and in many ways the most prosperous of them as well.

The discovery by the Portuguese of an alternative route to India, which enabled spices to be shipped direct from the East Indies to Lisbon, inevitably affected the trade in which Venice had hitherto enjoyed a monopoly and which supplied her greatest source of wealth; but the decline in her economic power was not as rapid as has sometimes been thought. At first the Portuguese were able to sell spices in Europe considerably more cheaply than the Venetians;[1] but when Portuguese and Venetians began to compete as purchasers in the spice-markets of the east, prices began to fall, and the Venetians were able to bargain as successfully as the Portuguese. Moreover, the Portuguese lacked the Venetians' type of commercial and industrial base upon which to operate. They could only offer bullion to the merchants of Goa, so that the profits from the spices they bought and sold had to pay for both the outward and return voyages; but the Venetians could take European goods out to the east, and the Arabs and Indians often preferred to trade for them. In the middle years of the century, there-fore, the Venetians could charge about the same as the Portuguese for their pepper, which had the advantage of not being spoilt by storms during the long voyage round the Cape of Good Hope. During the 1570s there was even a revival of the overland route through the Alps because of the interference with Portuguese and Spanish shipping by foreign privateers in the English Channel, and Venice benefited considerably through this situation.[2] By then, however, the Dutch were already beginning to engage in this trade themselves, and they were in a better position to supply western Europe with spices and also to take part in the growing export of timber and grain from the Baltic to the Mediterranean countries.[3] Venice began to lose her pre-eminence in this trade during this period, and at the same time her old-fashioned galleys were ceasing to be able to make their voyages to northern Europe. Nevertheless, she retained a great deal of her prosperity to the end of the century.

Without that prosperity, indeed, Venice would not have been able to assume and maintain her position as the centre of High Renaissance art in Italy during the second half of the century.[4] This was also made possible by the fact that, though Venice inevitably participated in the Italian Wars and was successively a member of the League of Venice, the League of Cambrai and the Holy League,[5] when the fighting was at last over she alone remained unconquered and politically independent. The Spaniards could not advance across her lagoons to subdue her, and she survived her troubles with the Turks.[6] She remained strong enough to resist complete domination by both Spain and the Counter-Reformation and so was unique in Europe.

The Duchy of Milan

To the west of Venice was the Duchy of Milan, which lay in the middle of the Lombardy Plain and was the natural focus of routes

[1] P. 67.   [2] P. 77.   [3] P. 312.
[4] P. 57.   [5] Pp. 140, 143.   [6] P. 292.

from western and central Europe as well as from all parts of Italy. Trade along these routes made it a thriving place of commerce; it was also one of the largest industrial centres of Europe both for textile production and metal work, particularly the manufacture of weapons and armour for which it was famous. Trade and industry had made it an important financial centre too. The international activities of its bankers during the Middle Ages is recalled to-day by the name of Lombard Street in the City of London, and they were still important in the sixteenth century.

From 1447 to 1480 the Duchy was under the brilliant and despotic rule of Francesco Sforza;[7] and it was an invitation to Charles VIII of France in 1493 by his successor as effective ruler of the Duchy, Lodovico Sforza, which helped to bring about the French invasion of the peninsula the next year, thus beginning the long Italian Wars.[8] During the struggle Milan was continually involved and became one of the most sought-after prizes in the contest between the French and Spanish armies, and for a time was held by the Swiss. The same natural position which had brought her such economic prosperity now made Milan also a place of great strategic value to either side. She was the gateway into Italy and of particular importance to Spain in maintaining her links with northern and central Europe.[9] Possession of the Duchy by one of the two kingdoms, thus denying it to the other, became an important object of the struggle.

The final retention of the Duchy by Spain under the settlement of the Treaty of Cateau-Cambrésis in 1559 was, therefore, a valuable part of her triumph. Thereafter Milan was the fulcrum of Spanish power in Europe, from which troops might be sent to subdue Italy, meet a Turkish threat, invade France or intervene in the Netherlands. The Duchy was ruled by a Spanish military governor and had to support a permanent garrison of Spanish and Italian troops. This imposed a heavy and bitterly resented burden of taxation upon the Milanese, but, on the other hand, the peace that Spanish rule finally brought them was greatly to their advantage. The Duchy was able to recover from the severe economic setback caused by the warfare of the first half of the century. The population increased, and the industries recovered and were able to take advantage of growing European markets and rising prices. The reign of Philip II was a period of expansion and prosperity for the Duchy before the disastrous plagues and wars of the seventeenth century.

The Republic of Florence

Between Venice and Milan was the Republic of Florence, which exercised control over most of Tuscany and owed much of its importance

[7] P. 125.   [8] P. 139.   [9] P. 146.

to its strategic position commanding routes not only west to Pisa and the sea, but also south to Rome and north-east across the Appenines to the northern Italian plain. At the close of the fifteenth century, the Medici family secured supreme power in the state, which became the focus of Italian literature and art.[10] The magnificent reign of Lorenzo de Medici (1469-92), however, was marked by resentment among many citizens at his destruction of the republican institutions of the state and at the heavy taxation made necessary by his lavish patronage of the arts. During the last years of his reign Girolamo Savonarola (1452-98), Prior of the Dominican Priory of San Marco in Florence, gained unrivalled ascendancy in the city with his eloquent and fiery preaching. The semi-paganism of the Italian Renaissance was completely at variance with Savonarola's conception of Christian spirituality and morality. He combined denunciations of the corruption of the Florentines and the immorality and worldliness of the clergy with calls for the restoration of republican government. Despite the wealth and magnificence of Florence, much poverty and ignorance existed in the city-state, worsened by outbreaks of the plague, and Savonarola's message found particular support among the poor and needy for whom it seemed to offer some hope. The ruling classes, however, feared his prophecies about the future, which were often in apocalyptic language and included the forecast of the coming of a French invasion as a scourge to purify the wickedness of the state.

When Lorenzo died in 1492, he was succeeded by his son, Piero, who allied himself with Naples against Milan.[11] When this led to the occupation of Florence by Charles VIII of France and the expulsion of the Medici, which seemed to fulfil Savonarola's prophecy, there was a rising in the city which received the support of the French. Savonarola established friendly relations with France in order to obtain paramount influence in the state and so establish a reformed republican constitution and accomplish a religious revival. The government of the Medici was replaced by a Grand Council of three thousand members on the Venetian model. The puritanical aspect of late fifteenth-century piety, which he in many ways typified, was spectacularly put into effect by the bonfires of vanities to which many people flocked to hurl costly ornaments, cards, dice, masks, carnival costumes and banned books and pictures into the flames. Jesus Christ was proclaimed King of Florence, and the state was dedicated to His Gospel to await the coming of the millenium which Savonarola declared was close at hand. Every effort was made to prepare the citizens for this time of judgment by regulation of their morals and pleasures, foreshadowing the later rule of Calvin in Geneva.

Savonarola's period of power, however, could not last. Popular support for him waned when Florence became isolated from the rest of

[10] P. 51.   [11] P. 139.

Italy and involved in a war, which lasted until 1509, to recover Pisa.[12] Moreover, success turned Savonarola to extremism, and when he delivered a violent personal attack on him, Pope Alexander VI was roused from his indifference and took action. In 1498 Savonarola was excommunicated and captured by some of the leading citizens, who handed him over to the papal commissioners. He was tried and found guilty of heresy and seditious teaching. He was strangled and burned in the market-square of the city together with two of his Dominican brethren. His support had largely come from the poor and under-privileged who had not been able to protect him. The millenarian regime in Florence failed as a generation later it failed again in Münster.

The death of Savonarola, however, did not produce any change in the constitution or foreign policy of Florence. She continued to be a republic and virtually a vassal of France until 1512 when the Medici were returned to power after the expulsion of the French from Italy, an event which meant exile for Machiavelli.[13] In 1527, after Francis I of France had formed the Holy League of Cognac and again invaded Italy, another rising in Florence expelled the Medici, and the republic was restored; but under the Treaty of Barcelona in 1529 Pope Clement VII, a Medici, was able to induce Charles V to agree to the restoration of his family to power. The city, strengthened by the fortifications designed by Michelangelo and defended by the militia formed through the influence of Machiavelli, only surrendered to the Spanish army after a siege of eight months. Thereafter the Medici had to rely upon Spanish protection for their continuance in power and displayed a complete subservience to Charles V and Philip II, which secured the cession to them of the free city of Siena and recognition of the title of Grand Duke of Tuscany granted by the Papacy.

The Republic of Genoa

At the foot of the Appenines and south-west of Milan was the coastal state of Genoa, which was ruled, like Venice, by oligarchies of merchants. During the Middle Ages she had been the equal of Venice and had fought with her for superiority. She had engaged in the overland spice trade through her Black Sea colonies of Amastris, near Trebizond, and Kaffa in the Crimea, but during the fifteenth century these had been conquered by the advancing Turks, who had deprived her also of all her settlements in the Aegean except Chios.[14] Yet she remained the second most important commercial city of the Mediterranean. With the loss of her trade in the Levant, she engaged in the trade between Spain and her colonies, and during the reign of Philip II her bankers became the main source from which the King acquired

[12] P. 143.   [13] P. 126.   [14] P. 286.

those loans so essential for the preservation of his possessions and the conduct of his foreign policy.[15]

These increasing financial and economic connections with Spain influenced Genoa's foreign policy during the sixteenth century. In the first part of the century, she had generally been in alliance with the French, which led to her being sacked and occupied by Imperial forces in 1522. She was retaken by the French in 1527, but the next year the Genoese admiral, Andrea Doria (*c* 1466-1560), fearful of the implications of French domination of the state, went over to Charles V with his fleet and secured the attachment of Genoa to Spain with important consequences for the Spanish cause in the Italian Wars.[16] Indeed, for the rest of his reign Charles came to depend so strongly upon Genoa for ships and money that he was careful always to maintain friendly relations with Andrea Doria, and towards the end of his reign warned his son never to break with the city-state. In the troubled years of Philip's reign Genoa acquired additional importance as the port at which the vital long land route to the Netherlands began. Under Spanish protection, therefore, Genoa was able to retain her independence throughout the century.

The Kingdom of Naples

The southern part of Italy was very different, politically and economically, from the north. It was occupied by the Kingdom of Naples, which was the only feudal kingdom in Italy, the land being held in large estates by turbulent barons, some of whom were of French and Spanish descent. In character it was not urban and commercial, but depended upon agriculture, particularly sheep-farming, and it lacked the prosperity of the north and the capitalist classes that went with it.

At the beginning of the sixteenth century it was divided into two parts.[17] Sicily and Sardinia had been ruled by the Aragonese royal family since the beginning of the fifteenth century, but Naples and the mainland had been secured by an illegitimate branch of this same royal house whose claims to the territory were bitterly contested by the legitimate line. From 1458 Naples was ruled by Ferrante I, the illegitimate son of Alfonso V of Aragon, and from 1479 Sicily belonged to Ferdinand the Catholic, King of Aragon and Castile. The rule of Ferrante was so oppressive that in 1485 he had to face a formidable baronial revolt in Naples. He was able to crush it and executed many of the barons, but others escaped into exile where they continued to intrigue against him so that his rule remained insecure. His position was further weakened by the papal claim to suzerainty over the kingdom. While he had the support of the Roman nobility, successive popes were allies of the Neapolitian barons.

[15] P. 116. [16] P. 148. [17] P. 23.

In 1492 Charles VIII of France accepted an invitation from some of the exiled Neapolitan barons to assert his claim to the Kingdom of Naples, which he had inherited from the last Duke of Anjou, and so initiated the Italian Wars.[18] Ferrante died in January 1494, during the French invasion of Naples, and was succeeded by his son, Alfonso II, of whom the French chronicler, Commines, said that, though not as dangerous, he was a worse man than his father, because 'never was any prince more bloody, wicked, inhuman, lascivious and gluttonous than he.' Deserted by his people, he resigned his throne in favour of his popular young son, Ferrante II, who had, however, to flee before the French to Sicily. Within a few weeks all the kingdom, with the exception of a few fortresses, was in French occupation; but this was destined to last only a very short time. Before the end of the summer of 1495, Charles VIII had been defeated and had left Italy. Ferrante II returned to Naples, but died in September and was succeeded by his uncle, Federigo. Naples had, consequently, been ruled by five kings within three years. The attempt by Charles VIII's successor, Louis XII, to divide Naples with Ferdinand of Aragon failed;[19] and from 1503 both parts of the kingdom were reunited under Spanish rule.

Naples and Sicily were each ruled by a Viceroy, one with his court at Naples and the other at Palermo, who were under the control at first of the Council of Aragon and then of the Council of Italy, which was created in 1555. Since, during the reigns of both Charles V and Philip II, this part of Italy was threatened by the naval activity of the Turks in the Mediterranean, the Spanish government naturally expected Naples and Sicily to make their own contribution towards the cost of their defence. This proved easier to enforce in Naples than in Sicily. While the Viceroy of Naples ruled with even more absolute power than the Governor of Milan, Sicily's long connection with the Crown of Aragon had bequeathed it an ancient constitution which preserved certain privileges and local rights. Taxation, therefore, rose rapidly in Naples, but Sicily remained almost as lightly taxed as Aragon. A sixteenth-century Italian saying maintained that 'the Spaniards nibbled in Sicily, ate in Naples and devoured in Milan'. Indeed, in seeking to secure the imposition of taxation, the Viceroys of Sicily were compelled to wage a losing contest against the nobility and the medieval estates; nearly all those who held viceregal office during the sixteenth century were recalled to Madrid because of the failure of their financial policy.

The Papacy

The pope was both the spiritual head of the western Church and an Italian prince as ruler of the Papal States, which lay across the centre of Italy from sea to sea.[20] As Italian rulers the chief aim of the popes during

[18] P. 274.   [19] P. 142.   [20] P. 23.

the fifteenth century had been to restore there the authority they had effectively lost during the long period of papal residence at Avignon in the time of the 'Babylonish Captivity'.[21] In fulfilling this policy they met with strong opposition within the Papal States. The city of Rome, despite the prestige it gained from having the Papacy established within its boundaries, preserved its ancient republican tradition, and the popes were so afraid for the safety of their lives in its crowded streets that they usually avoided it. Each town in the Papal States had its own local administrators who defied papal authority, and cities like Perugia and Bologna were practically independent, as were the power-ful Vicars of the Church in the Romagna. The leading Roman families, who had members in the College of Cardinals, chose the popes from their own numbers;[22] but at the same time, they were jealous of papal influence and did not hesitate to make use of their many opportunities of impeding it.

To overcome such resistance and enlarge their powers, the popes depended largely on their own relatives, appointing the clerics to be cardinals and granting lands and offices to the laymen. Sixtus IV, who was Pope from 1471 to 1484, developed the practice of nepotism to an extent never known before. He made two of his nephews cardinals (one of whom later became Pope as Julius II) and gave others lucrative appointments and secured marriages for them into princely families. Some of them, however, implicated him in political intrigues with the Italian cities, the results of which included the murder of a Medici and a war against Florence from 1478 to 1480. His pontificate showed the weaknesses of such a policy, particularly his own lack of experience (he had been a Franciscan friar before his election) and his lack of worthy relatives to promote. Another weakness was that the elective nature of the papal office made it impossible for any pope to found a dynasty. On the death of each pope, his relatives were immediately dismissed from the offices to which he had appointed them and replaced by those of the new pope. Moreover, since elderly men were generally elected pope, papal administrators had generally only a short period in which to establish themselves in office.

Nevertheless, by the later years of the fifteenth century, the popes had achieved considerable progress towards making the Papal States a despotism rather on the lines of the Duchy of Milan, and this process was taken a stage further during the pontificate of Alexander VI (1492-1503), who was born Roderigo Borgia and a Spaniard. He was the nephew of Pope Calixtus III (1455-58), who made him a Cardinal in 1456 and appointed him Chancellor of the Roman Church the next year. Alexander was the pope who divided the New World between Spain and Portugal in 1493 and secured the execution of Savonarola in 1498. He was also, like Sixtus IV, a generous patron of the arts, and

21 P. 38. 22 P. 43.

under him Rome was largely replanned and the Castle of St Angelo rebuilt. His election was largely secured through bribery, and he is best known for the efforts he devoted thereafter to enlarging the fortunes of the Borgia family. He was, however, a clever politician and an astute diplomat. As Chancellor of the Roman Church under several popes, he had gained great experience in the administration of the Papacy and was able to benefit from it. He was aware of the financial weakness of the Papacy and wanted to secure a large proportion of the revenue of the Papal States for it, and in seeking to aggrandize his family, he wished also to make his rule effective throughout the territory. Rivals and owners of coveted wealth were removed by poison or the sword. His chief agent in doing this was Caesar Borgia (1475-1507), his illegitimate son, who gained Machiavelli's admiration.[23] Alexander made him a cardinal in 1493, but he renounced this dignity five years later to serve his father in a military capacity. In the course of three campaigns between 1499 and 1502, he subdued the cities of the Romagna and established order and unity in the province, which he and his father planned to make into a family duchy. To further their dynastic ambitions, they co-operated with Louis XII in his invasion of Italy,[24] an indication of how the dynastic ambitions of the Papacy often contributed to Italian disunity.

The death of Alexander VI showed once again the effect of the elective character of the papal office upon the family hopes of its holders. After Pius III's brief pontificate of twenty-seven days, Giuliano della Rovere, Alexander's personal enemy, who had been living in hiding from him, mostly in northern Italy, became Pope as Julius II (1503-13). This proved fatal to the ambitions of Caesar Borgia, who was planning to conquer Tuscany; he had to leave Italy and eventually died fighting in the service of his brother-in-law, the King of Navarre. Julius reaped the harvest of his work and did much to centralize papal authority in central Italy. He took possession of Caesar's gains in the Romagna, and few of the ruling families retained control of their cities. Known as the 'Warrior Pope', he himself led a military expedition against Perugia and Bologna, both of which he compelled to submit to his authority.[25] Thereafter, he became involved in diplomatic enterprises and intrigues in connection with the League of Cambrai and the Holy League during the Italian Wars.[26] Under him the Papacy fell into such disrepute that the conciliar movement made itself heard again; Louis XII summoned a schismatic general council at Pisa in 1512;[27] and Julius had to call the Fifth Lateran Council at Rome to counter it.

Julius II, the politician and military leader, was also an imaginative patron of the arts and prepared the way for the election of Leo X (1513-21). Indeed, it was largely to meet the expense of the rebuilding

[23] P. 126.   [24] P. 142.   [25] P. 143.   [26] P. 144.   [27] P. 143.

of St Peter's, Rome, that Leo granted the indulgence which was to be the immediate cause of his conflict with Luther in Germany.[28] Otherwise he bore little resemblance to his predecessor. He had no liking for a policy which sought to aggrandize the Papal States through intervention in the tortuous events of the Italian Wars, and when Francis I launched a fresh French invasion of the peninsula, he was prepared to secure peace with him by agreeing to the Concordat of Bologna.[29] He was as ready as former popes to advance his family and to increase papal power in his territory, but he was too easy-going and pleasure-loving to concentrate with much determination upon such objects. 'God gave us the Papacy; therefore let us enjoy it' was his well-known remark, and he enjoyed it in a way which made Rome both the cultural centre of the Italian Renaissance and the city which increasingly shocked the spiritual sensibilities of those who still looked to the Papacy for a lead amid the problems facing the contemporary Church. Owing to Julius II's death, he presided over the Fifth Lateran Council, which, however, promulgated only a few minor reforms and left the main causes of the Reformation untouched.

When Leo X died in 1521, he was followed first by Adrian VI (1522-23), the last non-Italian pope, whose pontificate lasted little more than a year, and then by another Medici pope, his cousin, Clement VII (1523-34). He readily continued the patronage of artists and scholars in Rome, but at the same time he had been a capable papal Secretary of State and wanted to preserve the independence of the Papacy and reform its administration. Yet his character, though blameless morally, did not suit him for this task; he showed himself to be weak, hesitant and insensitive. His failure to support the movement for reform within the Church meant that it was during his pontificate that Protestantism was able to establish itself firmly in several countries, and his irresolute policy of procrastination over Henry VIII's wish to secure a divorce from Catherine of Aragon probably ensured that England renounced papal authority. Moreover, the time when the popes (and other Italian rulers) could hope to safeguard their independence by intriguing in the contest between France and Spain was coming to an end with the establishment of Spanish supremacy over the peninsula. His attempts to exploit Charles V's difficulties by joining with Francis I in the League of Cognac of 1527 brought its retribution in the shape of the Sack of Rome later that year and the acknowledgement of Spanish control over the Papacy in the Treaty of Cambrai two years later.[30] He spent the remaining years of his life, still unaware of the need for reform in the Church, opposing Charles V's wish for the summoning of a general council.

Henceforward, the Papacy remained firmly under Spanish domination, and the days when popes could hope to make themselves powerful

[28] P. 156.   [29] P. 145.   [30] Pp. 148-9.

temporal rulers, able to act independently and direct the course of international politics to their advantage, were over. This was shown in the pontificate of Clement's successor, Paul III (1534-49), who was a Renaissance pope in his patronage of the arts and promotion of nepotism, but showed that the prolongation of the authority of the Papacy was to be found in activities other than intervention in European politics.[31] He promoted reform within the Church, giving particular encouragement to the Society of Jesus and agreeing to summon the Council of Trent, but at the same time showing himself determined that it should not make concessions to the Protestants. He was followed by Julius III (1550-5) who led a worldly life, practised nepotism and was a protector of Michelangelo; he believed in reform, but was not energetic enough to do much beyond giving the Jesuits further assistance.

The inevitability of Spanish control of the Papacy was further shown by the attempt of Paul IV (1555-9) to break away from it, though he was the first of the Counter-Reformation popes, and the success of that movement depended, above all, on Spanish support.[32] In a way, he stood a better chance of succeeding in such a policy than some of his predecessors because the work of consolidating the authority of the pope over the Papal States, begun by Alexander VI and Julius II, had been continued by their successors, notably Clement VII (who had subdued Ancona) and Paul III (who had subjected Umbria and restored Camerino to the papal territories). The papal revenue was steadily improving, and Rome had recovered from the Sack of 1527. Yet, even with this assured power in his own dominions and adequate financial resources, his anti-Spanish policy failed completely.

For the remainder of this period, the papal office was held by a succession of Counter-Reformation popes.[33] Since Spanish ascendancy in Italy was now incontestable, the scope for independent action by the Papacy had become very limited. This, together with the firm establishment of their authority within the Papal States, meant that the popes became more concerned with maintaining and enlarging their power over the Roman Catholic Church as a whole during the process of internal reform, than with making any really effective incursions into European politics.[34] By thus adapting itself to changed circumstances, the Papacy was able to preserve and increase its authority within a restricted sphere. It could no longer seek to exercise a powerful sway over the rulers of western Europe or even of Italy, but its government of its own territory was more assured than ever; it had lost the acceptance of its spiritual leadership among the Protestant bodies, but was able to intensify its supremacy over the members of its own communion.

[31] P. 212.   [32] P. 213.   [33] P. 212.   [34] P. 218.

18

HABSBURG
AND
OTTOMAN

The founding of the Habsburg dynasty

The Habsburgs took their name from their ancestral castle on the River Aar in Switzerland, which they possessed from the tenth century. The owners of Habsburg Castle became Counts of Habsburg and gradually extended their territory into south-western Germany. The founding of their dynasty took place in 1282, when they obtained Austria, Styria and Carniola, which they ruled as archdukes; and in 1363 the Tyrol was bequeathed by its count to the family. Political ambition in the fifteenth century brought them election as Holy Roman Emperors, and, indeed, they succeeded in making the office practically hereditary in their family. From 1440, almost uninterruptedly, only the head of their house wore the Imperial crown. Meanwhile, they had acquired through marriage the kingdoms of Hungary and Bohemia, though these possessions were later temporarily to be lost. By the beginning of the sixteenth century, despite the absorption of their original family lands by the Swiss confederated cantons between 1386 and 1474, they had considerably increased their powers as Archdukes of Austria and were already the leading dynasty in Europe.

Their great weakness, however, lay in the elective nature of their Imperial position and the increasingly independent powers of the German princes who nominally accepted their suzerainty.[1] This imposed a formidable obstacle in the way of their making the Holy Roman Empire an absolutist state with centralized governmental institutions such as other rulers were perfecting. To do this they had to increase their own strength by treaties, alliances and, especially, marriages. By the late fifteenth century their efforts were on the way to success.[2] Most spectacular was their acquisition of the Spanish monarchy and its rich, extensive empire in 1496, but of more importance for their immediate purpose were the territories they obtained encircling Germany—the Netherlands and Luxembourg on the west

[1] P. 20.   [2] P. 187.

and Franche Comté in the Rhône basin—in 1477. These additions to Austria and the lands they already possessed in central Europe suggested that the princes of central Germany might soon be hemmed in by Habsburg territory and deprived of the possibility of foreign help. This consolidation and enlargement of the Habsburg family inheritance was weakened in its effect, however, by Maximilian's failure to achieve a corresponding success through organizing Imperial power in Germany; and when Charles V succeeded him, he was able to do little to check the drift towards disunity.[3]

On the other hand, the Habsburgs made their greatest territorial gain in the third decade of the sixteenth century. Hungary and Bohemia had been lost to them for more than a century, but they had not ceased to wish to regain these kingdoms and unite them with Austria, and this was finally brought about through the disastrous Battle of Mohacs in 1526.[4] But rather than a gain in strength, this acquisition immediately presented the Habsburgs with a dangerous problem and the first serious crisis of their dynastic career. The Turks advanced deep into Hungary, and the whole of central Europe seemed to lie open to their onslaught. Far from being in a position to rely upon his family lands to enable him to subjugate the German princes, Charles V had to adopt a conciliatory attitude towards them in the hope of persuading them to assist in protecting these lands.[5] The climax came only three years after the Battle of Mohacs with the siege of Vienna, and though the Habsburgs survived this threat to their existence, it had assisted in frustrating their political ambitions in Germany. Moreover, the danger from the Turks was to remain for more than a century. The union of Hungary and Bohemia with the Germanic Alpine lands, which was later to form a durable basis for Habsburg power, did not, therefore, achieve this in the later part of the sixteenth century. After 1555 the complications caused by the short-lived union between the Spanish Empire and the Habsburg family lands came to an end, but the Austrian Habsburgs were reduced to a position of considerable weakness and difficulty.

The Austrian Habsburgs

Although Charles V kept the direction of Imperial policy for himself until he abdicated, Ferdinand had for many years both controlled the daily administration of the Empire and ruled over the Habsburg family lands.[6] In dividing his dominions, Charles decided that the association of the Austrian Habsburgs with the Imperial office should be renewed, and in 1558 the Electors formally appointed Ferdinand as Emperor. Ferdinand, therefore, inherited the serious problems which had troubled Charles, and which he had left unsolved upon

[3] P. 196.   [4] P. 290.   [5] P. 163.   [6] P. 191.

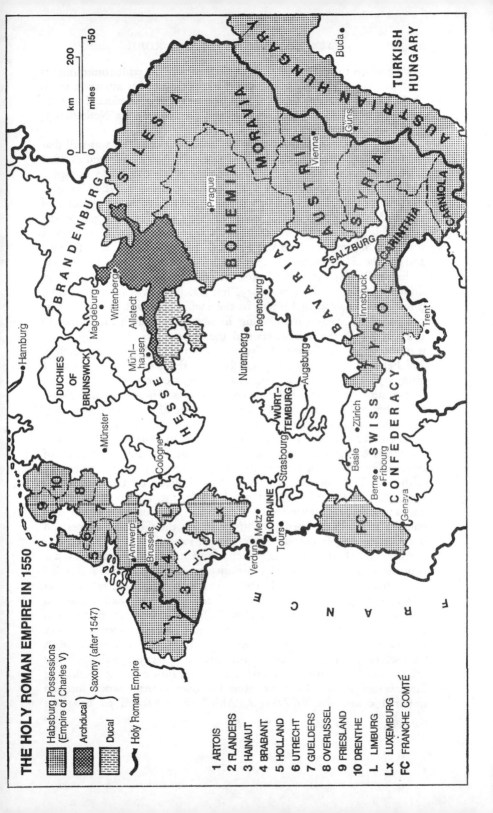

THE HOLY ROMAN EMPIRE IN 1550

Habsburg Possessions
(Empire of Charles V)

Archducal } Saxony (after 1547)
Ducal

Holy Roman Empire

1 ARTOIS
2 FLANDERS
3 HAINAUT
4 BRABANT
5 HOLLAND
6 UTRECHT
7 GUELDERS
8 OVERIJSSEL
9 FRIESLAND
10 DRENTHE
L LIMBURG
Lx LUXEMBURG
FC FRANCHE COMTÉ

150
200
km
miles

TURKISH
HUNGARY

AUSTRIAN HUNGARY

Buda

SILESIA

BRANDENBURG

MORAVIA

BOHEMIA

AUSTRIA

Vienna

STYRIA

Güns

SALZBURG

CARINTHIA

CARNIOLA

Hamburg

Prague

Magdeburg

Wittenberg

Allstedt

Münl-hausen

DUCHIES
OF
BRUNSWICK

HESSE

Münster

Regensburg

Nuremberg

BAVARIA

Innsbruck

TYROL

Trent

Cologne

WÜRT-TEMBURG

Augsburg

Zürich

SWISS

Strasbourg

Basle

Berne

CONFEDERACY

Antwerp

Brussels

LIÈGE

L

Lx

LORRAINE

Metz

Verdun

Tours

Fribourg

Geneva

FC

E
M
P
I
R
E

F
R
A
N
C
E

giving up his rule. It is true that he did not have the wide commitments that prevented Charles being able to concentrate his attention upon them, but at the same time the division of territories effected in 1555 deprived him of important possessions, particularly the Netherlands, with valuable revenues.

One of the most serious problems faced by Ferdinand was still that of the Turks. After the Battle of Mohacs, Hungary had been divided into three parts. Ferdinand took over the west, the Turks occupied the centre, and Zapolya held Transylvania in the east. When Zapolya died in 1540, leaving an infant son, John Sigismund, Ferdinand renewed his claim to the whole of Hungary. He besieged Buda, but Suleiman drove his forces away in 1541 and declared his support for John Sigismund. Two years later Suleiman resumed his offensive and advanced westwards and gained control of two-thirds of Hungary, including Transylvania. Ferdinand was faced with the danger of being driven completely from Hungary, but Suleiman was overtaken by a threat to the Ottoman Empire in the east. Ferdinand, however, was compelled to make a humiliating five-year truce with the Sultan in 1547 by which the Turks retained their conquests, John Sigismund was recognized as Prince of Transylvania under Turkish protection, and Ferdinand agreed to pay a tribute to the Sultan for the part of Hungary held by him. The expiration of the truce in 1552 was followed by skirmishes and raids between the two sides. These were indecisive, partly because Ferdinand had taken advantage of the period to strengthen his Hungarian frontier forces, but at the same time he was unable to extend his control over the kingdom, and in 1562 he had to renew the terms of the truce and agree to pay the accumulated arrears of tribute. For the rest of the century, the position was not fundamentally changed.[7] The defence of this eastern frontier of the Habsburgs remained a costly and debilitating burden for them, consuming almost the whole of the revenues of Carniola, Carinthia and Styria and compelling the Emperors to continue to ask the German princes and the Austrian and Bohemian noblemen for subsidies.

Another serious problem which confronted Ferdinand was the continued religious and political disunity in Germany. He had succeeded in negotiating the Religious Peace of Augsburg, but Protestantism was still making gains in the country.[8] Ferdinand, who had a Spanish upbringing, unhesitatingly supported the Counter-Reformation and gave it great encouragement by inviting the Jesuits to Vienna in 1551 and subsequently to Prague, from where they were able to establish themselves in Germany itself at Ingoldstadt in 1563.[9] In the political sphere, Ferdinand tried to create a rival institution to the ineffective *Reichskammergericht*[10] by converting his own court council into an Imperial court, the *Reichshofrat*. Although it proved to be more

[7] P. 292.   [8] P. 168.   [9] P. 169.   [10] P. 20.

efficient, it was mistrusted by the princes because of its complete dependence upon the Emperor, and it suffered from the same inability to compel acceptance of its decisions. Indeed, it was impossible to check the continuing decline of Imperial authority in Germany, and under Ferdinand the princes further increased their powers within their states and ignored the authority of Imperial institutions, including the Diet itself.

Ferdinand had also to deal with similar disunity in Hungary and Bohemia, and here again his power to do much was limited, owing to the strength of the nobility in both kingdoms. His attempts to control from Vienna that part of Hungary held by him were largely frustrated by the growth of Protestantism in the country. The Hungarian Church suffered from the usual spiritual deficiencies of the time and was dominated by the nobility. In addition, it was weakened by the death of almost half its bishops in the Battle of Mohacs and the seizure of much of its property by both Ferdinand and Zapolya in their various financial difficulties. In this situation, Lutheranism had been adopted widely by the German-speaking population, though the Magyar nobility mostly chose Calvinism with its opportunities for lay control of ecclesiastical affairs which enhanced their social prestige.[11] Ferdinand could do little beyond giving his support to the forces of the Counter-Reformation which were already establishing themselves in the kingdom.

After the Battle of Mohacs, the Bohemian Estates recognized Ferdinand's claim to the kingship, which they claimed was elective, but insisted that he must observe their ancient liberties, including religious toleration. Most of the people were Utraquists, observing communion in both kinds, vernacular services and other practices derived from Huss; but here also Lutheranism had been adopted by much of the German-speaking population, and in the late 1520s Anabaptism was introduced by refugees into Moravia, while from the 1550s Calvinism gained many adherents, particularly in the towns. The Estates also tried to gain important political concessions while Charles and Ferdinand were engaged in the Schmalkaldic War,[12] but the Battle of Mühlberg in 1547 so seriously undermined their position that Ferdinand was able to compel the Estates to accept the Bohemian monarchy as hereditary in the house of Habsburg and to replace the elected officials in the towns by royal ones, which meant that he now appointed nearly all their representatives in the Estates. He outlawed Anabaptism in the kingdom, but since the strength of the nobility was undiminished, and he needed financial help from them against the Turks, he could not take action against any other forms of Protestantism. Indeed, he induced the Papacy to allow communion in both kinds in the Habsburg lands to the laity in the hope that the

[11] P. 183.   [12] P. 164.

Utraquists would be reconciled to Roman Catholicism. He did, however, encourage the Jesuits to work in Bohemia, especially among the
greater nobility, many of whom had shown no enthusiasm for
Protestantism.

Upon the death of Ferdinand I in 1564, he was succeeded by his
eldest son, Maximilian II, who was a humanist and a patron of the
arts and believed in religious toleration and compromise. Moreover,
his political position was weakened by the subdivision Ferdinand had
made of his territories at his death among his three sons. Maximilian,
as the eldest, succeeded to Austria with Bohemia and Hungary, but
his second son, Ferdinand, received the Alpine province of the Tyrol
and the scattered remnants of the old family lands of south-western
Germany in Swabia and the Upper Rhine, while Charles, his third son,
was given the other Alpine provinces of Styria, Carinthia and Carniola.
Maximilian, therefore, was in no position to adopt an authoritarian,
intolerant policy within his dominions, even if he had wished to do so,
particularly as by now, even in Austria itself, most of the nobility
together with their peasants had become Lutheran and, by means of
their control of the Austrian Estates, were demanding religious
toleration. They knew that they were in a strong position, particularly
as the Emperor badly needed their financial assistance against the
Turks. Maximilian adopted a very tolerant policy, confirming the
privileges of the Austrian nobility, recognizing their right to freedom
of worship on their own estates and even sending for theologians from
northern Germany to advise the Lutherans in Austria on the organization of their worship.

Maximilian II died in 1576, and his eldest son, who became Emperor
as Rudolf II, was very different in character compared with his father
and grandfather. He had been educated in Spain and was a devoted
Roman Catholic and a patron of the arts, but he spent nearly all his
time in his hilltop castle at Prague amid astrologers, alchemists, artists
and charlatans.[13] He was able to do little in the way of measures against
Protestantism. He continued to need the support of the nobility
throughout the Habsburg lands. The price of his election to the Crown
of Bohemia was the acceptance of the 'Bohemian Confession', a single
statement of belief, which the Lutherans, Calvinists, Utraquists and
Anabaptists, alarmed by the progress of the Counter-Reformation in
the country, had drawn up in 1575. In Austria, he was assisted by a
peasants' revolt, which followed the heavy taxation consequent upon
the renewal of fighting against the Turks in 1593. When this had been
crushed, he had gained the support of the nobility and was able,
therefore, to take the first tentative steps to stop the growth of Protestantism. In 1597 Protestant preachers were expelled from Austria,
and the toleration of communion in both kinds, which had been

13 P. 104.

secured by Ferdinand I, was annulled. Meanwhile, in Styria the Archduke Charles had established a Jesuit university at Graz, and in 1591 his successor, Ferdinand, withdrew freedom of worship from both peasants and townspeople.

This support for the Counter-Reformation represented the hope among the Habsburgs that the restoration of religious unity might re-establish their political authority in both their family lands and the Empire; in the next century this hope contributed towards the outbreak of the Thirty Years' War in which they fought to secure that aim in Germany. The success of the Counter-Reformation in Germany, however, was not to assist their cause. The Roman Catholic princes showed themselves as determined as the Protestant ones to retain the independence from Imperial control which they had gained in the sixteenth century, and the real authority of the Habsburgs over the Empire was not to be revived. In their family lands, however, where their power had been so weak in the second half of the sixteenth century, the situation was different. There, once the Turkish threat had died away and Rudolf had been succeeded by more competent rulers, the Habsburgs were to benefit from the progress of the Counter-Reformation and gain the support of the nobility for the establishment of a strong administration under their direction.

The Ottoman threat to Europe

The threat of the Ottoman Turks to Europe, which was present throughout the sixteenth century, was nothing new. For generations Europe had feared for its safety in the face of their mounting conquests. The Turkish people came from beyond the Caspian Sea and were converted to the Mohammedan faith in the seventh century. Little is known about them until 1055 when one of their tribes, known as the Seljuk Turks, captured Baghdad. From this they went on to build up an empire in Asia which at its height included Mesopotamia, Asia Minor and Syria. Though the Seljuks successfully maintained their empire against the Crusades, it collapsed in the thirteenth and fourteenth centuries. Their place in Asia Minor was taken by the stronger tribe of Ottoman Turks, who took their name from Osman (Othman) Bey (d 1326), the Governor of western Anatolia in Asia Minor, who led their revolt against the Seljuks.

Under Osman's successors, who took the title of Sultan, the Ottoman Turks spread westwards across the Dardanelles and eastwards into Ankara, conquering all the Asiatic provinces that had once been included within the Roman Empire, and in 1354 they advanced also into Europe. They captured the city of Adrianople in 1361 and defeated the Serbian army in 1389 at the Battle of Kossovo, which brought a large part of the Balkans, including northern Greece, under their rule. Soon only the city of Constantinople and a few outlying and scattered dependencies were all that remained of the once-great Byzantine Empire founded in the fourth century by the Emperor Constantine as the Roman Empire of the East. By then Europe became alarmed, and an army, which included French, German and Hungarian troops, was sent to the Balkans, only to be defeated in 1396 at the Battle of Nicopolis, which brought about the subjugation of Bulgaria. Constantinople seemed doomed, but it was saved by the threat to the Asiatic dominions of the Turks by the Mongols under Tamerlane (Timur). The reprieve, however, was only temporary. The Turks turned towards Europe again in the early fifteenth century annexing Macedonia in 1430, and in 1453 they captured Constantinople and brought the Byzantine Empire to an end. The nature of the Turkish danger and the impotence of Europe to resist it were startlingly revealed.

The conqueror of Constantinople was Sultan Mohammed II, an able, ambitious soldier and also, unusually for his dynasty, a patron of artists and scholars. He renamed the city Istanbul and made it the capital of the Ottoman Empire. Then he went on to extend his dominions in several directions, taking Genoa's Black Sea colonies of Amastris in 1461 and Kaffa in 1475 and at the same time consolidating his rule in the Balkans, where he captured Mistra, Athens and the Morea between 1458 and 1460, Serbia in 1459, Bosnia in 1464 and Albania in 1479. These victories on land were not his only successes. Possession of the dockyards of Constantinople enabled him to build a fleet of galleys, which entered the Aegean Sea and led to the conquest of Lesbos from Genoa in 1462 and Negroponte from Venice in 1470. In 1481 he besieged Otranto in southern Italy and attacked the island of Rhodes, but his sudden death that year necessitated the abandonment of both these undertakings.

By then, except for the strip of the Dalmatian coast north of Albania which Venice still possessed, the entire Balkan peninsula south of the Danube and Sava rivers was part of the Ottoman Empire, and this was the position at the beginning of the sixteenth century since the death of Mohammed II brought about a lull in Turkish expansion. The Turkish monarchy suffered from the absence of a definite line of succession to the throne on the death of a Sultan.[14] Mohammed's elder son, Bayezid, secured the throne, but his brother, Jem, challenged him and took refuge in Rhodes, where the Knights of St John held him and in 1489 placed him under the control of Pope Innocent VIII. Bayezid paid the pope an annual pension on the understanding that Jem remained in captivity, but he dared not engage in a campaign anywhere so long as his brother might be freed and raise a revolt

[14] P. 109.

against him in some other part of the Ottoman Empire. Not until Jem's death in 1495 did Europe lose its valuable hostage, and Bayezid become free to take the offensive again.

The Ottoman Empire

The conquests gained in Europe by the Ottoman Empire were astonishing to contemporaries, and it was itself entirely without parallel among other states and empires. Indeed, much of its success was due to its unique political, social and military organization. The authority of the Sultan was greater than that of any European monarch.[15] It was supported by the religious sanction of Islam and made effective in its administration and the army by the all-pervasive institution of slavery. Since the members of the organ of government, the Ottoman Ruling Institution, were slaves from the chief minister, the Grand Vizier, downwards, they were subject entirely to his will as also were his sons and the women of his harem. These slaves, however, were likely to serve him well because he could express his satisfaction with them by rewarding them with privileges which might include judicial immunity and exemption from taxation. They could also dispose of their property as they chose, and their children might inherit their privileges. Indeed, to be the Sultan's slaves was regarded as an honoured position in society.

Slavery was widespread in the Ottoman Empire and, together with polygamy, formed the basis of the Turkish social structure, though the Turks themselves had no legally recognized class-differences. They formed a minority of the population in their dominions, amounting probably to no more than a third of the inhabitants, but their reliance upon slaves as administrators prevented their becoming a governing class. These slaves were obtained from neither Turkish nor Moslem peoples, but from Christians. Some were drawn from captives taken in battle—Slavs, Greeks, Albanians and Georgians—and some were bought from dealers. For important positions, religion and not race was the determining qualification. Numerous Christians among the subject peoples were prepared to abandon their faith to seek such well-paid administrative posts, and embassy officials—Italians, Hungarians and Germans—deserted their positions and became renegades for the same purpose. The most important method of obtaining slaves, however, was the system known as *devshirme*, which was a regular levy of boys from Christian families, mainly in the Balkan countries. It amounted to about a fifth of all Christian boys between the ages of ten and twenty in the Ottoman Empire and was imposed about once every five years. The boys were converted to Islam and received a thorough training to fit them for their future

[15] P. 108.

tasks. The ablest among them were trained for the Sultan's service, either in his household or in his government.

These boys, however, formed only a minority of the whole. Most of them received a military training and were enrolled among the *janissaries*,[16] who were a unique fighting force, the *élite* of the Turkish army and its most formidable troops, though in numbers they only formed a minority. The greater part of the army was provided by a system which had some affinities with the feudalism evolved in medieval Christendom but was designed to suit better the needs of the Turks as a conquering people. When the Turks occupied European territories, they dispossessed the native ruling hereditary nobility and divided the land into *timars* which were held by *sipahis*, who had either to serve in the cavalry themselves or provide a stated number of horsemen to do so. The *sipahis* rarely became settled landowners, however, and spent most of their time away with the armies on campaigns. Moreover, the *timars* were not hereditary fiefs; they were redistributed on the death of a *sipahi*, and a new Sultan might make a general re-allocation to allow for his expected military needs in the future. The *sipahis* as a class, therefore, were bound to be supporters of a forward policy of aggression, which would gain more and more land suitable for division into *timars*. Indeed, the entire social, political and military organization of the Ottoman Empire, resting upon official slavery and the exaltation of service under the Sultan, had been developed to meet the requirements of a national policy of militarism and conquest; government was always subordinated to the needs of the army.

Added to this was the religious zeal of Islam which inspired its adherents to wage war for its cause. Yet the Turks were tolerant in the countries they occupied. Forced conversion and persecution were rarely practised by them. Jews and Christians had to pay a special land-tax from which Moslems were exempt, but they were not hindered in the practice of their own religions. Protestants enjoyed a toleration denied to them in neighbouring Roman Catholic countries. The Greek Orthodox Church retained its privileges, and its bishops continued to perform their functions. Moreover, the peasants of the conquered countries found that the new *sipahis* made less heavy demands upon them for forced labour and dues than the former landowners. Indeed, the peoples of the Balkans seem to have been generally content under Turkish rule, particularly in the more mountainous and isolated districts where they could maintain much of their way of life and traditional customs; and this was a further measure of strength for the Ottoman Empire. Contentment was also induced by the light taxation and stable revenue, made possible by the fact that Ottoman territories were large enough to provide all that its society required.

[16] P. 131.

Economically, the Ottoman Empire remained largely undeveloped. It had no industry, and its trade was always largely in European hands. Nevertheless, the Turkish capture of Constantinople revived the city's commercial importance, and peace enabled the subject peoples of the Balkans and the Middle East to resume their trading activities. The possession of Constantinople also made the Turks a naval as well as a military power. Mohammed II's construction of a fleet of galleys was continued by his successors, and it became a formidable force in the Mediterranean later in the sixteenth century.

Since, by and large, the Ottoman Empire was much stronger than any single European state, the only opportunity that Christendom might have had to oppose the Turks successfully and exploit their weaknesses would have been for the western powers to unite for a concerted war against them. But such an alliance was never possible, the crusading impulse in Europe had died away. When Constantinople was menaced in 1453, the Bishop of Siena was one of the few ecclesiastics who sought to gain international assistance to save the city, but European monarchs gave him no support; Pope Nicholas V ordered the imposition of a tithe to finance a crusade, but its proceeds went into the papal treasury. Moreover, the Roman Catholic Church had little regard for the Greek Orthodox Church, whose bishops, in their turn, made it clear that they preferred the Sultan to the Pope. United action against the Turks became even less likely in the sixteenth century when Europe was dominated by the struggle between Habsburg and Valois in Italy. Francis I, after his defeat at Pavia, sought aid from Suleiman the Magnificent and began the traditional French policy of alliance with the Turks. Charles V believed that the Christian nations of Europe should unite behind him in resisting the Turks, but they were not prepared to contribute towards an undertaking which would weaken themselves and benefit the Habsburgs. The disunity of their opponents was as great an advantage to the Turks as their own strength.

The Ottoman Empire at its height

Even after the death of Jem in 1495, eastern Europe enjoyed a comparative respite from Turkish aggression. Bayezid defeated Venice at sea in 1503 and compelled the republic to relinquish its ports on the Morea, including Lepanto; but his attention had largely to be concentrated on conflicts with Syria and Egypt and the rising state of Persia. On his death in 1512, his youngest son, Selim, secured the throne and murdered his two brothers and eight nephews. During his reign of eight years, Europe continued to be left in peace by the Turks because he also campaigned in Asia, conquering Syria, Armenia, much of Kurdistan, northern Mesopotamia and part of Arabia and Egypt. Indeed, such a direction of the Turks' attention elsewhere was an important reason for the survival of Europe unconquered by them. Selim's successor, Suleiman the Magnificent, though the victor of Mohacs and captor of Buda, made far more extensive conquests in Asia.

The Ottoman Empire reached its height during the reign of Suleiman, who succeeded Selim in 1520 and was one of the greatest rulers of the sixteenth century. He was not only an outstanding soldier, but also an able administrator who doubled the revenue from his dominions and increased the size and efficiency of the army. He appointed capable Grand Viziers and other ministers and improved local government in the conquered territories. To his people he was known as 'the law-giver' because he sought to adapt the Moslem law-code to the needs of the enlarged, complex Ottoman Empire and was anxious to ensure that justice was administered fairly. He did a great deal to give the state the stability that it enjoyed for a long time after his death in 1566.

Upon becoming Sultan, he decided to strike at the two points where the Ottoman Empire was threatened. These were Belgrade, which menaced the safety of his northern frontiers, and Rhodes, which harassed shipping engaged in the valuable trade between Constantinople and Cairo. Both had resisted previous Turkish assaults, but he captured Belgrade in 1521 and Rhodes the next year. This meant, as Pope Adrian VI realized, that 'the passages to Hungary, Sicily and Italy lie open to him.' At first he was diverted by the need to defend his frontier with Persia, but his army urged him to advance from Belgrade—an indication of the constant military pressure on the Turkish government to go on fighting and conquering. In 1526, therefore, he crossed the Danube and destroyed the Hungarian army at the Battle of Mohacs.[17] The invaders then advanced northwards, took possession of Buda, entered Austria and prepared for an assault upon Vienna. Here, however, Suleiman encountered the difficulties that were increasingly being imposed on Turkish military operations in Europe by their long lines of communication and contemporary limitations upon transport. In May 1529 he left Constantinople, reached Belgrade in mid-July and arrived outside Vienna in late September, but by then the winter was approaching, and the campaigning season was nearly over. He failed to 'take the city by storm and had not the resources to mount a long siege. He had arranged for thousands of camels to be brought to the Danube for the purpose of bringing supplies to his army, but it took almost a month for the convoys to come to him. Heavy snowfalls made further operations impossible, and after eighteen days he had to make the long retreat to Belgrade, during which his

[17] P. 280.

troops suffered badly from the bitter cold. These circumstances, as much as the resistance of the city, had prevented his further advance into Europe.

The same circumstances foiled another attempt at capturing Vienna which Suleiman made in 1532. Then he was held up for three weeks by the resistance of the fortress of Güns, near the Hungarian border, 96 kilometres south of the city, and had to retreat in some disorder. Charles V, who was there himself, would have liked to launch a counter-offensive, but his German troops refused to go beyond the Empire, and the Italian situation again distracted his attention with news of an understanding between Pope Clement VII and Francis I.[18] The situation in central Europe had, in fact, reached a deadlock. Suleiman could not move into Austria, and Charles could not recover Hungary. Suleiman himself soon turned his attention eastwards. In 1534 he took Tabriz in Azerbaijan from the Persians and marched from there to Mesopotamia to take Baghdad. During this time, when the Turkish threat to Austria was in abeyance, Charles decided to take action against the Corsair pirates in the Mediterranean, whom Suleiman had realized would be valuable allies in threatening the sea-routes to Naples and Milan upon which the Spanish position in Italy depended.[19] Charles V's commitments in Italy and Germany again, however, prevented him exploiting his success in capturing Tunis by going on to take Algiers. The victory improved Habsburg morale, but the Corsairs continued to raid shipping in the Mediterrenean.

Soon after his return from his eastern campaign, Suleiman in 1536 signed a treaty with Francis I. Both rulers realized that they could best strike at Charles in the Mediterranean. During the winter of 1536-7, when Francis had renewed his contest with Charles, the Corsairs were allowed to have the port of Marseilles as a base. Charles attempted to take the offensive again in 1541 by capturing Algiers, but this time he did not succeed. Two years later Francis allowed the Turkish and Corsair fleets to use Toulon and establish a slave-market there to dispose of the captives they had taken while raiding the Italian coast.[20] The alliance with Suleiman, however, brought Francis little gain and lost him the support of his allies, while the Turks found it difficult to maintain a fleet over a thousand miles away from their naval bases. Nevertheless, the Turks continued their activity in the Mediterranean, capturing Tripoli in 1551 and repulsing Philip II's attempt to recapture it in 1560, but they still could not hope to operate effectively far enough westwards to threaten Spain and Italy seriously. The Danube valley remained the most serious battleground.

War had been resumed in the Balkans in 1540 by Ferdinand in an attempt to regain all of Hungary, but the venture did not go in his

[18] P. 149.   [19] P. 200.   [20] P. 150.

favour.[21] Only the threat of renewed war in Persia probably saved
Ferdinand from losing Hungary entirely to the Turks. For the rest of
his reign, however, Suleiman did not attempt to advance further into
Hungary. He had captured Gran in 1543, which gave him a much-
needed base north of Belgrade, the absence of which had weakened
him so badly in 1529. He was content now to fortify it, together with
Buda and Belgrade, and, particularly as Ferdinand was at the same
time fortifying his part of Hungary, was content to consolidate his
hold on the Balkans rather than attempt to extend his conquests in
Europe. He followed the same policy in the east. On renewing the
war against Persia in 1548, he made conquests which extended the
frontier from the Black Sea to the Persian Gulf, but made peace in
1555. Here again problems of distance and transport made it very
difficult to wage war. Although he had reached the limits of his
expansion against Persia, he had, as in the Balkans, provided his
territories with a firmly-held frontier. There were indications, indeed,
that the growth of the Ottoman Empire was nearing its end. One of
these occurred in 1565 when Suleiman, encouraged by the Spanish
defeat off Sicily in 1560, embarked on his last great venture in an
attempt to capture Malta, to which the Knights of St John had gone
after the fall of Rhodes, but he had to withdraw after the combined
Turkish and Corsair fleets besieging the island had failed to prevent
its relief by Spain.[22]

Nevertheless, when Suleiman died in 1566, the Ottoman Empire
had attained the height of its power and almost its greatest extent.
It included the whole of the Balkan peninsula and the Danube valley
almost up to the boundary of the Empire, only a strip of the Dalmatian
coast and the mountainous principality of Montenegro not having
been conquered by them. To the north-east, the Black Sea was surrounded by Turkish territory with the exception of a district to the
east occupied by Circassians. From Asia Minor, Turkish possessions
stretched eastwards beyond Baghdad and Mesopotamia to the Persian
border. The Turks held the northern coast of Africa, including Egypt,
and most of the islands of the Mediterranean and the Aegean, the
important exceptions being Crete and Cyprus (which were still
Venetian) and Malta; the eastern Mediterranean was dominated by
their naval power.

The decline of Ottoman power

Though the dynasty of the Sultans maintained its position and lost
no territory after the death of Suleiman, a number of serious weaknesses
began to appear in the Ottoman Empire from about the middle of the
sixteenth century. These originated in the character of the sultanate

[21] P. 282.   [22] P. 246.

itself, the absolute powers of which made it the centre of the whole Turkish system of government. These powers were supplemented by the institution of the harem, which freed it from family attachments, and the right of a new Sultan to kill his brother on his accession, which safeguarded him from the claims of pretenders; but Suleiman was persuaded by his favourite wife, Roxolana, to murder his son by an older wife to secure the throne for her incompetent son, who succeeded him as Selim II and from whom were to descend an almost unbroken line of equally incompetent sultans. Indeed, the period after the death of Suleiman became known as that of the 'rule of women'. The sultans gave themselves to effeminate and luxurious pursuits; the harem acquired a growing influence in public life; favourites obtained high imperial posts and sold others to the highest bidders; palace ladies, minors and officials, unable to undertake military service, were appointed to be holders of *timars*. At the same time, the Ottoman Empire experienced serious financial difficulties. It shared in the inflation caused by the general 'price revolution' of the time, which caused its government to depreciate the currency in an effort to meet its expenses; and this added to the confusion within the empire.

Inevitably the government of the Ottoman Empire deteriorated. Under Selim II, Rustem Pasha, who was appointed Grand Vizier through Roxolana's influence, set a pattern of corruption which was followed by his successors in office. At the same time, the ending of the years of conquest changed the character of the civil administration. Almost continual warfare had enabled it to maintain its numbers by recruiting renegade captives who became effective higher officials, but it could now no longer do so. At its head it became merely a palace service staffed by eunuchs, possessing considerable power, but unable to prevent the increasing autonomy gained in the provinces by governors and pashas, many of whom were able to make their office hereditary and became virtually independent lords.

Even more debilitating was the effect of peacetime conditions upon the organization and discipline of the army, which depended upon an empire perpetually at war to keep it powerful and effective. The *sipahis* became unable to maintain their numbers owing to the way the *timars* were now distributed. Already the traditional composition of the janissaries had been affected as a result of Suleiman's wars in which their losses had been heavy in the arduous fighting of both eastern and western campaigns. The *devshirme* system could not produce sufficient recruits to make good their casualties. Moslem children were accepted in increasing numbers, and Turkish families began to regard service with them as a good career for their sons. Even before the end of Suleiman's reign, the janissaries obtained the right to marry, and on the accession of Selim II they gained the further right of admission to the corps for their sons. As inflation continued, they demanded higher pay, and when they did not obtain it, as in 1589, they mutinied. They began also to take part in politics, and during the reign of Selim's successor, Murad III (1574-95), they obtained the execution of ministers who opposed them. In the absence of fighting, they became an armed corporation, many of whose members were engaged in civilian occupations, but claimed special social privileges and were relieved of active service by the issue of veterans' certificates. Even Jews obtained admission to their numbers in order to enjoy their privileges.

The first sign of the Turkish decline came about through the political inability of Selim II. During the time when Turkish assistance to the insurgent Moriscos might have been an effective blow against Spain he ignored their appeal for help and decided instead to attack Cyprus.[23] The island fell to the Turks, but the episode brought upon them the crushing defeat at Lepanto. Nevertheless, the Turkish fleet made good its losses and even captured Tunis in 1574. Control of the eastern Mediterranean and possession of northern Africa was retained by the Ottoman Empire, which, though now static, managed to maintain its boundaries. Indeed, these were even extended in the east. When the Persians renewed war on the Turks in 1578, Murad III conducted a campaign in which he conquered Georgia and Azerbaijan, gains which Persia had to recognize in 1590. This enabled Murad to launch an offensive against the Habsburgs, which was continued by his successor, Mohammed III (1595-1603). The war was to continue into the seventeenth century and was to end with no change in the territories held by either side. The Turks, despite large-scale use of their resources, failed to make any further expansion in the Balkans. The threat to Europe was over.

[23] P. 247.

19
MUSCOVITE
RUSSIA

Kievan Russia

The history of Russia is usually taken to begin in the ninth century with 'the coming of the Varangians', groups of Vikings who moved along the great rivers of western Russia, first as pirates and traders and then as conquerors of the scattered Slav tribes settled there. They established a number of warring principalities stretching from Novgorod to Kiev. Soon Kiev established its supremacy and brought some sense of unity to the tribes, which was strengthened by the introduction of Christianity among them.

In 988 Prince Vladimir of Kiev was baptized and enforced conversion on his boyars or nobles, making his principality the religious and political centre of Russia. He had seen the need of a common culture if unity were to be achieved and also that religion and culture were inseparably united. He had come under the influence of Byzantine culture for there were already strong trading-links between Kiev and Byzantium. It was, therefore, the Byzantine version of Christianity that he adopted, and the Greek Orthodox Church was established in Russia. This was to be of very great importance in the history of the country. Greek Orthodoxy was to be a powerful instrument in assisting the princes of Kiev in their attempted unification of the Russian lands. The eastern Church had never, unlike the western Church, been able to gain any independence for itself. The Byzantine Empire had never had to contend with the claims of any such authority as the Papacy. The emperors had absolute sway over the Church in their dominions, and Russian rulers were able to assume this position. Greek Orthodoxy in Russia was from the start a powerful support for the monarchy.

Another effect, however, of the adoption of Greek Orthodoxy by Russia was to initiate her separation from Europe. Byzantine culture and religion, which reached its height in the tenth century, certainly brought to Russia at the time of her conversion a large measure of western influence, but the growing rift between the Roman and Greek

Churches inevitably acted strongly in favour of her exclusion from the west, a process intensified by the Mongol invasion and Russia's subsequent expansion eastwards. In the Middle Ages the Russian people were semi-Asiatic and isolated from European civilization; and in the sixteenth century she was not to become an important state nor take any significant part in European affairs. Moreover, she remained almost unaffected by the great developments which brought about a new Europe between 1400 and 1700. She developed no large-scale commerce and gained no energetic middle-class; she had neither Renaissance nor Reformation and took no part in the rise of the scientific spirit.

The expansion of the Russian principalities was halted in the thirteenth century when the Mongols, known to the Russians as the Tatars, swept from Asia across the Russian plain and established themselves as overlords of the country under the name of the Golden Horde. The next century, Lithuania took advantage of the situation to seize Russian territory in the west of the country. This was the end of Kievan Russia. The Tatar domination lasted altogether for two and a half centuries and had an influence long after it was over. The devastation and the payment of tribute imposed upon the people impoverished the country terribly; industry and commerce were extinguished, and the culture and prosperity of the towns were destroyed. The isolation from the west was intensified, and Russia became uniquely and lastingly a backward country. Another consequence was the rise of Russian despotism and the spread of serfdom. Both became an essential feature of Muscovite Russia, and both came into being, in their different ways, through the effect of the times upon the lives of the people.[1] The Mongol conquest also strengthened the Church and encouraged its reliance upon temporal support. The Tatars, even after their conversion to Islam in the earlier years of the fourteenth century, were tolerant in matters of religion and favoured the Church as being likely to preserve the obedience of the people to their rule. The Church, and especially its monasteries, became wealthy and ready to acknowledge the authority of the Tatars as the overlords of the Russian bishops as well as of the princes.

The growth of Muscovy

During the fourteenth century, the power of the Tatars in Russia began to decline, and the small principality of Moscow gained in strength through its advantageous geographical position in the centre of north-eastern Russia, which encouraged commercial development and protected it from Tatar raids. At the same time, its princes followed an ambitious, resourceful and consistent policy and gradually extended

[1] P. 80.

its scattered possessions, achieving supremacy over neighbouring principalities. They were able to make use of two developments which assisted their policy. In 1326, the Metropolitan of the Russian Church, who had previously moved from Kiev to Vladimir, now established himself at Moscow, so making it the religious centre of the country. Two years later, Ivan I (called the Money-Bag), Prince of Moscow, secured the right to collect for the Golden Horde the tribute payable to them over a large part of Russia, and this proved a powerful way of asserting Muscovite influence and supremacy. In 1380 Dmitry Donskoy, Prince of Moscow, at the head of a coalition of Russian princes, defeated the Tatars at the Battle of Kulikovo on the Don, and though they retaliated by sacking Moscow, the principality had taken an important step towards establishing itself as the leader against the foreign conqueror.

The rise of the Muscovy Kingdom, determined to assert itself as the ruler of all Russia, began with the accession as Prince of Moscow of Ivan III, commonly known as Ivan the Great, in 1462. His contribution towards this development was made through five main achievements: his extension by war and diplomacy of Muscovite control of large new areas of Russian lands; his strengthening of his territories against the Tatars; his marriage into the family of the last of the Byzantine emperors; his establishment of contacts with the west and encouragement of European influence; and his consolidation of the power of the Muscovite monarchy. In extending the lands ruled by Moscow, Ivan's greatest success was the annexation of the city of Novgorod and its dependent territory between 1478 and 1489. Novgorod had been able to remain comparatively unmolested throughout the Mongol conquest and had become prosperous through trade with Scandinavia and the German towns of the Hanse. To ensure that it should no longer be a rival to Moscow, Ivan sacked it, transported many of its leading citizens and expelled the representatives of the Hanse. From 1490 he was engaged in warfare against Lithuania with the object of recovering the Russian territory she had seized. He succeeded in making important gains from her and in extending his frontier westwards, though he was not able to capture the important cities of Smolensk and Kiev. In all, he more than trebled the size of Muscovy during his reign so that by his death in 1505 it stretched from the Ural mountains to Lithuania and from the Arctic to the River Don.

In his determination to strengthen his territory against the Mongols, Ivan achieved notable successes. The Tatars of Kazan, who had broken away from the Golden Horde in 1438, raided Moscow incessantly, but in 1469 he mounted a campaign against them and reduced them to passivity. He was able also to come to an agreement with the

Tatars of the Crimea, who had similarly gained their independence, and he secured a temporary immunity from attacks by them. And in 1480 he ceased to pay tribute to the Golden Horde, so becoming a sovereign, independent ruler.

In 1469 Pope Paul III, in the vain hope of promoting the union of the eastern and western Churches and securing Russian help against the Ottoman Turks, suggested to Ivan that he should marry his ward, Sophia Palaeologa, the niece of the last Byzantine Emperor, Constantine XI, who had been killed on the walls of Constantinople by the attacking Turks in 1453. Ivan accepted this offer, which clearly enhanced his prestige and claims. He now added the Byzantine double-headed eagle to his insignia and adopted much of the elaborate Byzantine ceremonial in his court. He regarded himself also as the only true ruler over all Christians, and he supported the claim, now being made by the Russian Church, that Moscow was the holy city, 'the third Rome', the successor to Rome conquered by the barbarians and Constantinople taken by the Turks. This idea became as important in the political ideology of the Muscovite state as another idea also being adopted at this time, that of 'gathering the Russian land' from the invader and the conqueror.

In 1486 Maximilian, the Holy Roman Emperor, offered to confer upon Ivan the title of king, but he declined it since he already considered himself the equal of any ruler. 'We have been sovereign in our land,' he told the Emperor, 'from our earliest forefathers, and our sovereignty we hold from God.' From 1480 he had, indeed, used the title of 'tsar', a Slav contraction of the Latin 'Caesar', which signified a ruler who owed no allegiance and paid no tribute to any foreign authority. At first he did this cautiously, only in relation to the Hanseatic cities and other weaker neighbours, but before the end of his reign he was signing all state documents 'Ivan, by the Grace of God, Tsar of All Russia' (which expressed the Byzantine conception of the sovereign as divinely sanctified in his office), though his grandson was to be the first to adopt this title officially.

Since Sophia Palaeologa was half-Italian by birth and education, it was natural that she should wish to bring some of the influence of the Renaissance to bear upon the primitive city of Moscow, and Ivan encouraged her since this would give it a dignity and splendour worthy of the capital of his new realm. She brought to Moscow a number of Italian architects and builders, who constructed much of its citadel, the Kremlin, with its strange mixture of architectural styles. Among the edifices they erected within its walls were the Uspensky Cathedral (the Cathedral of the Assumption) in which the tsars were to be crowned, the Granovitaya Palace and a new court of stone in place of the old timbered buildings. Indeed, intercourse between Russia and the west was established in a number of ways during Ivan's reign. Scholars, who came to Russia after the fall of Constantinople, brought Latin culture which became better known than ever before. He himself inaugurated a new period in Russian relations with Europe by deliberately multiplying contacts with it. He employed several military and other western experts, and thereafter the need for artificers, gun-founders and specialists of all sorts was increasingly appreciated in Muscovy.

The rise of Moscow and the union of Russian territory under its control received general support from the people, who longed for peace and security and were ready to support the rule of a strong prince who would secure this for them. His military victories, therefore, placed Ivan in a good position to strengthen his authority in the Muscovite state, but he was opposed by the hereditary nobility, the boyars. Traditionally they occupied an important position in the government of the Principality through the Duma of Boyars, the chief executive council which claimed to share authority with the Prince. The greatest of them, the princely boyars, had themselves once been independent rulers and were now subjects of the Muscovite Tsar, but all retained extensive privileges. They were not compelled to render military or other service in return for their hereditary estates, and they enjoyed the 'right to depart', which allowed them freely to transfer their allegiance from one prince to another.

Both the drive towards despotism and the need of the expanded state for officers and administrators led Ivan to seek to reduce the powers and privileges of the boyars, and establish the principle that the holding of land involved loyalty to the Tsar and the obligation of service to him. In response to this, the boyars during the later fifteenth century developed the *Mestnichestvo*, a complicated system of official ranking intended to safeguard their status. It established a fixed order of precedence among noble families, which was applied rigidly to official appointments to prevent a boyar performing a duty lower than any which had ever been performed by a member of his family. The system placed impossible restrictions upon the Tsar who found himself unable to use the most able or experienced men in important posts in his service. At the same time, it brought about rivalries and jealousies among the noble families which, in fact, prevented any effective common action to preserve their powers and privileges.

In this situation, Ivan began an important new development designed to diminish the strength of the boyars and to consolidate the position of the Muscovite monarchy. He initiated the creation of a new class of landowner, the service nobility, whose name indicated their status and duties. In return for military or other service, this nobility was granted the life tenure of estates created out of royal, confiscated or newly-conquered lands. Thus, over sixteen hundred service nobility were granted estates in the lands left by the eight thousand families who were moved from Novgorod to Moscow, and frontier lands were generally distributed among this new nobility. Some of these estates were large, able to maintain a family of officers and a hundred or more peasant troops, while others could only support one or two fighting-men; but all were held at Ivan's pleasure and could be recalled whenever he wished. Moreover, the members of this nobility were appointed in growing numbers to the Duma of Boyars together with clerks, who were mostly the sons of priests, until they had a majority over the boyars; and the Duma was reduced to the position of a consultative and advisory body under the Tsar. Such developments left the boyars an angry, resentful class, ready for an opportunity to reassert themselves.

Another consequence of these developments was to encourage the growth of serfdom in Russia. During the years of the Mongol conquest, the need of the peasants for protection and their indebtedness caused by the burden of the Tatar tribute led them to turn to the landowners for assistance. The terms on which they received it commonly included their being bound to perform obligations in the shape of working on the land of their patron or granting part of their produce to him, and thus they were prevented from moving elsewhere. When estates were allocated to the service nobility, the labour of the peasants was often essential if the conditions under which these estates were held were to be fulfilled, and so these peasants, too, were prevented from moving elsewhere. In this way, and at a time when it was beginning to decline in many European countries, serfdom was accorded an increasingly important part in the Russian social and political system.

Towards the end of Ivan's reign the ill-feeling between the service nobility and the boyars produced a dispute over the succession to the throne which threatened to imperil the unity of the Muscovite state. When his son, Ivan, died in 1490, the boyars favoured his grandson, Dmitry, as the heir to the throne, but the service nobility preferred his second son, Basil, and in 1497 they plotted to kidnap Dmitry. At this threat to his authority, Ivan beheaded their leaders and recognized Dmitry as his successor, only to change his mind in 1502 and transfer his choice to Basil.

When he came to the throne in 1505, Basil III proved himself to be a strong and able ruler, who continued his father's policy of extending the Muscovite kingdom and building up his power at home. In some ways, events were not as favourable for him as they had been for his father. In particular, the Tatars of the Crimea resumed their hostilities, and several times their raids reached as far as the walls of Moscow. He was able, however, to renew the war against Muscovy's most serious opponent, Lithuania, and to annex Smolensk in 1514. In the administration of his kingdom, he was naturally not inclined to show much favour towards the boyars, who had tried to exclude him from the throne. He carried their exclusion from active participation in state affairs further by resorting to the appointment of secretaries with functions similar to those who were being appointed by the monarchies of western Europe. He continued also to grant estates to the service nobility on terms which continued the enserfment of the peasants in many parts of Russia so that numbers of them took to running away to join the Cossacks, the lawless frontiersmen who lived as adventurers and plunderers in southern and south-eastern Russia, especially along the Don and in the Lithuanian-controlled Ukraine.

Ivan the Terrible

On Basil's death in 1533 his son, Ivan IV, who has become known to history as Ivan the Terrible, succeeded to the Throne. He was then only three years old, and his mother, Helena, became Regent. She was an ambitious and forceful woman and did not lack courage. For a time, advised by her lover, Prince Obelensky, she was able to maintain order and succeeded in crushing a rebellion against her authority, but when Ivan was only seven she died suddenly, possibly poisoned by a group of boyars plotting to seize power. No one was formally appointed Regent in her place. Ivan now reigned in name, but the great boyars were determined to exploit the situation to their advantage.

For over a decade, during Ivan's minority, rival factions of boyars struggled for power and tried to reverse the developments of the previous two reigns which had more and more relegated them to a position of inferiority in the state. Obelensky was arrested and murdered. The Shuisky family dominated the Duma and gradually overcame their opponents. They ransacked the Muscovite treasury and took over royal estates for distribution among their supporters. Throughout Russia the district garrisons did as they liked and plundered towns and villages. It was one of the periods known as the Time of the Troubles in Russian history.

During these years, the treatment the young Tsar received from the Shuisky family undoubtedly affected his character for the rest of his life. His nurse and the few boyars he trusted and liked were taken from him. No one was responsible for his care, and he lived in the palace in the Kremlin as best he could, often cold and hungry. 'What suffering did I endure,' he was to write twenty-five years later, 'through lack of clothing and through hunger.' On state occasions, he made ceremonial appearances, seated on the throne in bejewelled robes, while the boyars bowed deeply before him, but he lived in constant fear that he might be seized and murdered. His only solace was reading.

He was able to get hold of some history books and read with special attention the lives of caesars, khans and despots.

Ivan never forgot the indignities and sufferings he underwent during those years. He became only too familiar with scenes of violence and brutality; rival groups of boyars even fought and killed each other in the halls of his palace. Moreover, the Shuiskys encouraged him to take up cruel pleasures. With his companions he threw dogs, cats and other small animals to their death from the high walls and towers of the Kremlin. Another favourite pastime was to gallop on horseback through the streets of Moscow knocking people down and slashing at them with their whips. He was encouraged also to indulge, as he grew older, in drinking and debauchery. As a result of such experiences, he grew up with a hatred of those who had ill-treated him and an appetite for power combined with a deep-seated sense of insecurity which made him always suspicious and mistrustful of those around him. He had also revealed in his character a love of cruelty and torture which was to possess him overwhelmingly in his later years. Yet he possessed at the same time an intelligence and determination which were to enable him to make the tsardom a lasting, highly-centralized absolutism in the country.

When he was thirteen, Ivan suddenly turned upon his chief tor-mentor, Andrei Shuisky. He had him murdered by the palace servants and his body thrown to a pack of hounds. This, however, was not the end of the rule of the boyars. A rival family, the Glinskys, seized power, and the anarchy continued for another three-and-a-half years. Thirty of the Shuisky supporters were immediately hanged on roadside gibbets. In January 1547 Ivan had himself crowned with Byzantine ceremony, not simply as Prince of Moscow, but as Tsar of All Russia. Through this action he proclaimed that Muscovy was the heir to Byzantium as the defender of Orthodox Christianity and that his power was derived from God alone. Having been crowned, Ivan decided upon marriage. Following the old Muscovite custom, boyar families were ordered to produce their daughters for inspection by royal officials, and about a thousand were selected to go to Moscow from whom the Tsar would make a final choice. He chose Anastasia, the daughter of the old but comparatively obscure family of Romanov. She became the only person able to have any control over him.

So far the government of the country had remained in the hands of the Glinskys, who were able to continue to do as they chose as long as they deferred to Ivan's whims, and he was now obsessed by his newly-gained power. Soon after his coronation, seventy citizens of Pskov petitioned him against the wrongs inflicted upon their city by the district governor appointed by the Glinskys. He regarded this as sedition. He poured hot wine over their heads, singed their hair and beards with a candle and ordered them to lie naked on the floor. They were probably saved from immediate execution by the news that a fire had broken out in Moscow. A large part of the city was destroyed before it was extinguished. A group of discontented boyars accused Prince Yury Glinsky, Ivan's uncle, of having caused the fire through witchcraft and incited the mob to seize and murder him. With this the rule of the Glinskys came to an end, and Ivan at the age of seventeen was able to assume control of the state at last.

The period of reform

The action of the Moscow mob deeply shocked Ivan because it was apparent that the popular antagonism was partly directed against him personally. He disliked having to share the unpopularity of the Glinskys, and he typically turned away from his cruelty and vindictiveness to adopt a policy of moderation and reform. He gathered round him a group of advisers known as the Chosen Council, who mostly came from the service nobility and not the boyars. He relied particularly upon the Metropolitan of Moscow, the Archpriest Sylvester, who was the court chaplain, and the Chamberlain, Alexei Adashev, a man of high ability and humble origin.

During the later 1540s and throughout the 1550s the Chosen Council carried out a number of reforms with the object of strengthening and centralizing the power of the government under the Tsar over the extended territory of the Muscovite state and of increasing the powers of the service nobility at the expense of the boyars. In 1549 the service nobility were freed from the jurisdiction of the district governors and empowered to judge the peasants on their domains. A year later the practice which allowed the governors to 'feed' off the people, extorting as much money as they could, was abolished, and they had to share the control of the district assizes with the service nobility. In 1555 all taxes were to be paid directly to the royal treasury, instead of first to the governors, and districts were empowered to elect councils to take over the work of the governors.

In 1550 Ivan summoned the first *Zemsky Sobor* or assembly of the land, which consisted of members of the Duma of Boyars together with important administrators and representatives of the Moscow merchants. This was an appointed, not an elected body, and its purpose was to approve the decisions of the Tsar, but it was allowed to present grievances, and Ivan listened to them. The most important reform he produced in conjunction with it was the new legal code of 1550, which included measures to appoint better judges and combat corruption, and the establishment of a permanent bureau to receive petitions. Another code laid down moral and educational requirements for the clergy, and this was accepted by an assembly of the Russian Church.

During these years Ivan also sought further contacts with the west. He employed a German administrator named Schlitt to recruit a considerable number of foreign technicians for Russia, and among the foreign inventions introduced during his reign was the first printing-press, which was set up in Moscow by Ivan Federov in 1553 and produced books in Greek, Italian and German. In 1565, however, Federov and his partner, Peter Mstislavtsev, were driven out of Russia into Lithuania by religious purists who objected to their printed version of the Gospels, but Ivan was able to invite them back to Russia in 1574, and they produced the first complete printed version of the Slavonic Bible in the town of Ostrog. Ivan also was able to extend trade with western Europe. In 1553 an English ship sailed by Richard Chancellor reached the White Sea. Ivan declared that other ships would be welcomed to Russia, and when the Muscovy Company was formed in London two years later, he granted it a charter conferring privileges on English merchants in Russia. The first exchange of ambassadors between London and Moscow followed soon afterwards, and English mining and medical specialists were engaged for service in Russia.

Finally, Ivan took the first steps towards the establishment of a standing army by bringing into being in 1550 the Streltzi ('the ones who shoot'), a permanent body of regular infantry armed with muskets bought from the west. They were mostly recruited from the more prosperous townspeople and lived apart in their own quarters in Moscow. They were exempt from taxation, even on the trades or handicrafts in which they were allowed to engage between their tours of duty or campaigns. At first they numbered three thousand, but as they acquitted themselves well in Ivan's wars, more were recruited, and by the end of the sixteenth century there were some twenty thousand of them garrisoning towns all over the country. At the same time, large numbers of the sons of the service nobility were granted estates near to Moscow on condition that they took on their father's service under the state, for which they received regular payments in money as well as land.

The coming of war

These military reforms were intended to prepare for the renewal of war to liberate further Russian territory. Ivan's immediate aim was the capture of Kazan, the great Tatar fortress situated near the junction of the Rivers Kama and Volga. With an army of 100 000 men, German engineers and the first cannon to be used in Russia, he reduced Kazan in 1552. Four years later, Astrakhan, at the mouth of the Volga, was taken. Russia now possessed the whole of the River Volga, along which were built in the following years the cities of Samara, Saratov and Tsaritsyn (later to be well known as Stalingrad). Control had been secured of the great trade routes to the Caspian Sea and central Asia, and expansion eastwards towards the vast spaces of Siberia was at hand. The Tatars of the Crimea remained unconquered, however, and Adashev and Sylvester now urged him to attack them, but Ivan thought it wiser not to commit his troops against their well-fortified positions and he did not want to risk becoming involved in a war against the Turks since these Tatars had an alliance with Suleiman the Magnificent.

Moreover, he had decided to turn his attention to the north-west. Eastern expansion inevitably intensified the problem of Russia's relations with the west, increasing both her need of help and her sense of danger from Europe. The Baltic powers tried to block Russian contacts with the west and repeatedly stopped the passage of experts whom Ivan engaged in Europe. In 1547, for instance, 124 foreign technicians, intended for service in Russia, were detained in Lübeck, and when Ivan asked Elizabeth I of England for assistance in procuring experts from her kingdom, King Sigismund Augustus of Poland urged her to refuse, saying, 'Up to now we could conquer him because he was a stranger to education and did not know the arts'. Moreover, Russia needed access to the Baltic, since the port of Archangel on the White Sea, only ice-free from June to October, was inadequate for any large-scale trade with the west.

The Russian way to the Baltic was checked by the Teutonic Knights, a German feudal order possessing Livonia, the coastal region between Sweden and Poland. In 1558 Ivan invaded Livonia and at first met with considerable success, occupying much of eastern Estonia and capturing the port of Narva on the Gulf of Finland, which brought the desired access to the Baltic.[2] In 1560 his troops went on to invade central Livonia, but by then the other Baltic powers had become alarmed by the Russian conquests. In 1561 Poland compelled the Teutonic Knights to cede Livonia to her, while the next year Sweden took possession of the port of Reval, in response to an appeal by its citizens for protection, and claimed possession of the whole of Estonia. By then Ivan was at war with Poland, and his campaign in the Baltic had run into serious difficulties.

The reign of terror

During this military failure in Livonia, Ivan was reverting to his former suspicions and brutality. In 1553 he had been seriously ill and

[2] P. 310.

had ordered the Chosen Council to accept his infant son as heir-apparent, but Adashev and Sylvester, fearful of a renewal of anarchy during a royal minority, had advised him to nominate his cousin, Prince Vladimir. He never forgave them for this, and their opposition to his Livonian campaign increased his resentment. In 1560 he dismissed them both and brought the Chosen Council to an end. Soon afterwards Anastasia died. All restraints on his conduct were thus removed, and he was subject to a loneliness which increased his fears. His former advisers and even their families and servants were murdered or exiled. He acted with particular ruthlessness towards the boyars, whom he had always hated, murdering two princely boyars on the same day as they attended church. In 1564 the Russian army was defeated by the Poles in Livonia, and its commander, Prince Kurbsky, defected to Lithuania. This had a devastating effect upon Ivan. He believed that the boyars hated him and were plotting his downfall. That winter he left Moscow for the small town of Aleksandrov, about 96 kilometres away, and announced his intention to abdicate, but he sent two letters to be published in the capital. In one he assured the people of Moscow of his affection for them, and in the other he denounced the boyars and the clergy for opposing his authority. The citizens and merchants, alarmed at the prospect of anarchy through the absence of the Tsar, invited him to come back on his own terms.

He had left Moscow a powerfully-built, alert, handsome man with a full head of hair, but now he returned bald, stooped and unkempt, prematurely aged by some sort of mental breakdown. He announced that for the safety of the state and himself he would set up a private establishment with a special guard for himself. This was called the *Oprichnina*, from the Russian word meaning 'apart'. It was, in effect, an autonomous principality for himself within the Muscovite kingdom, such as had existed in the days of the Mongol conquest. Towns and districts all over Russia, comprising eventually almost half the country, were included within it; some parts of Moscow were in it, and some were not. The rest of the country was to be governed by the Duma of Boyars, but in the *Oprichnina* the Tsar ruled as its proprietor. Ivan's purpose seems to have been to provide himself with the security he desperately needed by establishing a domain under his direct and personal control. At first a thousand and later up to six thousand of his loyal followers, the oprichniks, were given estates taken from the boyars and other landowners and were often given powers to exact servile labour from their tenants.[3] Some of the boyars were given compensation in frontier areas to the south, but more frequently they had to search for free lands themselves with their families in the bitterly cold winter of 1565-6. It has been generally accepted that his

[3] P. 80.

purpose in doing this was to destroy the power of the boyars, but recent research has shown that his confiscation of estates was so capricious as to make it doubtful whether he had such a clear plan.

The role of the oprichniks, who wore a black uniform and rode black horses with an emblematic broom at their saddlebows, was to strike at any whom Ivan feared or suspected. Boyars and their servants were tortured and executed. Merchants and townspeople were plundered. All processes of law were ignored. When the Metropolitan Philip rebuked the Tsar for his cruelties, he was taken from the Uspensky Cathedral to a monastery where he was strangled in 1569. Fearing treachery from Novgorod, Ivan had batches of the population, men and women, young and old, systematically butchered every day for five weeks in 1570; sixty thousand citizens were said to have died, and the river was choked with their bodies. In 1571 the Tatars of the Crimea took advantage of the confusion to attack Moscow and burnt down the whole city except the Kremlin. The oprichniks had failed to defend the city, but two years later the boyars and local service nobility checked another raid only 80 kilometres south of the city.

This and the deteriorating military situation in Livonia added to the mistrust Ivan had come to feel about the oprichniks, some of whom had been discovered to be plotting against him. Typically, he abolished the *Oprichnina*. Most of the oprichniks were deprived of their estates and had to accept other lands on service tenure. Many of the old landowners were allowed to return to their estates, and the service nobility who had defeated the Tatars received further grants of land. The process was a disorderly one, which lasted for a long period, impoverishing the land and weakening the military forces of the country.

The years of the *Oprichnina* had lasting social and economic consequences. Not only had the oprichniks often been given increased powers to exact compulsory labour from their tenants, but also the dispossessed boyars who had to take up land in the border areas, and the oprichniks who then sometimes succeeded them, secured labour by imposing servile exactions upon the peasants.[4] To escape this situation, many joined the bands of peasants who were already migrating to colonize the lands eastwards towards the Lower Volga or southwards among the Cossacks. This led to a depopulation in central Russia, around Moscow, which seriously weakened the state economically and militarily. Ivan, therefore, had to support landowners in imposing serfdom as a means of obtaining labour on their estates. Most peasants, not bound to landowners by economic dependence, still had the legal right to move to another estate after the autumn harvest, during the week before and after St George's Day (26th November). He forbade them to do this in 1581 and repeated the

[4] P. 80.

prohibition in later years. Such action inevitably made the nobility interested supporters of the tsarist despotism. At the same time, Muscovy gained important new territory when some eight hundred Cossacks in 1582 crossed the Urals, defeated the Tatar forces, largely because they possessed firearms, and so began the colonization of Siberia.

The later years

Meanwhile, the campaign in Livonia had become a long war of attrition. In 1563 the Russian army captured Polotsk and penetrated into Lithuanian territory as far as the capital, Vilna, but the years of terror crippled further military effort. For a time, Poland was not ready to undertake a full-scale war, but the situation was transformed by the union of Poland and Lithuania in 1569 and still more by the election of Stephen Bathory as King of Poland in 1575.[5] Russia was now unable to withstand the combined onslaught of Poland and Sweden, particularly while the threat from the Tatars of the Crimea remained. Bathory recaptured Polotsk in 1579 and carried the war deep into Muscovite territory. Only the stubborn resistance of Pskov saved the whole of the ancient Russian lands of the north-west from conquest. In the north, Sweden had occupied almost all the southern coast of the Gulf of Finland by 1581. Ivan could do nothing but accept papal mediation in 1582, which resulted in the humiliating Treaty of Yam Zapolsky. He had to renounce all the Lithuanian territories he had gained and all claims to Livonia. The next year he finally ceded the whole of Estonia to Sweden. Ivan's venture in the north-west had failed, and Russia was left with even less of the Baltic coast than she had possessed before the war.

The bitterness of defeat plunged Ivan into alternating periods of depression and outbreaks of rage. During one of these outbreaks in 1582 he killed his eldest and favourite son, Ivan, by striking him with the iron-tipped staff which he always carried. He himself died in 1584. There had always been two sides to his character and deeds. During the earlier years of his reign, an English traveller in Russia had written, 'No prince in Christendom is more feared of his own than he is, nor better loved.' Amid his tyranny, misrule and cruelty, Russians feared the threat of domestic anarchy and foreign invasion which seemed to be the alternative to his rule, and they supported his desire to continue the policy of his predecessors in strengthening the position and prestige of the tsardom and 'gathering the Russian land'. And so the achievements and consequences of his reign must be regarded as mixed. Poland and Sweden thwarted his attempt to expand in the north, but the Tatars were weakened, and the important drive towards the south and the east was begun. The capture of Kazan compensated

[5] P. 324.

for the loss of Narva. Trade with Europe through Baltic ports was not achieved, but the discovery of the White Sea route by the English and his encouragement of the Muscovy Company began a growing commerce at first with England and later with the Netherlands as well.[6] The establishment of the *Oprichnina*, together with the cost of the long war in Livonia, disrupted the state, exhausted the treasury, depopulated the countryside and prepared the way for the wholesale imposition of serfdom upon the peasantry in the next century. But Ivan centralized the government under the tsardom, secured its place in the political and religious life of the nation and weakened the factious boyars by the encouragement of a new nobility, bound to serve the tsars and united to them in strong self-interest. Without Ivan the Terrible, collapse through foreign invasion, internal dissension among the feudal nobles or attacks by the Tatar hordes might have been the fate of Russia.

The sixteenth century closed in Russia with the end of the old Muscovite dynasty and a Time of Troubles even longer and more catastrophic than the period of Ivan the Terrible's minority. The death of his oldest son meant that Ivan was succeeded by a younger son, Theodore, who was weak in mind and body. He was, Ivan himself had said, better suited to be a bell-ringer in a convent than to reign as Tsar of Russia. The effect upon a political system which depended so much upon the capability of the ruler was inevitable. The remnant of the boyars began to plot to seize control of the throne, but they were at first too weak and disunited to succeed. Power passed to one of the recently-elevated service nobility, Boris Godunov, who was of Tatar origin, and whose sister was married to Theodore. While he was Regent, order was maintained in the state, and he was able to continue many of Ivan the Terrible's policies. The service nobility were supported against the boyars; the prohibition of peasant migration was upheld; the Metropolitan of Moscow was made a Patriarch, entirely independent of Constantinople, in 1589; English merchants were given further privileges to encourage them to increase their commerce through the White Sea; fortified towns were established in the south as a protection against Tatar raids; and the war against Sweden was resumed with the result that in 1595 Russia regained the Finnish territories lost by Ivan. In 1591 Theodore's younger brother, Dmitry, died in suspicious circumstances, and when Theodore died without an heir in 1598, Boris Godunov was elected Tsar by the *Zemsky Sobor*. The ambitions of the boyars, disputed claims to the throne and foreign intervention then combined to initiate a Time of Troubles which was to last beyond the first decade of the seventeenth century and yet, in the end, serve to proclaim the durability of the tsardom established by Ivan the Great and Ivan the Terrible.

[6] P. 78.

THE
BALTIC
LANDS

The Baltic

Despite the efforts of Ivan the Terrible, Russia did not succeed in making herself a Baltic power until the later seventeenth century. In the sixteenth the sea was dominated by those countries on its western side—Scandinavia and Poland—and between them and Russia were marked differences in culture, religion, language and custom. During this century, however, these western countries were divided religiously when all Scandinavia became Lutheran, and Poland was eventually regained by the Counter-Reformation; in addition the political disputes among them were inspired by such serious rival ambitions and interests that they were pushed to the point of war.

The conflict, largely caused by the rivalry between Denmark and Sweden, was precipitated by Ivan the Terrible's attack on the Teutonic Knights and capture of Narva in 1558.[1] The Teutonic Knights were founded in the early thirteenth century as a German military order, one among several originating with the Crusades, and at the beginning of the sixteenth century they possessed Prussia, Livonia and Estonia. In 1525 the Grand Master, Albert of Brandenburg, created a sensation by becoming a Lutheran and secularizing the Prussian possessions of the Order.[2] As a condition of accepting this change, Sigismund I of Poland took over West Prussia; and East Prussia was made into a duchy with Albert as its hereditary ruler doing homage for it to the Polish monarchy. The Teutonic Knights then only possessed Livonia and Estonia and were unable to offer an effective resistance to Ivan's intervention. Since Narva was the main port through which goods from western Europe were exported into eastern Europe, its occupation by Russia had far-reaching consequences in the Baltic. Not only did Poland occupy Livonia, but Sweden's claim to the whole of Estonia resulted in the Northern Seven Years War.[3]

When the war ended in 1570, the peace conference included representatives of England and Scotland and even of Spain. This was an

[1] P. 305.   [2] P. 163.   [3] P. 315.

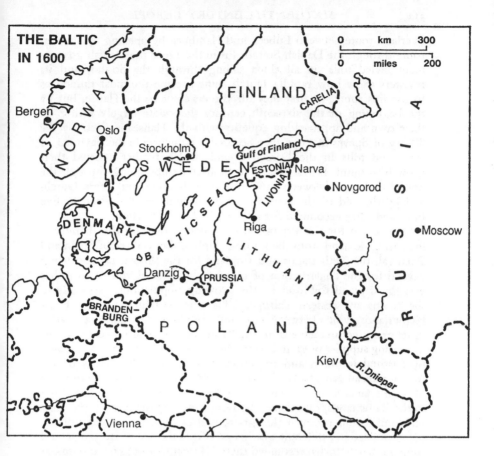

THE BALTIC IN 1600

indication of the increasing importance of the Baltic and particularly of the Baltic trade. In the fourteenth century, the Hanse, the association of north German trading towns, had gained virtual domination of this trade. Of the Hanse's member towns, the most important was Lübeck, which was separated by a narrow neck of land from Hamburg on the North Sea and so could dominate the trade between the Baltic and the Netherlands. Lübeck retained much of its importance in the Baltic until its naval defeat by the Danish fleet in 1535.[4] This brought to an end its attempts to use the internal troubles of the Scandinavian countries in order to regain its political power.

By then the Hanse was losing its commercial pre-eminence in the Baltic. Sailors from Holland and Zeeland had entered the North Sea, at first to fish herring, for which there was a good demand in Europe on fast days and in the winter when meat was short, and then to move into the carrying trade. They quickly reduced the importance of the

[4] P. 318.

overland route between Lübeck and Hamburg by opening up the sea-route through the Danish Sound. From the 1490s the Danish government levied tolls on all ships sailing through the Sound, and its registers show how rapidly Dutch ships became the most numerous to use this route. At first they hired their ships to the Hanse, but by the beginning of the sixteenth century they were largely acting on their own and approaching equality with the Hanseatic fleet. By the Treaty of Speyer in 1544, they secured a reduction in the payment of taxes and tolls in the Danish Sound, which further assisted their growth in numbers. Of the three thousand ships going through the Sound each year between 1560 and 1569 three-quarters were Dutch, and by the end of the century, when the number had risen to five thousand, they accounted for an even higher proportion.

One reason for this expansion of Dutch trade with the Baltic was increasing demand from the leading shipbuilding centres of Spain and Portugal, the Netherlands and England for the timber, tar and hemp needed for the construction of merchant and naval vessels. Another was the demand for food by the growing populations, especially in the towns of western Europe. This was particularly true of the Netherlands, which between 1562 and 1569 imported almost a quarter of its grain requirements from the Baltic, but Spain also had to import increasing supplies of grain because her own agriculture was dominated by pastoral farming, and the cities of Italy and other parts of the Mediterranean came to need such imports as well, particularly in times of famine, such as occurred in 1575 and again in 1590-1. Peasant farming in the Baltic lands, especially when organized on the lines of the 'new serfdom', could produce this grain, and east Germany and Poland, being situated in a different weather area from the rest of Europe, could supply it when the harvest failed there. The cargoes of grain and timber were taken through the Danish Sound at first to Antwerp and, from the middle of the century, increasingly to Amsterdam from where they could be re-exported to southern Europe. The Dutch developed this trade even while fighting for their independence against Spain, despite the opposition of their Calvinist preachers;[5] during this time also they were entering the Mediterranean and taking away the trade of the Venetian galleys which had hitherto monopolized this route.[6]

The growing economic and political importance of the Baltic had inevitably a profound effect upon the Scandinavian countries, which could hope to be in a position to dominate it and benefit from tolls upon its trade. The kingdoms of Denmark, Sweden and Norway had been united since coming under the common regency of Margaret of Denmark through the threefold Union of Kalmar of 1397.[7] By the beginning of the sixteenth century, however, the Swedish nobility had become opposed to the rule of her successors because they feared

[5] P. 264.   [6] P. 269.   [7] P. 24.

that their rights were endangered by a tendency towards monarchical absolutism, and the union came to an end during the reign of Christian II (1513-23). The King's execution of those opposed to the union in the 'Stockholm bloodbath' of 1520 provoked a revolt the next year led by Gustavus Vasa, a Swedish nobleman who, with the help of Lübeck and a rebellion by the Danish clergy and nobility, re-established the country's independence and was elected King as Gustavus I in 1523 by the Riksdag (Diet). The disunity and subsequent struggle for power in the Baltic by Denmark and Sweden dominated the political situation in the Baltic from the Northern Seven Years War onwards and ended with the brief period during the next century when Sweden became a great European power and the Baltic was a Swedish lake.

Sweden

The Swedish monarchy, to which Gustavus I was elected in 1523, lacked both political power and financial resources. The elective nature of the monarchy had enabled the nobility in the past history of the country to increase their privileges each time they chose a new king, and their control of the council gave them an important share in the government of the country. In addition, they owned about a fifth of the land and were exempt from taxation. The Swedish Church possessed another fifth, and just over a half belonged to the peasantry, who were represented as an estate in the Riksdag. The amount of land owned by the Crown was rather more than a fifth, and its income was insufficient to meet the needs of administration and justice.

If the Crown were to strengthen its authority, it would have to be at the expense of its aristocratic and ecclesiastical rivals, and the Swedish episcopate was largely filled by the chief noble families. Gustavus supported the Reformation, therefore, for political and financial reasons, but except for Stockholm, where German influence was strong, Protestantism was slow in making progress among the people. The crisis came in 1527 when he demanded at the Riksdag of Westerås the alienation of ecclesiastical property to the Crown. The bishops appealed to the Papacy for support against him, but he compelled them to give way by threatening to abdicate, and by the Ordinances of Westerås all land belonging to the bishops, cathedrals and monasteries was placed at his disposal for confiscation or religious use. The Riksdag of Westerås decreed also 'that God's Word may be purely preached everywhere in the realm,' that all priests should be subject to civil jurisdiction and that all appointments to ecclesiastical posts should be made only with royal approval, though the method adopted gave the bishops some independence.[8] During the later years of the reign of Gustavus, Lutheran influence was extended in the

[8] P. 110.

Swedish Church, largely under the influence of Olavus Petri, a priest who had studied at Wittenberg and was Archbishop of Uppsala from 1531 to 1573. The Swedish Mass Book, Lutheran in doctrine and structure, was adopted in 1531, the Swedish Bible was published ten years later, and papal authority over the Church was formally renounced in 1544. The culmination of the process, however, did not come until after the death of Gustavus, when in 1572 a synod at Uppsala adopted the Confession of Augsburg in its unaltered form of 1530. Nevertheless, the Swedish Church never formally declared its adherence to Lutheranism. It retained its bishops and much of the old ceremonial in its services. It continued to regard itself as the national church of the kingdom and was accepted as such by the Swedish people from whom came no martyrs for the retention of papal authority.

Having secured his power by establishing royal control over the Church and gaining much of its wealth, Gustavus I now set out to stabilize the position of the Crown. His threat to abdicate in 1527 had made it clear to the nobility that his kingship probably was the only alternative to anarchy in the country and the resumption of Danish rule, and he had gained the support of many by distributing some of the confiscated ecclesiastical property among them. This and the support he received from the other estates of the Riksdag made it possible for him to obtain the acceptance of the Succession Pact, which replaced the elective monarchy by one that was hereditary in the house of Vasa, so depriving the nobility of their opportunity to exploit each vacancy of the throne to their own advantage.

Though, except for a short war against Russia, Gustavus kept Sweden at peace, he did much to build up the strength of his newly-independent kingdom. He subsidized manufacturers of arms and munitions and gave grants for the establishment of new iron furnaces and forges and arranged for the engagement of German artisans to work in them. He increased the size of the navy and in 1544 founded a compulsory military reserve among the peasants, who were formed into trained regiments that could be called up in time of war, so providing Sweden with a unique type of native army, although she continued to have to rely upon mercenaries, mainly as specialists.

On his death in 1560, Gustavus was succeeded by his eldest son, Eric XIV. Gustavus had been content to retain good diplomatic relations with Denmark, whose possession of both coasts of the Sound controlled Sweden's communications with western Europe and with Lübeck which still managed most of her foreign trade. Eric, however, believed that Sweden should assert herself in order to avoid being encircled and to gain a share of the trade of the Baltic. Russia's conquest of Narva and Reval's appeal to Sweden gave him the opportunity to intervene in Estonia.[9] Its possession would be an important step

[9] P. 305.

towards providing Sweden with an empire on the Baltic and securing control for her of Russian trade with the west.

His action, however, had unforeseen consequences. It worsened Swedish relations with Denmark and Poland, both of whom also had territorial ambitions there. Moreover, in an attempt to insist that Russian trade should henceforward pass through Reval under Swedish control, he blockaded Narva through which the Hanse could now trade directly with Russia, and so he aroused the hostility of Lübeck. The situation was further complicated by the civil war Eric was waging with his half-brother, John, who had married Catherine Jagiello, sister of Sigismund II of Poland, and he had his own ambitions in Livonia. Eric defeated and imprisoned him in 1563, but the episode was a further cause of enmity with Poland and encouragement for Denmark to take action against him.

Such conflicting political and commercial ambitions produced the Northern Seven Years War from 1563 to 1570 in which Sweden fought Poland, Denmark and Lübeck, although the formal occasion for war was provided by Frederick II of Denmark, who had succeeded the pacific Christian III in 1559 and displayed the emblem of Sweden in his coat of arms as a sign that he still claimed to rule over the country;[10] Eric took up the implied threat to Swedish independence. It was a lengthy war in which Sweden had to endure a Danish blockade and was only able to survive because her new navy succeeded in keeping open the vital routes to northern Germany and so prevented her from being completely deprived of supplies. Years of hostilities produced a general stalemate with both sides approaching exhaustion, but the strain finally unhinged Eric's uncertain mind. He became subject to persecution mania; he began to mistrust the nobility, and in 1567 he had several of the most prominent executed. The nobles revolted, imprisoned and deposed him and replaced him by his half-brother who ruled as John III. The new king at once set about obtaining peace for Sweden. The Treaty of Stettin in 1570 nullified Eric's plans for Swedish expansion in the Baltic. She did retain Estonia, but the intention that she should control Russian trade had to be abandoned together with the hope of wresting control of the Sound from Denmark.

John's wife, Catherine Jagiello, was a Roman Catholic, and he was himself a learned theologian, who hoped to reconcile Lutheranism and Roman Catholicism. Moreover, Catherine's mother was Bona Sforza of Milan, who had left her a considerable fortune, but since this was in Sicily and detained by Philip II of Spain, papal influence would be needed to induce him to release it. In addition, either John or his son, Sigismund, might hope eventually to be elected to the Polish throne if Roman Catholic support could be secured. In 1576 he issued the 'Red Book', which was a liturgy he himself devised to combine the

[10] P. 319.

Lutheran and Roman Catholic forms of service, and ordered the Swedish Church to use it. He also persuaded Pope Gregory XIII to send envoys to Stockholm, but to no purpose since the Papacy would not listen to his suggestions that special concessions should be allowed in Sweden, such as the marriage of the clergy, services in the vernacular and communion in both kinds. His plans for religious reconciliation did not receive any support in Sweden either, and he was wise enough not to risk his possession of the throne by persisting in them.

Though John had brought the Northern Seven Years War to an end, he did not intend to relinquish Eric's policy towards the Baltic and Russian trade. He renewed the war against Russia, but met with no success until Stephen Bathory was elected King of Poland in 1575 and conquered Livonia. This made it possible for Sweden to take the offensive, and with the capture of Narva in 1581 she gained control of all the strategic positions in the Gulf of Finland. Two years later Ivan the Terrible had to recognize Swedish possession of the whole of Estonia. On the death of Bathory in 1586, John strengthened his alliance with Poland by securing the election of his son, Sigismund, to the Polish throne, which resulted in the union of the two countries when Sigismund succeeded his father as King of Sweden in 1592. This development had obvious advantages for Sweden's ambitions in the Baltic since union with Poland would give her the support of a country which also was a natural opponent of Russia.

The Swedish nobility, however, viewed it with misgiving. Eric XIV and John III had both already aroused their opposition by governing the country through secretaries, who were mostly not of noble birth, and now they feared the capture of the Swedish Church by the Counter-Reformation and the establishment in the kingdom of a Roman Catholic monarchical absolutism, since Sigismund had been brought up by his mother in the strictest Tridentine orthodoxy. Before he left for Poland in the autumn of 1587, Sigismund had been compelled to accept the Statutes of Kalmar, which provided that the union of the crowns should not affect Sweden's political or religious independence and that during his periods of absence in Poland the kingdom was to be governed by a council of regency consisting of seven noblemen. The succession of Sigismund to the Swedish throne in 1592, however, coincided with the election to the Papacy of Clement VIII, who resolved to make use of the occasion for the conversion of the country. When Sigismund visited Stockholm the next year, he was accompanied by a papal nuncio and Roman Catholic attendants. The Riksdag were determined to preserve the Swedish Church from papal control, and the nobility wished to impose further restrictions upon the power of the monarchy. The opposition found a leader in John's brother, Charles, and Sigismund, after vainly attempting to establish himself in power with the assistance of Polish troops, was compelled finally to return to Poland in 1598, leaving the country to be ruled by Charles and a council of noblemen. The next year Sigismund was deposed, and Charles governed the country although he was not crowned (as Charles IX) until 1604.

The deposition of Sigismund had important consequences, nationally and internationally, for Sweden. It marked the survival of the power of the Riksdag and the nobility and ensured that future Swedish monarchs would have to rule as constitutional kings. It ensured also that Sweden would remain a Lutheran country and that the advance of Roman Catholicism in the Baltic was checked. Poland had been won for the Counter-Reformation, but Scandinavia was henceforward to be secured firmly for Protestantism. Finally, Charles IX wished to continue to strive for Swedish supremacy in the Baltic and was involved in war with both Poland and Denmark. He secured a Swedish foothold on Livonia, but died in 1611, at the outbreak of hostilities with Denmark, leaving the accomplishment of the policy to the great Gustavus Adolphus.

Denmark

The Swedish revolt of 1521 against the Danish monarchy came at a time of religious and constitutional difficulties in Denmark. Christian II was a vigorous, ruthless ruler, who had shown his ambition by marrying the Emperor Maximilian's grand-daughter, Isabella, and he wished to strengthen and centralize the power of the monarchy. He attempted to do this by promoting the interests of the townspeople and the peasants, whom he released from serfdom, in order to gain their support against the nobility and the clergy. This led him also to support the cause of Lutheranism, which was establishing itself in the country by the early 1520s. The Swedish revolt, however, caused him to abandon an anti-clerical policy because he hoped for the support of his brother-in-law, Charles V, in suppressing it; but his position was undermined by a rebellion of the Danish nobility and clergy. He had to flee from the country, and in the spring of 1523 the nobility offered the throne to his uncle, the Duke of Schleswig-Holstein, who became King Frederick I.

Schleswig-Holstein had already become Lutheran, and the movement continued to spread in Denmark, particularly through the country's trading links with northern Germany. Since, however, Frederick partly owed his position on the throne to the Danish bishops, he was not able to come out into open opposition to the Church. He was careful to retain the support of the nobility as well, and when they saw that he had abandoned his nephew's alliance with the townspeople and the peasants, they realized that they no longer needed the support of the bishops and were prepared to favour a religious policy that might bring them a share of ecclesiastical lands. This made it possible for Frederick to refuse to comply with the demands of the bishops that Lutheranism should be repressed, and the Reformation was able to continue to make progress in the country. In 1526 the Diet of Odense decided that bishops should no longer be appointed by the Papacy, but by the Crown which should also receive all fees previously sent to Rome, that the clergy might be allowed to marry and monks to leave the cloister; in addition, changes in worship were to be tolerated in Denmark until a general council was summoned to make a final decision for the whole Church. In the later years of his reign, Frederick might have more actively promoted the Reformation in Denmark, but in 1531 the exiled Christian invaded the country, and though Lübeck supported Frederick, he had to rely upon financial help from the Danish Church as well.

Political and religious matters reached a crisis on Frederick's death in 1533. He had brought up his son, who succeeded him as Christian III, as a Lutheran and had married his daughter to Albert of Branden-burg. The bishops sought to regain their power by opposing Christian's succession, and nearly three years of civil war followed during which the Crown had to contend also with risings by the towns and peasants (caused by resentment at royal favour to the nobility) who were supported by Lübeck, and with a revolt in Norway. By 1536, however, he had triumphed in his kingdom, had subdued Norway and declared her to be a Danish dependency and had inflicted a decisive defeat upon Lübeck.[11] The Church was left unpopular and at the mercy of Christian, who was determined to destroy its power and seize its property for the replenishment of the royal treasury which had been depleted during the troubles. In 1536 ecclesiastical lands were confiscated, and the episcopacy was abolished. The old bishops were replaced by seven superintendents, who were, however, given the title and territorial designation of bishops. Lutheran theology and Danish services were adopted. Three years later a Church Order arranged for the government of the Church under the Crown.[12] These changes in the Danish Church were generally popular, but when Christian extended them to Norway and Iceland, where Protestantism had made little headway, they were resented as a means of strengthening Danish overlordship, and their imposition was only achieved after considerable violence.

During the years after 1536, when he was engaged in accomplishing his religious settlement and restoring the financial stability of the Crown, Christian III was anxious not to threaten his position by becoming involved in a war. He renounced the Danish claim to the Swedish throne and was able to benefit from the equal desire for peace

[11] P. 311.   [12] P. 110.

entertained by Gustavus I of Sweden.[13] He wished to accomplish a settlement also with the Emperor Charles V, who still resented the exclusion of Christian II and his descendants from the Danish throne, and eventully he was reconciled with him at Speyer in 1544. This pacific policy, however, did not survive his death in 1559 and his succession by Frederick II.

Such a policy was not acceptable to Frederick II, whom a recent historian has called 'a brutal extrovert'. He wanted war and revived the Danish claim to the Swedish throne, which was resented by Eric XIV, who became King of Sweden in 1560. This served, amid the situation produced by Swedish intervention in Estonia, to bring about the Northern Seven Years War in 1563.[14] When it ended with the Treaty of Stettin in 1570, Denmark had successfully resisted Swedish aims in the Baltic, but at considerable cost. Frederick was in no position to engage in further warfare, and until his death in 1588 he devoted himself to other interests, including patronage of the astronomer, Tycho Brahé.[15] Indeed, the financial strain imposed upon Denmark by this contest was an omen for the future. It was to be succeeded by further warfare between her and Sweden and she was to cling tenaciously to her control of the Sound, but her greatest days in the Baltic were slowly but inexorably passing away in the face of the challenge from new and rising powers.

Poland

The Poles, a Slav people inhabiting the plains watered by the Oder and Vistula, consolidated themselves into an organized kingdom under German pressure during the later tenth century. The kingdom, however, was weakened by divisions of its territory among the sons of successive monarchs, and this political disunity lasted until early in the fourteenth century. During the reign of Casimir the Great (1333-70), the power of the monarchy was increased by bringing the separate provinces under royal administration, and immigrant Jewish traders and German craftsmen developed commerce and industry in the country. This brought a prosperity which was reflected in the splendour of Casimir's court at Cracow and the university he established there in 1364 at which the astronomer Copernicus (1473-1543) was later a student.[16] Casimir died without a male heir, and so did his successor, his nephew, Louis of Hungary. In 1382, therefore, the Polish nobility accepted Jadwiga, the daughter of Louis, as their queen and then arranged her marriage with Jagiello, Grand Prince of Lithuania, which was a large state lying immediately east of Poland and extending from the Baltic nearly as far as the Black Sea. It had increased its territory during the thirteenth century by expanding across south-west Russia,

[13] P. 315.   [14] P. 104.   [15] P. 104.   [16] P. 103.

after the devastation of the Mongol invaders, but now it was threatened by the Teutonic Knights from their bases in Prussia and Estonia. The personal alliance with Poland, therefore, was welcome to the Lithuanians, and in 1410 Polish military assistance enabled them to defeat the Knights at the Battle of Tannenburg in East Prussia.

The personal nature of the union was emphasized in 1492 on the death of Casimir IV. The Polish nobility elected one of his sons to be their king, but the Lithuanian nobility, who had long believed that successive rulers had not bestowed their favours fairly upon them, chose another son as Grand Prince of Lithuania. The two countries remained apart for nine years, but the union was restored in 1501 when the Polish nobility elected the Grand Prince of Lithuania to the Polish throne.

The continued danger from the Teutonic Knights was the main reason for the resumption of the union. Casimir IV had, after a war of thirteen years, compelled them to cede West Prussia, including the port of Danzig, to him by the Peace of Thorn in 1466 and to pay homage to him for East Prussia, but after his death they had been able to regain the whole of Prussia for themselves. Not until 1525 was Sigismund I able to secure possession of this territory for Poland again as the price of recognizing Albert of Brandenburg's secularization of the Prussian lands of the Order.

Sigismund I, who succeeded his two brothers, sons of Casimir IV— John Albert (1492-1501) and Alexander (1501-6)—and reigned from 1506 to 1548, was an able King, and his diplomatic success in Prussia removed a dangerous threat to Poland's northern frontiers. But she was a land of many frontiers.[17] The Ottoman Turks had established themselves on the coast of the Black Sea and raided Polish and Lithuanian territory, but the rise of Muscovite Russia presented the most serious danger to her security. The aim of 'gathering the Russian land' particularly impinged upon Lithuania, which had occupied so much of it in the past. Ivan the Great made considerable gains from her, and Basil III took Smolensk.[18] Sigismund made many attempts to recover the city, but he was ominously unable to benefit from Basil's harassment by the Tatars of the Crimea, and his failure was very much due to the internal difficulties he had to face.

Though he was the ruler of two great states, his position was weak in both because the monarchy of Poland and the principality of Lithuania were alike elective. They had not shared in the general development experienced by monarchical systems elsewhere by which the hereditary had come to replace the elective principle. In both countries the monarch was chosen by its Diet, and Sigismund I was unable to change this arrangement. He was only able to get them to agree to his son's succession. They would not abandon the principle of election itself, and the only lasting result of his attempt to abrogate it was to prevent the election of a ruler in the future who was likely to repeat his attack on the institutions of the countries.

Both diets were dominated by the nobility, whose power, therefore, was immense, particularly in Poland, where they formed about ten per cent of the population and enjoyed extensive political and economic privileges. In the national Diet of Poland, the Senate or upper house was controlled by twenty or thirty great noblemen and the House of Deputies or lower house by the lesser noblemen. The powerful noblemen had large estates and were hereditary rulers of the palatinates into which the kingdom was divided; they had their dependants among the numerous lesser noblemen, over whom they exercised a more than semi-feudal authority. These lesser noblemen met in the local assemblies or dietines, which they dominated.[19] The result of this was that the King of Poland was, as a witty Irishman declared, indeed a King of Kings and Lord of Lords, since he had no better than companions and equals for his subjects. He was likely to have little more power than the ability to dispense patronage to self-seeking and often traitorous noblemen. At the time of his election and then subsequently when he faced national crises and needed money, he would find that the nobility were determined to use the situation to their advantage. Sigismund I started his reign with unusually serious difficulties because his father and his brothers had been compelled to grant numerous concessions to the nobility whose support they needed for their wars. In particular, Alexander had accepted the law of 1505, known as the Nil Novi, which asserted, 'From henceforward nothing new may be established by us or our successors, without the full consent of the council and delegates of the lords, which might be harmful to the State or to the harm or injury of any private person or directed towards the change of the general law and public safety.'

The economic power of the nobility was becoming greater by the beginning of the sixteenth century because of the growing demand for grain in western Europe.[20] To take advantage of this, they were able to impose, as elsewhere in eastern Europe, the demands of the 'new serfdom' upon the peasantry.[21] Gradually they diminished the rights of their tenants and brought them more directly under their control and discipline. In 1493 and 1511 the monarchy had to agree to make new laws which deprived peasants of their right of appeal on a nobleman's estate from verdicts of his court to royal judges, though they retained it on royal estates. With this power, lords could do more and more as they wished with the peasants, reducing their share of common land, forbidding them to move to other estates, increasing their money dues and exactions of field-work and subjecting them to the Russian practice of corporal punishment. The towns were able to preserve

---

[19] P. 123.   [20] P. 312.   [21] P. 80.   L

most of their freedom from noble control, but the citizens had to engage only in trade; they were forbidden, in 1496, to own land in the countryside, where the supremacy of the landed gentry was thus legally assured.

While the nobility were adding to their powers as landowners and serf-owners, they were also able during the reign of Sigismund I to augment their political privileges. In 1520 he had to agree that the members of the House of Deputies should in future no longer be elected but appointed by the dietines, a change which strengthened the noble control of the Diet; in 1538 he was forced to grant, as part of the concessions he made to secure the election of his son, that all new kings, after his son's reign, were to be chosen by the entire nobility and not merely by the Diet. Yet such gains by the nobility did little to add to their willingness to support the interests of the state. When, at the beginning of his reign, Sigismund set out to build a line of forts to check Turkish raids into the south-eastern territory of Poland and Lithuania, the nobility opposed his request to the Diet for grants to finance the undertaking almost to the point of open rebellion, and their attitude remained the same throughout his reign.

During Sigismund's reign, the impact of the Reformation made itself felt in Poland and Lithuania. These countries, with their history of migration and conquest, differed from the rest of western Europe in that religious diversity already existed in them before the advent of Protestantism during the sixteenth century. Most of the people belonged to the western Church, though there was quite a large Jewish minority in the towns, and there were many members of the Greek Orthodox Church in Galicia and of the Russian Orthodox Church in Lithuania. Casimir the Great had obtained from the Papacy the right to appoint bishops, who were mostly worldly-minded noblemen. Lutheranism appeared in Danzig as early as 1518, and thereafter it spread rapidly in Cracow, Posen, Lublin and other towns in which there were German inhabitants, especially after East Prussia became a Lutheran duchy in 1525, and Polish pastors were trained there at the University of Königsberg. Sigismund, anxious to retain his ecclesiastical powers, issued several edicts against heresy, but they were rarely enforced owing to the indifference of the nobility. Only when it led to peasant or urban revolts did they support him, notably in 1525 when the artisans of Danzig seized control in the name of Luther, and Sigismund captured the town by military attack, beheaded six of the leaders of the movement and fined the city council.

While Lutheranism did not appeal to the Polish nobility, Calvinist ideas, which entered the country early in the reign of Sigismund (Augustus) II (1548-72) did and were rapidly adopted by them.[22] They added to their political demands the claim for religious toleration.

[22] P. 183.

Sigismund II had a Calvinist wife, the sister of Prince Radziwill, and was prepared to be tolerant, though he feared that the demands of the nobility would lead to further political disunity. He was as able a ruler as his father, but was no more able to resist their demands. In 1555 he had to agree to the abolition of the jurisdiction of the ecclesiastical courts, and in 1558 the bishops were excluded from participation in the election of the King. Apart from such ecclesiastical measures, Sigismund had to make other concessions, the most important being in 1562 when he recognized the possession by the nobility of all royal lands which they had illegally obtained since 1504.

Sigismund was prevented from withstanding the demands of the now mainly-Protestant nobility because he needed their support in the long and costly war against Russia begun by Ivan the Terrible's invasion of Livonia in which Sweden had fought for a time as well.[23] This threat, in fact, demanded greater unity than was possible under the personal union of Poland and Lithuania, especially as the Lithuanian nobility remained discontented, and those who belonged to the Russian Orthodox Church were ready to turn to Ivan. In 1569, therefore, the Union of Lublin united Lithuania to Poland with a single King and Diet. This made Poland a stronger state, but the monarchy was weakened, since Sigismund had to agree to extend to the Lithuanian nobility the numerous privileges enjoyed by the Polish nobility, consequently limiting royal power in Lithuania as much as in Poland.

The war in Livonia was still in progress when Sigismund II died in 1572, leaving no heir and bringing to an end the Jagiellon dynasty in Poland. The whole of the nobility, some 40 000 in number, assembled in Warsaw to assert their newly-gained right to choose a successor. The Roman Catholics wanted Ernest, the son of the Emperor Maximilian II, and many Lithuanians favoured Ivan the Terrible. Eventually, the throne was offered to Henry, Duke of Anjou, partly as a compromise and partly in the hope of obtaining French help against Russia. On his arrival in Poland he was presented with the Henrician Articles by the nobility, requiring him to respect their privileges, and also a new statement, the *pacta conventa*, which declared, 'If the King act against these laws, liberties, articles and conditions or does not fulfil them, he thereby makes the nobles free of the obedience and fealty they owe him.' To these constitutional provisions was added for Henry's acceptance also the Confederation of Warsaw, an agreement for mutual toleration drawn up by the Roman Catholic, Orthodox and Protestant leaders, 'As there is great discord in this kingdom touching the Christian religion, we promise, in order to avoid sedition such as has come to other kingdoms . . . that all of us of differing religions will keep the peace between ourselves and shed no

[23] P. 305.

L*

blood.' Henry reluctantly accepted these conditions and was crowned early in 1574, but after less than five months in Poland he departed in the summer as soon as he heard of his accession to the French throne as Henry III.

This time the unexpected death of Maximilian II made possible the choice of Stephen Bathory, Prince of Transylvania, who married Anna, a sister of Sigismund II. He had already shown himself to be a forceful ruler and experienced soldier, and he was now able to make use of the greater strength of the united Poland to defeat Ivan completely.[24] In internal matters, he was faced with a changing religious situation. The Counter-Reformation was now exerting an ever-stronger influence in Poland. In 1565 Sigismund II had allowed the Jesuits to enter the country; they established four colleges during his reign and another eight during Stephen's reign. Through these they were able to promote higher standards of morality and pastoral efficiency among the clergy and to win over many noble families which had become Protestant. They were assisted, at the same time, by the continuing disunity among the Polish Protestants. Stephen was tolerant by nature and had sworn to observe the requirements of both the Henrician Articles and the Confederation of Warsaw, but he was himself a devoted Roman Catholic and anxious to see the Church reformed along Tridentine lines. He assisted the Jesuits and gave strong encouragement to the progress of the Counter-Reformation in the country.

On Stephen's death in 1586, the nobility again chose a foreign prince as King of Poland—Sigismund, son of John III of Sweden. Their hope was that he would bring them Swedish help against Russia, but this was frustrated by his deposition from the Swedish throne.[25] In Poland, Sigismund III's main aim was to forward the advance of Roman Catholicism, and he was prepared to use all possible means of doing so. Only Roman Catholic noblemen received government posts, and this stimulated the conversion of Protestant families, including the Radziwills.[26] In their turn, Roman Catholic noblemen brought about the conversion of their tenants and peasants. Royal judges supported Roman Catholic claims for the restoration of ecclesiastical property, and during his reign the parish churches were recovered in every town except Danzig. This policy, together with Sigismund's attempts to increase the power of the monarchy, in 1606 brought about a revolt by a group of the nobility, who were supported by the Protestants. Civil war raged for three years, and was only ended by Sigismund reaffirming his acceptance of the principle, contained in the *pacta conventa,* that a king could be deposed if he ruled unconstitutionally. Poland, therefore, was to enter upon the seventeenth century with her constitutional weaknesses as serious as ever and badly prepared to face the threat from new and rising powers in Central Europe and the Baltic.

[24] P. 308.   [25] P. 317.   [26] P. 323.

BIBLIOGRAPHY
GENEALOGICAL TREES
AND
INDEX

BIBLIOGRAPHY

General histories

The Cambridge Modern History: vol. I, *The Renaissance* (1902); vol. II, *The Reformation* (1903); vol. III, *The Wars of Religion* (1905).

The New Cambridge Modern History: vol. I, *The Renaissance 1493-1520* (1971); vol. II, *The Reformation 1520-59* (1958); vol. III, *The Counter Reformation and the Price Revolution 1559-1610* (1971).

The Fontana History of Europe: J. R. HALE, *Renaissance Europe 1480-1520* (1971); G. R. ELTON, *Reformation Europe 1517-59* (1969); J. H. ELLIOTT, *Europe Divided 1559-98* (1968).

R. H. BAINTON, *The Sixteenth Century* (1952).

V. H. H. GREEN, *Renaissance and Reformation 1450-1660* (2nd edn. 1964).

H. GRIMM, *The Reformation Era* (1954).

H. G. KOENIGSBERGER and G. L. MOSSE, *Europe in the Sixteenth Century* (1973).

R. LOCKYER, *Habsburg and Bourbon Europe 1470-1720* (1974).

D. MALAND, *Europe in the Sixteenth Century* (1973).

The Renaissance

J. BURCKHARDT, *The Civilisation of the Renaissance in Italy* (Eng. trans. 1951).

P. BURKE, *The Renaissance* (1964).

J. HUIZINGA, *The Waning of the Middle Ages* (1924).

L. MURRAY, *The High Renaissance* (1967).

L. MURRAY, *The Late Renaissance and Mannerism* (1967).

P. and L. MURRAY, *The Art of the Renaissance* (1963).

P. MURRAY, *Architecture of the Italian Renaissance* (1963).

R. H. BAINTON, *Erasmus of Christendom* (1969).

J. HUIZINGA, *Erasmus of Rotterdam* (1952).

H. M. PHILLIPS, *Erasmus and the Northern Renaissance* (1949).

The Reformation and Counter-Reformation

O. CHADWICK, *The Reformation* (1964).

A. G. DICKENS, *Reformation and Society in Sixteenth-Century Europe* (1966).

R. H. BAINTON, *Here I Stand: A Life of Martin Luther* (1955).

A. G. DICKENS, *Martin Luther and the Reformation* (1967).

E. G. RUPP, *Luther's Progress to the Diet of Worms* (1964).

E. G. RUPP, *The Righteousness of God* (1953).

O. FARNER, *Zwingli the Reformer: His Life and Work* (1952).

J. RILLIET, *Zwingli, Third Man of the Reformation* (1964).
F. WENDAL, *Calvin* (1965).
E. W. MONTER, *Calvin's Geneva* (1967).
J. T. MCNEIL, *The History and Character of Calvinism* (1967).
A. G. DICKENS, *The Counter-Reformation* (1969).
H. O. EVENNETT, *The Spirit of the Counter-Reformation* (1968).
G. W. SEARLE, *The Counter-Reformation* (1974).

Social and economic history

The Cambridge Economic History of Europe: vol. IV (1967).
E. J. HAMILTON, *American Treasure and the Price Revolution in Spain 1501-1650* (1934).
M. WEBER, *The Protestant Ethic and the Spirit of Capitalism* (Eng. trans. 1930).
R. H. TAWNEY, *Religion and the Rise of Capitalism* (1947).
H. R. TREVOR-ROPER, *Religion, the Reformation and Social Change* (1967).

Political thought

J. W. ALLEN, *Political Thought in the Sixteenth Century* (1928).
W. F. CHURCH, *Constitutional Thought in the Sixteenth Century* (1941).
H. KAMEN, *The Rise of Toleration* (1967).
F. CHABOD, *Machiavelli and the Renaissance* (Eng. trans. 1958).
J. R. HALE, *Machiavelli and Renaissance Italy* (1961).
J. H. FRANKLIN, *John Bodin and the Rise of Absolutist Theory* (1973).

The scientific revolution

MARIE BOAS, *The Scientific Renaissance 1450-1630* (1962).
H. BUTTERFIELD, *The Origins of Modern Science 1300-1800* (1957).
A. R. HALL, *The Scientific Revolution 1300-1800* (1954).
H. KEARNEY, *Origins of the Scientific Revolution* (1964).
H. KEARNEY, *Science and Change 1500-1700* (1971).
A. G. R. SMITH, *Science and Society in the Sixteenth and Seventeenth Centuries* (1972).
A. WOLF, *A History of Science, Technology and Philosophy in the Sixteenth, Seventeenth and Eighteenth Centuries* (3 vol., 3rd edn. 1962).

Overseas expansion

C. R. BOXER, *The Portuguese Seaborne Empire 1415-1825* (1973).
C. R. BOXER, *The Dutch Seaborne Empire* (1973).
C. M. CIPOLLA, *Guns and Sails in the Early Phase of European Expansion* (1966).

G. R. CRONE, *The Discovery of America* (1969).

J. H. ELLIOTT, *The Old World and the New 1492-1650* (1970).

J. HEMMING, *The Conquest of the Incas* (1970).

H. INNES, *The Conquistadors* (1970).

J. H. PARRY, *Europe and a Wider World 1415-1715* (1949).

J. H. PARRY, *The Age of Reconnaissance* (1963).

J. H. PARRY, *The Spanish Seaborne Empire* (1973).

Diplomacy and warfare

G. MATTINGLEY, *Renaissance Diplomacy* (1955).

M. MALLETT, *Mercenaries and their Masters: Warfare in Renaissance Italy* (1974).

SIR CHARLES OMAN, *History of the Art of War in the Sixteenth Century* (1937).

F. L. ROBERTSON, *Evolution of Naval Armament* (1968).

J. A. WILLIAMSON, *The Age of Drake* (5th edn. 1965).

Spain and Portugal

W. C. ATKINSON, *A History of Spain and Portugal* (1960).

B. CHUDOBA, *Spain and the Empire 1519-1643* (1952).

J. H. ELLIOTT, *Imperial Spain 1469-1716* (1963).

H. V. LIVERMORE, *History of Portugal* (1947).

G. MATTINGLEY, *The Defeat of the Spanish Armada* (1959).

A. S. TURBERVILLE, *The Spanish Inquisition* (1949).

France

J. HERITIER, *Catherine de Medici* (Eng. trans. 1963).

J. E. NEALE, *The Age of Catherine de Medici* (1943).

N. M. SUTHERLAND, *The French Secretaries of State in the Age of Catherine de Medici* (1962).

A. W. WHITEHEAD, *Gaspard de Coligny, Admiral of France* (1904).

M. WILKINSON, *A History of the League* (1929).

Germany and the Empire

E. ARMSTRONG, *The Emperor Charles V* (2 vol., 2nd edn. 1910).

K. BRANDI, *The Emperor Charles V* (Eng. trans. 1939).

F. L. CARSTEN, *The Origins of Prussia* (1954).

F. L. CARSTEN, *Princes and Parliaments in Germany* (1959).

HAJO HOLBORN, *A History of Modern Germany. The Reformation* (1965).

R. W. SETON-WATSON, *Maximilian I* (1902).

Italy

C. M. ADY, *A History of Milan under the Sforza* (1907).

C. M. ADY, *Lorenzo de Medici and Renaissance Italy* (1956).

M. DE LA BEDOYERE, *The Meddlesome Friar: The Story of the Conflict between Savonarola and Alexander VI* (1957).

H. G. KOENIGSBERGER, *The Government of Sicily under Philip II* (1951).

F. SCHEVILL, *A History of Florence* (2nd edn. 1961).

The Netherlands

P. GEYL, *The Revolt of the Netherlands* (1932).

C. V. WEDGWOOD, *William the Silent* (1944).

C. WILSON, *Queen Elizabeth and the Revolt of the Netherlands* (1970).

Russia

J. D. CLARKSON, *A History of Russia from the Ninth Century* (1962).

J. L. I. FENNELL, *Ivan the Great of Moscow* (1961).

I. GREY, *Ivan the Terrible* (1964).

N. V. RIASANOVSKY, *A History of Russia* (1963).

The Ottoman Empire

M. S. ANDERSON, *The Eastern Question 1423-1774* (1966).

P. COLES, *The Ottoman Impact on Europe* (1968).

R. B. MERRIMAN, *Suleiman the Magnificent* (1944).

DOROTHY M. VAUGHAN, *Europe and the Turk* (2nd edn. 1967).

The Baltic

The Cambridge History of Poland: vol. I (1950).

E. H. DUNKLEY, *The Reformation in Denmark* (1949).

M. ROBERTS, *Essays in Swedish History* (1967).

M. ROBERTS, *The Early Vasas: A History of Sweden 1523-1611* (1968).

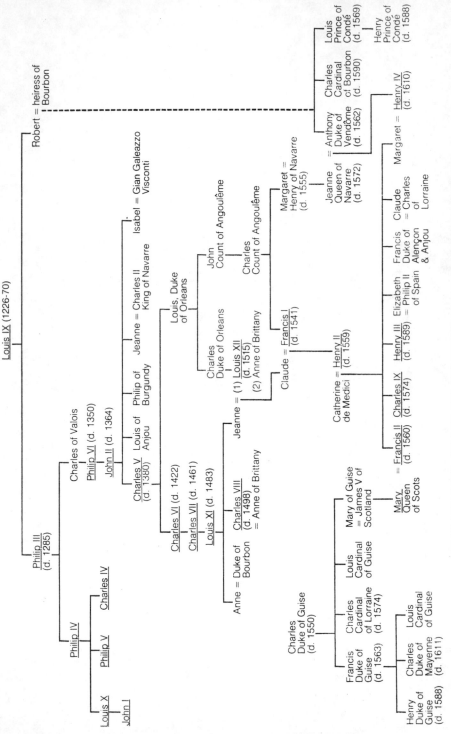

THE HOUSES OF VALOIS, BOURBON, NAVARRE AND GUISE

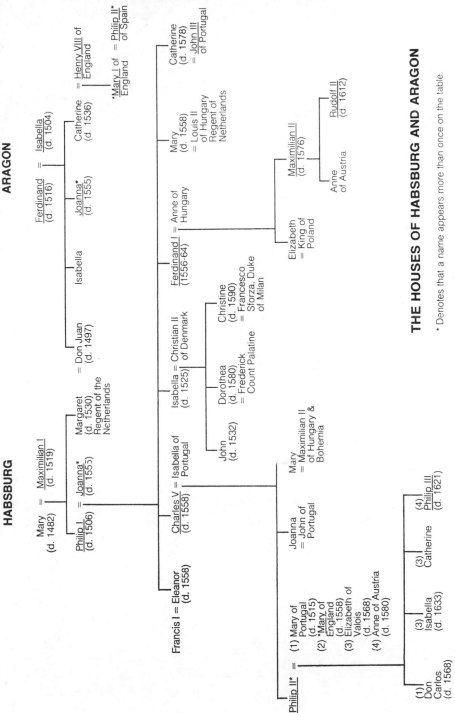

THE HOUSES OF HABSBURG AND ARAGON

HABSBURG

ARAGON

Mary
(d. 1482) = Maximilian I
(d. 1519)

Philip I
(d. 1506) = Joanna*
(d. 1555)

Margaret
(d. 1530)
Regent of the
Netherlands

Ferdinand = Isabella
(d. 1516)   (d. 1504)

Isabella

Joanna*
(d. 1555)

Catherine
(d. 1536)
= Henry VIII of
England

Mary I of = Philip II
England   of Spain

Francis I = Eleanor
(d. 1558)

Charles V = Isabella
(d. 1558)   of Portugal

= Don Juan
(d. 1497)

Ferdinand I = Anne of
(1556-64)   Hungary

Mary
(d. 1558)
= Louis II
of Hungary
Regent of
Netherlands

Catherine
(d. 1578)
= John III
of Portugal

Isabella = Christian II
(d. 1525)   of Denmark

John
(d. 1532)

Dorothea
(d. 1580)
= Frederick
Count Palatine

Christine
(d. 1590)
= Francesco
Sforza, Duke
of Milan

Elizabeth
= King of
Poland

Maximilian II
(d. 1576)

Anne
of Austria

Rudolf II
(d. 1612)

Mary
= Maximilian II
of Hungary &
Bohemia

Joanna
= John of
Portugal

Philip II* =
(1) Mary of
Portugal
(d. 1515)
(2) *Mary of
England
(d. 1558)
(3) Elizabeth of
Valois
(d. 1568)
(4) Anne of Austria
(d. 1580)

(1)
Don
Carlos
(d. 1568)

(3)
Isabella
(d. 1633)

(3)
Catherine

(4)
Philip III
(d. 1621)

* Denotes that a name appears more than once on the table.

INDEX